MW01709083

INSTRUMENT

INSTRUMENT

PHOTOGRAPHS BY **PAT GRAHAM**
FOREWORD BY **JOHNNY MARR**

CHRONICLE BOOKS
SAN FRANCISCO

For my son, Huw, and
my father, William Graham

Copyright © 2011 by Pat Graham.
Foreword copyright © 2011 by Johnny Marr.
All rights reserved. No part of this book may be reproduced in any form without written permission from the publisher.

Library of Congress Cataloging-in-Publication Data
Graham, Pat, 1970–
Instrument / photographs by Pat Graham ; foreword by Johnny Marr.
p. cm.
ISBN 978-0-8118-7474-8 (hardcover)
1. Musical instruments—Pictorial works. I. Title.
ML89.G73 2011
784.19—dc22
2011005948

Manufactured in China

Designed by Suzanne LaGasa
Pre-press photo editing and technical support by Owen Richards
Image calibrations by Ben Norton

10 9 8 7 6 5 4 3 2 1

Chronicle Books
680 Second Street
San Francisco, CA 94107
www.chroniclebooks.com

CONTENTS

FOREWORD

This is a book about relationships. The relationship between musician and instrument, craft and machine, artist and muse, friend and companion.

There are a lot of myths and ideas about the relationship between a musician and an instrument; all of them true, and all of them are here. As you will see, some musicians carry their instrument through life with them like a precious object to be protected and treasured; some artists rely on their instrument to do the work in a way that only that particular guitar, or snare, or keyboard can do; while others take it for granted that the instrument they acquired all those years ago will always do what they do together, like a companion or sibling, no question, no option.

Pat Graham understands that all of the above is true for each of the musicians in this book. I've travelled with Pat on trains and planes, in cities and stations, and I can't ever think of a time when he wouldn't be holding his camera. I've seen him taking pictures before he climbed in a tour bus bunk and then again as he got out of the bunk the next morning. It's because he has exactly the same relationships with his own instrument that he understands all of this stuff, and why he had the idea for this book in the first place. That, and the fact that he's a brilliant artist in his own right, who takes photographs that are completely unique and memorable.

The first picture I saw for this book was the shot of Ian MacKaye's SG pickups. It struck me immediately as a portrait, art for sure, and definitely more than just a photo of a part of a guitar. It was a portrait of something that had a story, a soul even, and a relationship with someone.

This is also of course a book about amazing photographs, one that's taken a lot of hard work and dedication to make happen. It's a testament to the respect that these musicians have for Pat Graham that they were prepared to present their most treasured instruments and share their stories for him and his camera. I'm glad and proud that he's done it.

—Johnny Marr

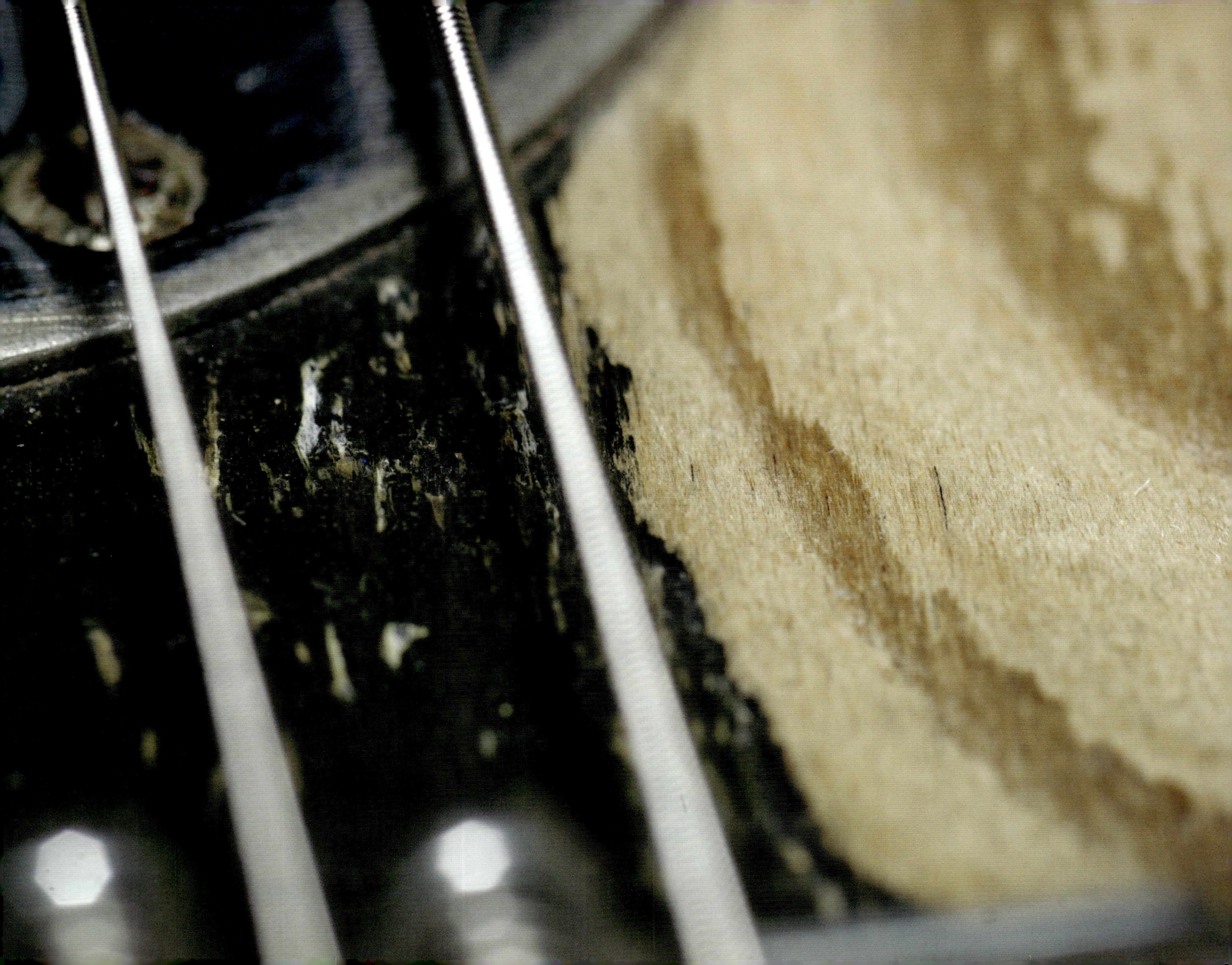

INTRODUCTION

The instruments are things most people don't think about much while at a concert or listening to their favorite records. I spend so much time with musicians that people invariably ask me if I play an instrument. My answer is always the same: I love music, but I leave the music to the experts. What inspired me to start taking photos of bands were the people playing the music and the instruments they were playing.

I have always thought the best music photos are ones of someone doing something to a guitar, a bass, or a set of drums. I love shots of an artist enraptured with his or her instrument, completely lost in the moment.

Some of my favorite music photos—Jim Marshall's shot of Jimmy Hendrix setting his guitar on fire at the Monterey Pop Festival; Charles Peterson's photo of Kurt Cobain upside down on stage playing his guitar circa 1992—are interesting to me not only because of the musicians and the events, but also because of the instruments that are central to the scene. These photos inevitably leave me wondering how the instruments survived and what they look like now.

Musicians form an incredible bond with their instruments. It's a relationship that often has plenty of ups and downs. The instruments and musicians travel the same miles and play the same shows. The instruments, of course, are also "gear," and as such they are abused as they travel, slammed around in the underbellies of planes and buses. And to make matters worse (or better) the instruments are also battered, drenched with sweat, stood upon, punched, screamed into, and frequently abused (or caressed) as they are being played until they make just the right sound. Sometimes musicians take a beating, too.

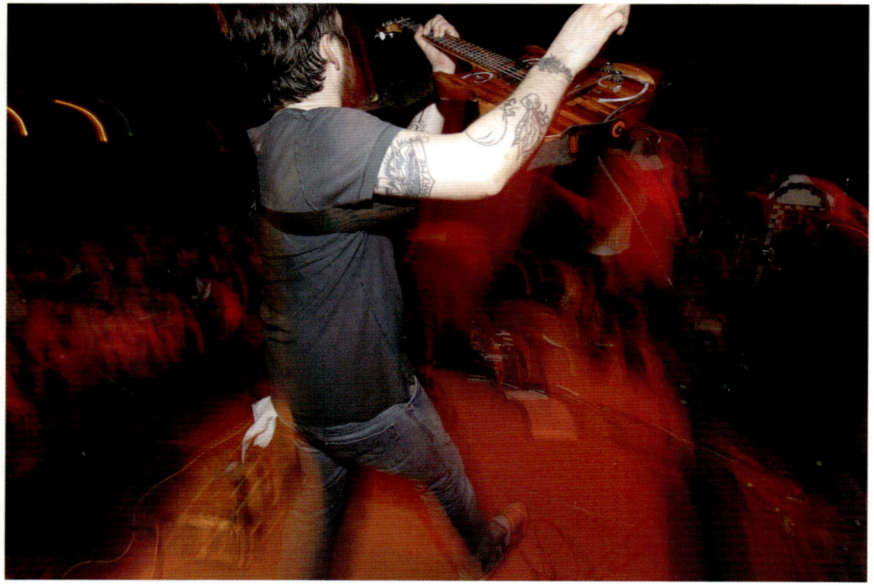

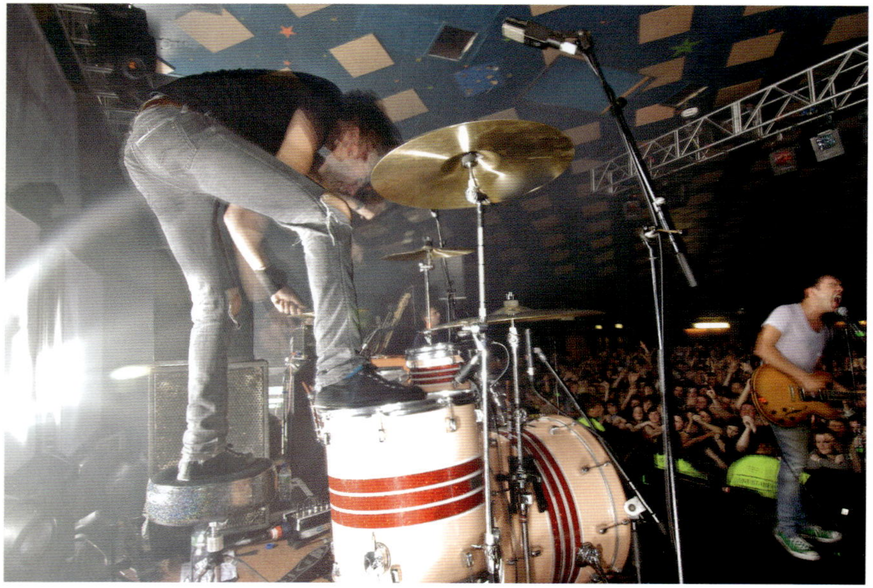

I love to watch and photograph Isaac Brock. Over the years, I have seen him elicit the craziest sounds from his guitars through movement and bending, twisting and screeching. His is a very physical relationship in which the instrument and artist test each other's limits.

It's not only guitarists who behave this way. While on tour with The Cribs, I watched Ross Jarman, their tall and lanky drummer, rain abuse on his drum kit night after night. At one point, he stood on one kick drum while beating the other with a drumstick, all the while keeping his balance. It added to the visual aspect of The Cribs live experience, and to the music.

Johnny Marr is another of my favorite guitarists to shoot, and he has shown me how close the relationship between guitar and musician really can be. I have always appreciated that Johnny has his guitar in hand or nearby before every gig. He and his guitar leave the dressing room as a unit before every performance. I have even caught him brushing his teeth before a show with the guitar hanging in its rightful place, firmly in his grasp.

To me, this relationship between musician and instrument creates not only the basis for great music, but eventually a beautiful, tangible landscape. I was amazed to see the way a small cut on Modest Mouse drummer Joe Plummer's hand created a wonderful abstract image on a drumhead by the end of a gig.

It's also fascinating to see the way the repetitive motion of playing a guitar erodes the wood of the instrument. The sounds drawn from worn musical instruments can be inspired and emotive, and the visual images of these instruments can also provoke intense visceral responses.

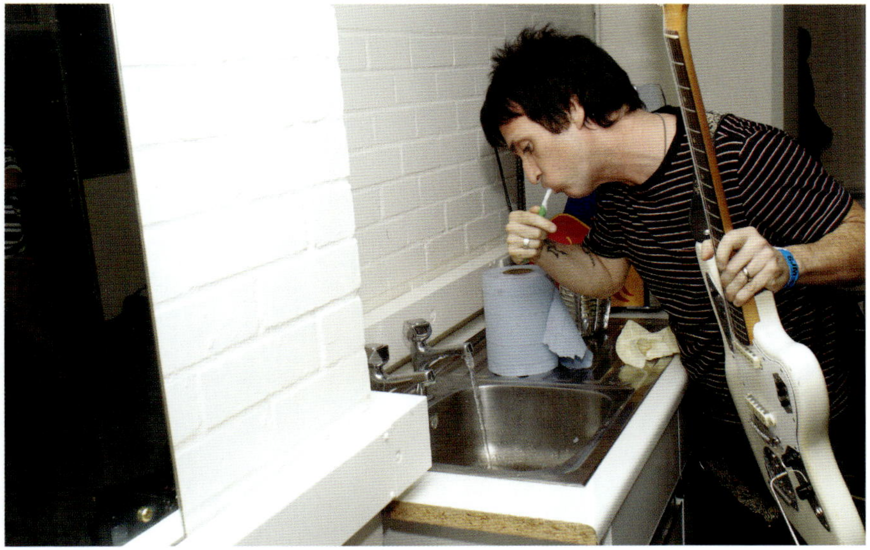

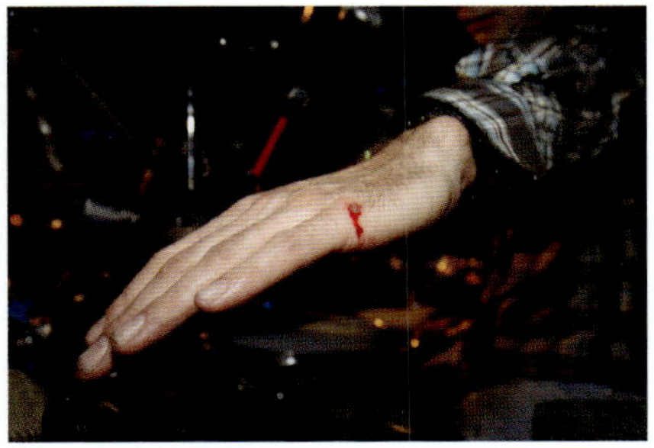

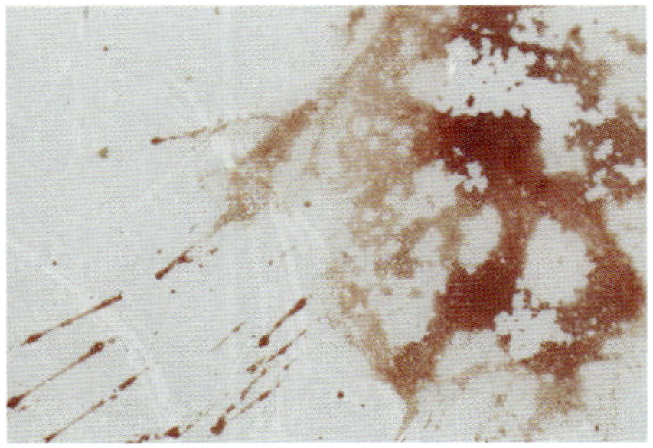

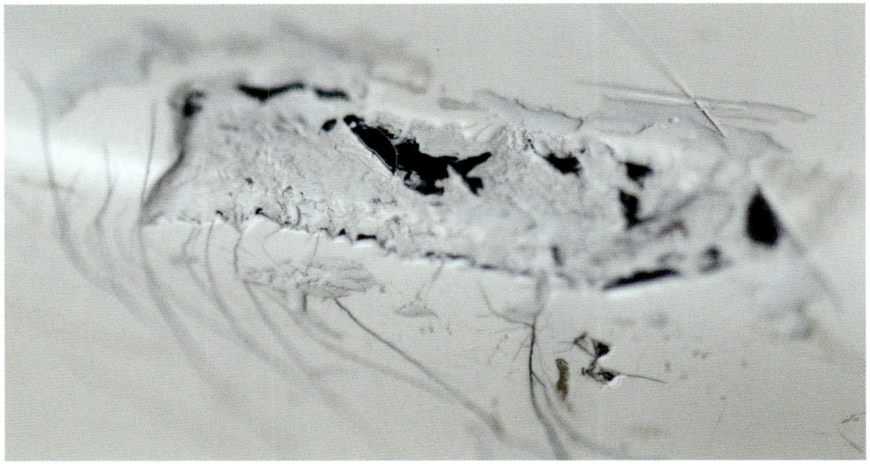

In 2001, I was asked to photograph Ian MacKaye for *Guitar World* magazine. The brief instructed me to shoot Ian and his white Gibson SG. I didn't want to make a corny portrait of Ian standing there holding his instrument. Instead, I set out to shoot Ian and his guitar in the style of a landscape, featuring the surface of the instrument. Ian described his SG as "a piece of art." With the cracks, abrasion, and varied color fading created by Ian playing it relentlessly over the years, the guitar had become sculptural. The resulting photographs were, to my eye, as intense and abstract as Fugazi's music. I was immediately hooked on the idea of the instrument as a musical landscape, and I wanted to see and photograph the surface of as many of the instruments that were used to produce my favorite music as possible.

Creating music is a very personal experience, yet musicians love to share their music with other people. Most of the instruments pictured in this book carry personal stories about their owners, and I'm very lucky to have been given the opportunity to both photograph the instruments and document their hidden narratives.

JAMES MERCER

The Shins, Broken Bells
Harmony Silvertone Jupiter guitar
Gibson J-50 guitar

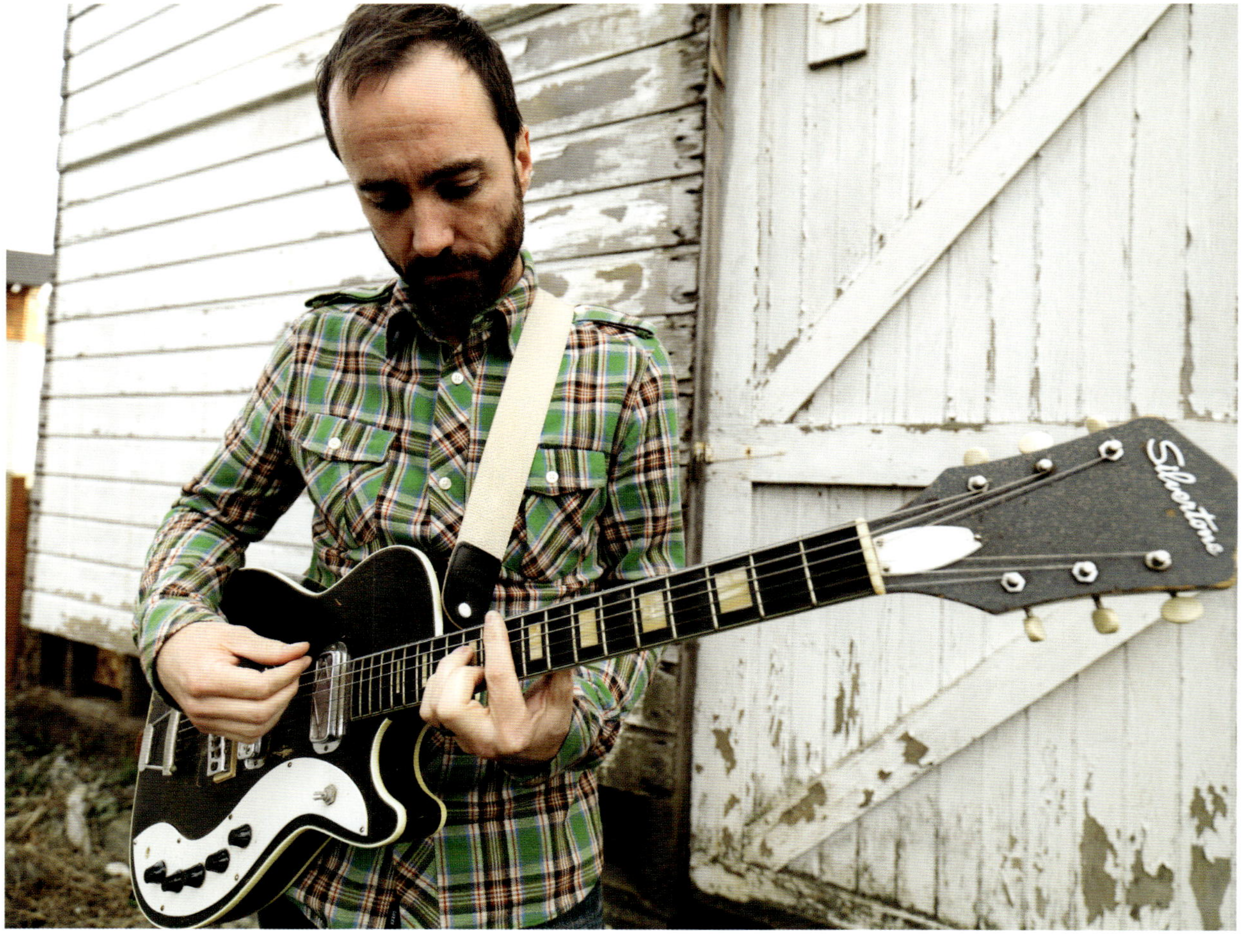

The Jupiter is my guitar. It's the one that I got signed with. It has beer stains and sweat stains and is corroded and abused. It was designed and manufactured by Harmony in the '50s for students and kids, then labeled Silvertone and sold by Sears in the mid-'60s. Thirty years later I traded a stolen guitar for this one and added the fancy bridge. It has Dearmond pickups that sound amazing, and its short scale gives it a wobbly sound that keeps you guessing.

The Gibson was given to me by my father. He bought it used in Honolulu around the time I was born. It is scarred from his use and from a time when it fell off the top of our VW camper as we drove down the road. Still sounds great though. It's the instrument I write most my stuff on and is the most natural feeling object I've ever held.

Both are on all the records, but not every song. Most all acoustic stuff I do is with that J-50.

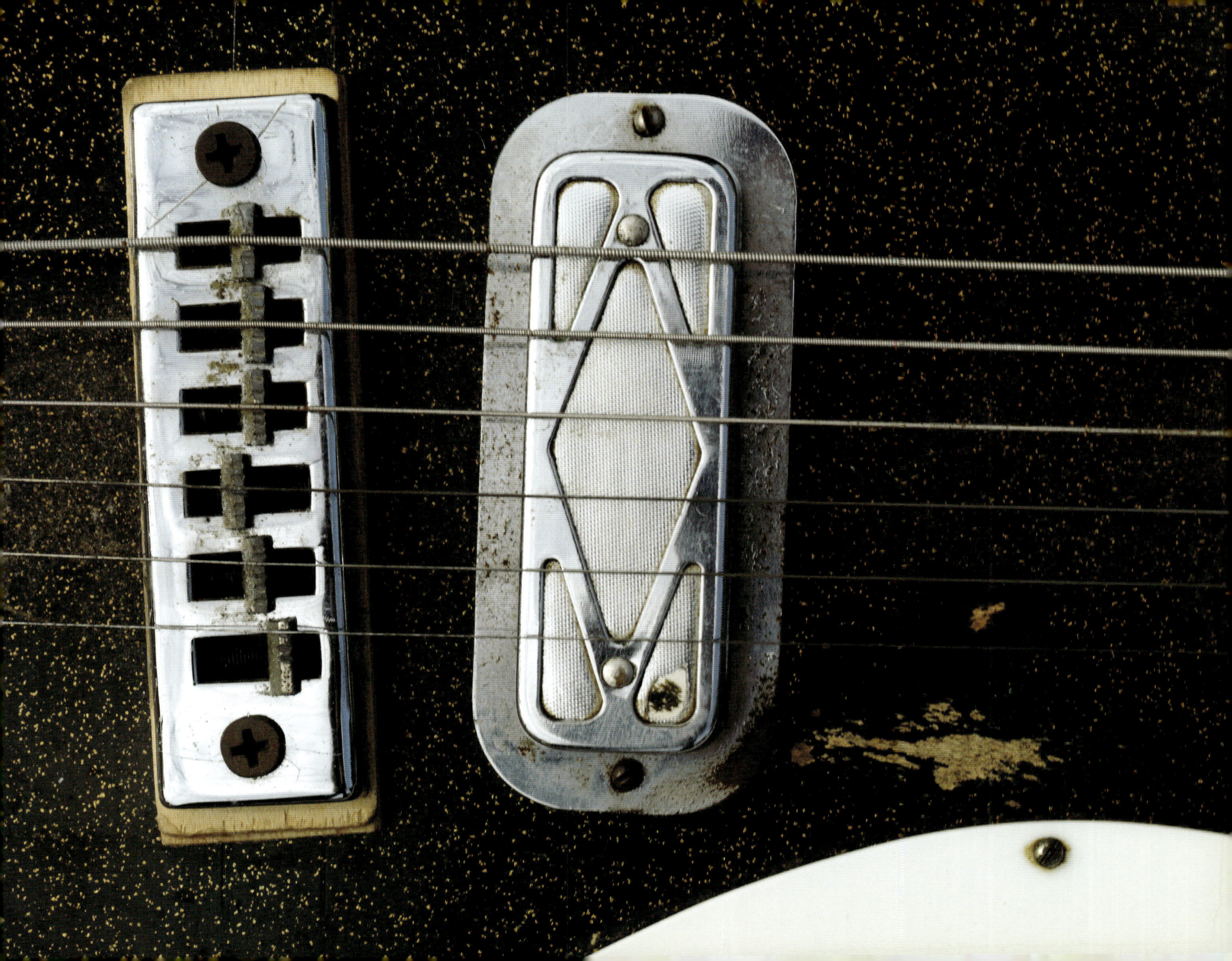

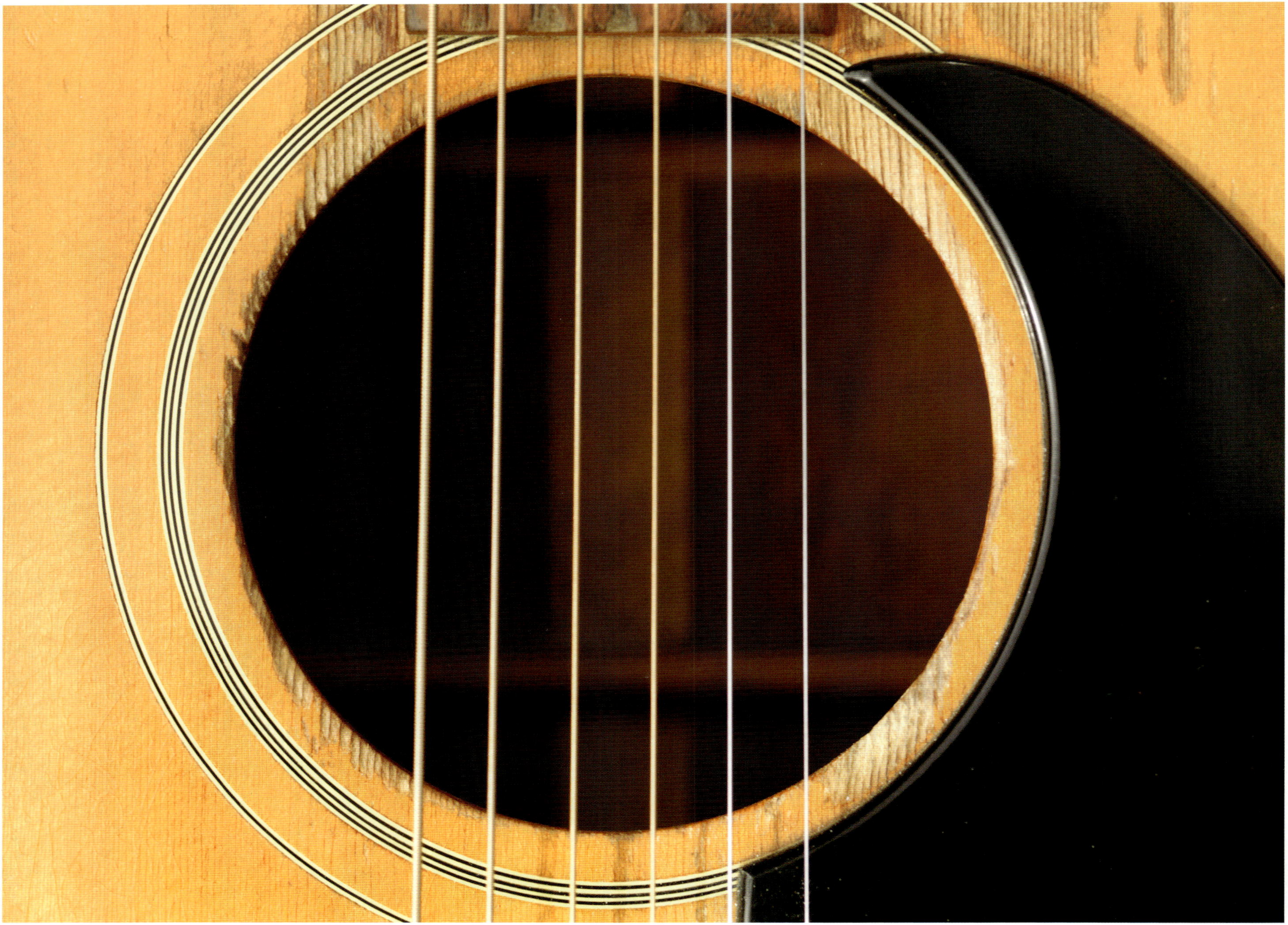

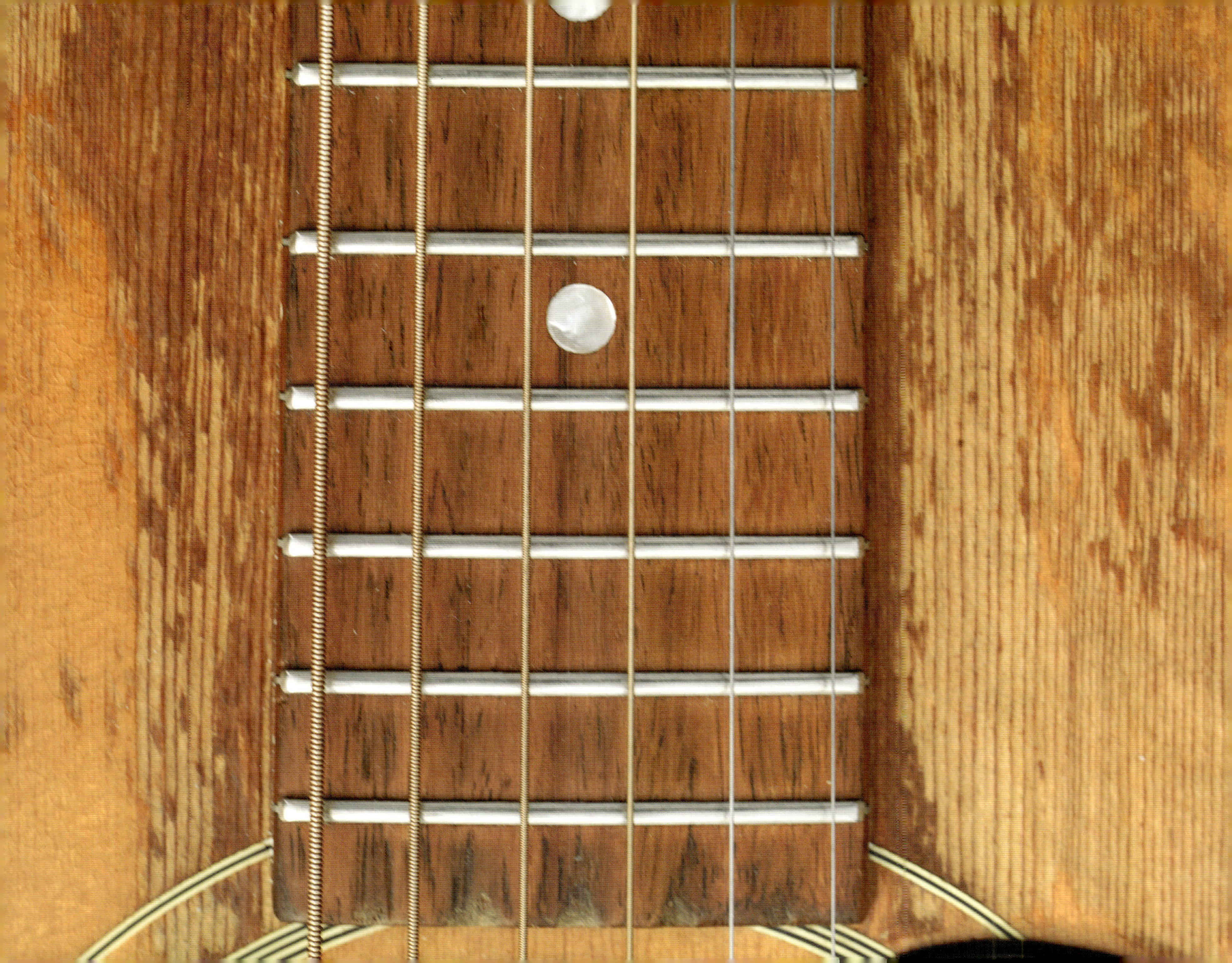

COLIN NEWMAN

Wire

Ovation Breadwinner guitar

It would be wrong for anyone to assume that just because I've played guitar in some fashion for a number of years I know anything about guitars. Yeah, I know the basics—the names of the strings and their order, the names of half a dozen chords, etcetera, plus a bunch of half-knowledge like "don't fiddle with the whammy bar 'cause it'll go out of tune," and which way to turn the knobs so they are all on full, and so on. However, for me the guitar has always been a means to an end, a way to provide bits of the music you can't get any other way, an input source to a set of sound treatments—but above all, it's a fashion accessory!

In 1977, the white Ovation Breadwinner was the perfect fashion accessory for me. Onstage I wore a black suit and white shirt. A white, interestingly shaped guitar—perfect! The fact that the guitar was intended for and originally pitched to country music stars totally passed me by. Wire was playing in London's Charing Cross Road area, and we had a budget from our initial EMI advance to buy new gear, so the cost was abstract—to be honest I have no idea how much it cost. The notion of testing it out in the shop was anathema to me. People who work in guitar shops always want to demonstrate that they are so much better guitarists than the customers, and for me, how useful any instrument can be comes down to the context it's used in, so I just turned up the amp as loud as I could and whacked out an E-chord drone. Sounded okay to me.

Although the guitar is actually made of wood, it's finished with a kind of matte vinyl finish that suggests it's plastic, and which has yellowed over the years. The fretboard is very black, also showing no sign of its wooden origin. In 1977, it looked smart, urban, modern, and ever so slightly alien. Anything but musicianly! To see it best in action, check out the *Wire on the Box: 1979* DVD of us on the German *Rockpalast* TV show. Its iconic status was such that, for years, people who knew nothing about guitars would ask about "that white guitar."

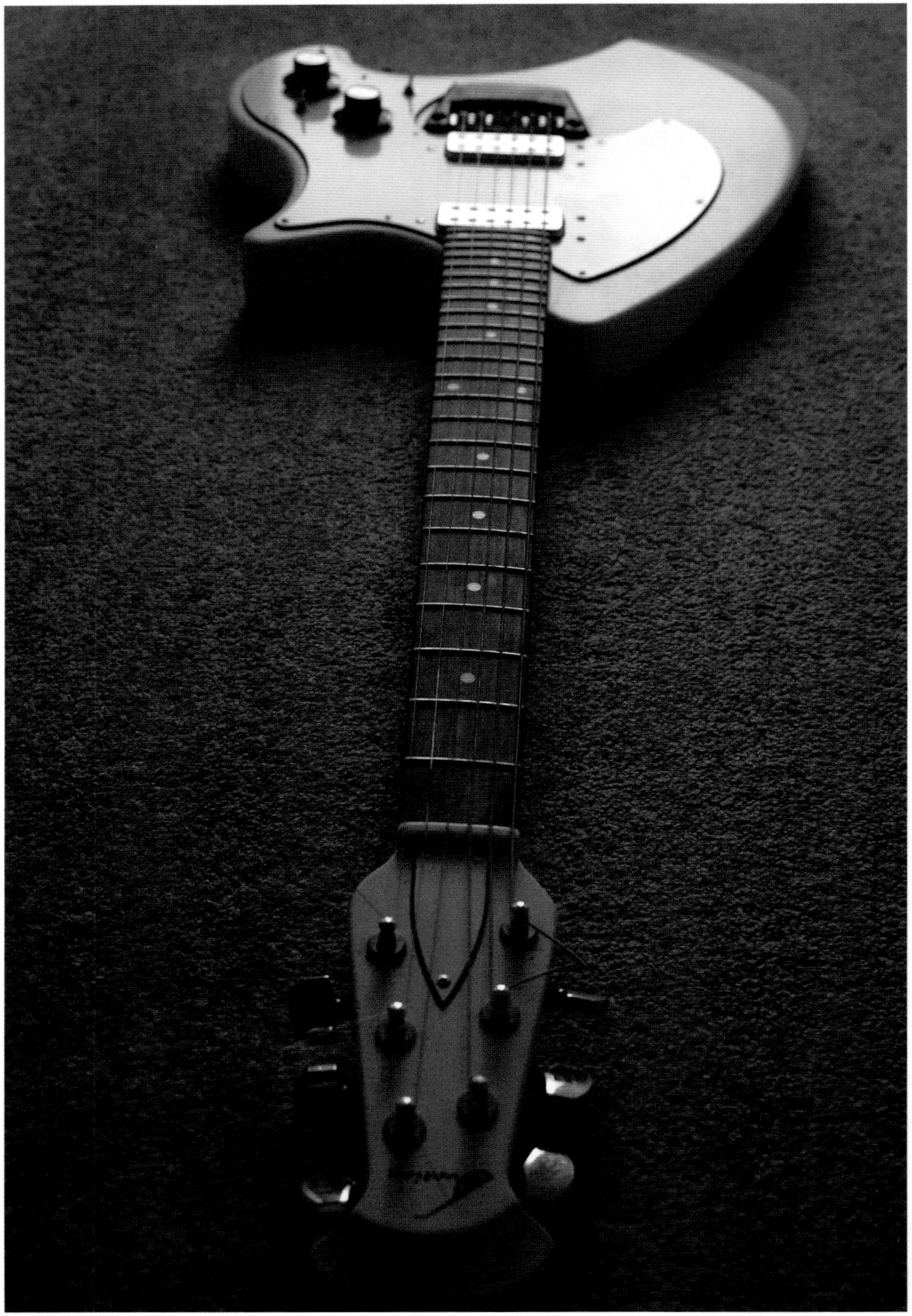

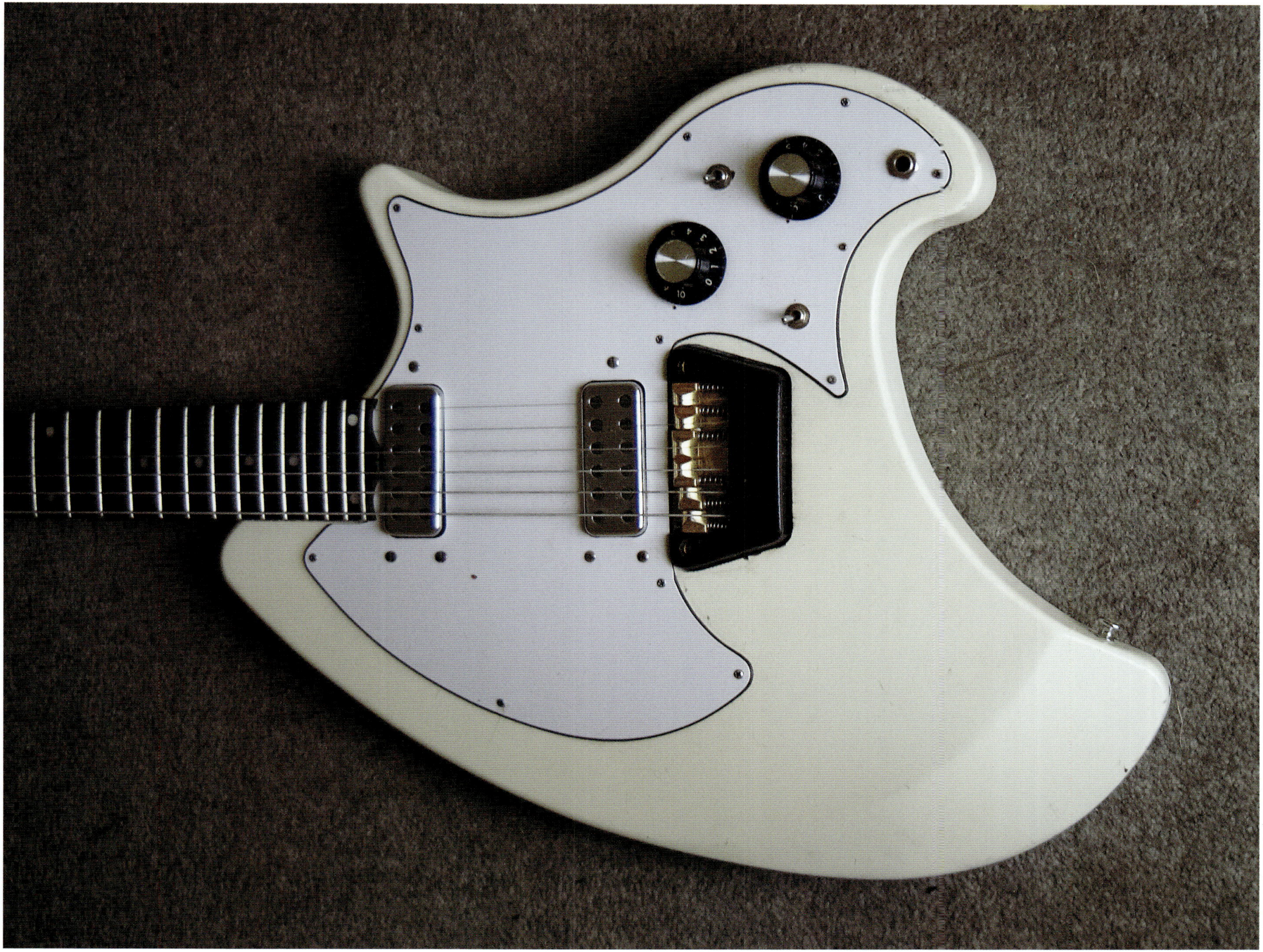

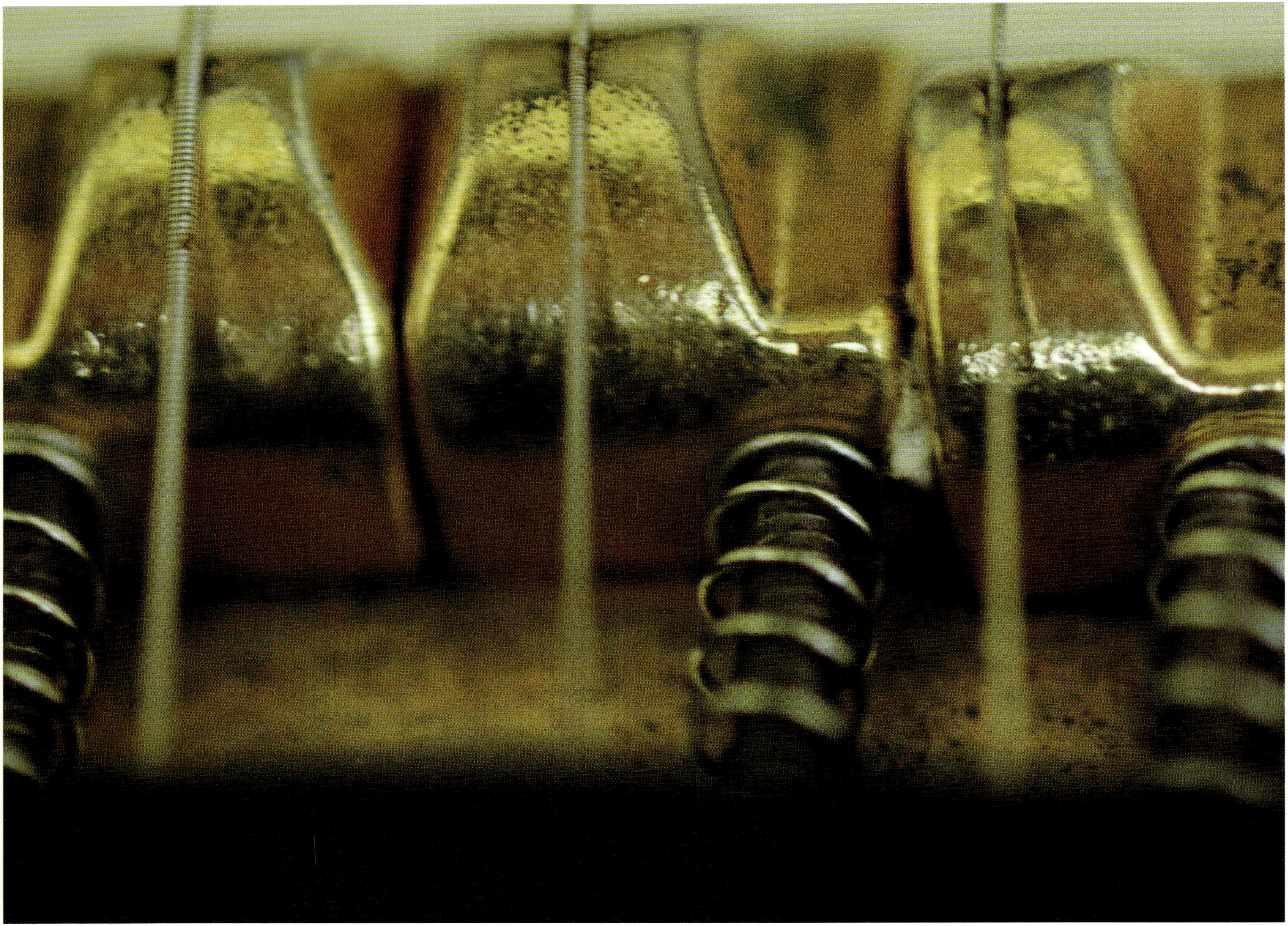

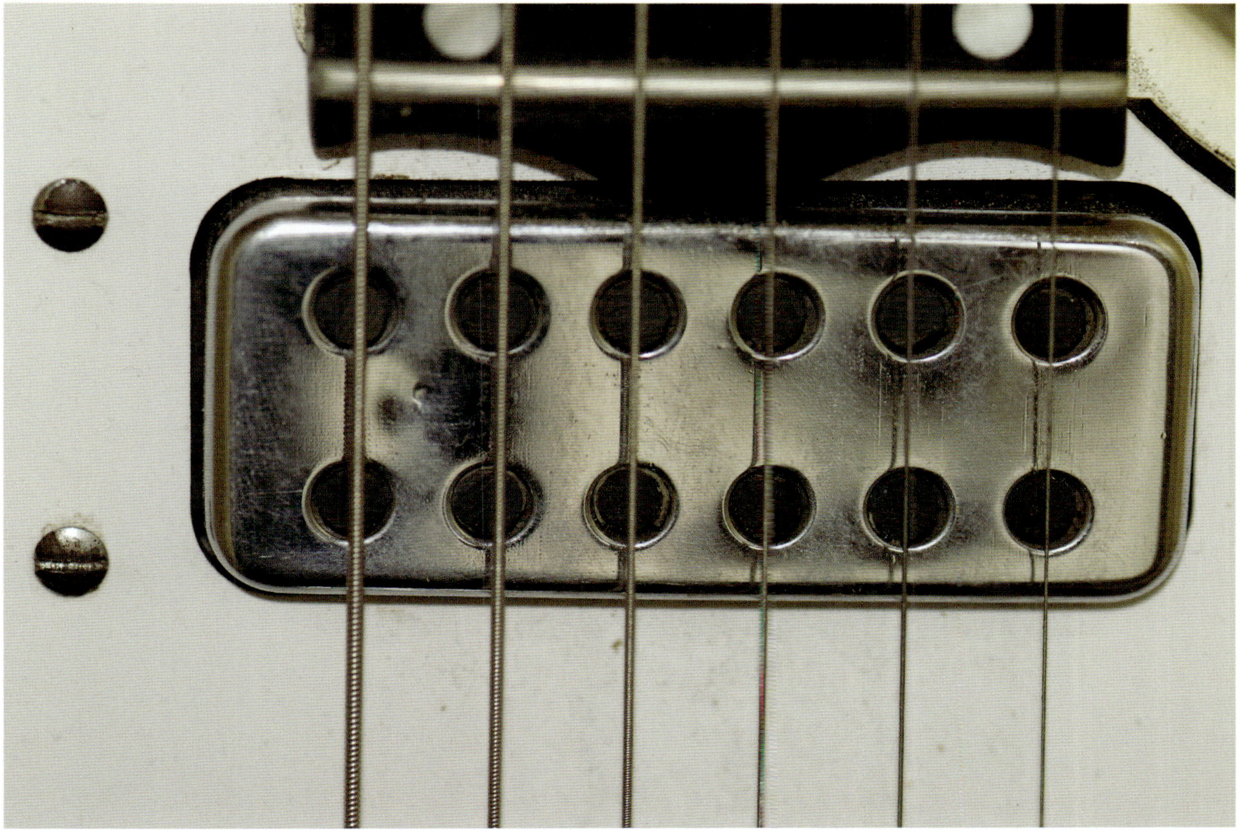

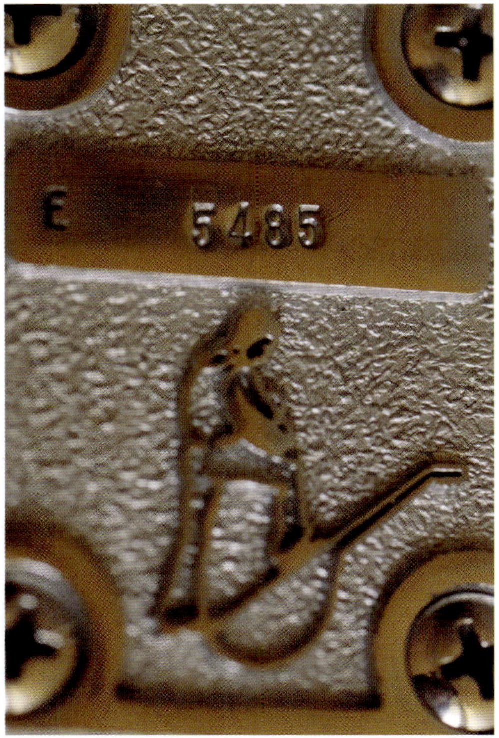
E
5485

JAMES CAUTY

Space, The KLF, The Orb

Floppy disks
Floppy disk drive
Akai S-900 sampler

Before we had the S-900, we had to rely on DJs to fly in the samples we wanted, usually slightly out of time and pitch. After acquiring the sampler, we could fly in our own samples, also slightly out of time and pitch. Those were the days when you couldn't see the music on a screen; you had to listen to the break beats to try and get them in synch.

This Akai S-900 was purchased with the royalties from a record called *Doctorin' the Tardis,* released in 1988. Prior to that we used borrowed equipment. It was the sampler of choice at the time, I think, because it had the longest sampling time, about one minute—much better than the one and a half seconds on the Greengate DS3 sampler.

We used the S-900 and S-950 on *Chill Out, Space*, KLF's "What Time Is Love?," "3 a.m. Eternal," and everything else up until about 1990.

All our equipment was badly mistreated both technically and conceptually; that's why none of it works any more. The samplers were left out all night on a beach in Scotland and never really recovered from the salty air. I did take one to the synth service center, and they found a small colony of mushrooms growing inside.

The floppy disks contain the samples for all the KLF records that were ever made.

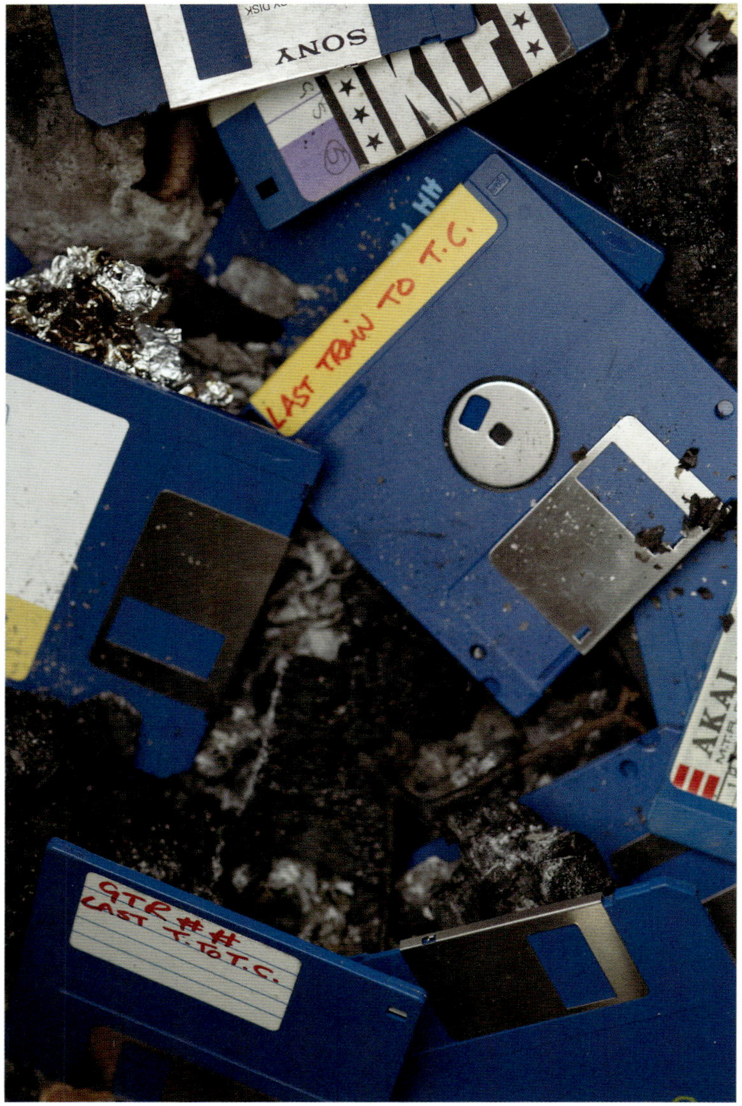

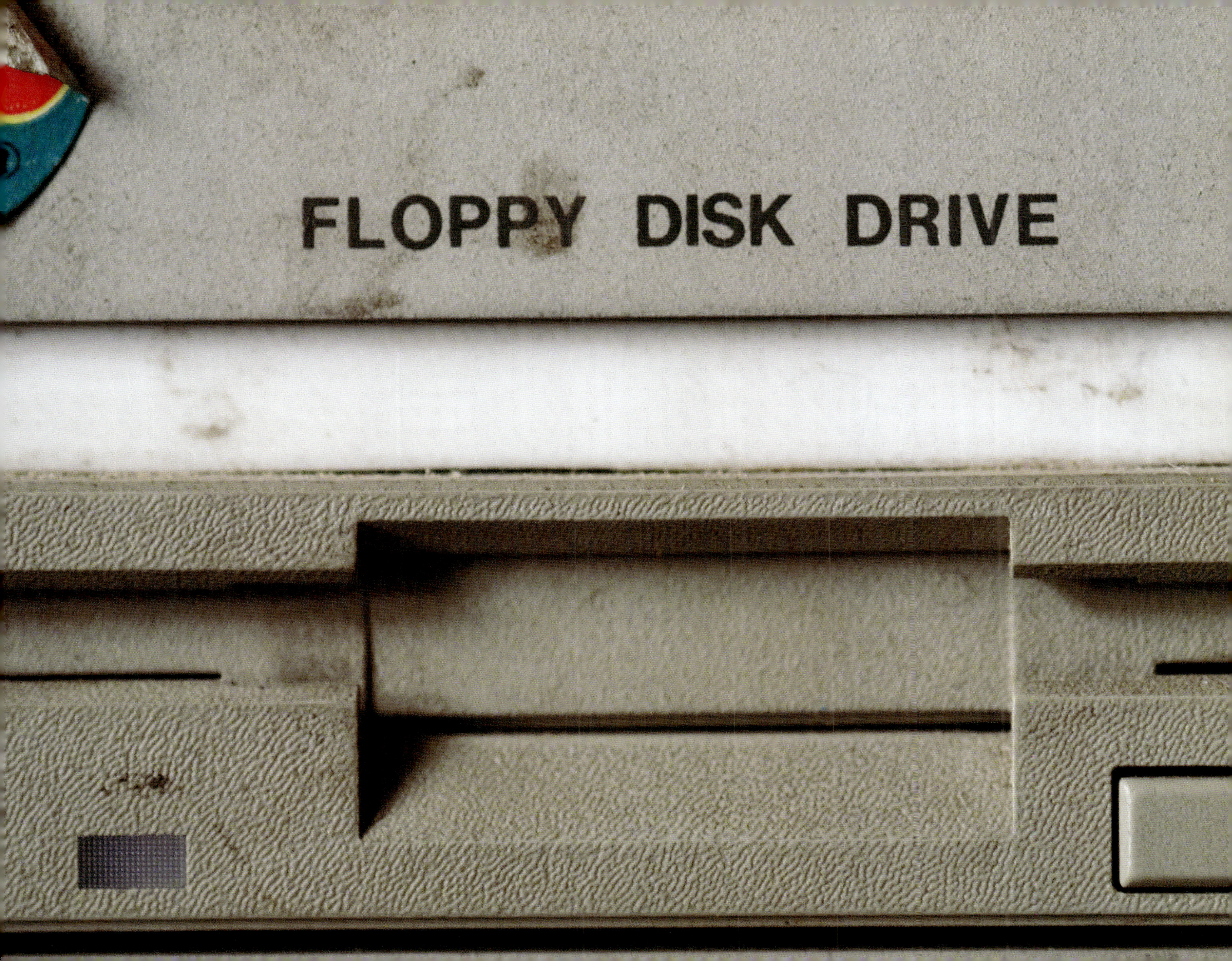
FLOPPY DISK DRIVE

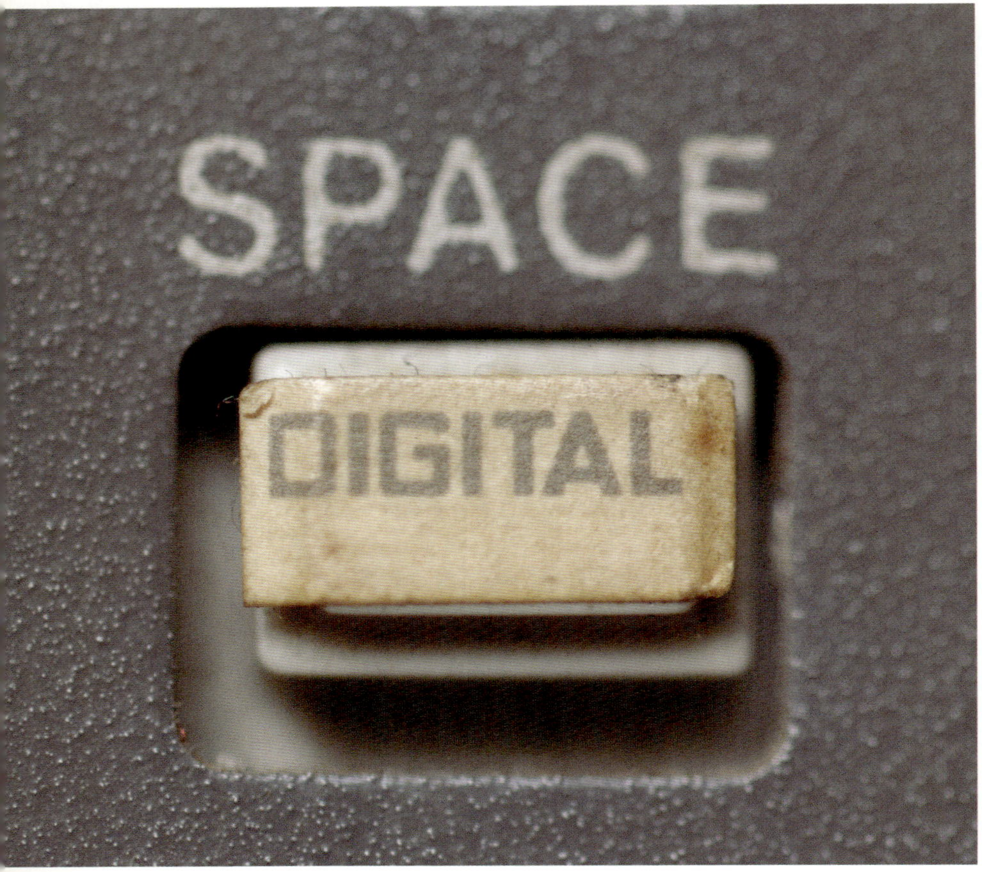
SPACE
DIGITAL
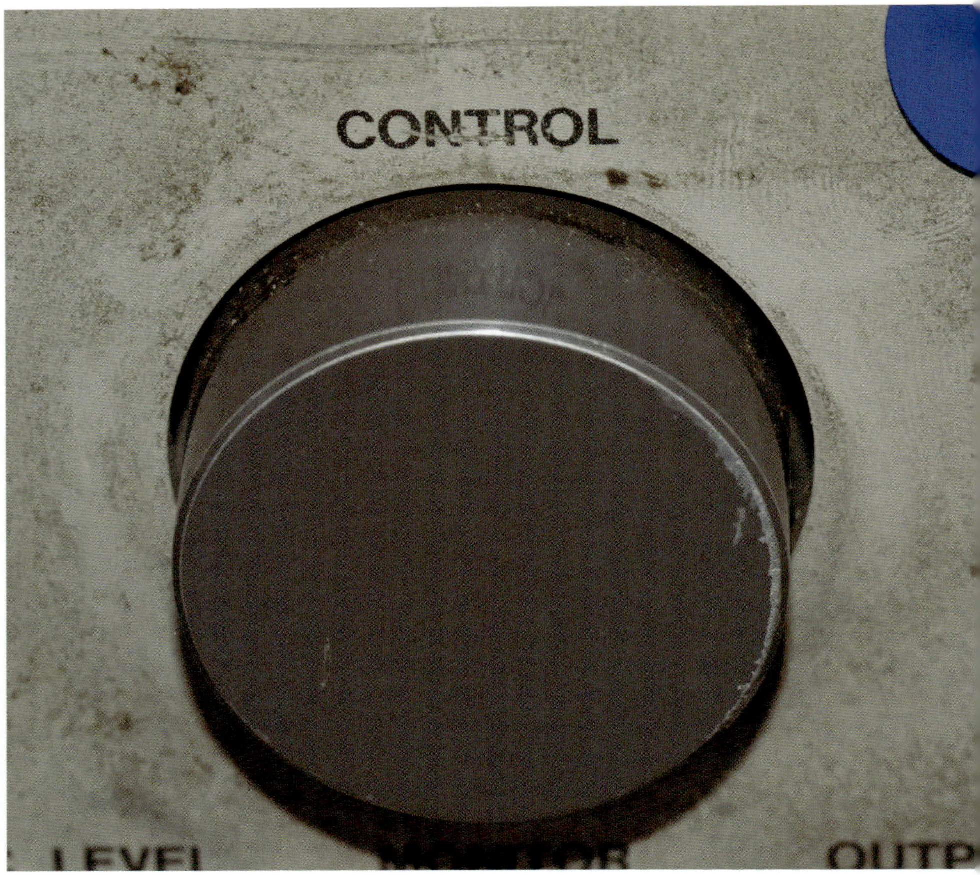
CONTROL

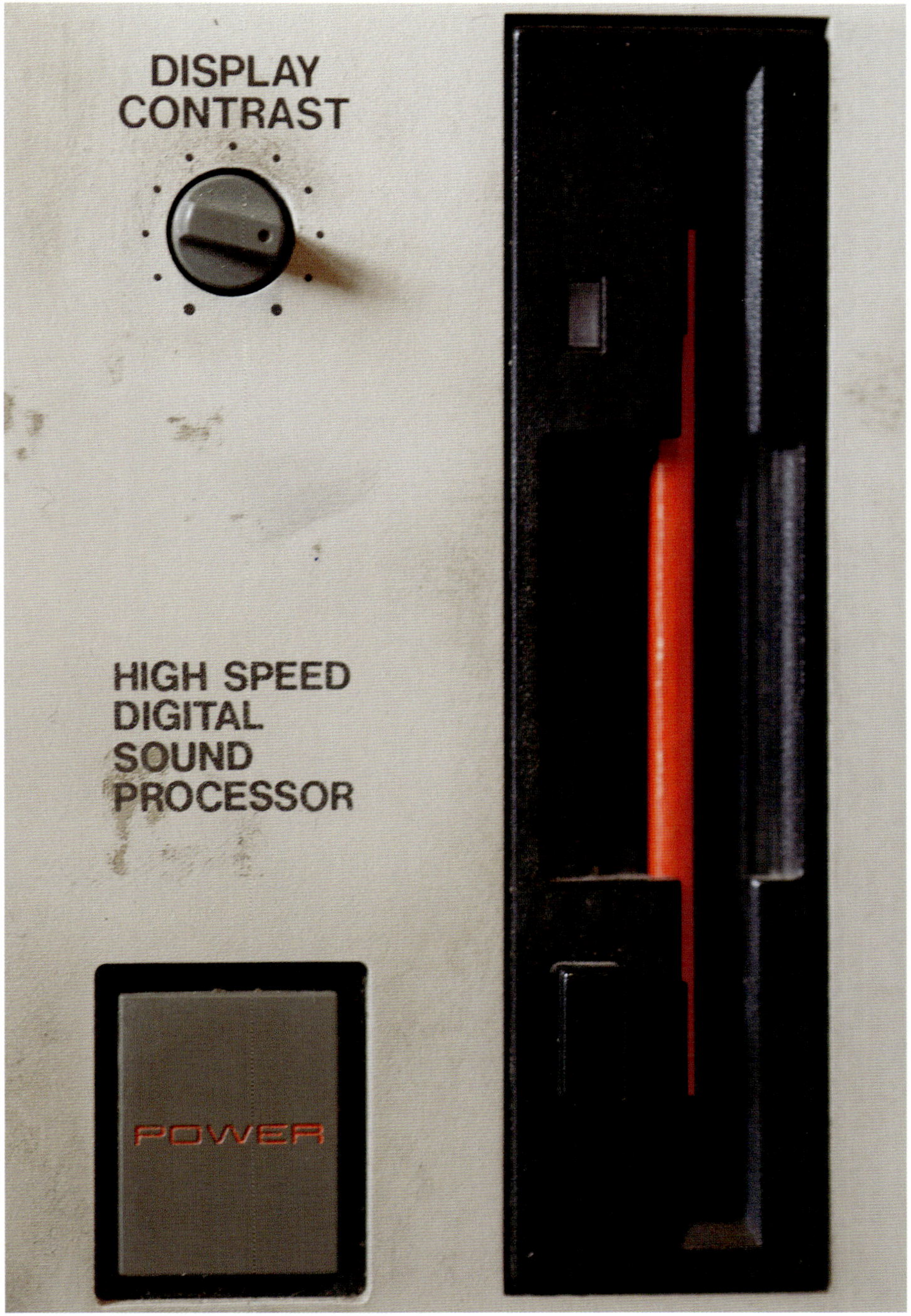
DISPLAY
CONTRAST
HIGH SPEED
DIGITAL
SOUND
PROCESSOR
POWER

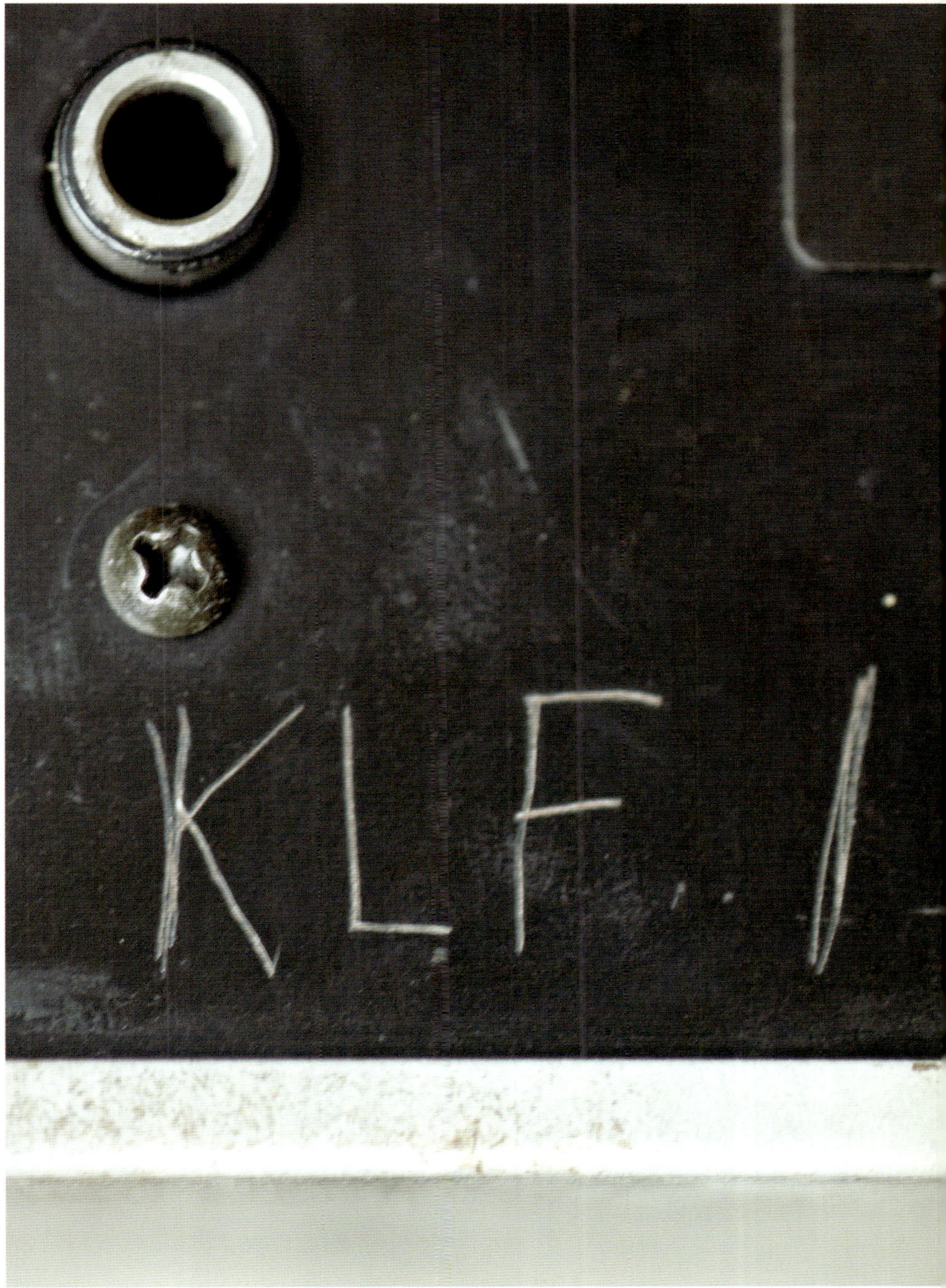
KLF 1

JOHN REIS

Rocket from the Crypt, Drive Like Jehu, Hot Snakes, Night Marchers
Fender Telecaster guitar

This guitar was once Jimmy Ferrelli's [Jimmy Ferrelli and the Panty Hounds] and was given to their merch guy, Mac [McCaughan, later of Superchunk] and then to Pen [Rollings, of Honor Roll]. Pen gave me the guitar in the late 1990s to keep me from drooling on him.

I recorded some later Rocket stuff on it, I don't remember exactly what. I used it on most of the Hot Snakes recordings, and I play it live with the Night Marchers. I write with it. Don't know exactly which songs, but lots for sure. Hundreds of hits.

Most of its war stories come courtesy of video footage I have seen of Pen playing it in the final days of Honor Roll. Man, it looked like he was trying to break that block of wood with every stroke, and then he threw it across the stage to careen off the stage decorations. To say it was well worn in before I got it would be a severe understatement. Personally, I wrap it in crushed velvet after every show and treat it like gothic royalty. Sometimes when I'm feeling naughty, I don't purchase an extra ticket for it on flights, and I put it in a dog crate and make it fly down below with the sedated house pets. I do change the electronics every tour due to sweat damage.

It's a fine axe, the nicest I have ever owned. It is a part of me, like my tongue or hair.

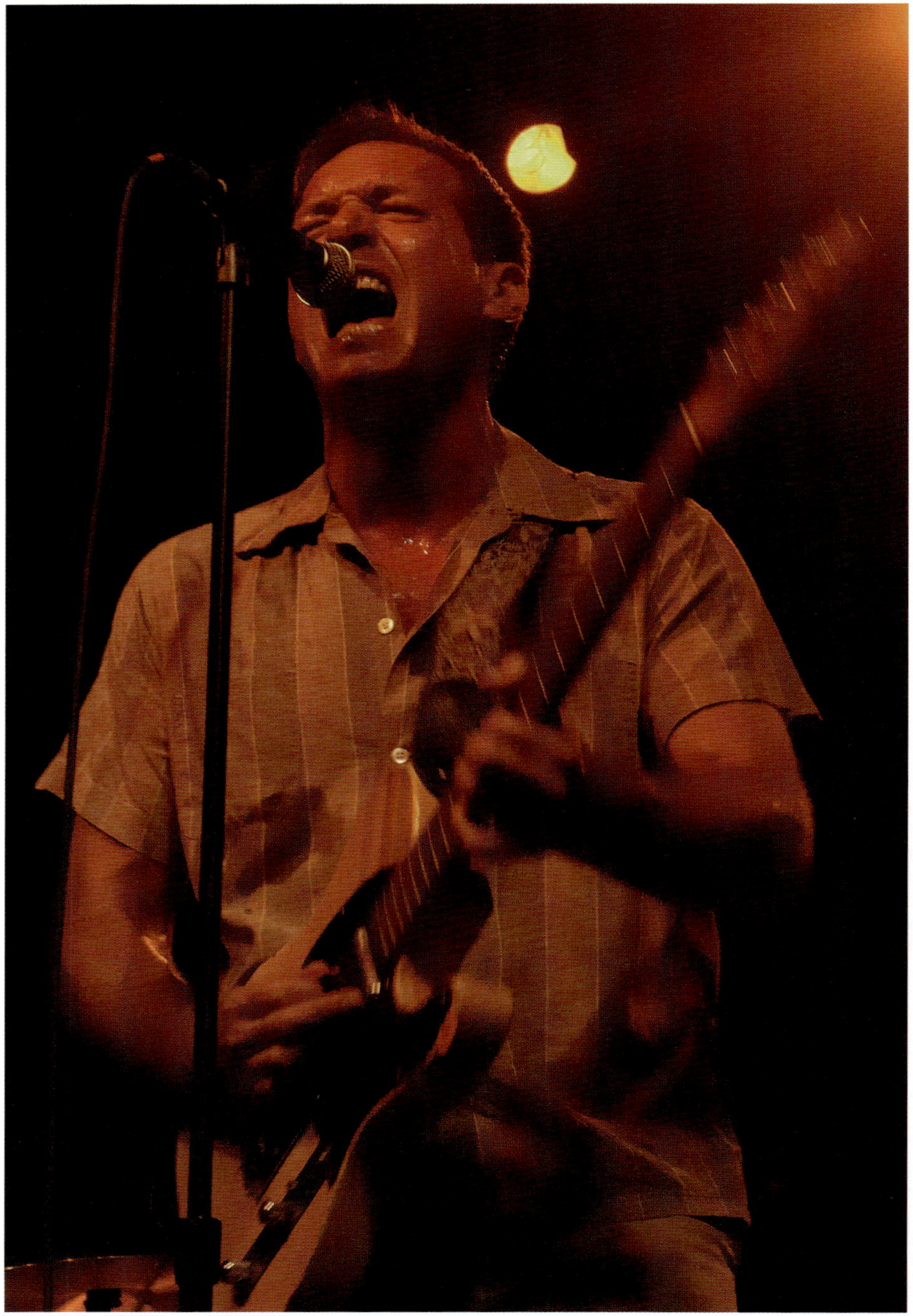

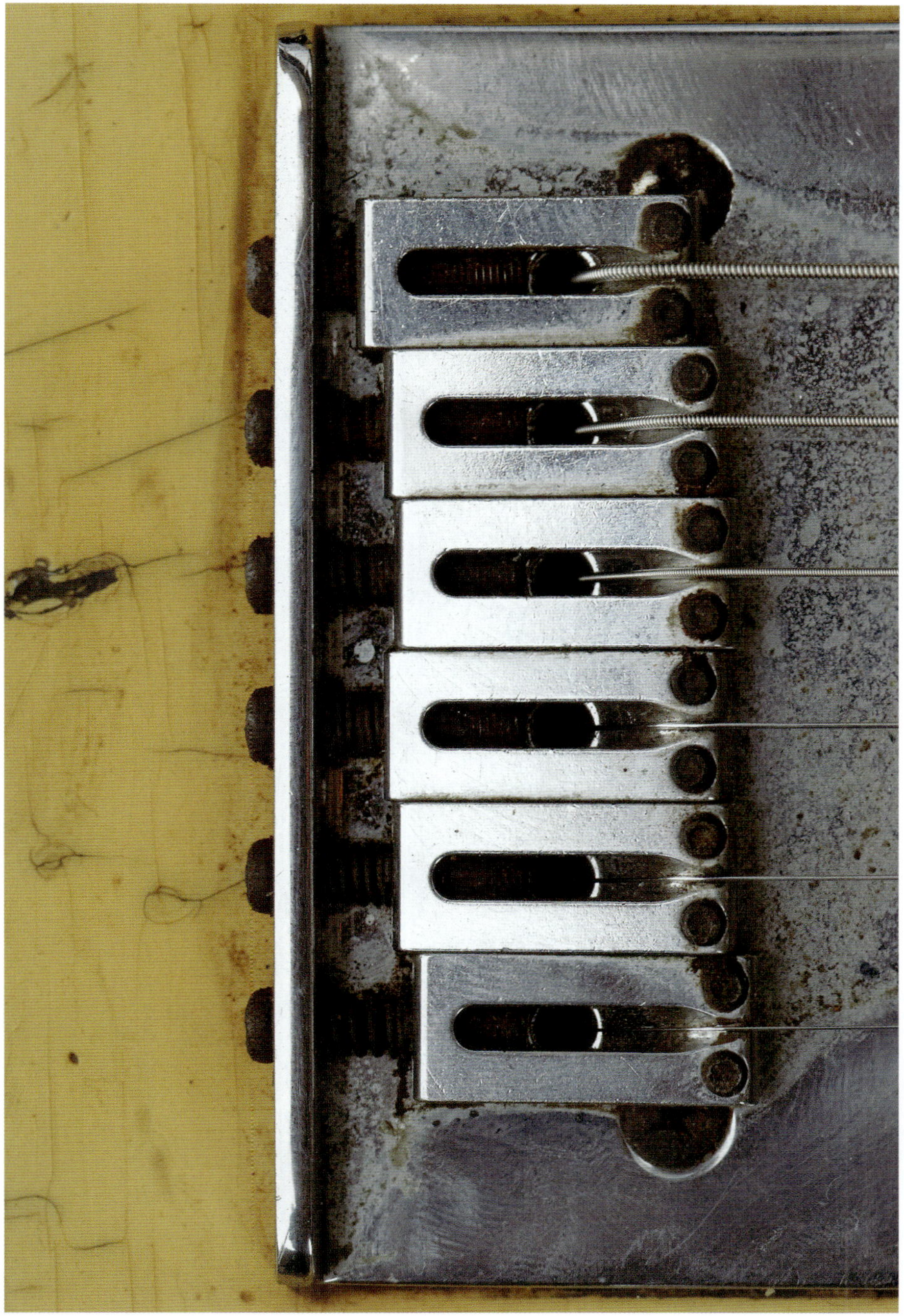

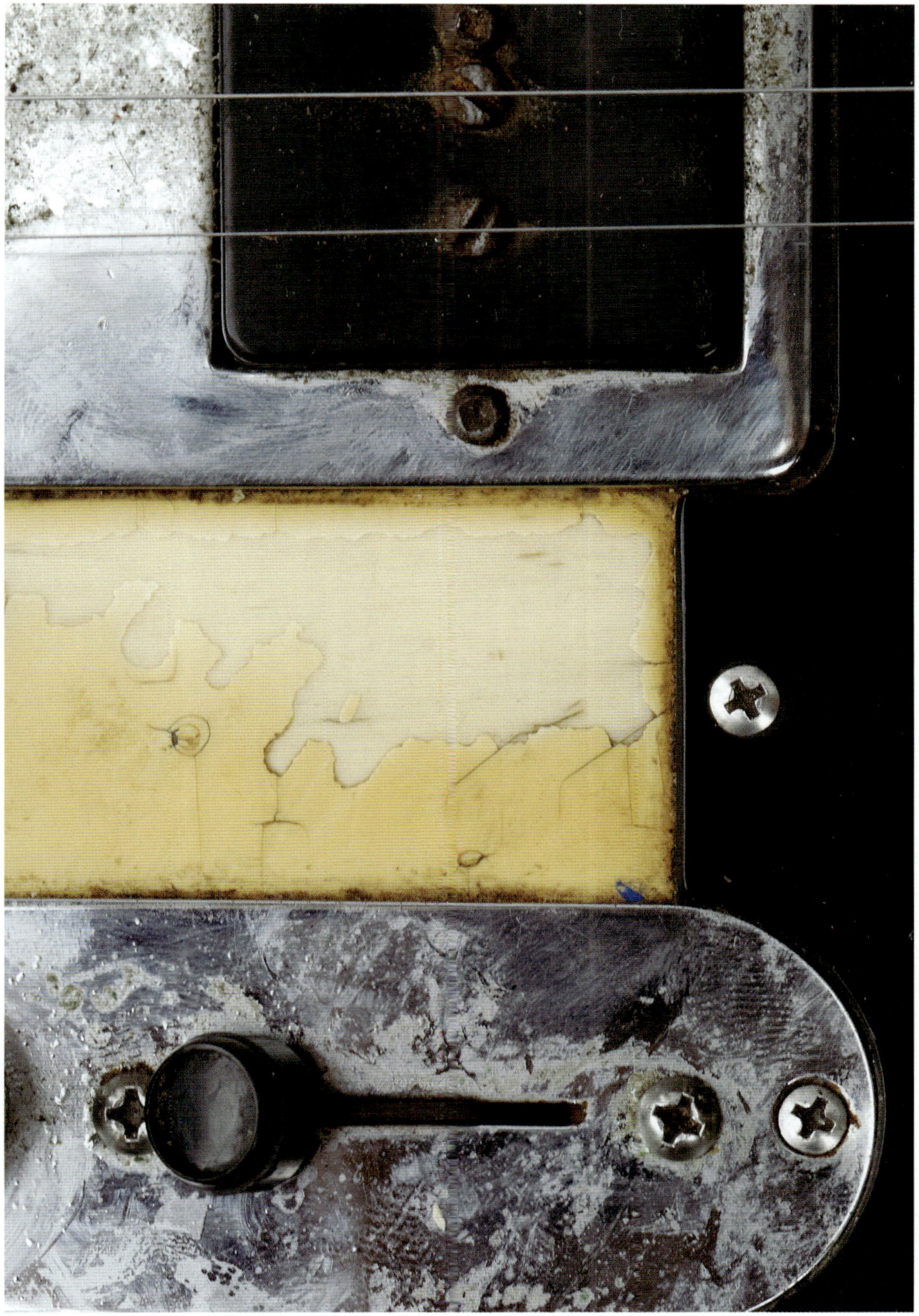

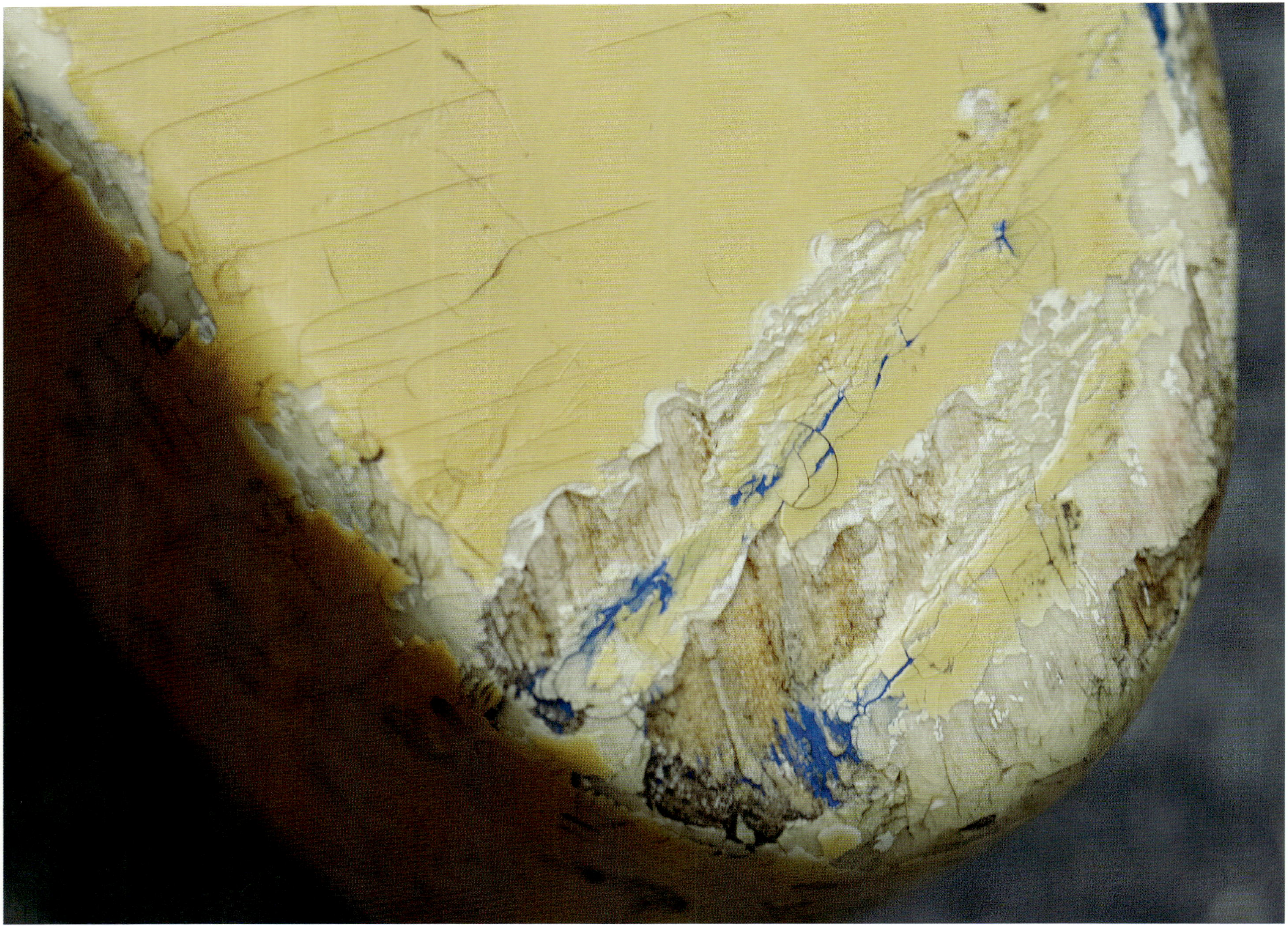

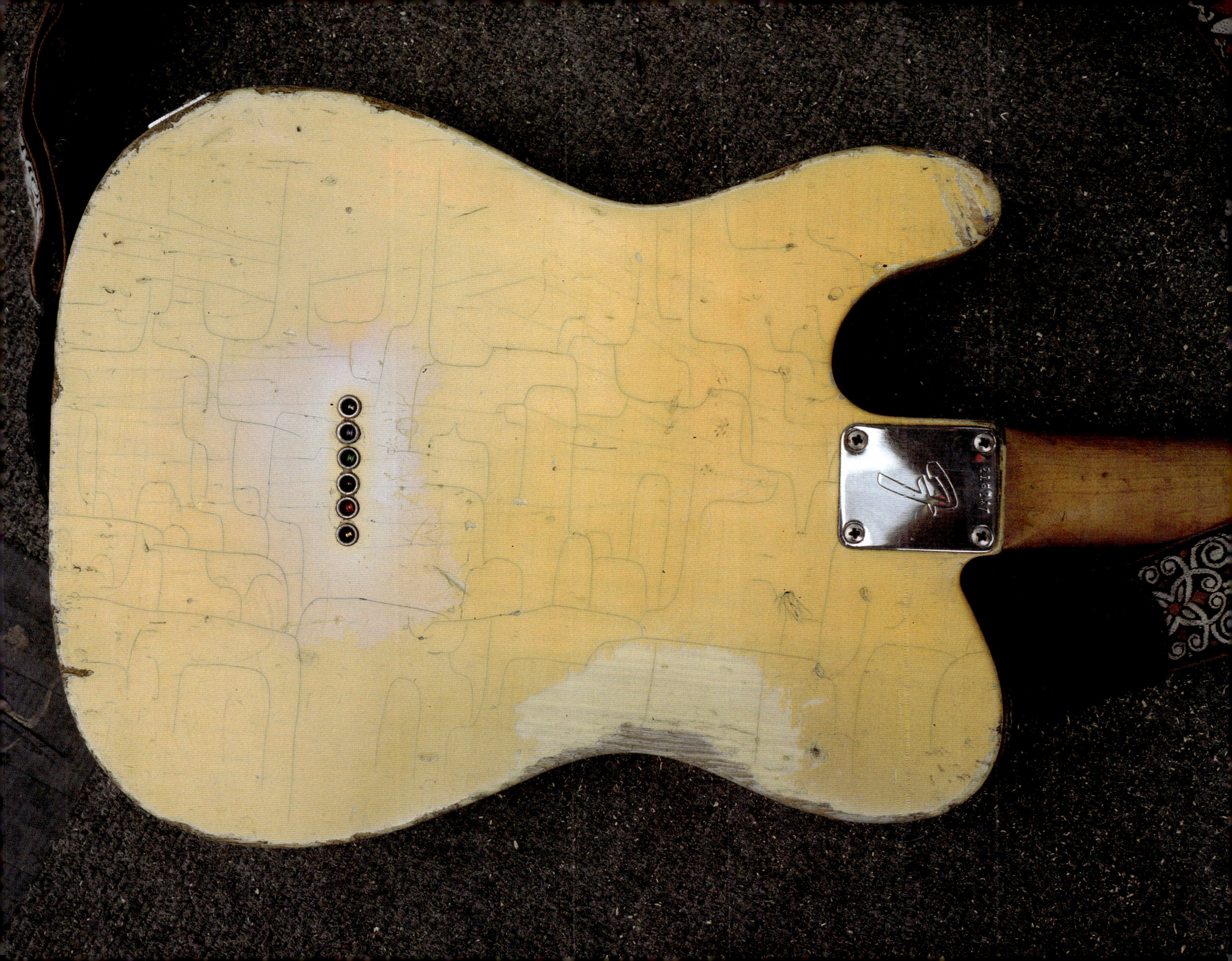

JUSTIN VERNON

Bon Iver
National Reso-Phonic guitar

I bought this guitar from a guy here in a music shop in Eau Claire, Wisconsin. The serial number on the guitar body dates it to between 1929 and 1931, nobody knows for sure. I bought it for $400 and had minor restoration done to it.

When you put this guitar in an open-D tuning . . . I've never ever heard a harmonic sequence resonate so purely on any instrument. It lights up an entire wooden room with sparkles and notes that feel like you are listening to one of those $30,000 speaker systems. It's just beautiful.

It literally wrote a song for me, a song called "Skinny Love," which was a really important song for our band and our first record. The guitar seemed to exist to write that song, although it has been around for eighty years and who knows where it has been. It makes me feel humble in its presence because I know it's older than me, and that it has brought more music to the world than I ever will have the time to make. I will never get rid of it, and I take it everywhere that I go.

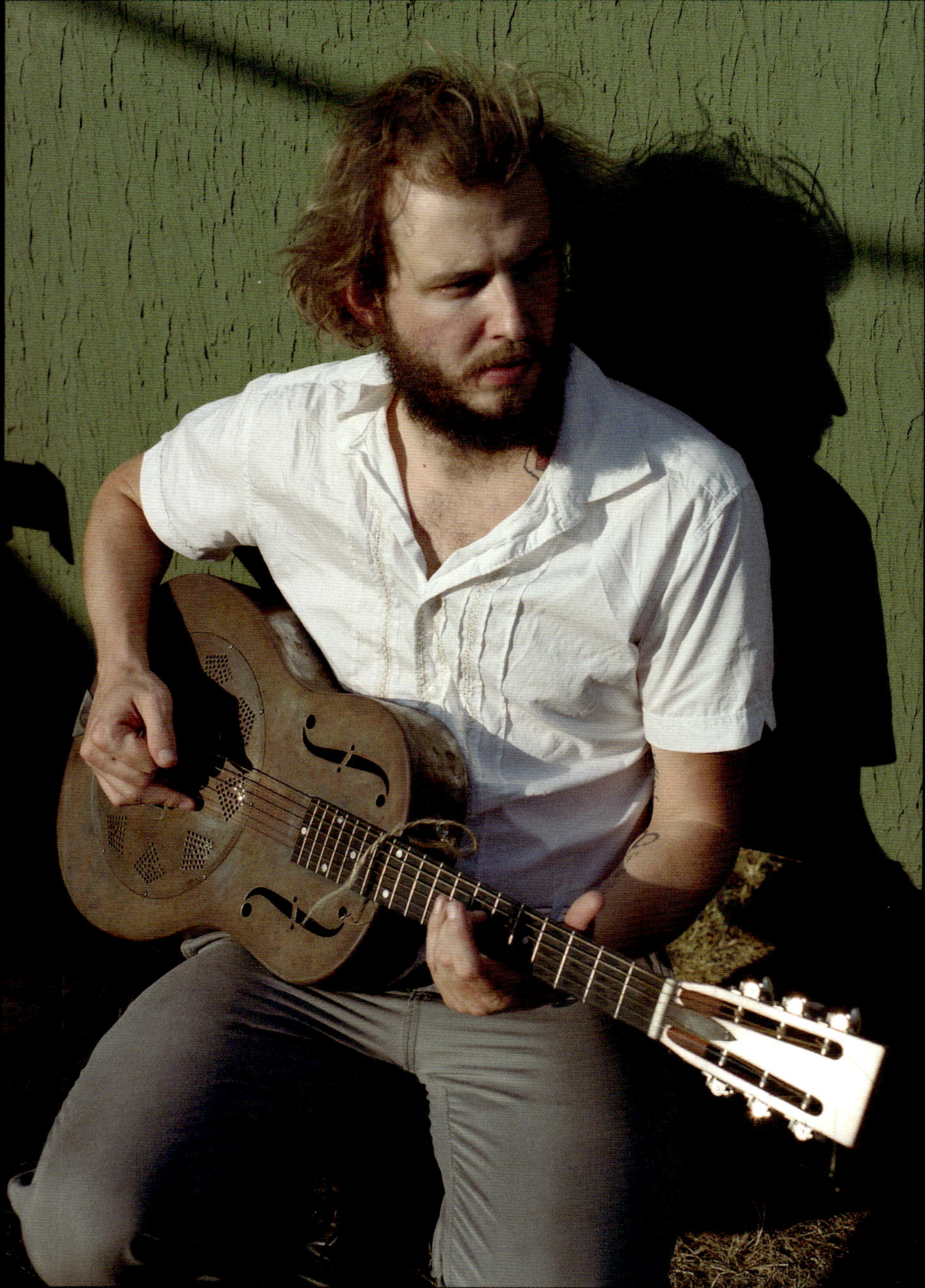

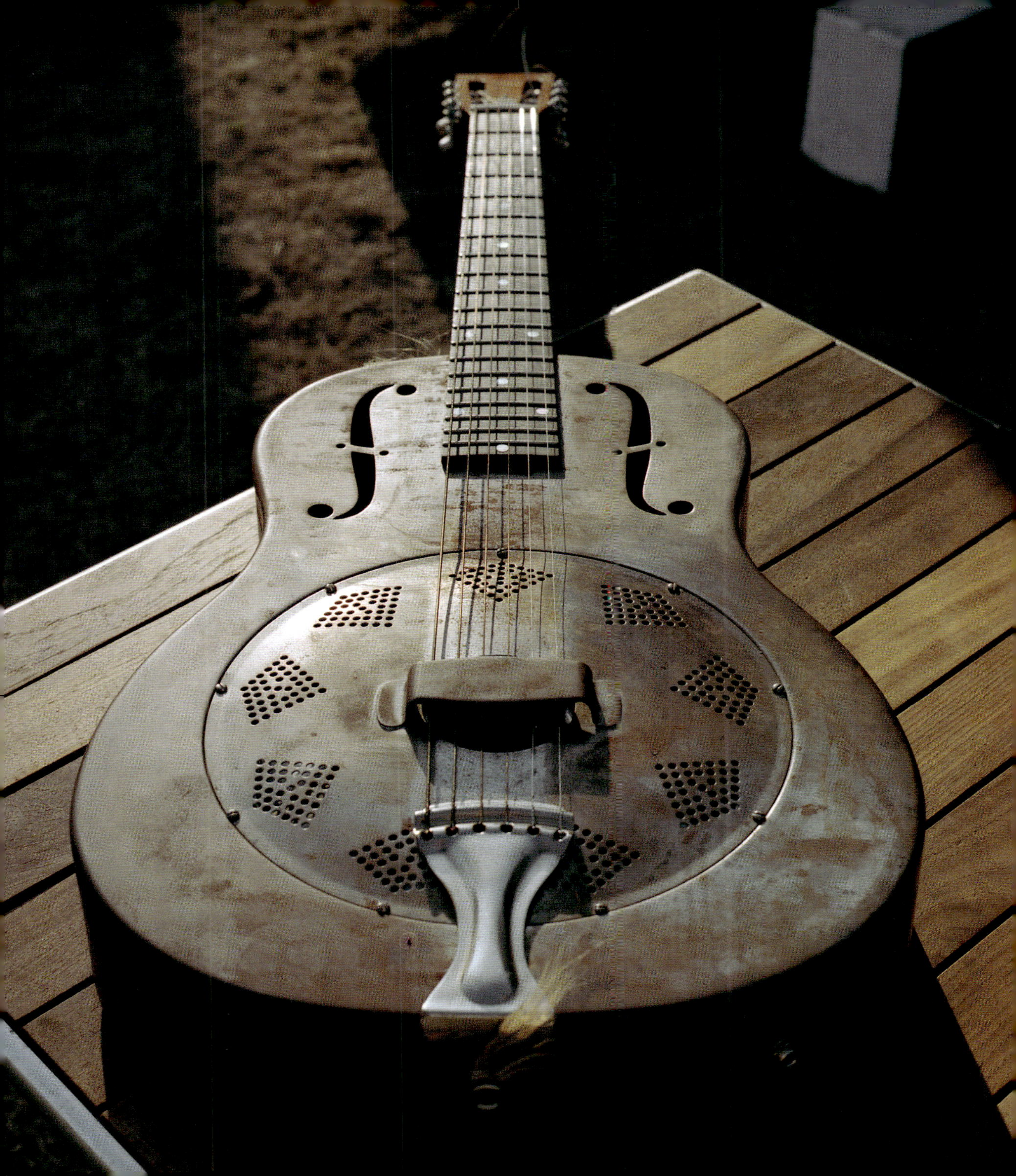

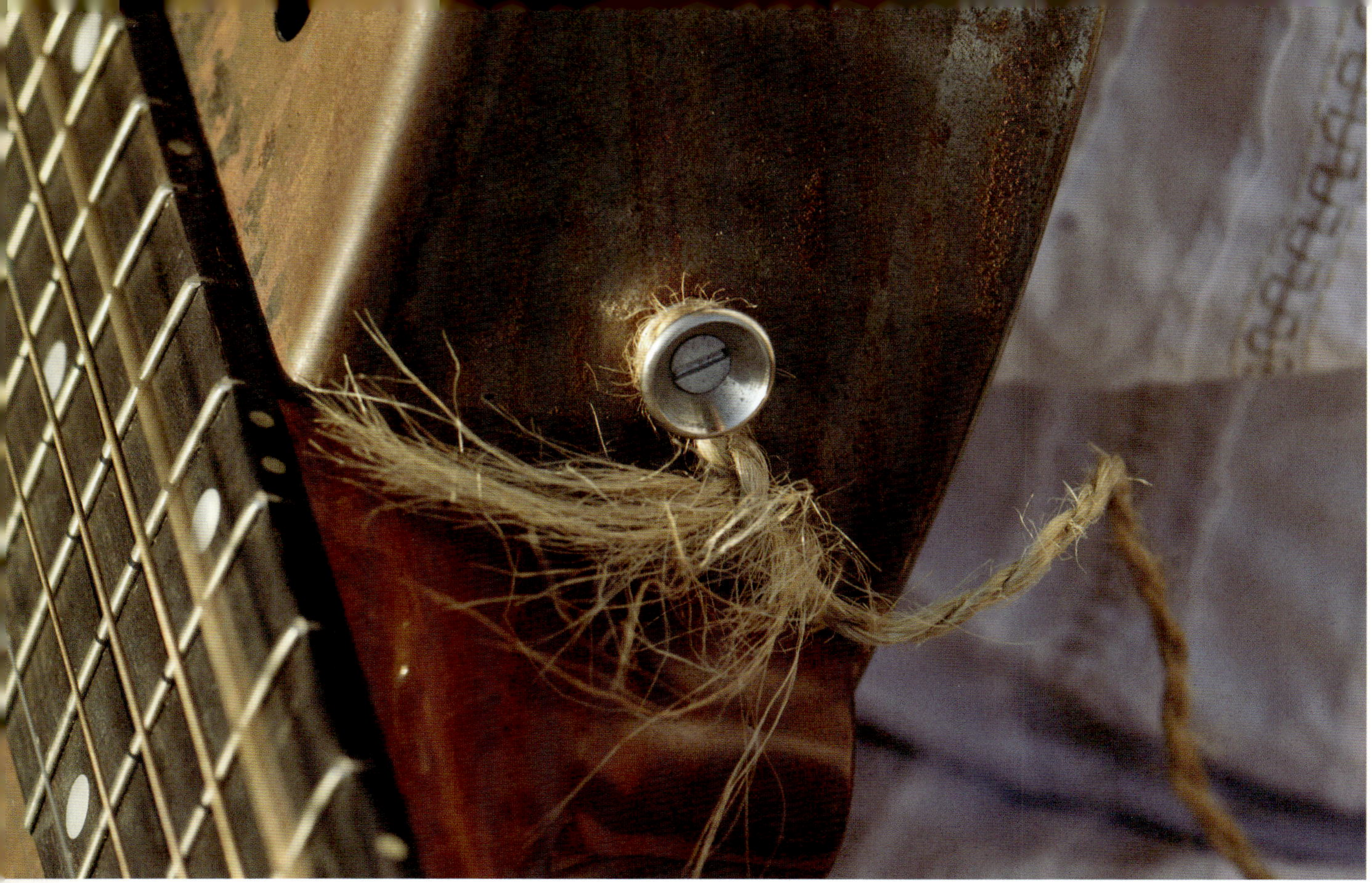

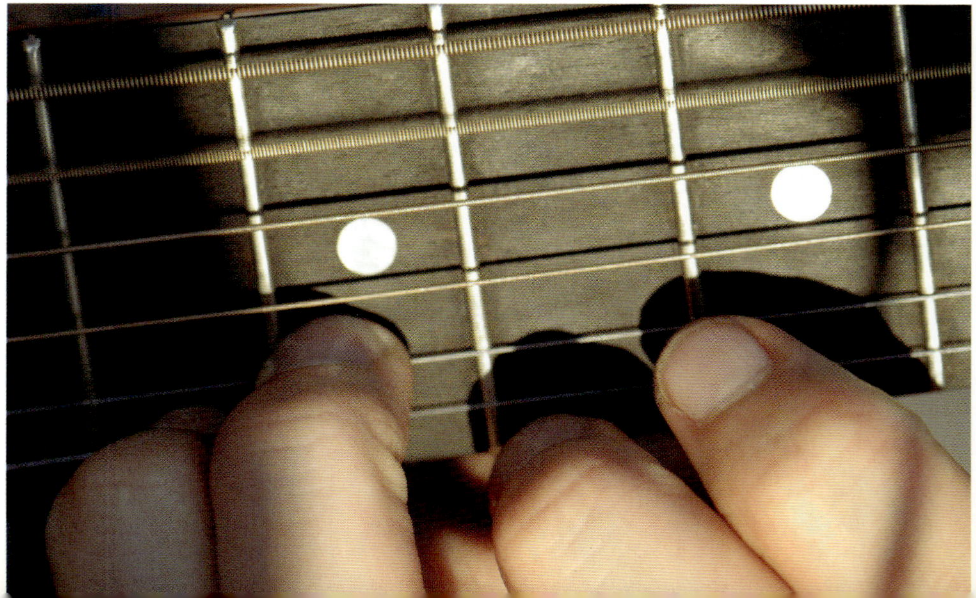

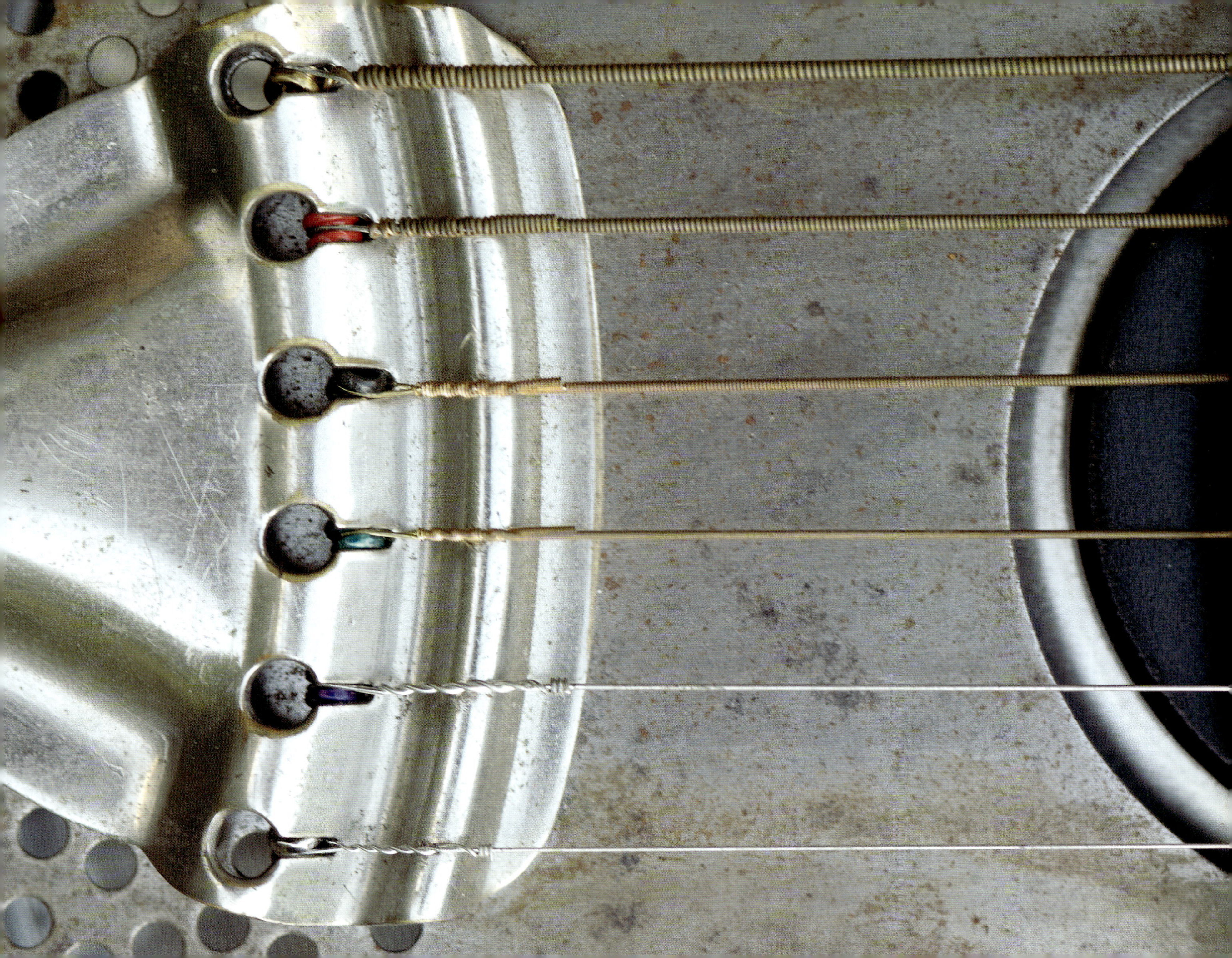

IAN MACKAYE

Minor Threat, Fugazi, The Evens

Gibson SG guitar

I only really used two guitars in Fugazi. The first one was a brown SG, which I bought in the mid-1980s. The second was a white SG I traded a Marshall head [amp] for five or six years later—and this became the one I really developed a relationship with. I had this idea with Fugazi that I was going to have one guitar and one amp and one cable, not use any effects, and just try to get as many tones and sounds as I could by physically manipulating the instrument. I respond to limitations, so when I put myself into a situation with few options, I have to work a lot harder, and that always engages me. This particular guitar became my main instrument.

Now, I am glad I had two guitars, because I quite often broke one. I never purposefully smashed my guitar, but I really put it through its paces, and often it would just fall apart. You can see that there are two or three crack lines on the neck . . . Fugazi was doing a show in Green Bay, Wisconsin, in '89, and I was playing the song "Burning." In the song, there's this sort of siren-like feedback in the chorus, which involves me getting a tone and then really waving the neck back and forth to get the pitch to change. I was going back and forth to get that tone, and suddenly the guitar just went off. I couldn't figure out why there was no sound; then I realized that I had hit the head of the guitar against the top of a banister and it had snapped the head clean off, so the strings had no tension. It was kind of a drag, you know, that was kind of an absurd moment. But I have to say, when you are using things and they break, it's kind of beautiful in a weird way, because you are actually using them.

Another time, we did a show just north of San Diego, a really great gig. I remember at one point, playing guitar and just spinning in a circle, around and around, and I hadn't taken into consideration that the cable was wrapping around my leg, so I had basically hog-tied myself, and fell flat on my face and broke the neck off the guitar. I think there is a video of that where you can see me from the side, and I just take a nosedive. I smashed in the jack, too. You can see where we had to put a metal plate on where the jack had destroyed the wood.

Playing with Fugazi, I perspired in a way that was kind of unbelievable, and when we played, my guitar would quite often just shut down because of the amount of sweat that ran into the pickups. I would have to change guitars at some point because of the amount of sweat. On the back of the guitar, you can see that the way I beat it against my chest or my stomach or whatever wore off all the paint.

You can clearly see where the pick is always hitting. The guitar strap is actually a seat belt that came out of a van Fugazi bought in 1988. We removed the middle seats, and the lap belt was the perfect length, and I just bolted it onto the guitar.

This guitar actually is easier for me to play than any other, and this certainly has been a central part of using it. I didn't record with this guitar, because it had problems with the strings hitting the frets—it was wrecked—so I usually used the other guitar for recording. But in terms of playing and performing, this was always my chosen one. I am not a particularly materialistic dude. I don't really give a damn about things that much, but this guitar for me is irreplaceable. It has just been through so much that it's just like a fellow traveler for me.

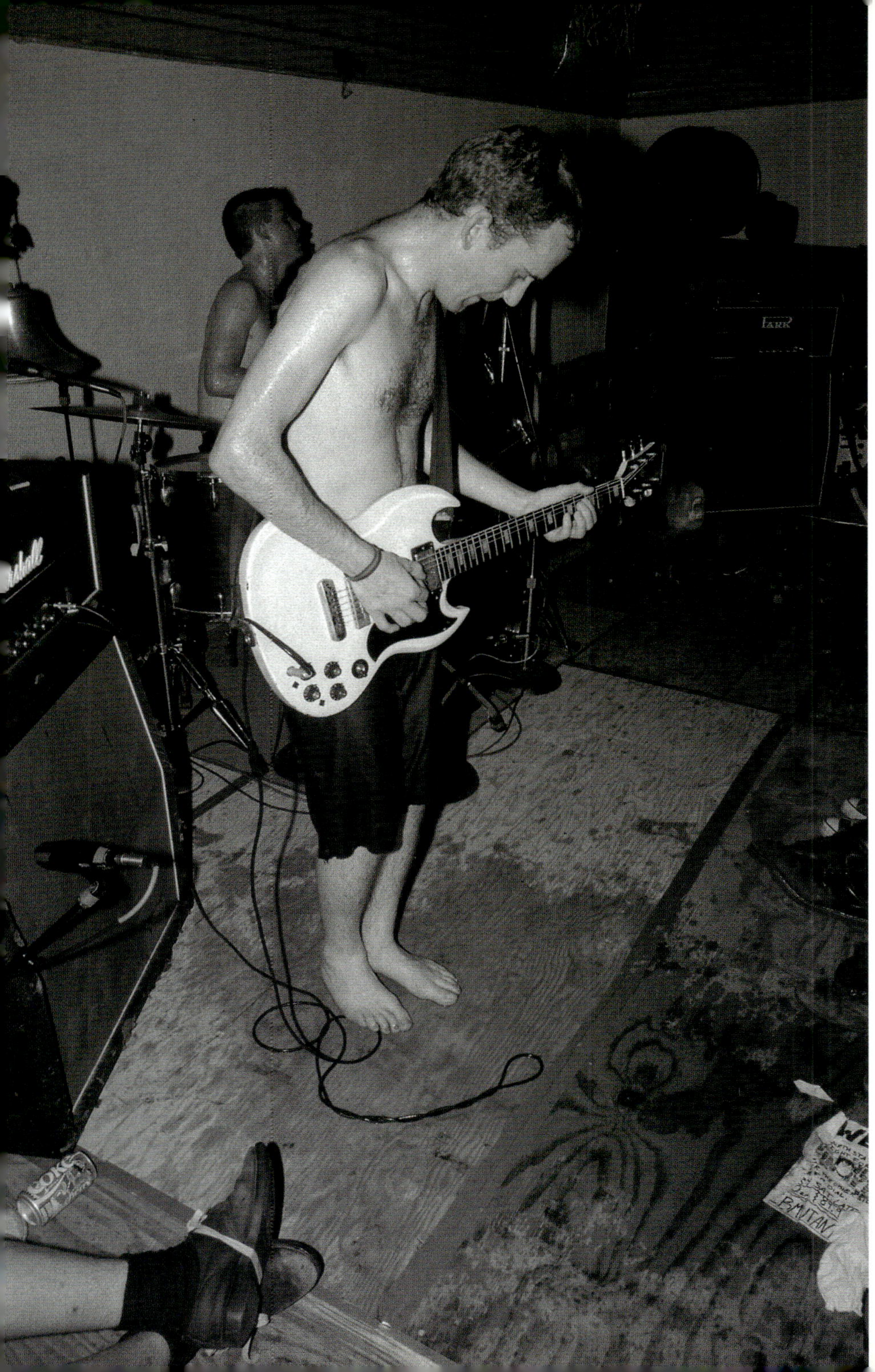

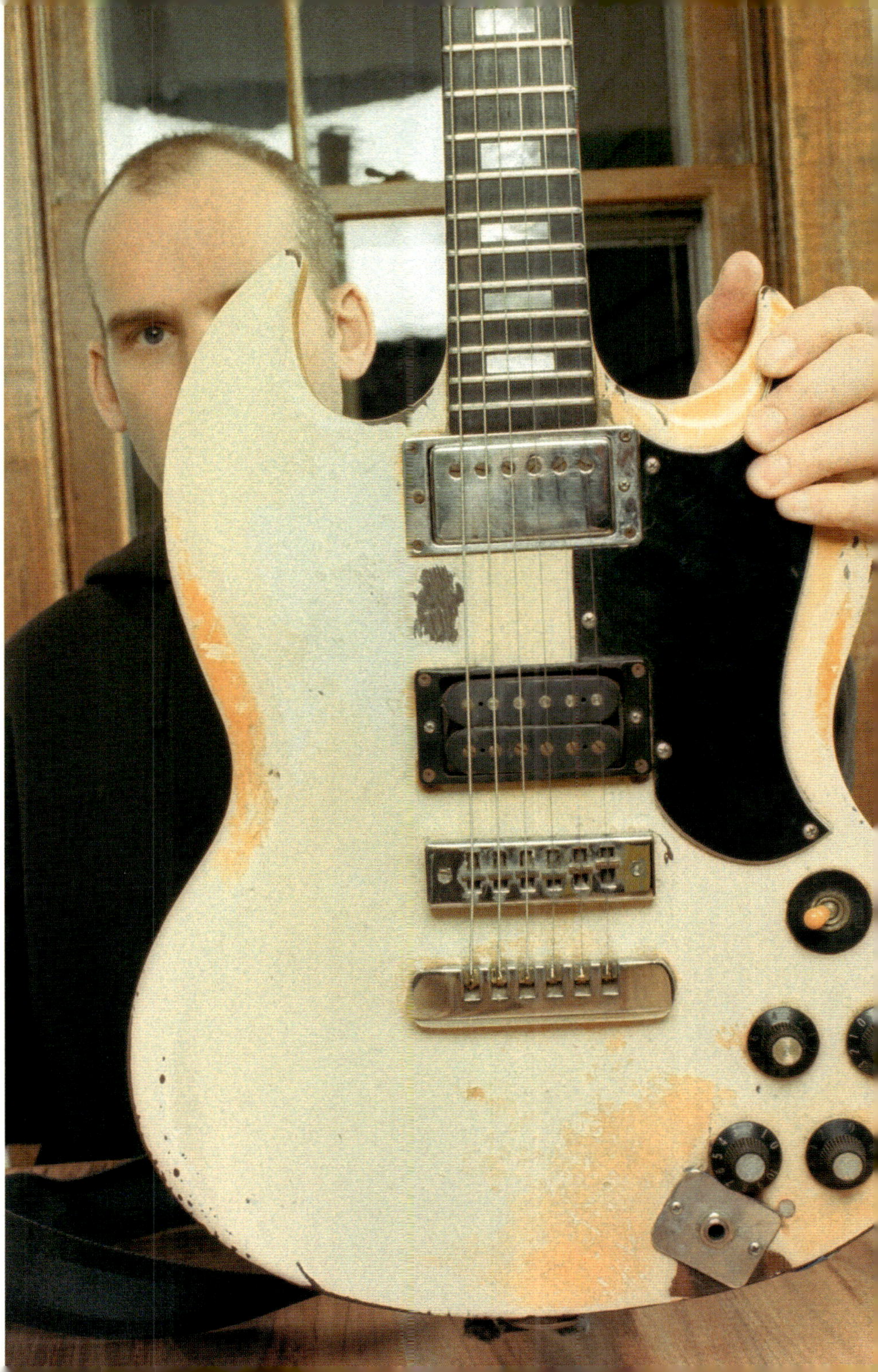

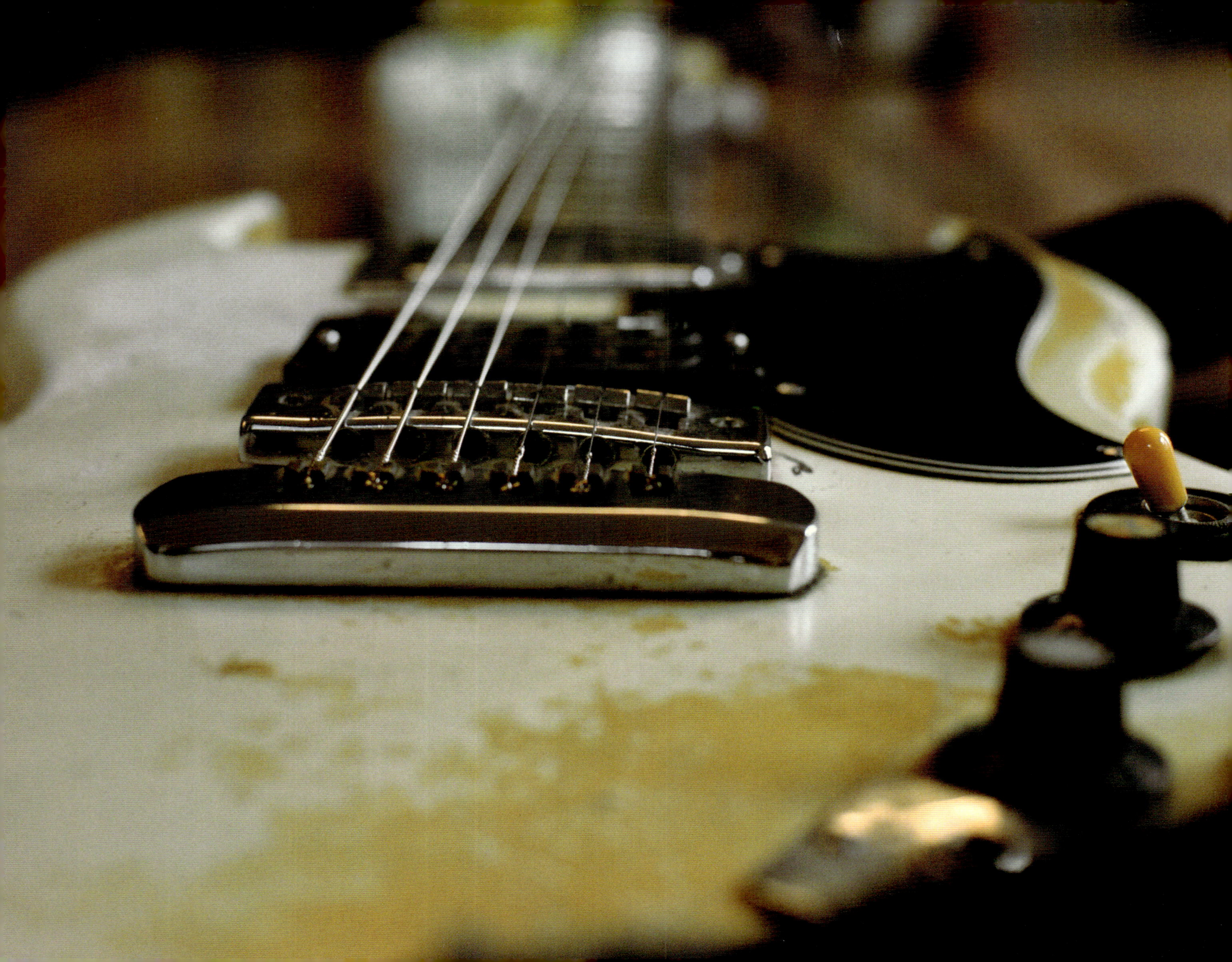

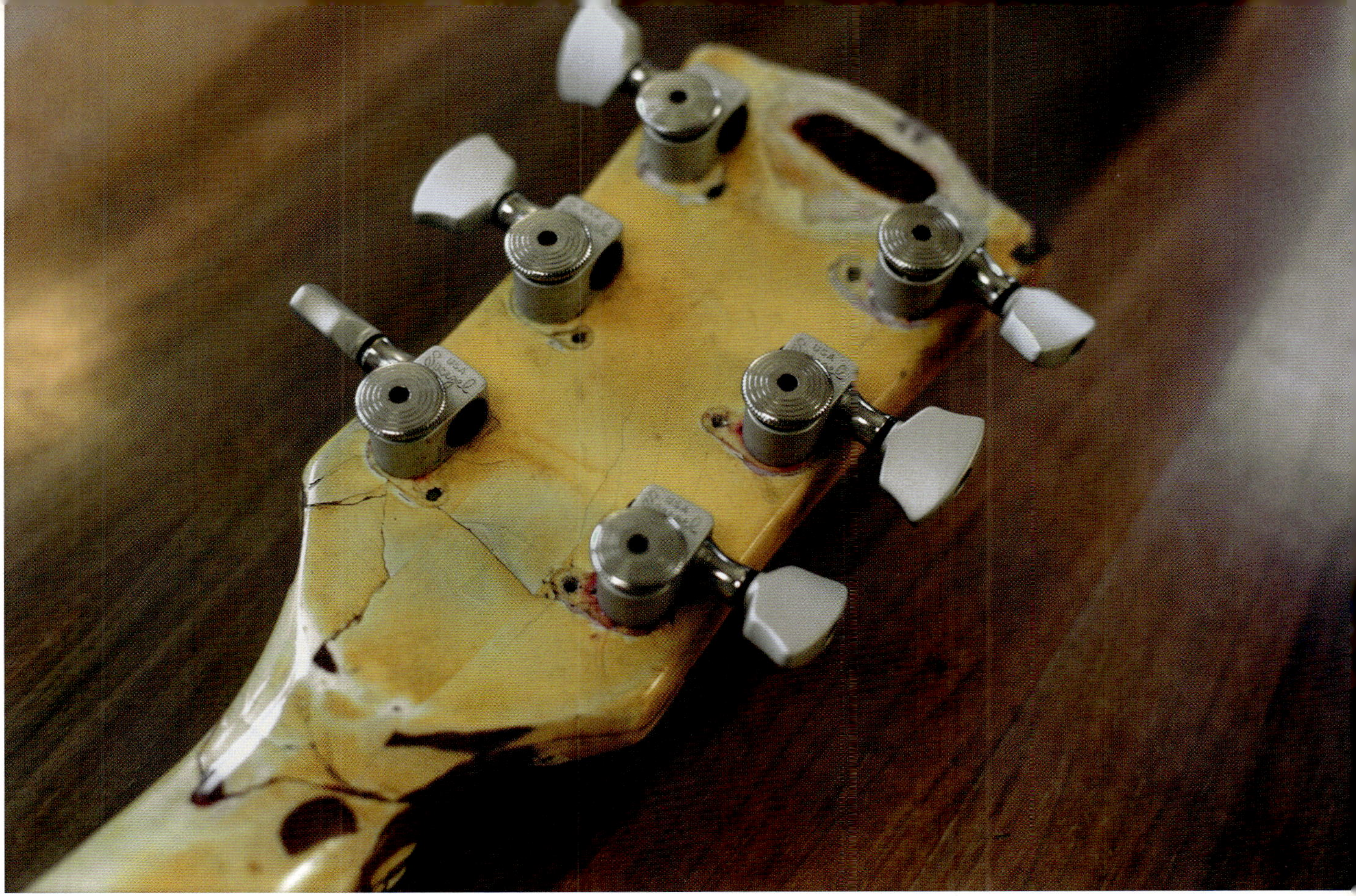

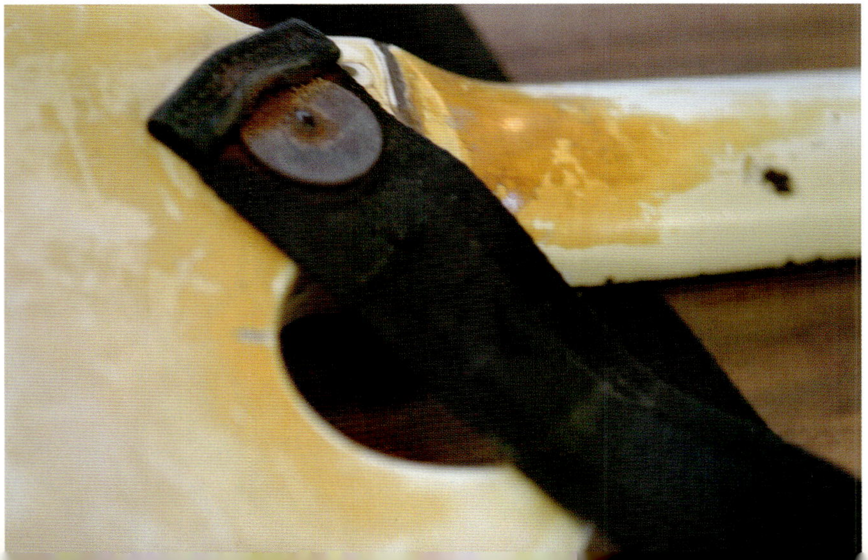

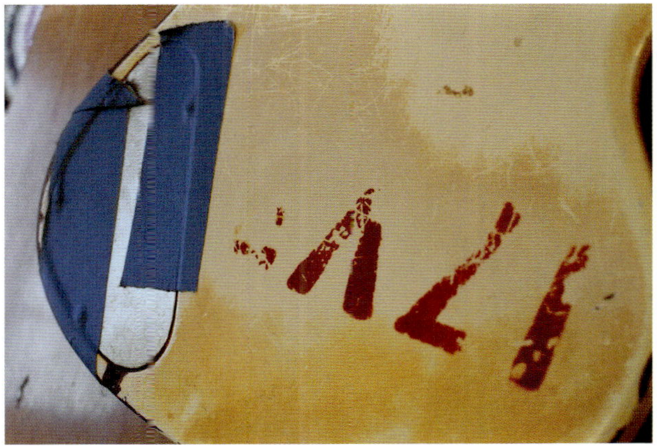

JOHN DOE

X

Fender Jazz bass

John bought this bass in 1971 in Baltimore, where he grew up. He wrote every X song on this bass. He's playing it in Penelope Spheeris's movie about the L.A. punk scene, *The Decline of Western Civilization,* and in W. T. Morgan's fantastic X documentary, *The Unheard Music*. In that film, he's sitting on his bed writing "Real Child of Hell" with it. This model of bass manufactured now has black sparkle with subtle glitter through it, but in the '70s it had a different look. John later went to the Fender Precision bass that he plays now.

—Rick King

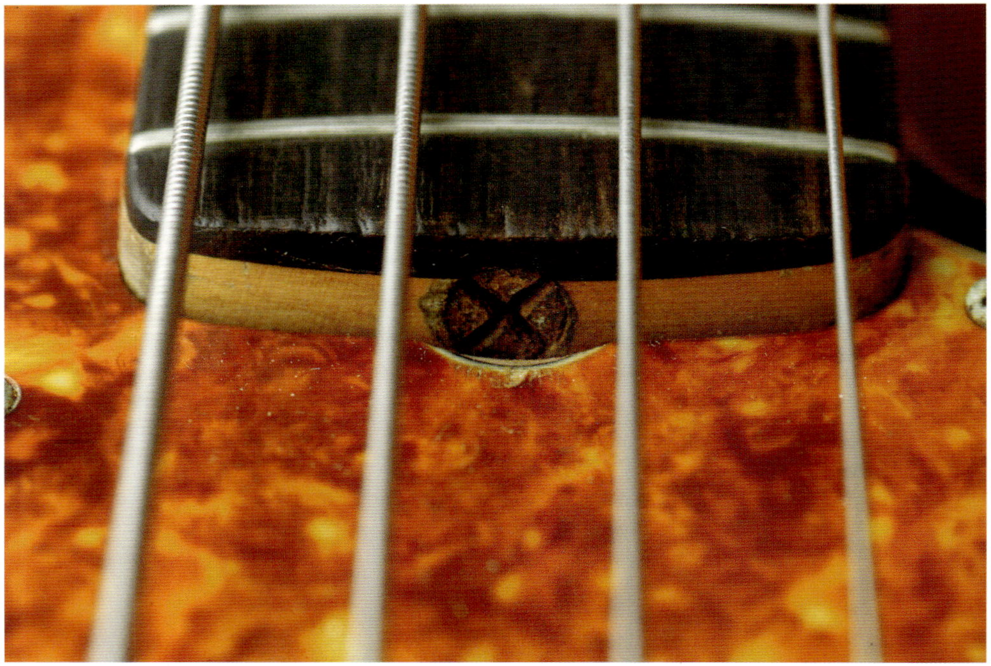

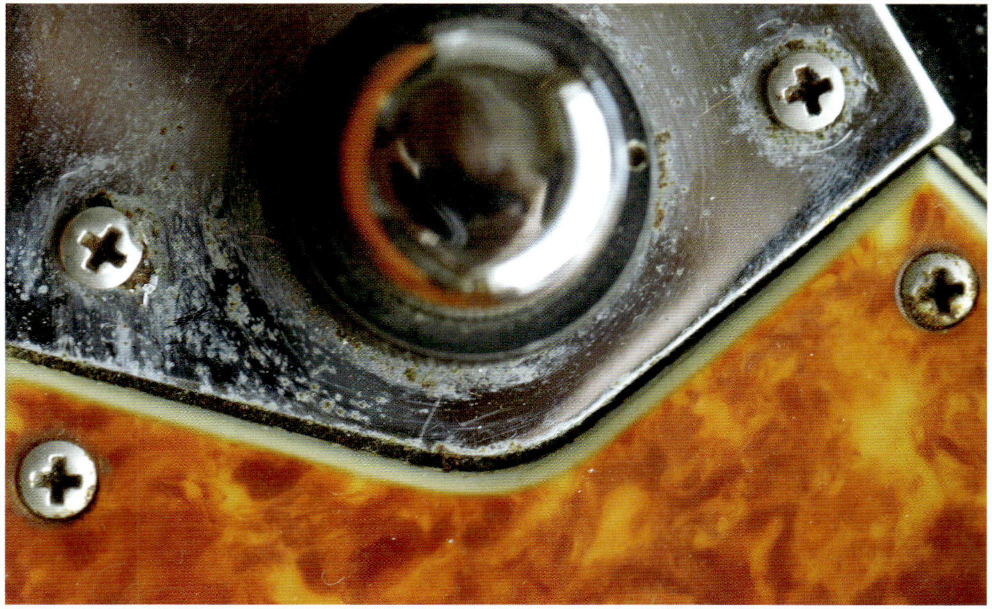

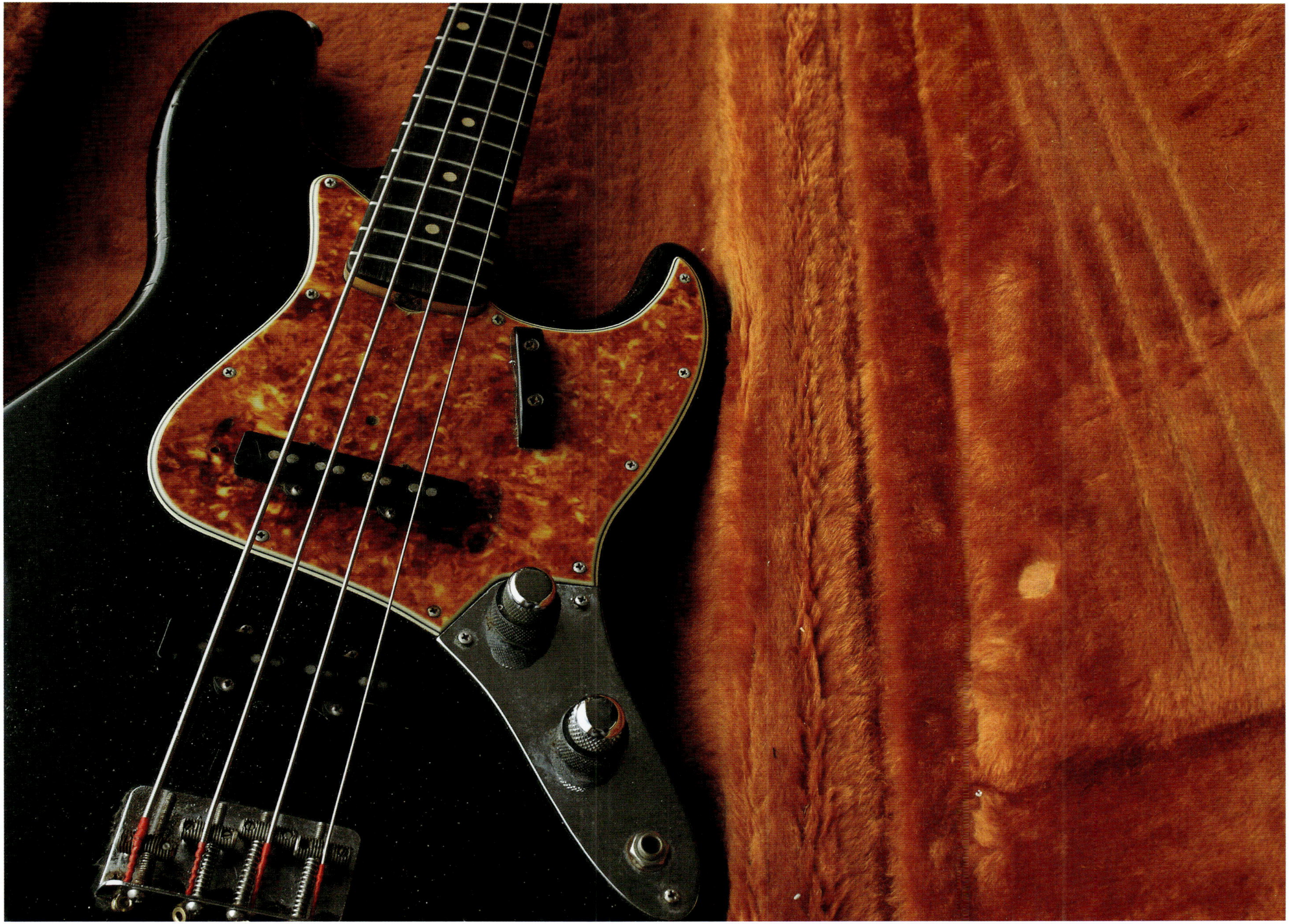

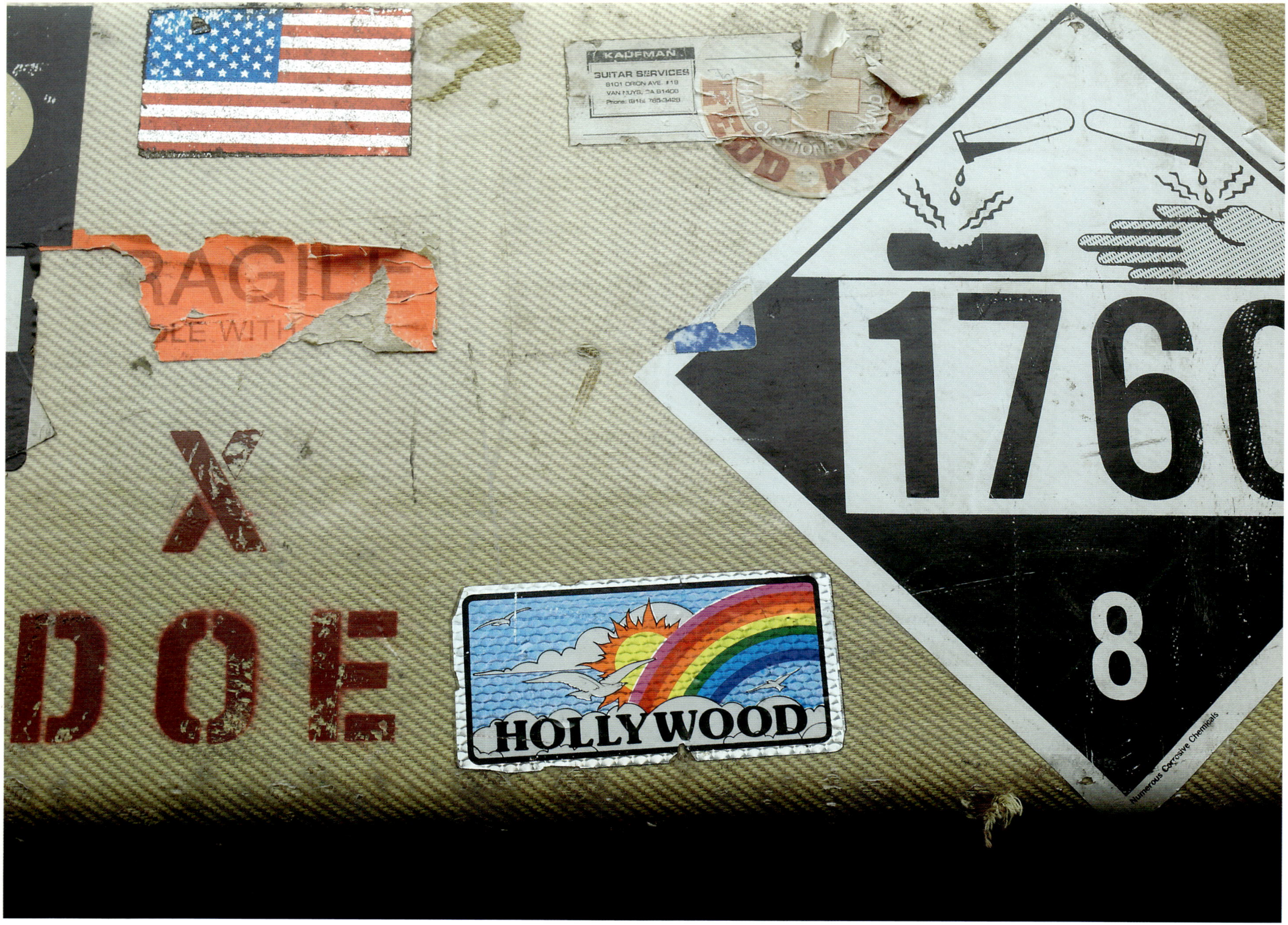
KAUFMAN
GUITAR SERVICES
8101 ORION AVE. #18
VAN NUYS, CA 91406
Phone: (818) 785-3428
1760
8
Numerous Corrosive Chemicals
X
DOE
HOLLYWOOD

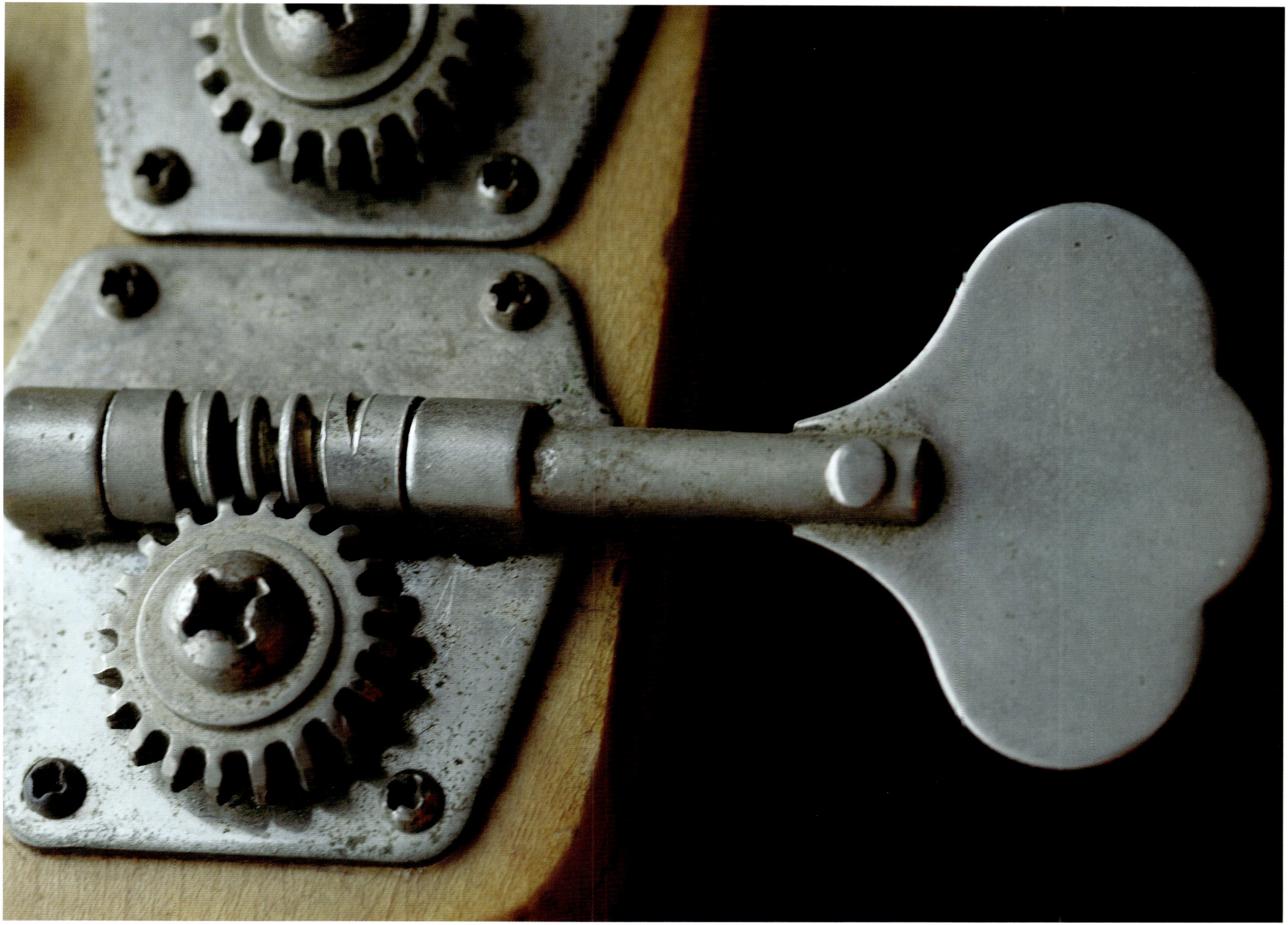

IAN CURTIS

Joy Division

Vox Phantom VI guitar

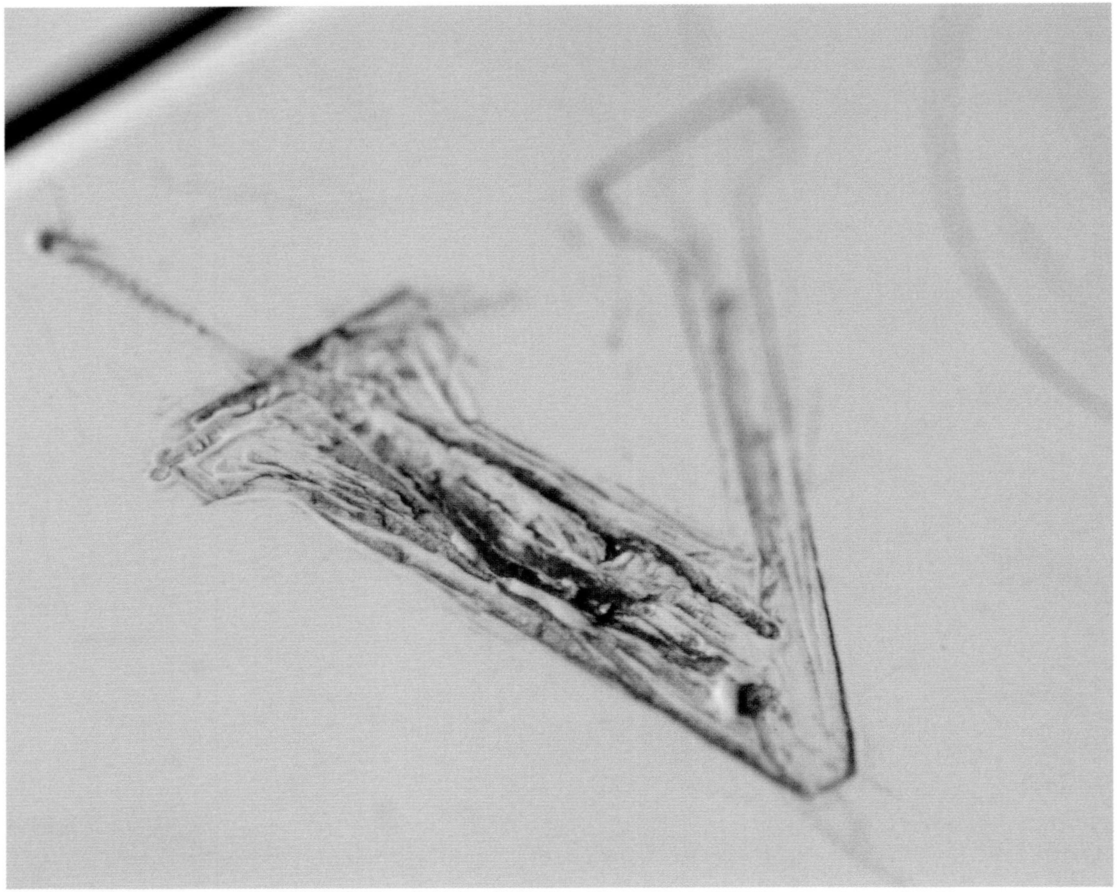

Ian really liked this guitar. The Phantom had tons of effects built into it, as an added bonus. It had a pause unit, and a thing called the *replat*. When we got the guitar, half the effects didn't work, and we were thinking, "What the hell is the replat?" We got the guitar repaired, and it turned out that *replat* is actually *repeat*—it was just a misprint. The guitar has a battery in it, and if you press the buttons in the wrong combination it will go into self-oscillate mode and start to make this strange twittering sound that Ian liked very much. It is a pretty wacky guitar.

Ian didn't really want to play a guitar, but for some reason we wanted him to play it. I can't remember the reason now. It sounded like some of the thinner guitars on the Velvet Underground tracks, clean and jangly. I think Ian used to play only on "Love Will Tear Us Apart" . . . no I'm wrong, there was another track, too. Maybe "Heart and Soul"? I do remember Ian used to play just one chord, which was D. We showed him how to play D and we wrote a song. I wonder if that's why we wrote "Love Will Tear Us Apart," you could drone a D through it. I think he played it live because I was playing keyboards. On the record, I played guitar, a twelve-string Echo guitar, an Italian guitar that actually sounded pretty good.

To pick it out, I think we all just went to a record shop and said, that one looks cool, get that one, and he said, yeah, I like that. I kept the guitar after he died, kept it under my bed in a case and then gave it back to his daughter when she came of age.

We did use it on a couple of New Order recordings. The one I remember is "Everything's Gone Green." On the rhythm guitar part on that song, you can hear this guitar. It just plays the D chord. That's a joke . . .

—Bernard Sumner

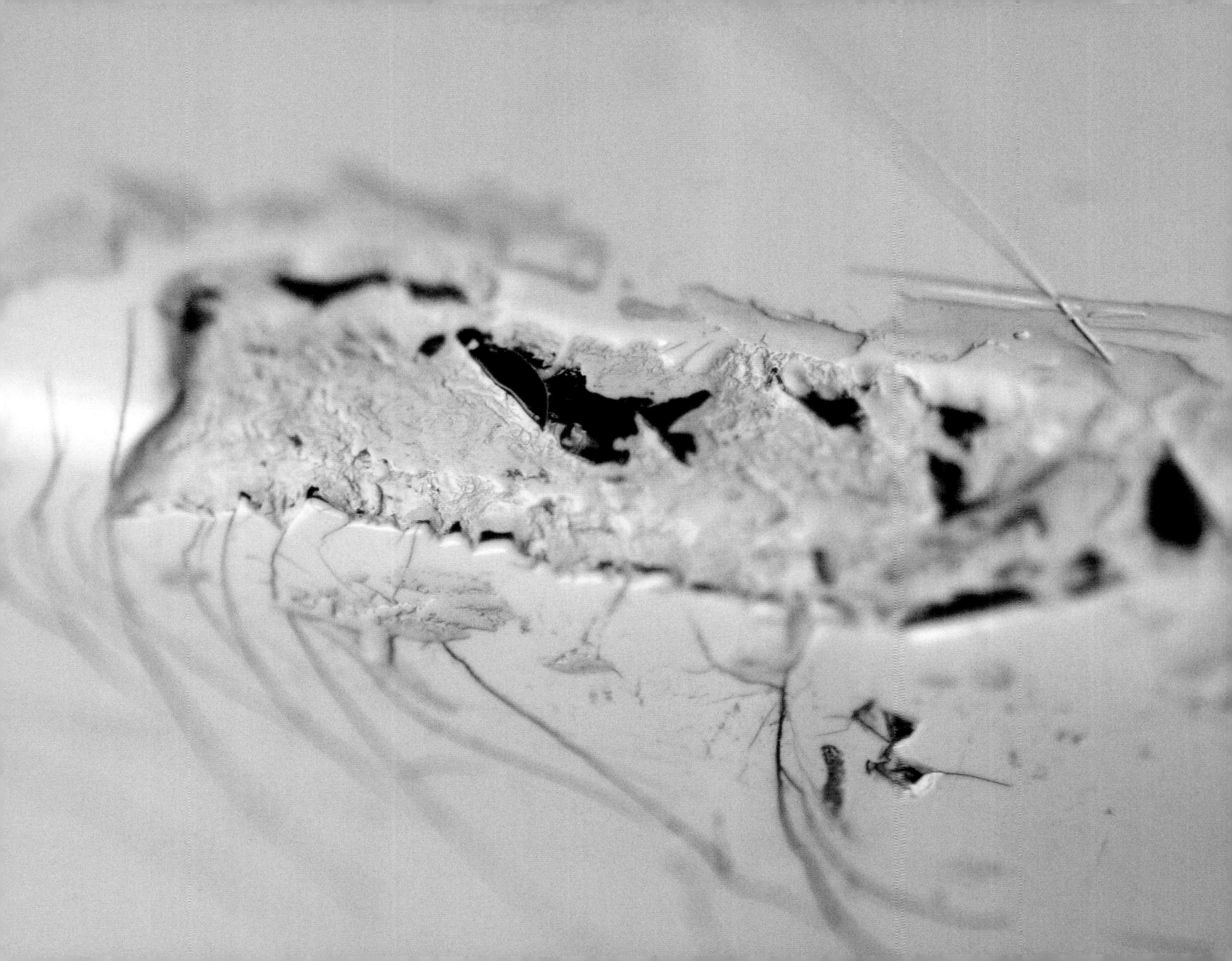

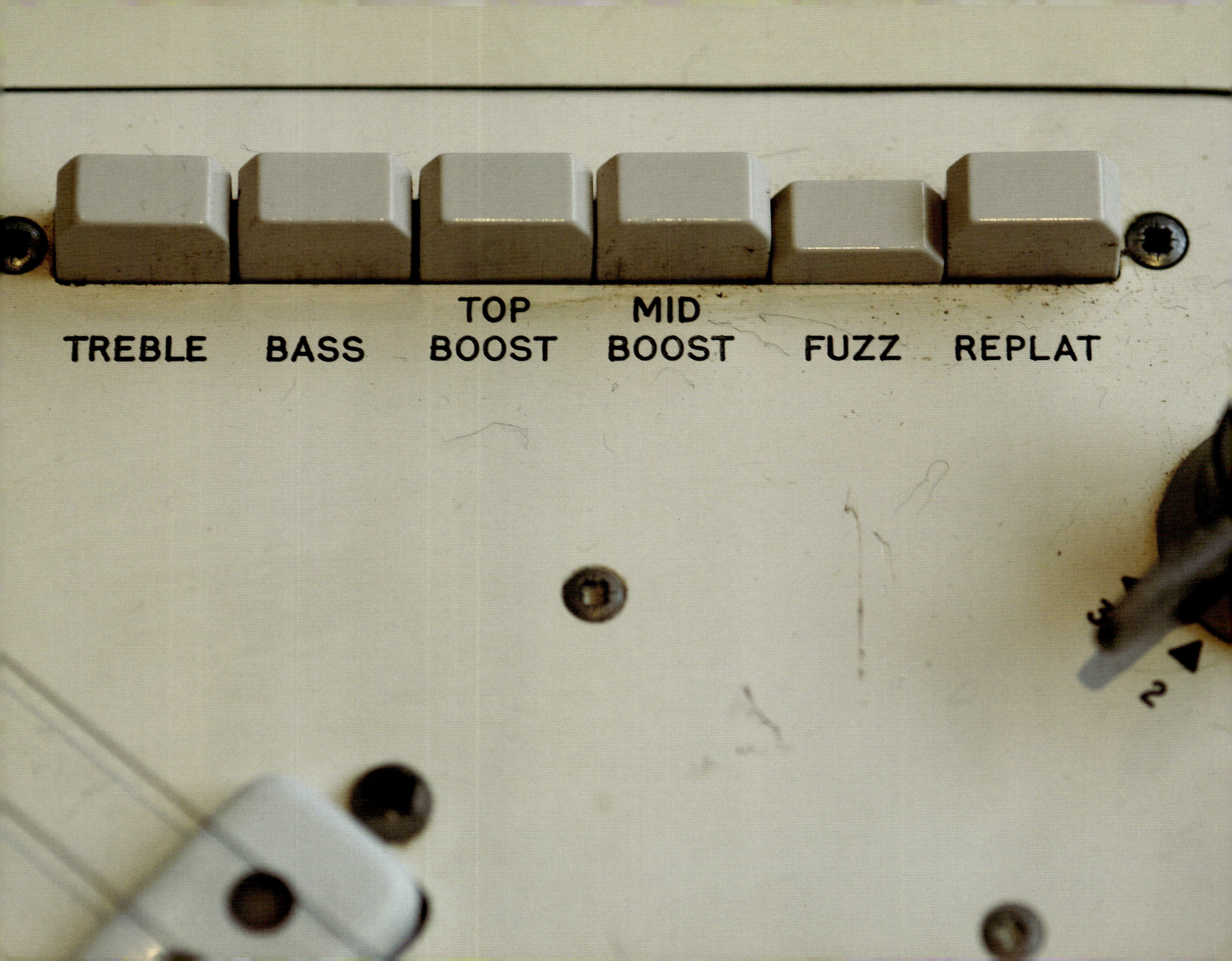
TREBLE
BASS
TOP BOOST
MID BOOST
FUZZ
REPLAT

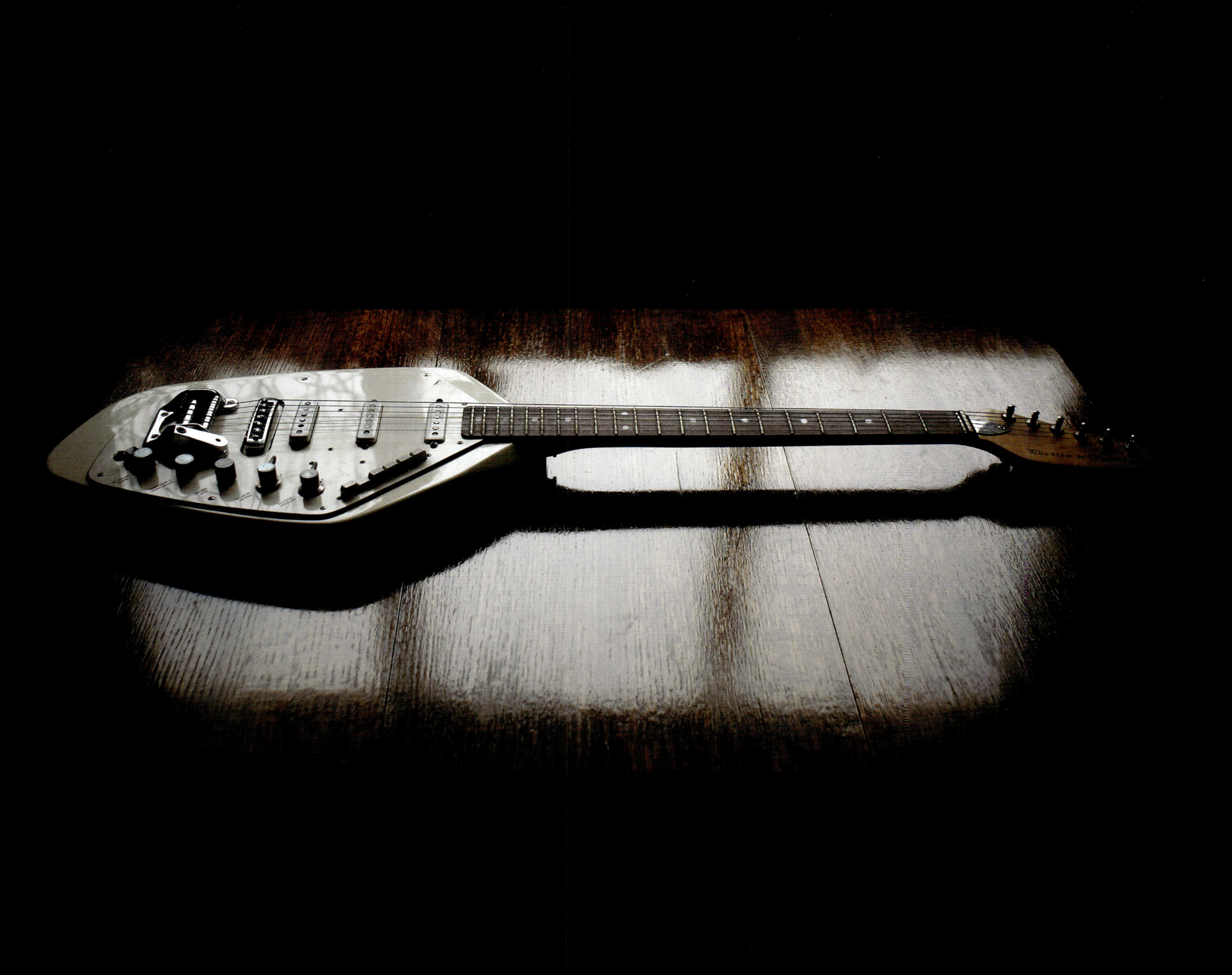

JOHNNY MARR

The Smiths, Electronic, The The, Modest Mouse, The Cribs

1963 Fender Jaguar guitar
1959 Gibson 355 guitar

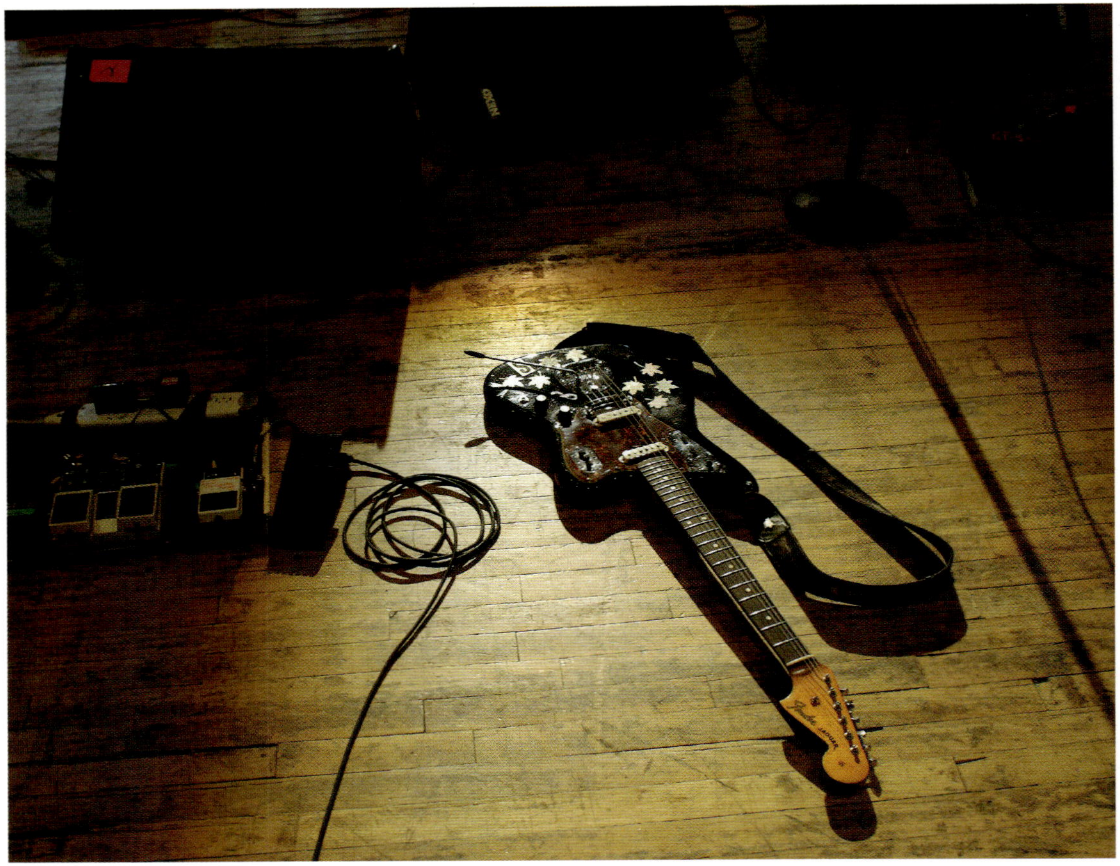

A lot of my favorite Fender guitars are 1963 L series Stratocasters. It's the year I was born. Nineteen sixty-three is my favorite year.

When I got this Jaguar from Isaac [Brock] it was in quite a bad state, so I gave it some love and took care of it and gave it a setup. I decorated it one night when I was making the Modest Mouse album *We Were Dead* in Mississippi. The 8 stands for Scorpio—my birthday is Halloween, which is in the eighth sign of the zodiac. The S is to remind me of my daughter, Sonny, the N is for my son, Nile, and the A is for my wife, Angie. The flowers I got from Walmart at 3 o'clock in the morning when I was bored.

When I started playing with Modest Mouse, I thought, "Well, I'm going to have to have a big sound to do this." I saw this black Jaguar, it was dusty and not working, a pickup was broken. I plugged it in, and it was just a huge sound; Guitarzilla.

I like the Jag because it is a little restrictive to play, and that's a good thing. I have to work with the limitations of the guitar. It gives me quite a strong direction. It's too feminine to play many power chords. That's what appeals to me about the Rickenbacker as well. They sound really good, clear, and clean, and a lot of guitars don't sound that great clean; they need the amplifier to do 30 to 40 percent of the work. As a machine, the Jaguar does what a Strat does, but with more of an all-encompassing sound, and I can pretty much do everything I want on it. I ended up playing a Fender Jaguar exclusively for the next five years. I still do.

I met Sire Records boss Seymour Stein in late 1983 when the Smiths were about to sign to the legendary New York label. Seymour told me that he had once gone to a guitar store on 48th Street with Brian Jones to get him a guitar when the Rolling Stones were in town, so I suggested that if I signed with Sire he should buy me a guitar. We signed the contract on January 2, 1984, and true to his word, Seymour took me down to We Buy Guitars on 48th and bought me the 1959 Gibson 355. I took it back to the Iroquois Hotel and wrote "Heaven Knows I'm Miserable Now" and "Girl Afraid." It became my main guitar for quite a while, and I'm told it inspired Bernard Butler and Noel Gallagher to buy one of their own. It's still one of my favorites.

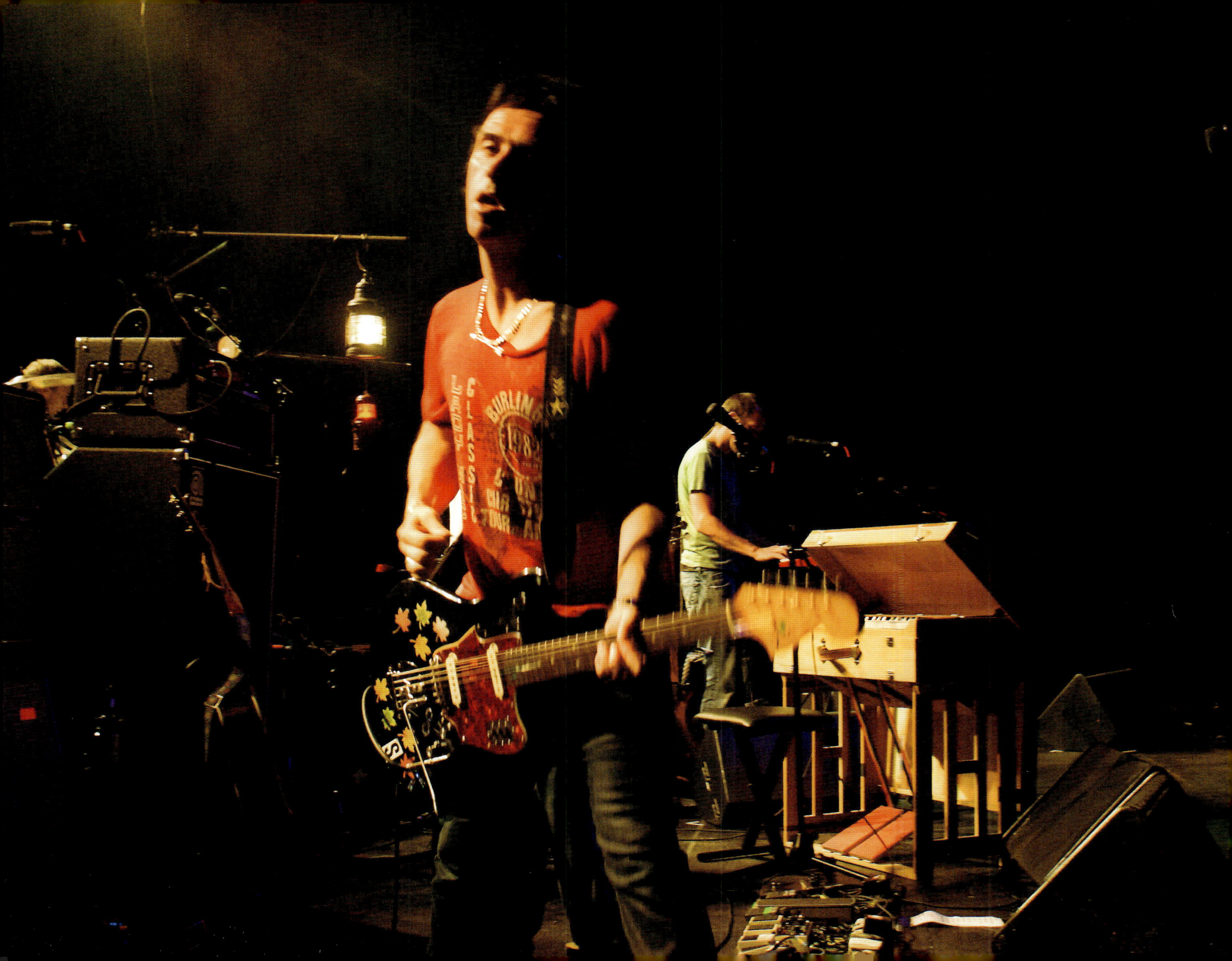

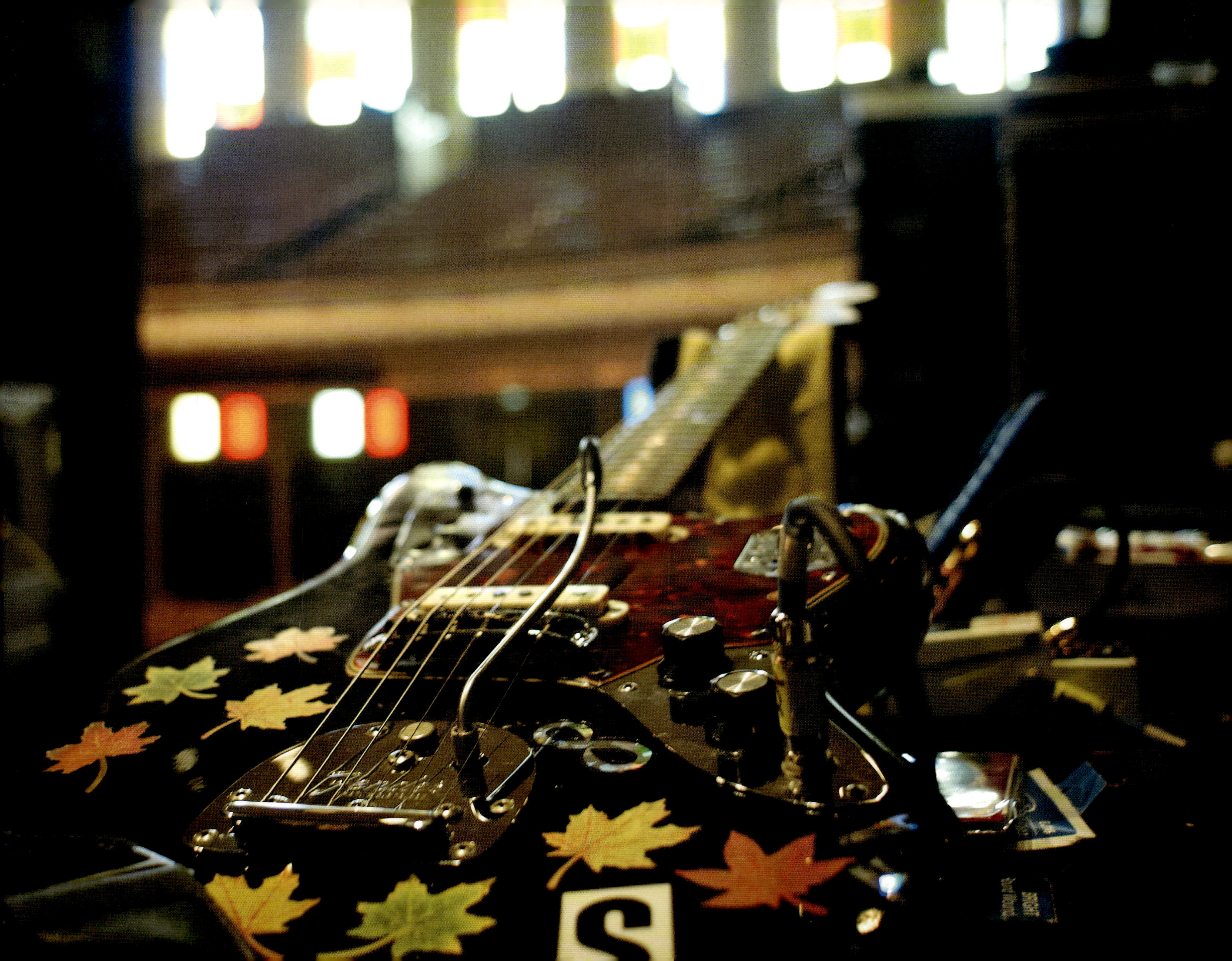

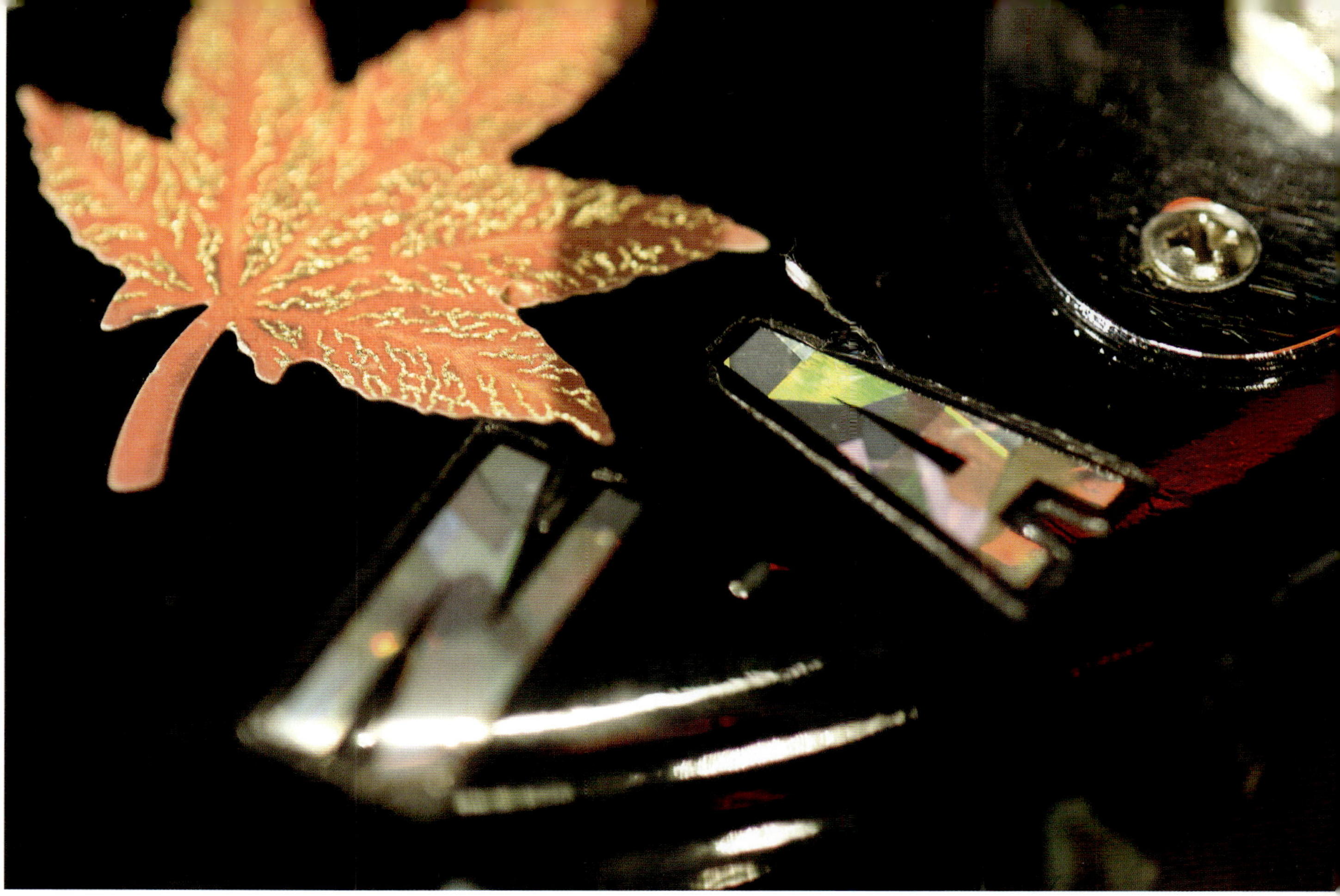

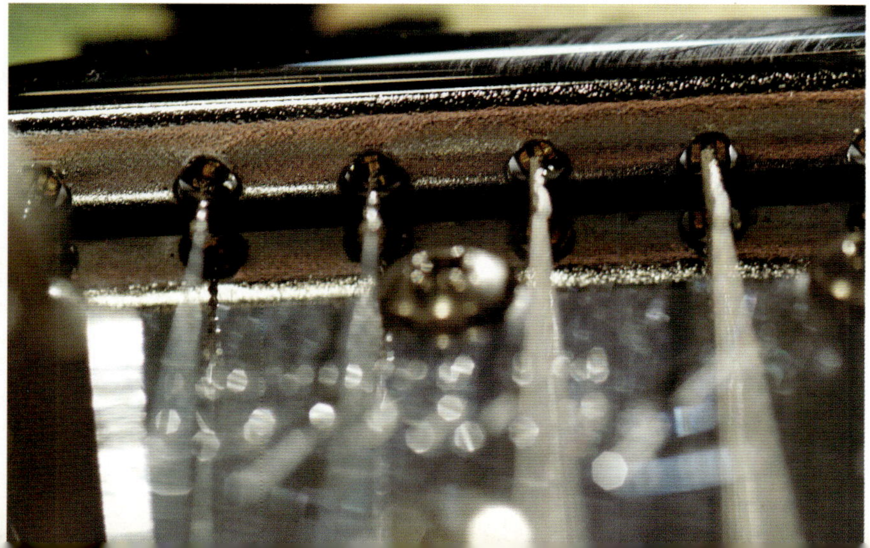

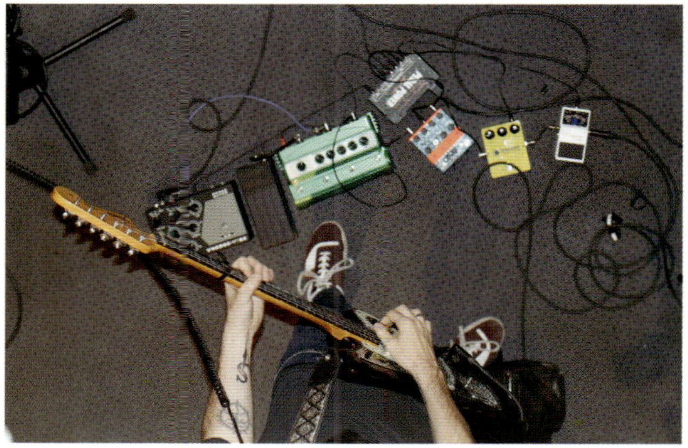

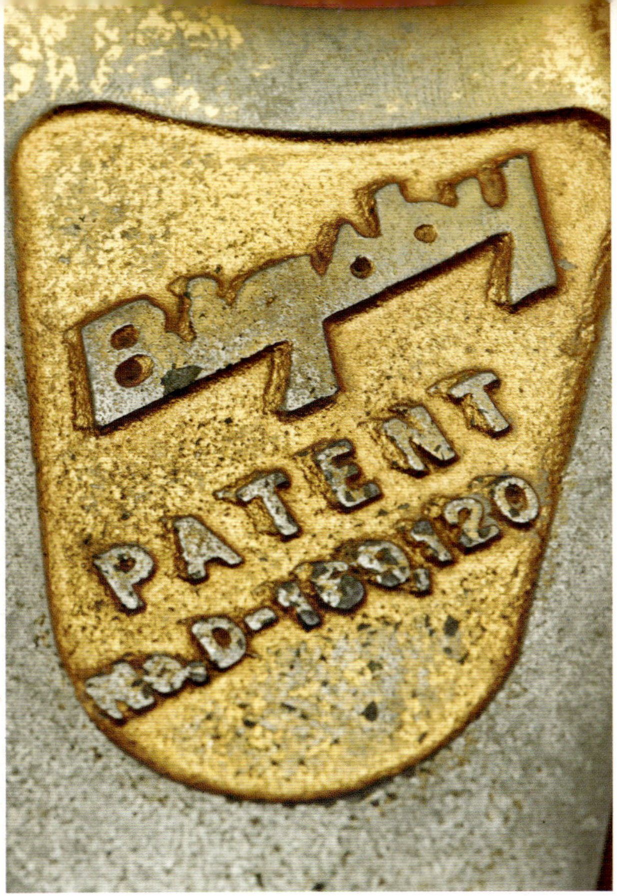
Bigsby
PATENT
No. D-169,120

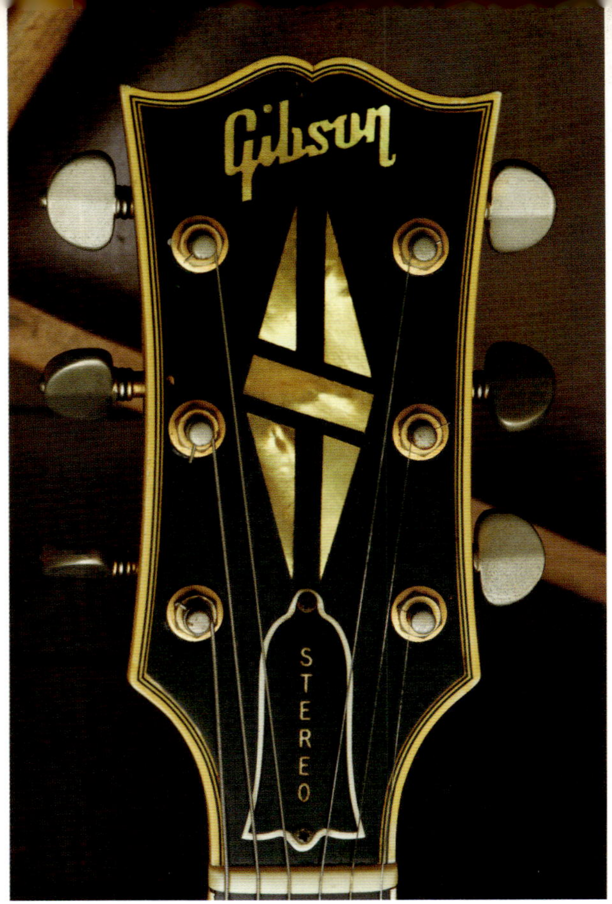
Gibson
STEREO

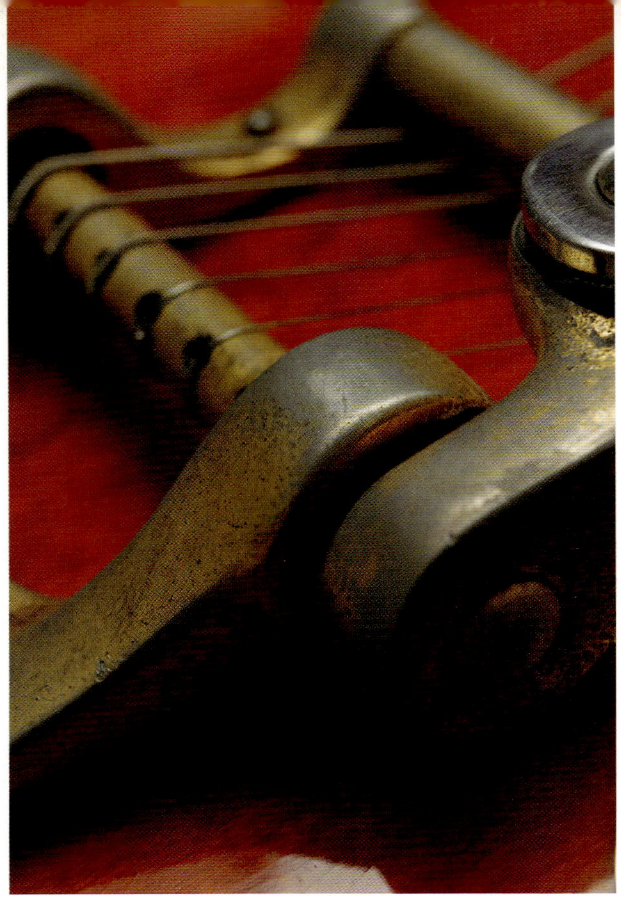

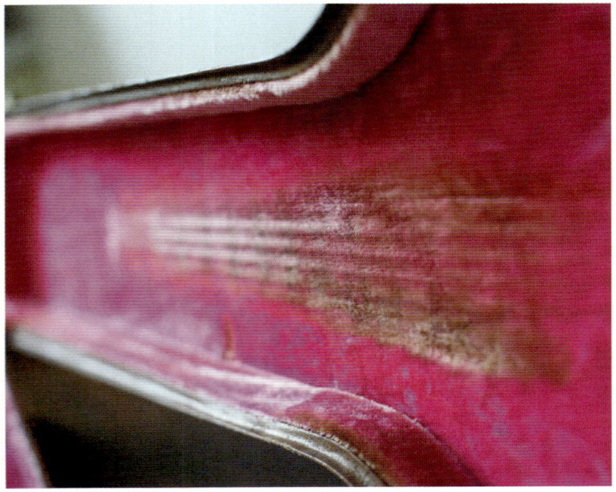

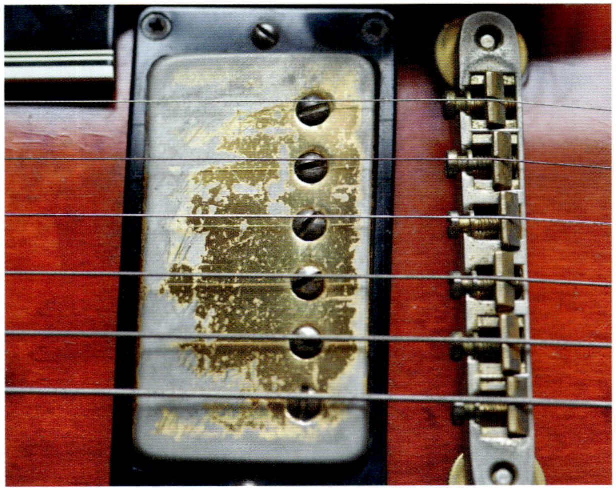

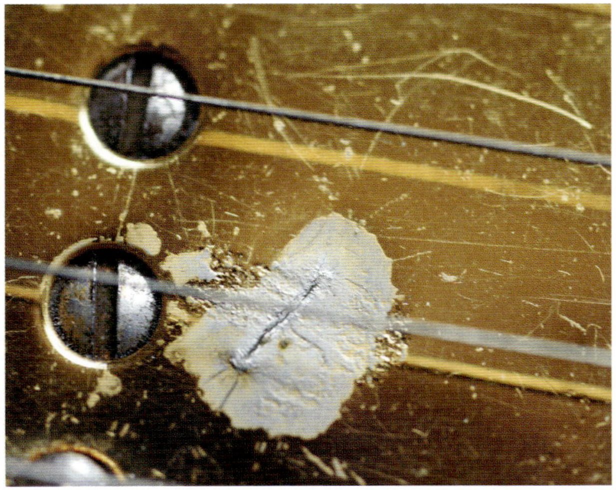

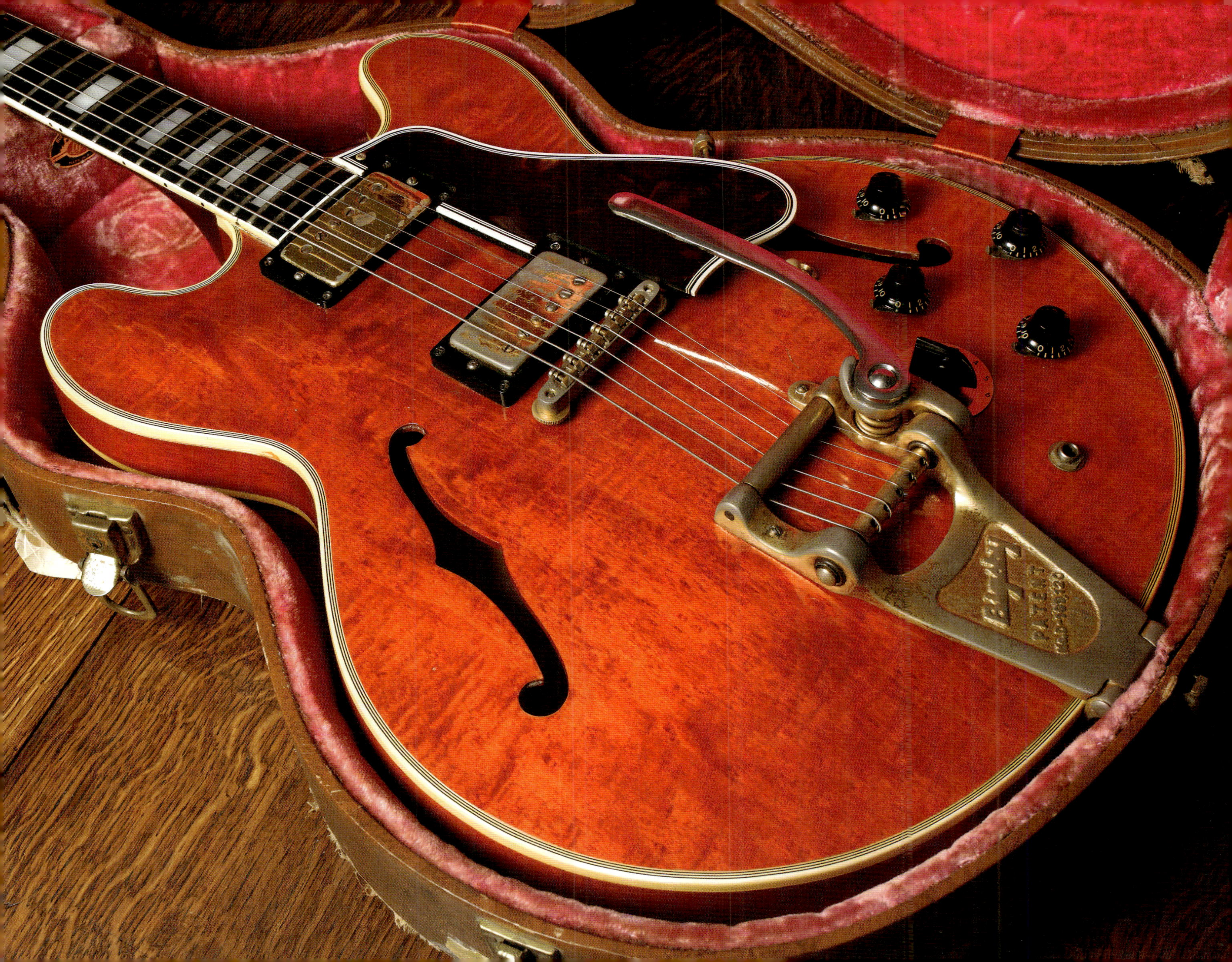
PATENT

TODD TRAINER

Shellac
Ludwig Black Beauty snare drum

A Ludwig Black Beauty, drenched in blood, sweat, and tears.

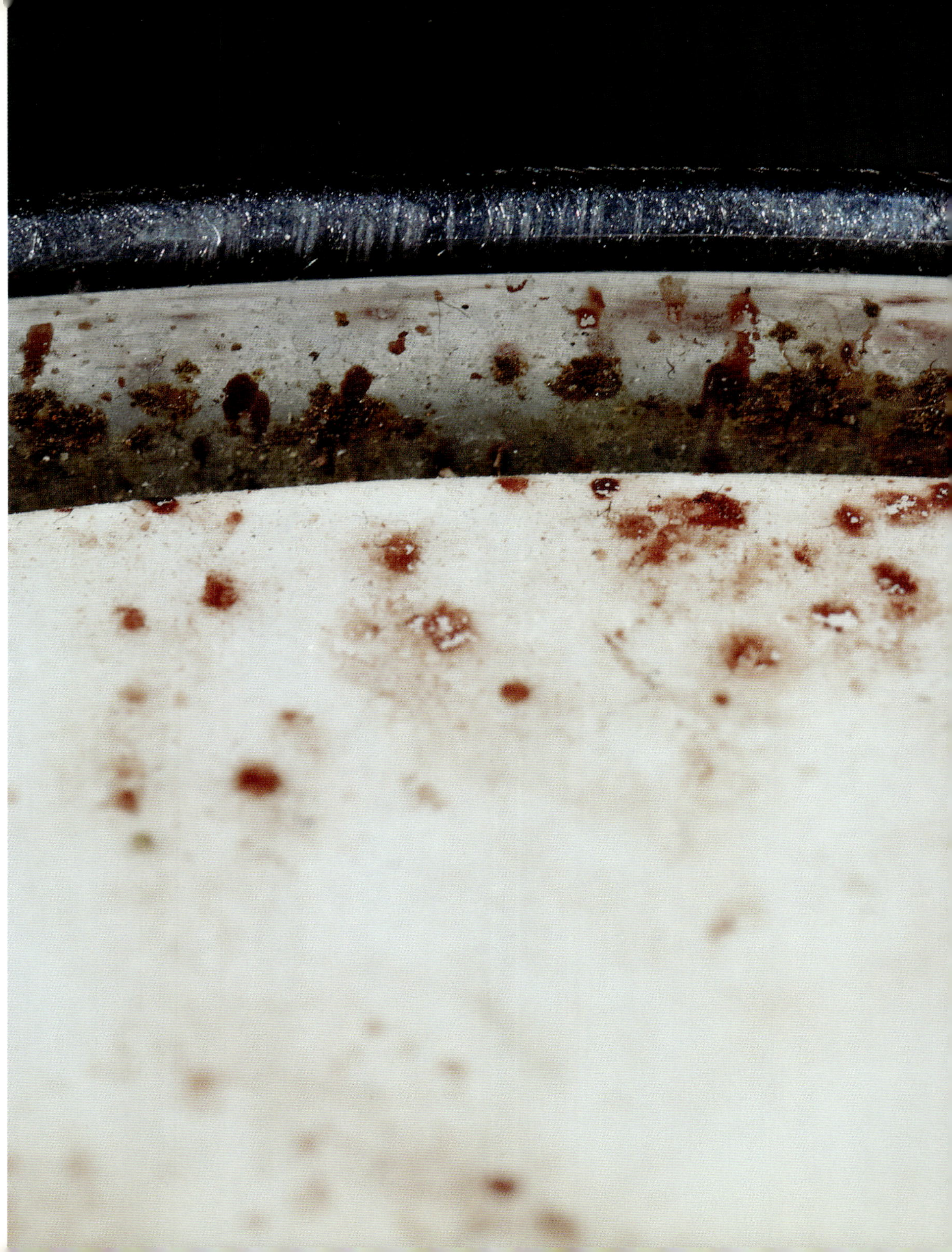

JOE PLUMMER

Modest Mouse, The Sads, The Shins

C&C drums and various percussion instruments

I had these C&C drums made for me in 2006; they're mahogany, and some of the best drums I've had. I've always liked the basic three-piece setup, so when I am playing kit only, this is what I'm used to. As for all the other stuff, that was a natural expansion of my kit that grew and grew. All the percussion and hand drums and clanky metal things are what I use to weave through and/or collaborate with JG [Jeremiah Green, also drummer for Modest Mouse]. I toured with these drums from 2006 on, and wrote and recorded "The Whale Song" and "Satellite Skin" on them.

The blood that you see in the photo of my hand (see page 11) is from the outside of my left pinky knuckle. I go through phases of hitting it on the hi-hat cymbals, and once I do, I seem to constantly reopen the wound. It takes a few days off for it to heal, and if it doesn't, Isaac has superglued it for me once or twice. That seems to work. I don't generally hit my hand on the hi-hats, but once the cut is open, it happens over and over again. Some sort of psycho-mental-muscular apprehension feedback loop mixed with Murphy's Law. I've also spilled lots of drinks on the drums. I'm surprised the hardware isn't totally rusted out. I tend to snack at sound check, so there are probably a lot of food crumbs in all the nooks and crannies between the hardware and the wood, too.

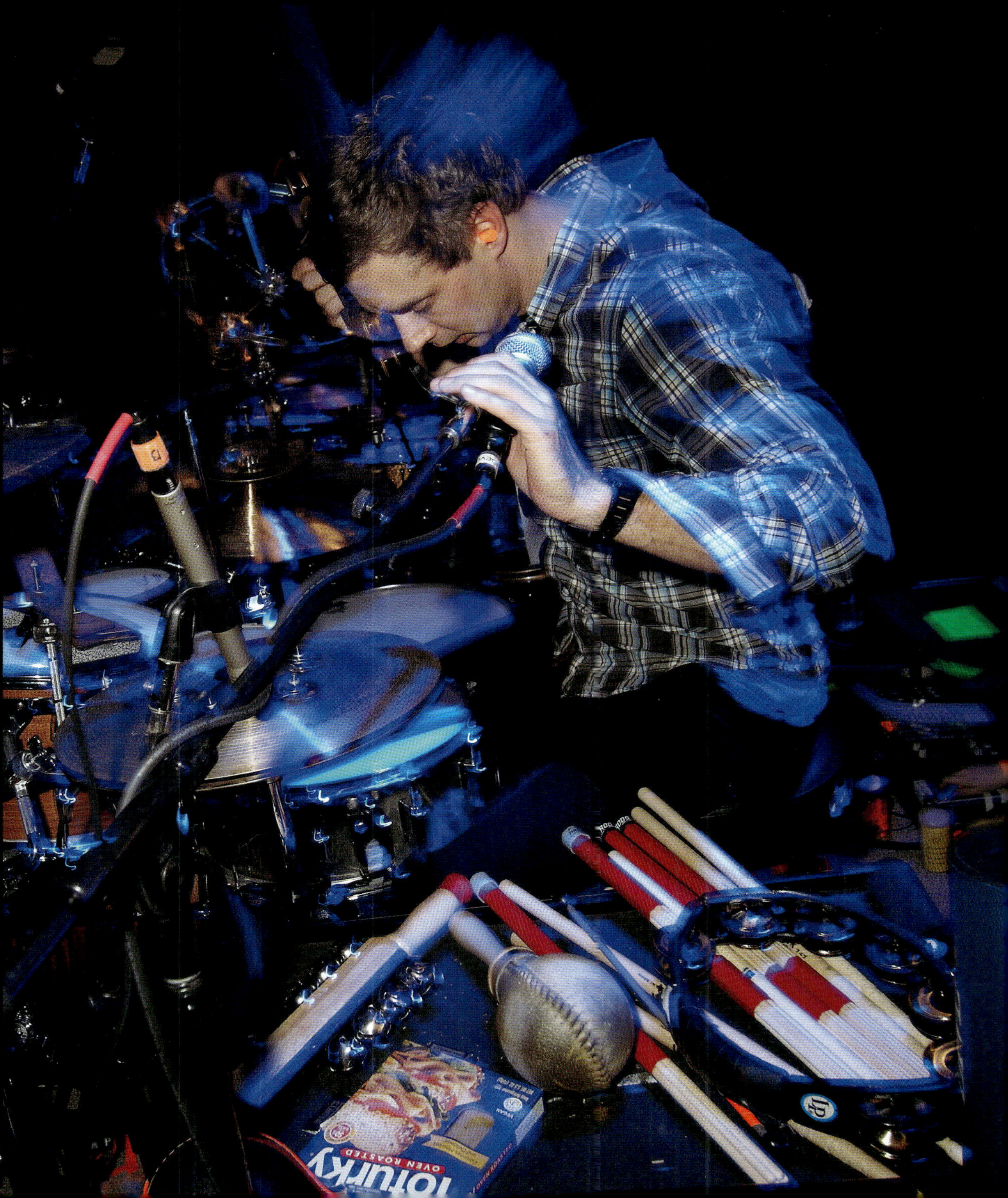

BILLY CHILDISH

The Pop Rivets, The Milkshakes, Thee Headcoats, The Chatham Singers, The Buff Medways

Klira guitar
Buff Medway Cadillac guitar
Valco Airline guitar

My Nana Lewis brought this guitar for my elder brother in 1969 or '70. It was secondhand and came with a practice amp. My brother played in a school group, doing blues/ Hendrix/Zeppelin–type stuff. I learned to play on it and used it in the Pop Rivets in '79, played it live with them on "Bo Diddley" and "To Start—to Hesitate . . . to Stop!" It was on the first Milkshakes record, and then had a rest until Thee Headcoats.

The Buff Medway guitar was made by my friend Fabian in '98. I like the design—it's the design after Bo Diddley's Cadillac guitar. It's on the last Headcoats LP, all the Buff Medways stuff, and some blues.

The tail piece is of an Airline guitar I got my wife to buy in Seattle ten years back. I wanted her to get it because Steve Turner from Mudhoney used to lend me a similar model to do blues shows when we were in Seattle and I dug the sound. I broke it chucking it on the floor during an argument. I used it on some Chatham Singers recordings, too.

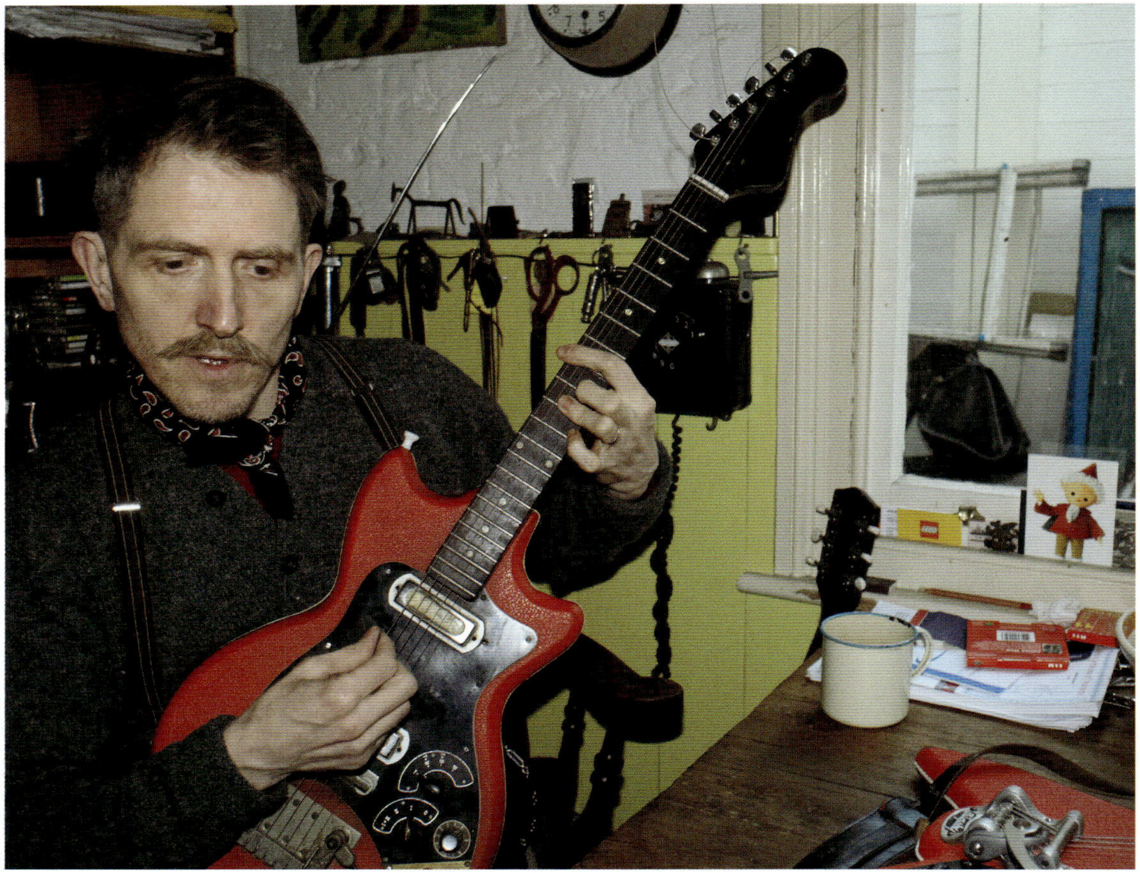

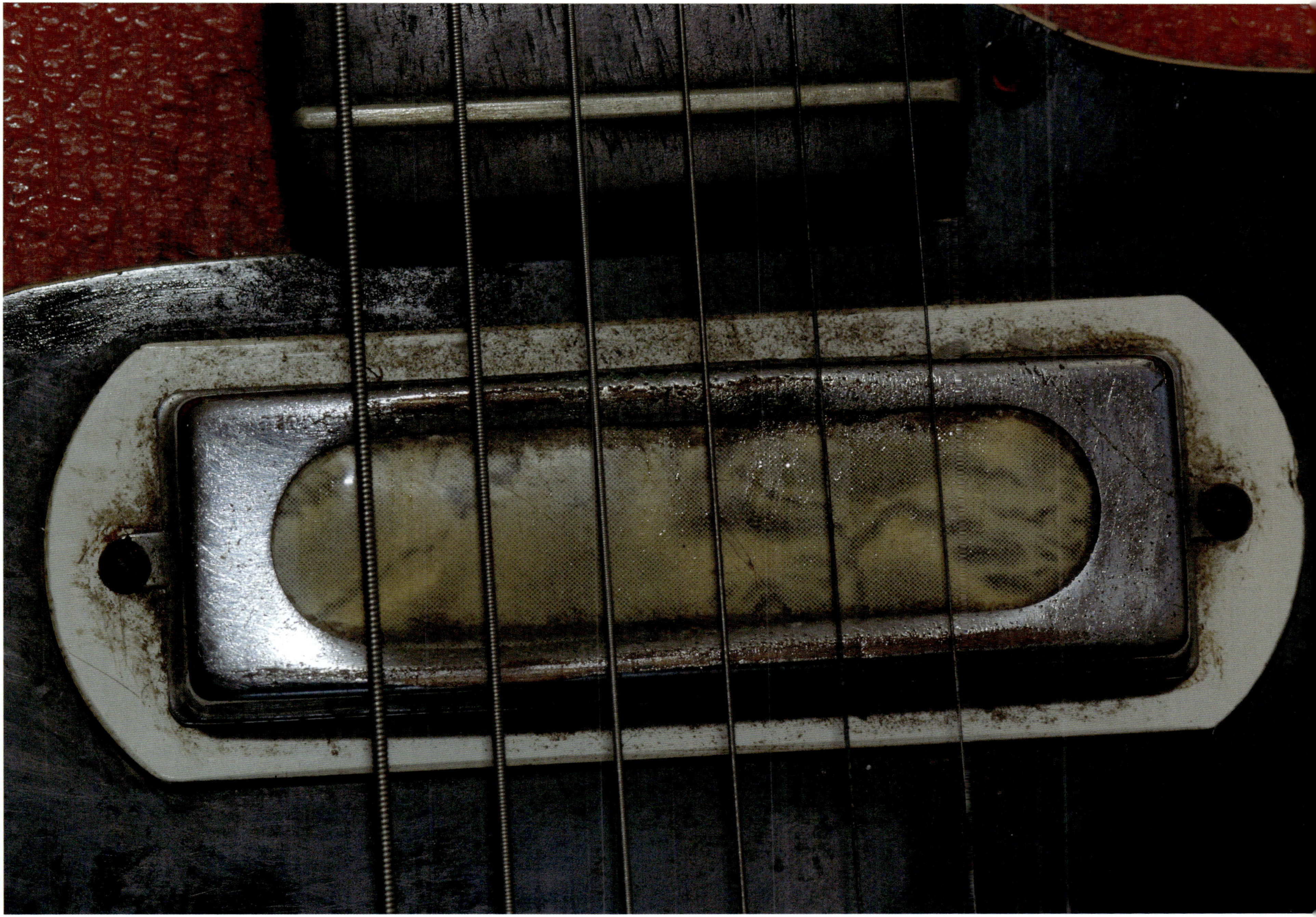

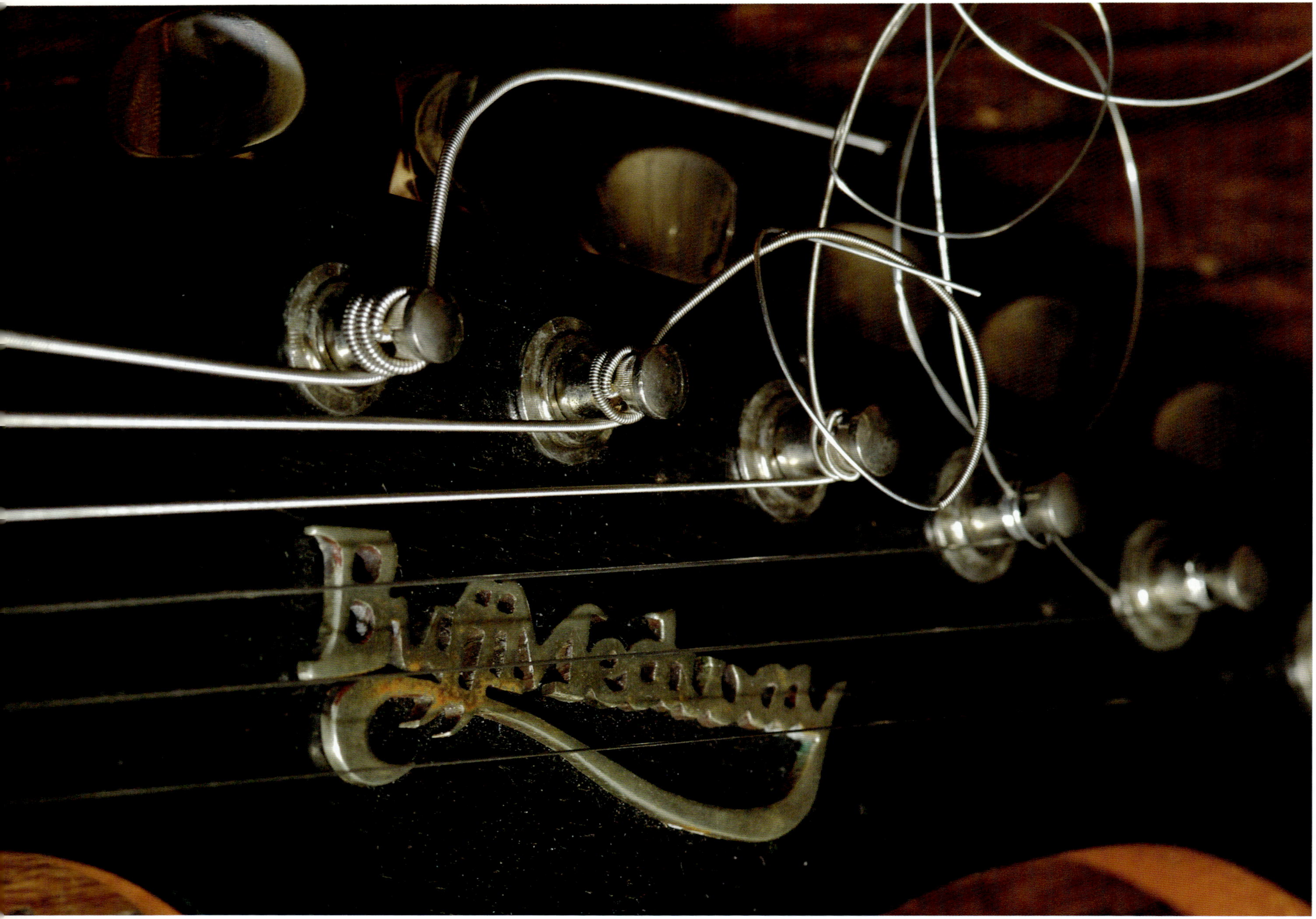

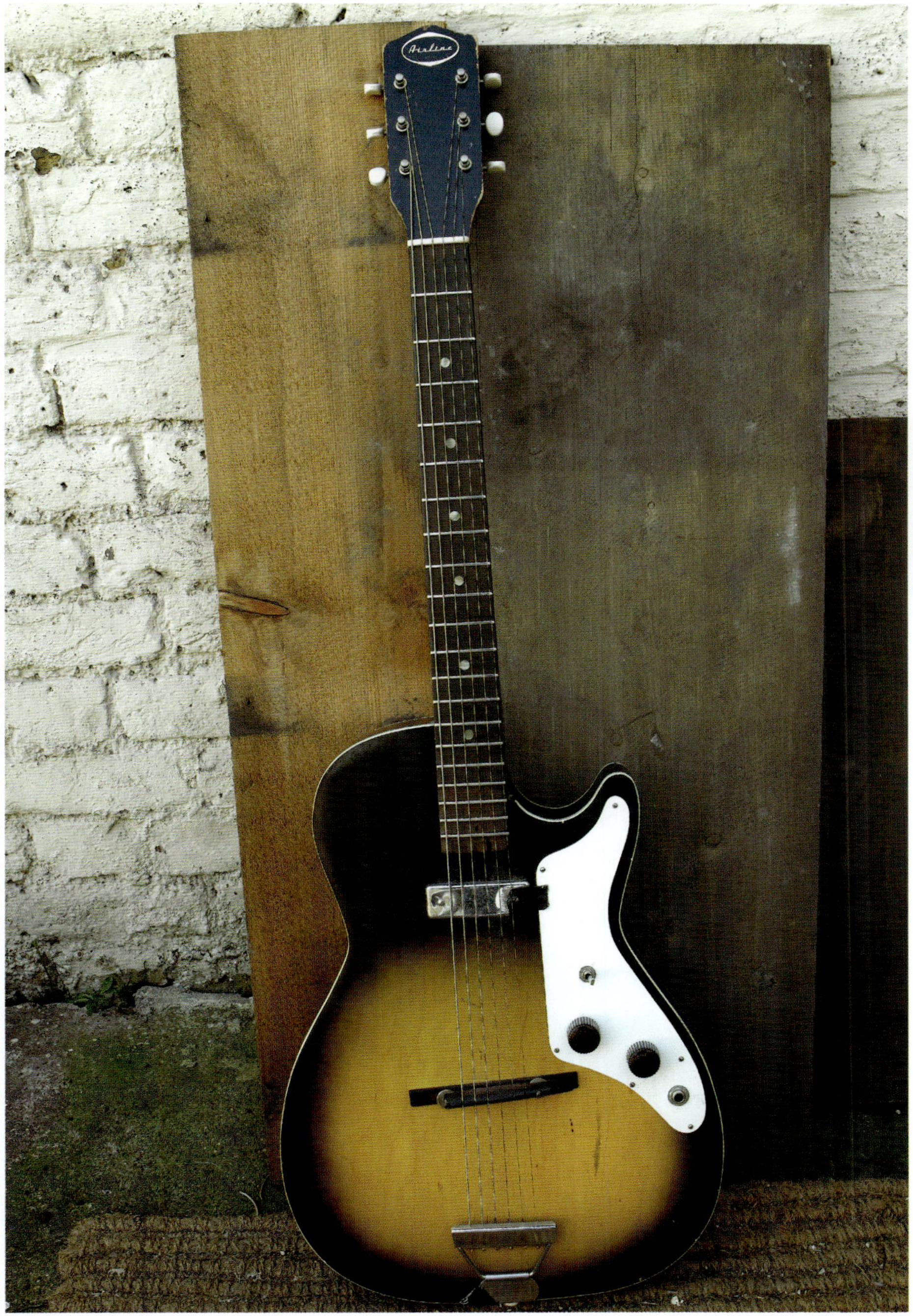
Airline

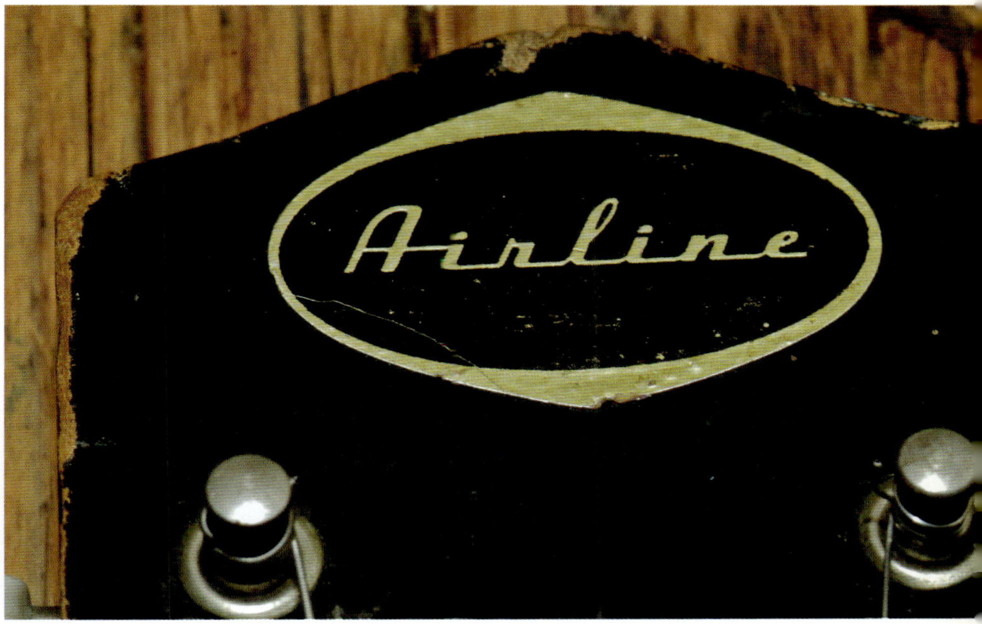
Airline

DOUG MARTSCH

Built to Spill
1987 Fender Stratocaster guitar

My girlfriend at the time, Laurie, bought me this guitar brand new in 1988 or '89 when she sold her first house. I'd been playing a Les Paul that my brother, Martin, had traded his car for on my behalf, but it wouldn't stay in tune. I didn't know anything about guitars, so Kevin at Old Boise Music recommended the Strat. I've played this guitar on every record I've made. I've taken it on every tour except one or two around 2005, when I took my new Telecaster that our sound guy Ian made for me. I have a Gibson acoustic my wife gave me in '98, and I mostly use that for writing, but prior to that I wrote everything on my Strat. In 1999, we were on TV as part of a tour in New York, and I wrote KARENA and BEN on my guitar to say "Hi" to my wife and son, but the paint has been rubbed off at the top of the body by my forearm from years of strumming.

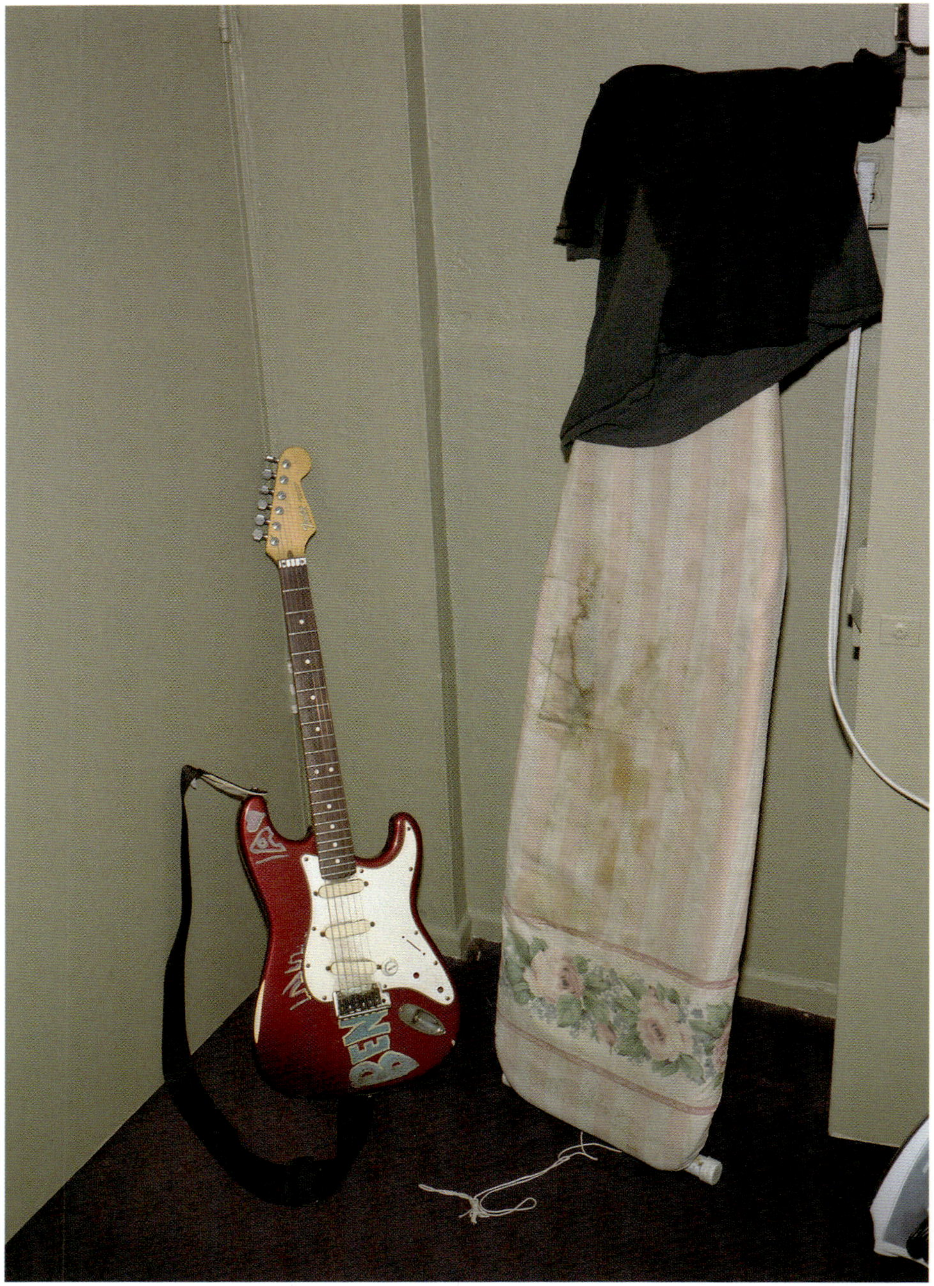

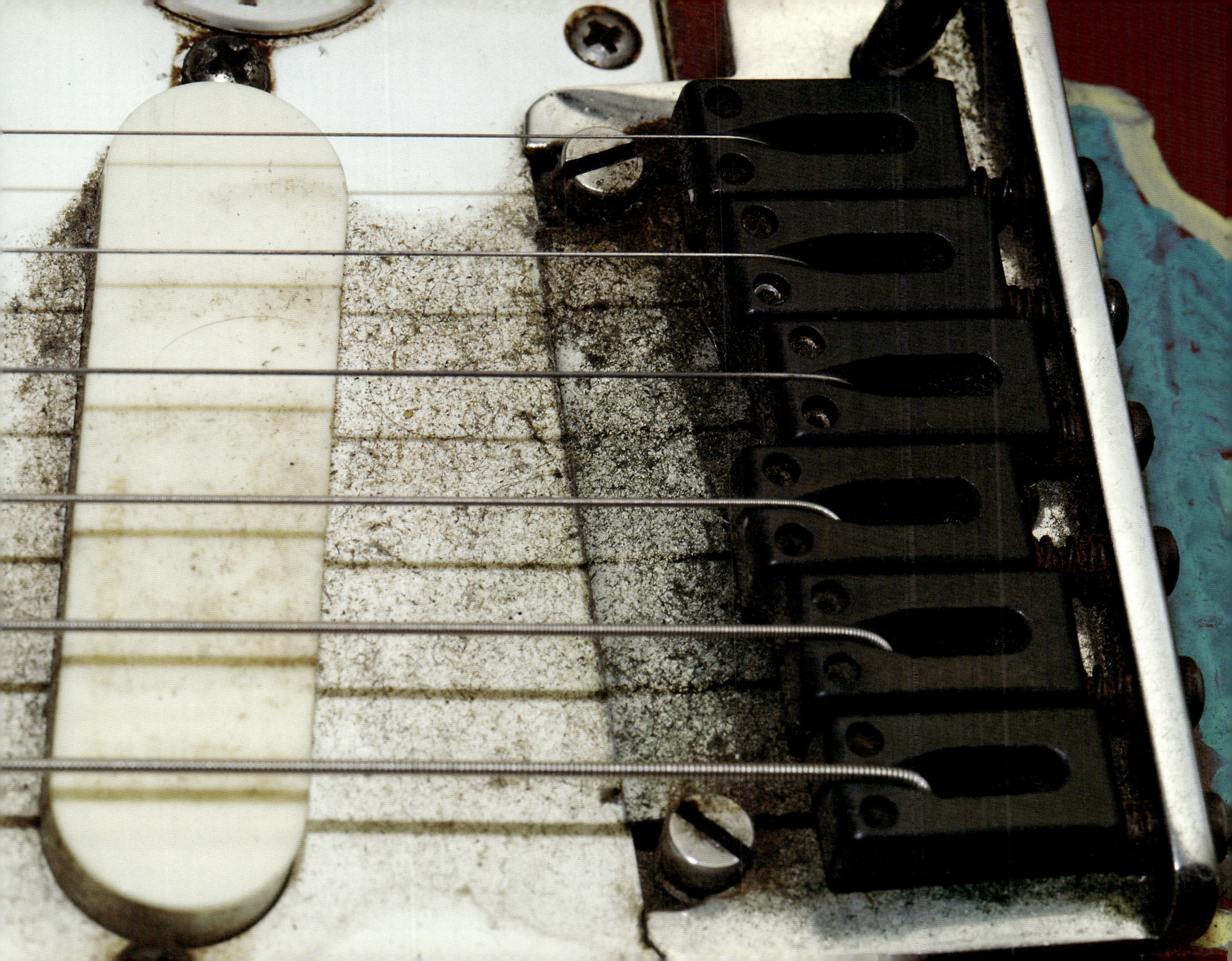

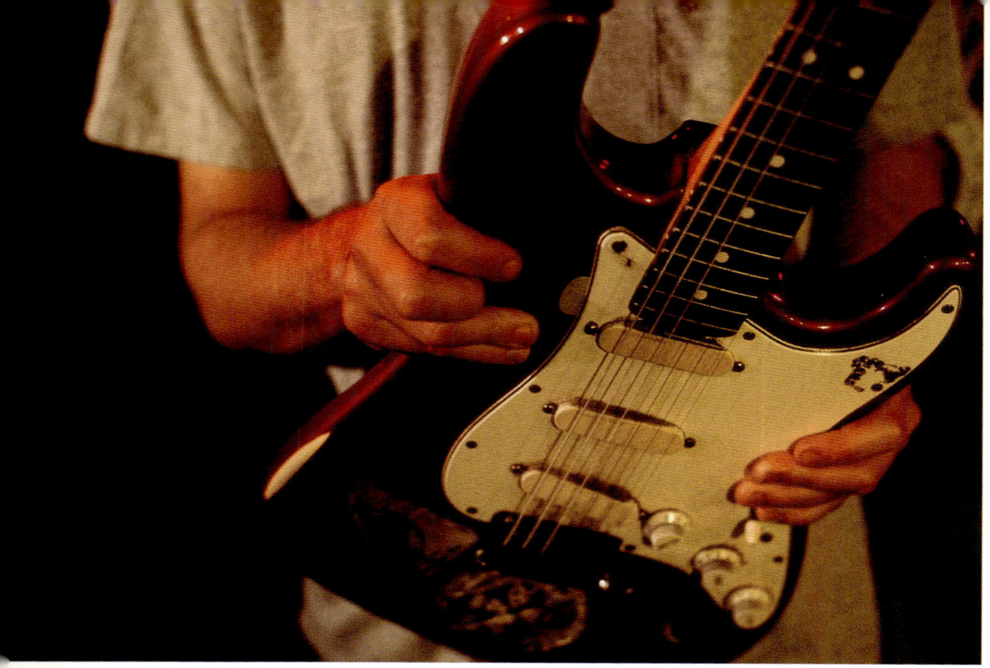

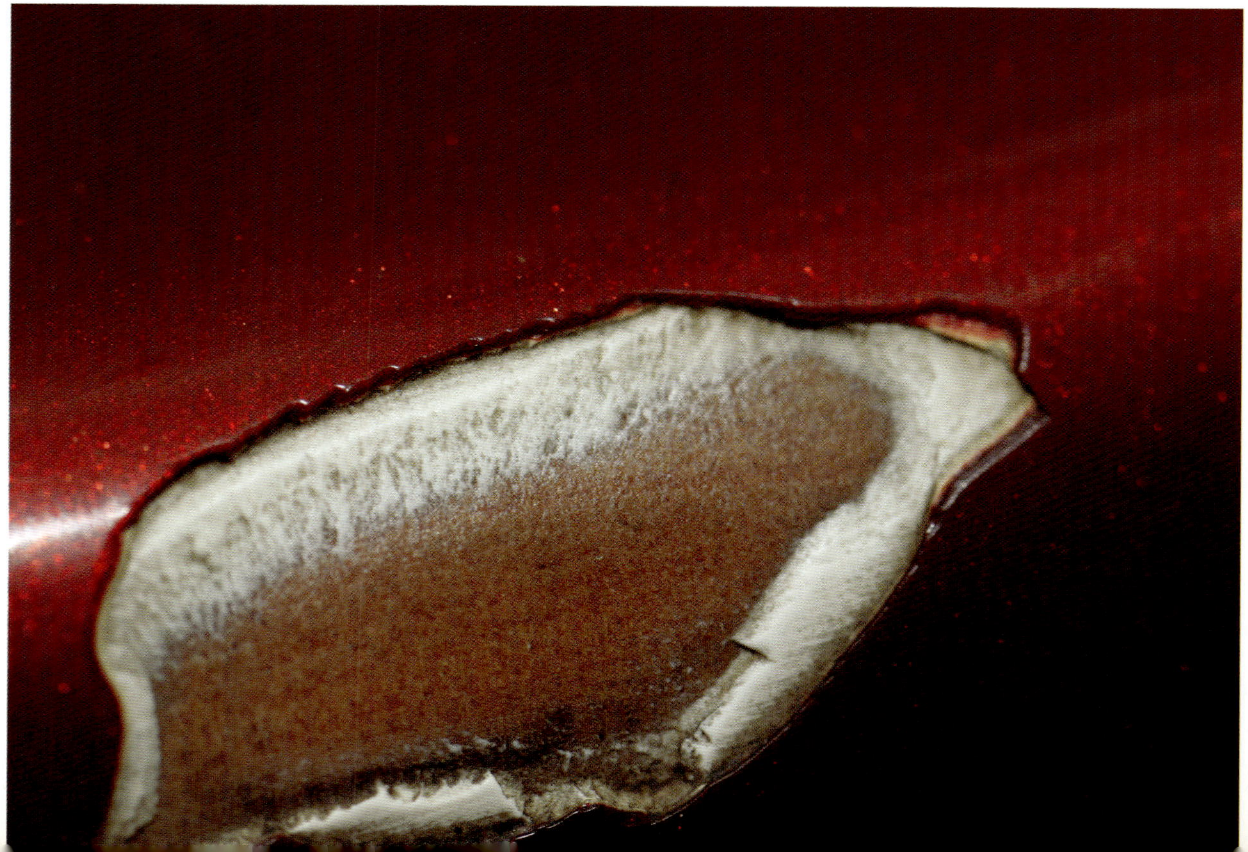

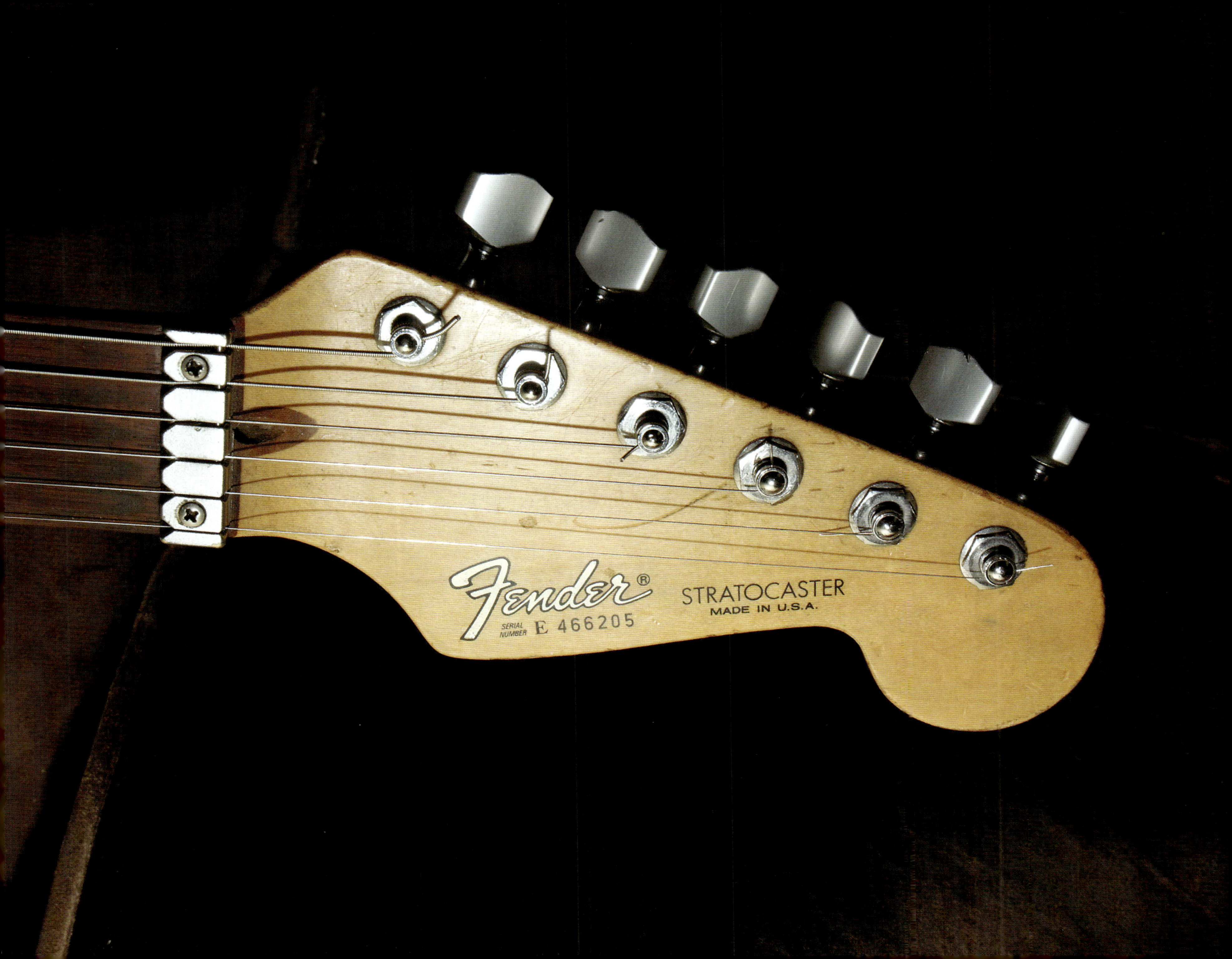
Fender®
SERIAL NUMBER E 466205
STRATOCASTER
MADE IN U.S.A.

ISAAC BROCK

Modest Mouse
Wicks custom guitars

Early on, the guitars I played were the cheapest ones I could find that had the Floyd Rose tremolo, which was found almost exclusively on cheesy metal and glam-rock guitars. They were really hard to keep in tune, and impossible when I removed the apparently necessary locking nuts on the necks. (I had taken off the locking nuts because they made changing a string during a show really time consuming.) I spent about a year and a half playing with a pair of needle-nose pliers in place of the locking nuts because I could get the pliers on or off in a single motion.

Any time I had a problem with one of these guitars, I'd take it to Brian Wicks, a repair guy at a local instrument shop, and he slowly started developing a better system for me. We started by sawing off and sanding out all the little fine-tuning screws and the layers of bullshit—the little fine tuners were cutting my hands and arms. He then installed locking tuners, which I think had come on the market right around then. Good-bye needle-nose pliers!

The problem with modifying cheap guitars was that the back of each one had a slightly different warp. I bend notes with the whammy bar using the side of my hand to push and my pinky wrapped behind it to pull. The slight variations in the guitars often made it very hard for me to play the way I liked. Brian came up with a prototype that, after it was modified by a couple of people along the way, developed into what I use now. He also began making guitars for me that I could really get the sound and harmonics out of that I wanted. He knew I have a tendency to be rough on guitars, so you almost can't break these. It's great!

The guitar with the vines on the neck—wood inlay on wood, a nice touch—was the first of four that Wicks made for me. I am still playing and touring with it. The one with bees on it is the one I've been using the most because we made some sonic tweaks that I like. The bees are inlayed because I wish I could play a hive of bees.

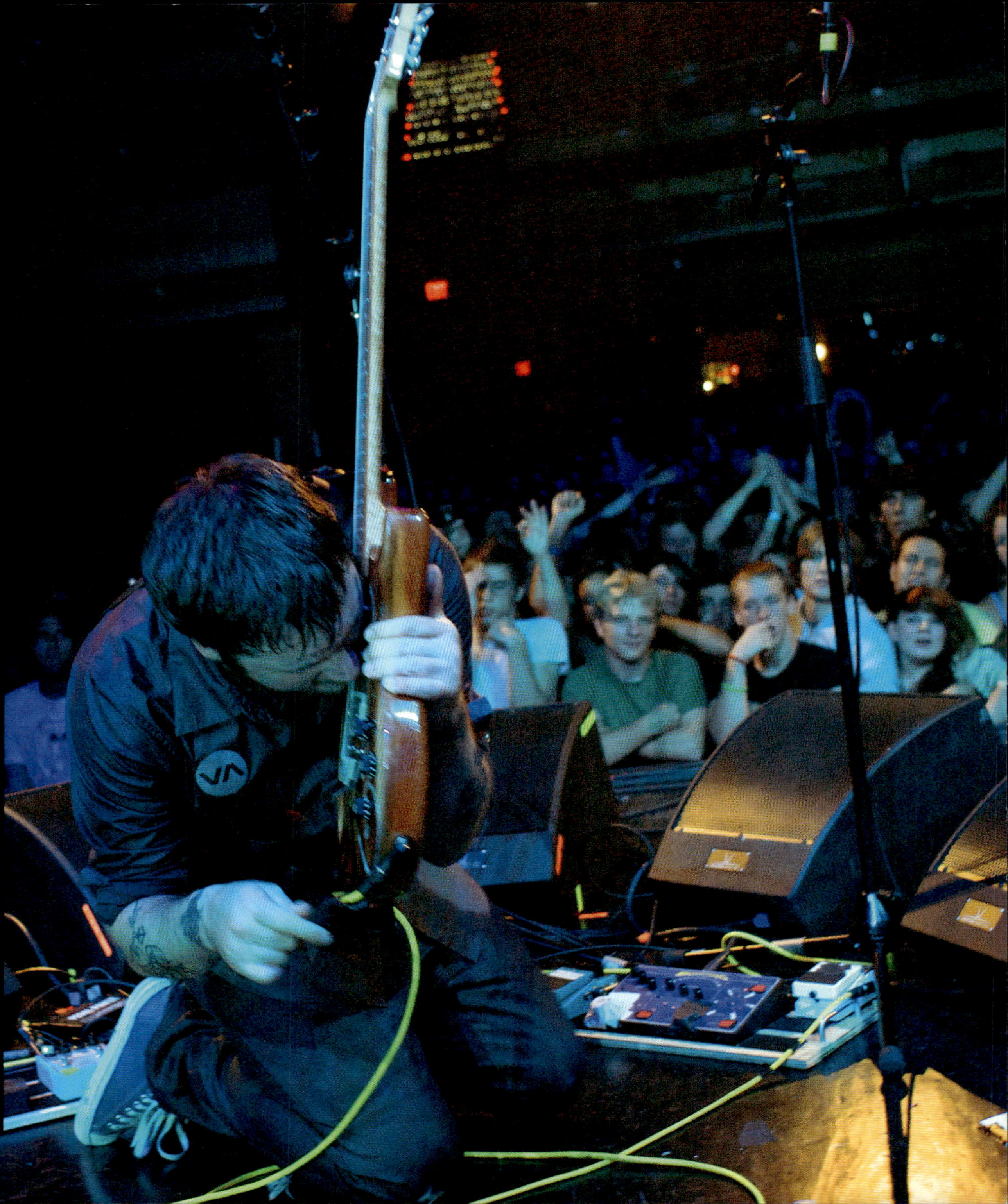

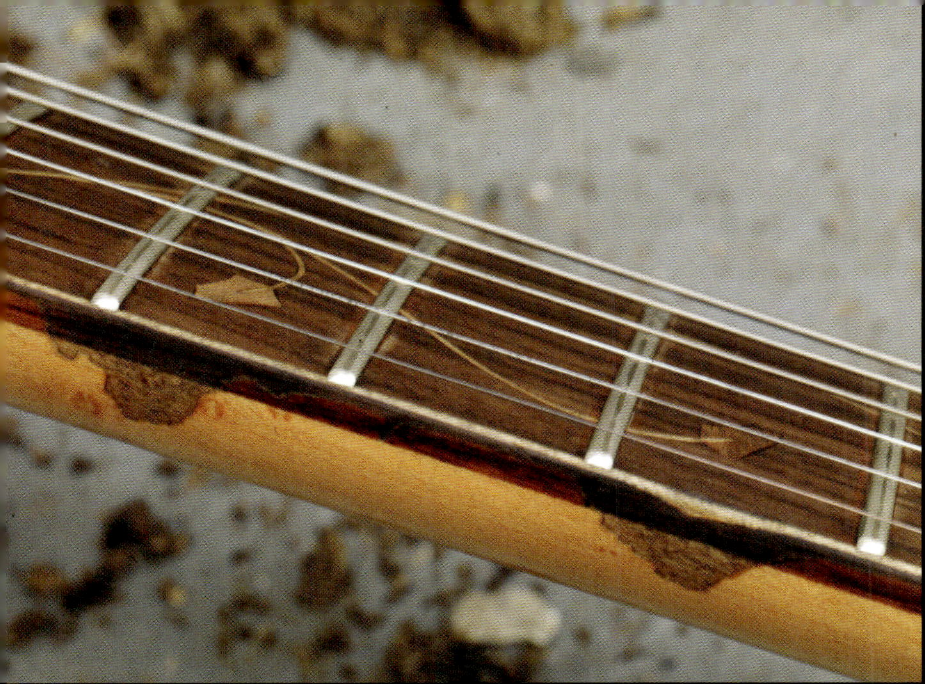
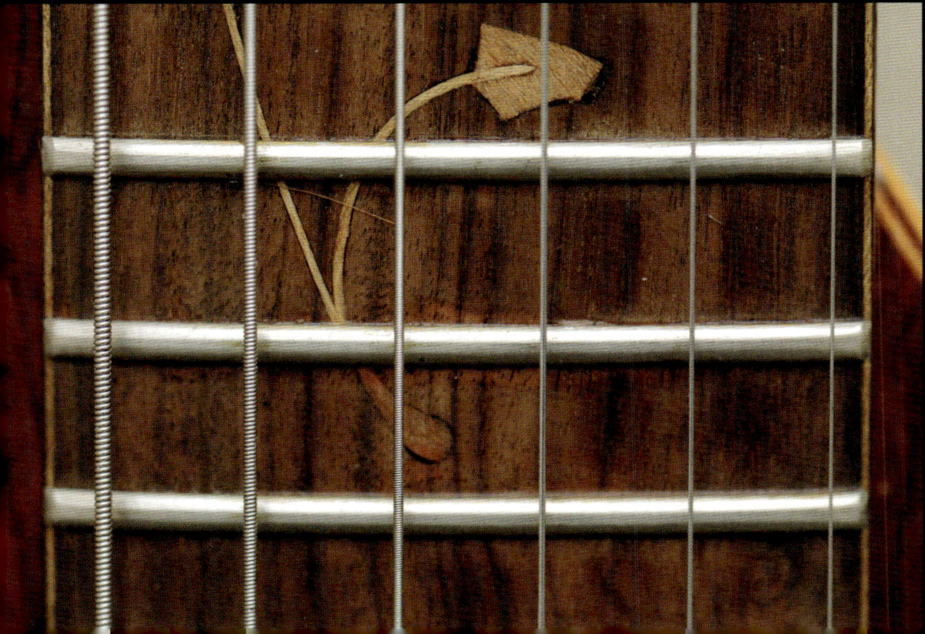
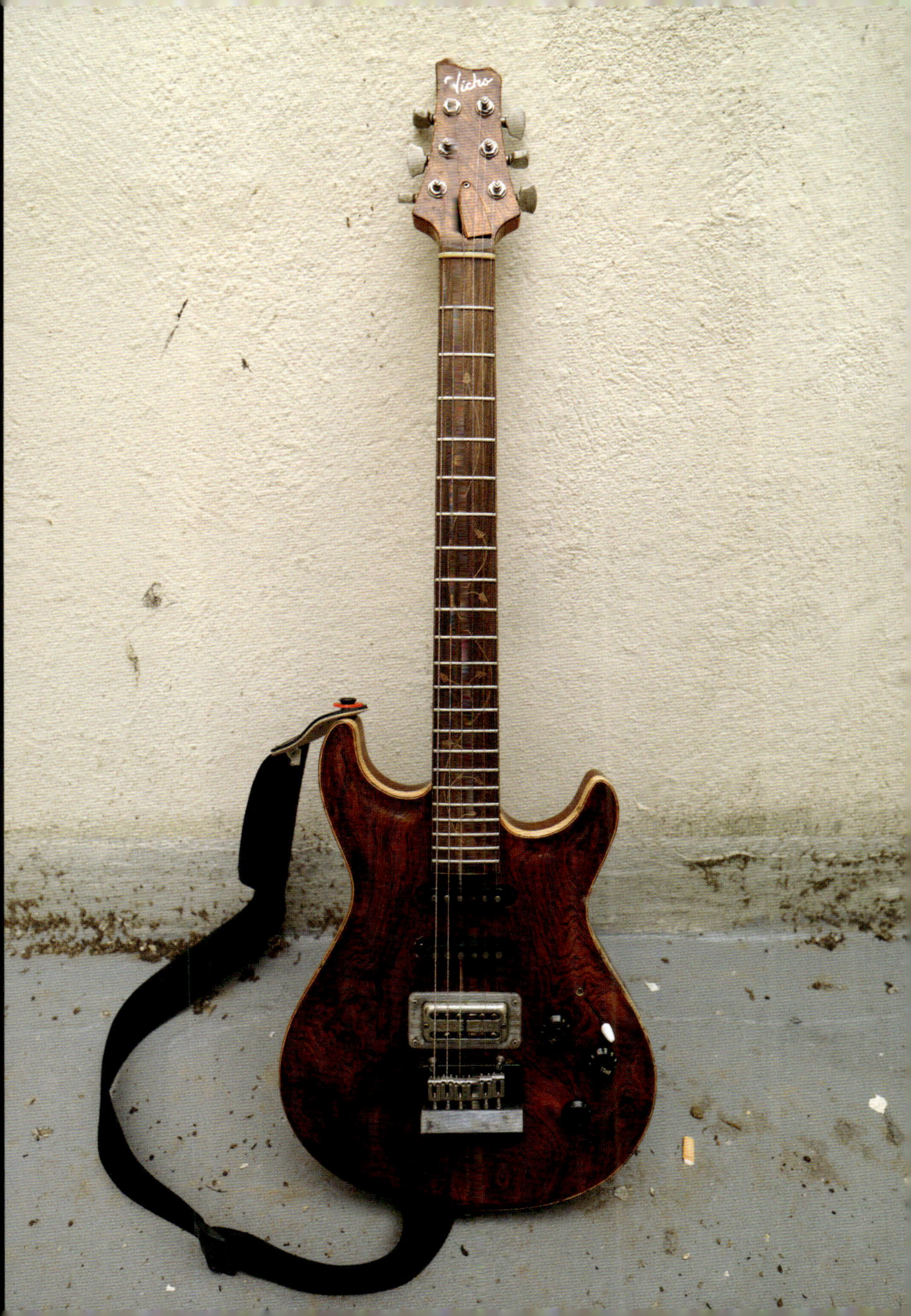

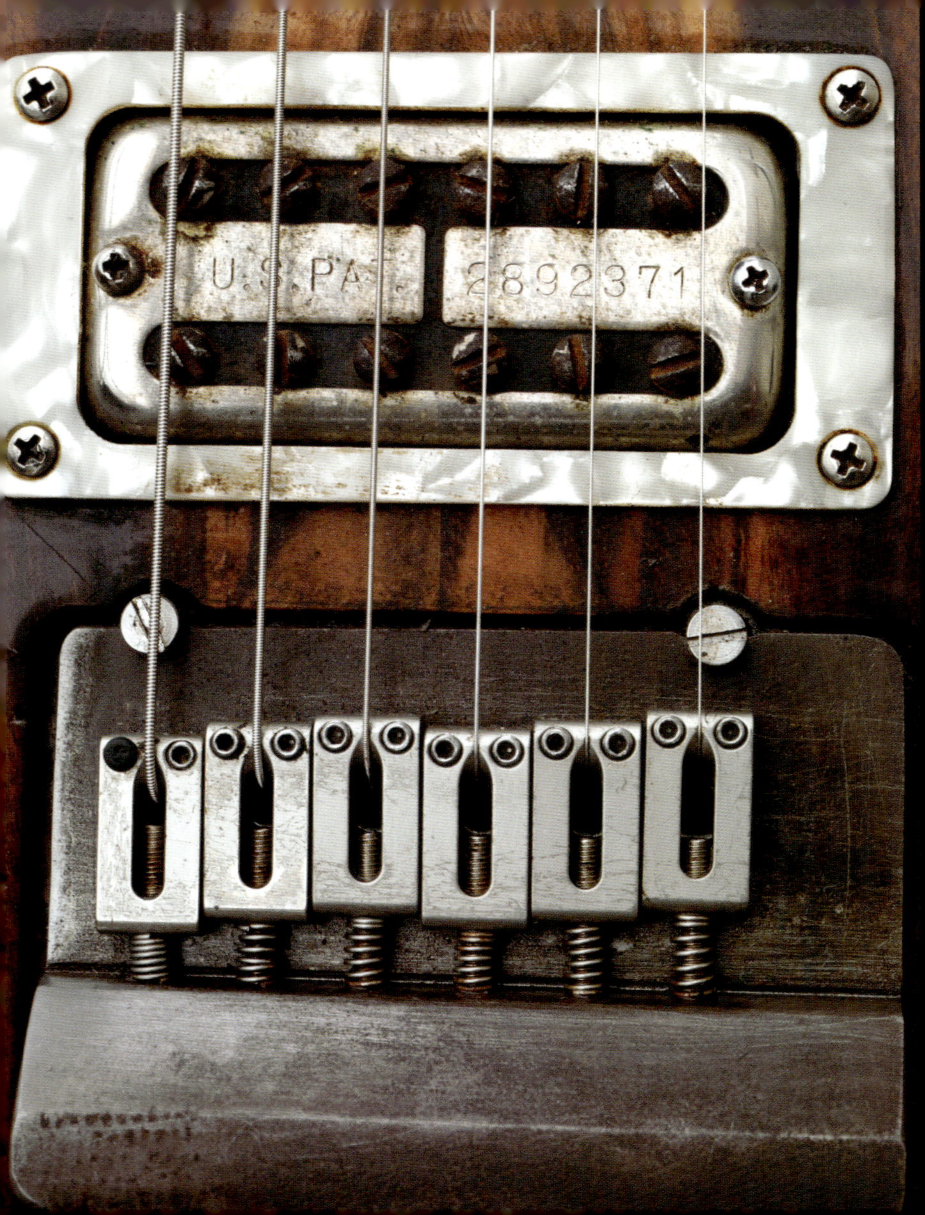
U.S.PAT.
2892371

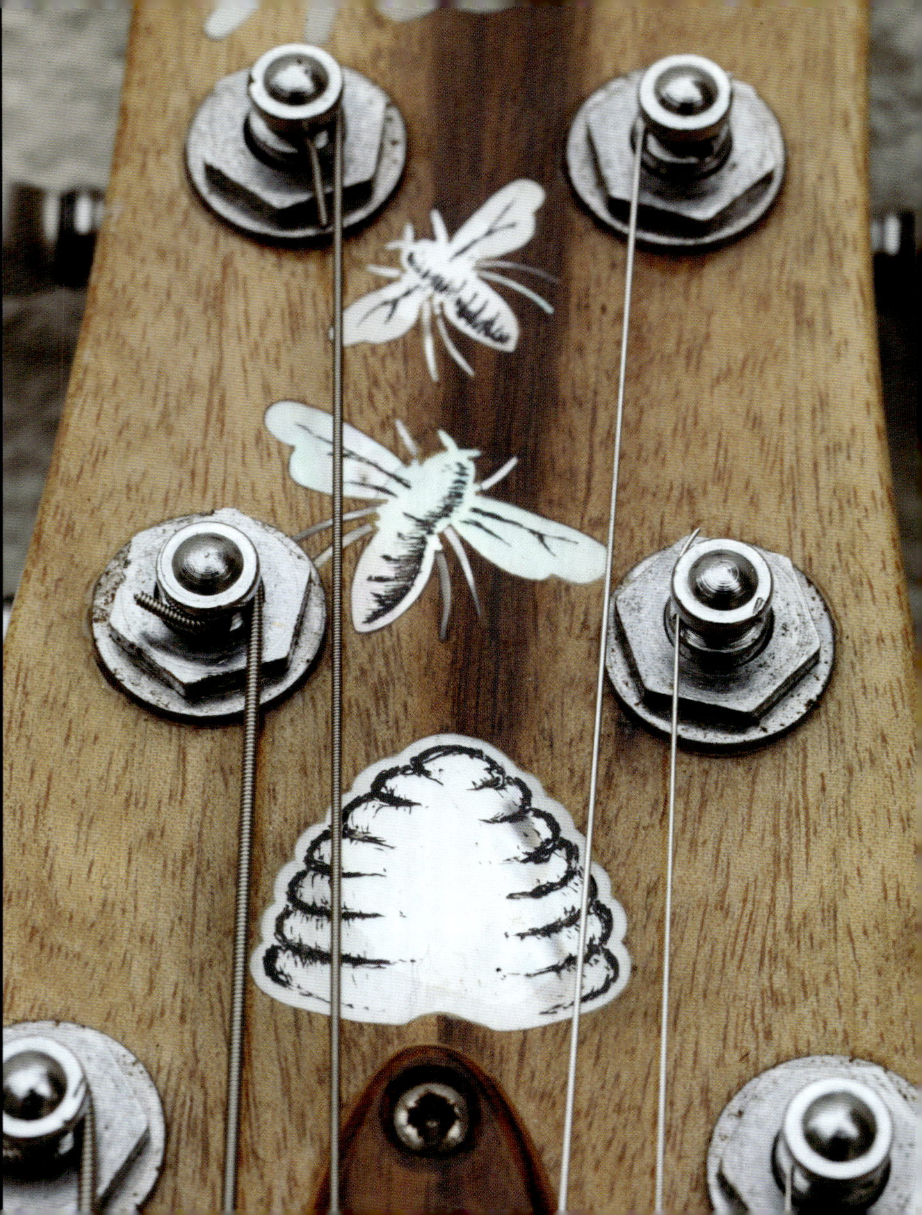

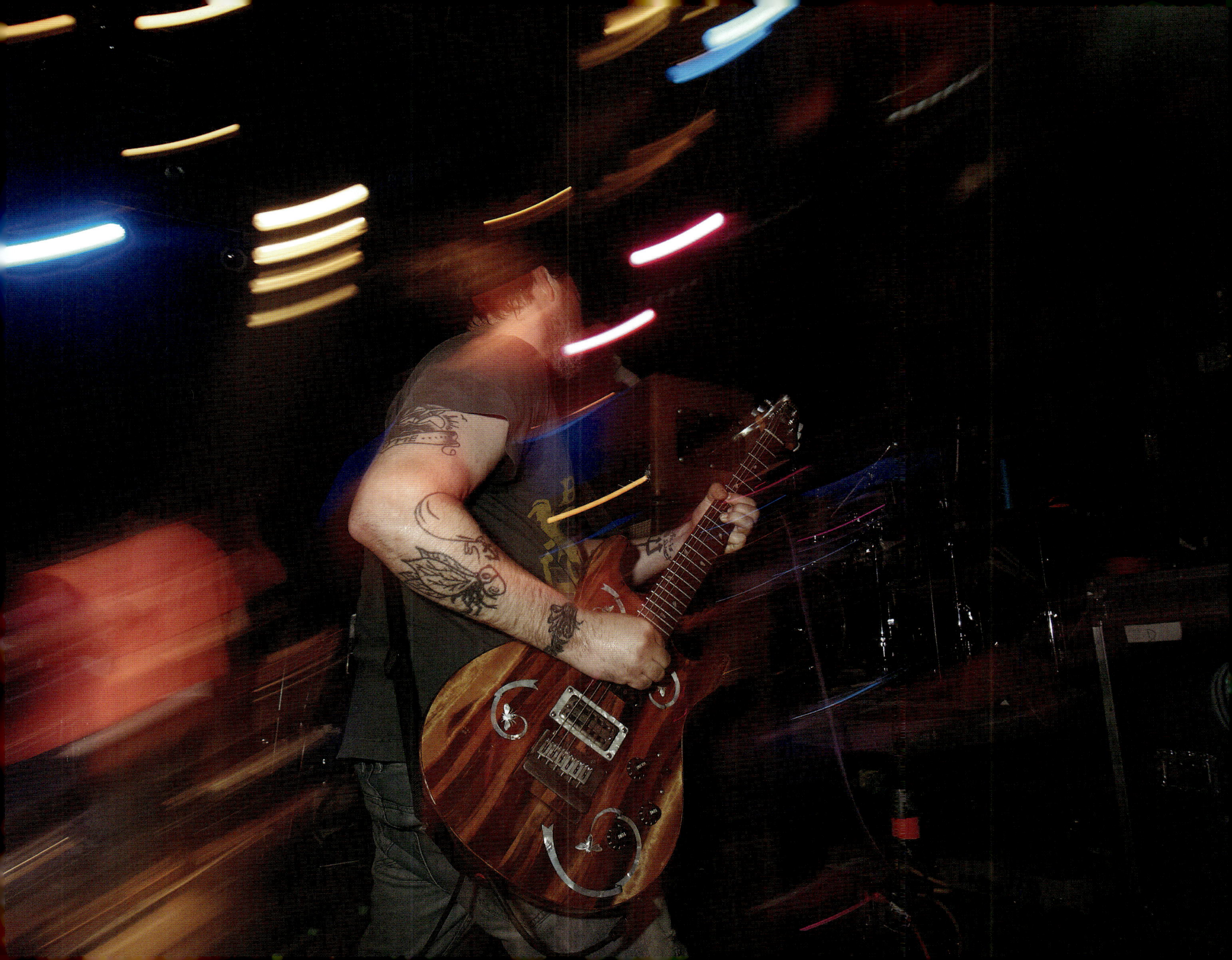

JEREMIAH GREEN

Modest Mouse

C & C drum set and various percussion instruments

This is a C & C clear acrylic drum set. It was born in Kansas City.

My friend Davie customized this trash can. It has been to many countries, and there is a webcam in it. It sounds like a trash can.

This is a noisy tree made by Gregg Kepplinger, from Seattle, and a bell with a feather for making it fly. The metal makes a trashy sound.

These are pom-poms in a drum. They bounce around.

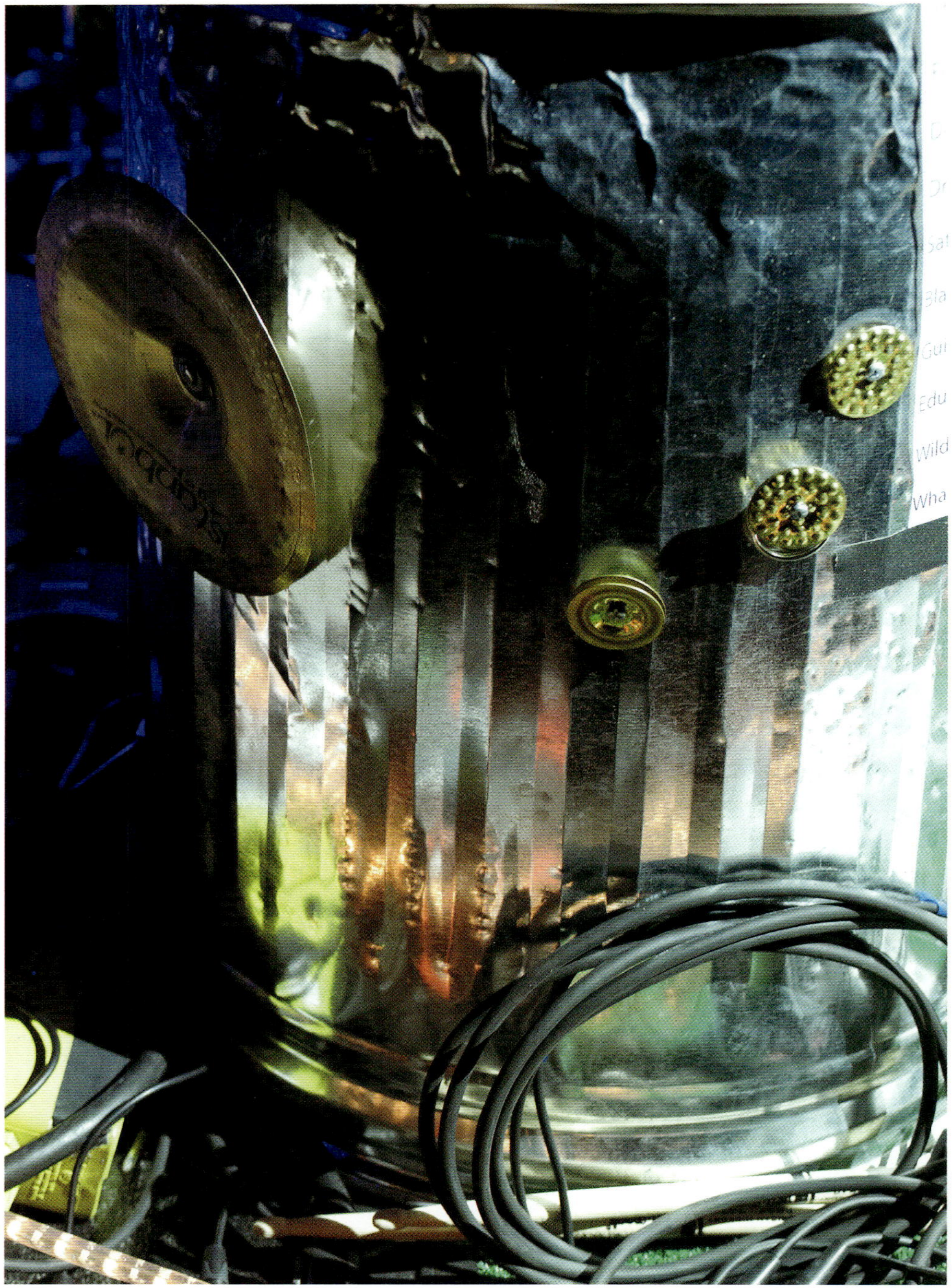

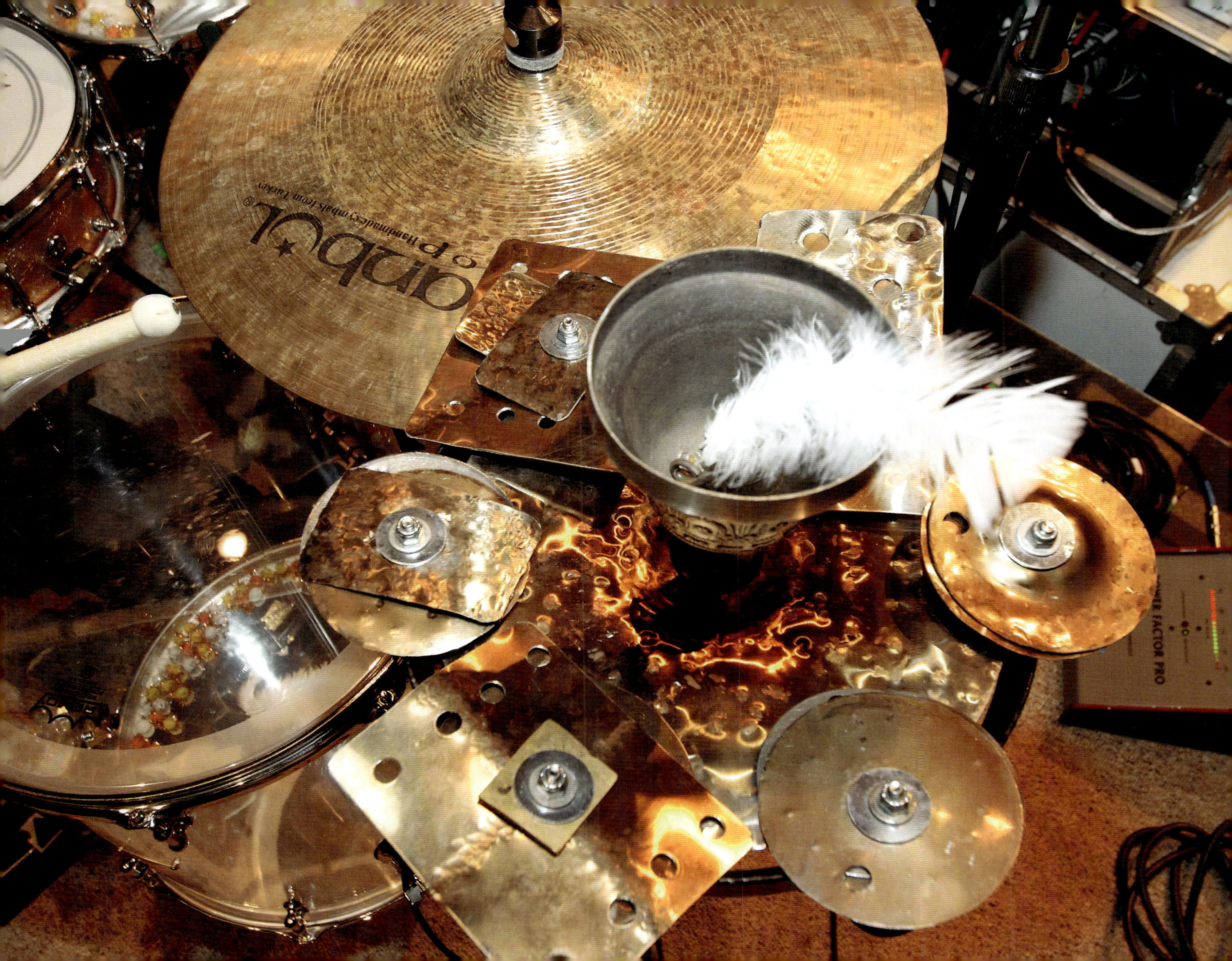

JOHN McENTIRE

Tortoise

Deagan Commander vibraphone
Fender Rhodes 54 electric piano
Clavia Nord Lead 2 keyboard

This vibraphone is a Deagan Commander, purchased from Century Mallet Instrument Services here in Chicago, around 1998. Century's Gilberto Serna installed the custom piezo pickup system in it, and it has performed admirably considering the copious amounts of abuse it has withstood and thousands of miles traveled. For the last several years, we have been trying to find any possible excuse to prune it from the live setup, but it seems that no matter what, it remains firmly in the ranks. At least for the time being.

Our keyboard rigs have always been a means to an end—portable solutions for emulating sounds on recordings that are (generally) produced by instruments that are totally impractical for touring. And to that end, we have almost always employed variations on the following triumvirate: an electric piano (specifically a Rhodes), a synthesizer, and a sampler. We used this particular Rhodes for many years, and at 54 keys (and only 90 lbs!) it seemed absolutely tiny and lightweight compared to hauling around a 73 Suitcase. The Nord Lead 2 replaced the venerable Moog Source, also around 1998, and had the benefits of polyphony and a much broader array of tones (though arguably not as "good" as the Moog). This particular Nord was lost during a night drive in 2001 in Europe: somehow the door to our trailer came unhitched while en route to Fribourg, Switzerland, and a good deal of our backline was strewn about the autobahn for several hundred meters. We thought all of it had been recovered, but alas, we were wrong. I can only hope someone found that thing and made good use of it, flightcase and all. Fast forward to 2011, and our key rig is now two MIDI controllers, a Dell Inspirion Netbook running Reason, and a couple FX pedals . . . my, how things have changed.

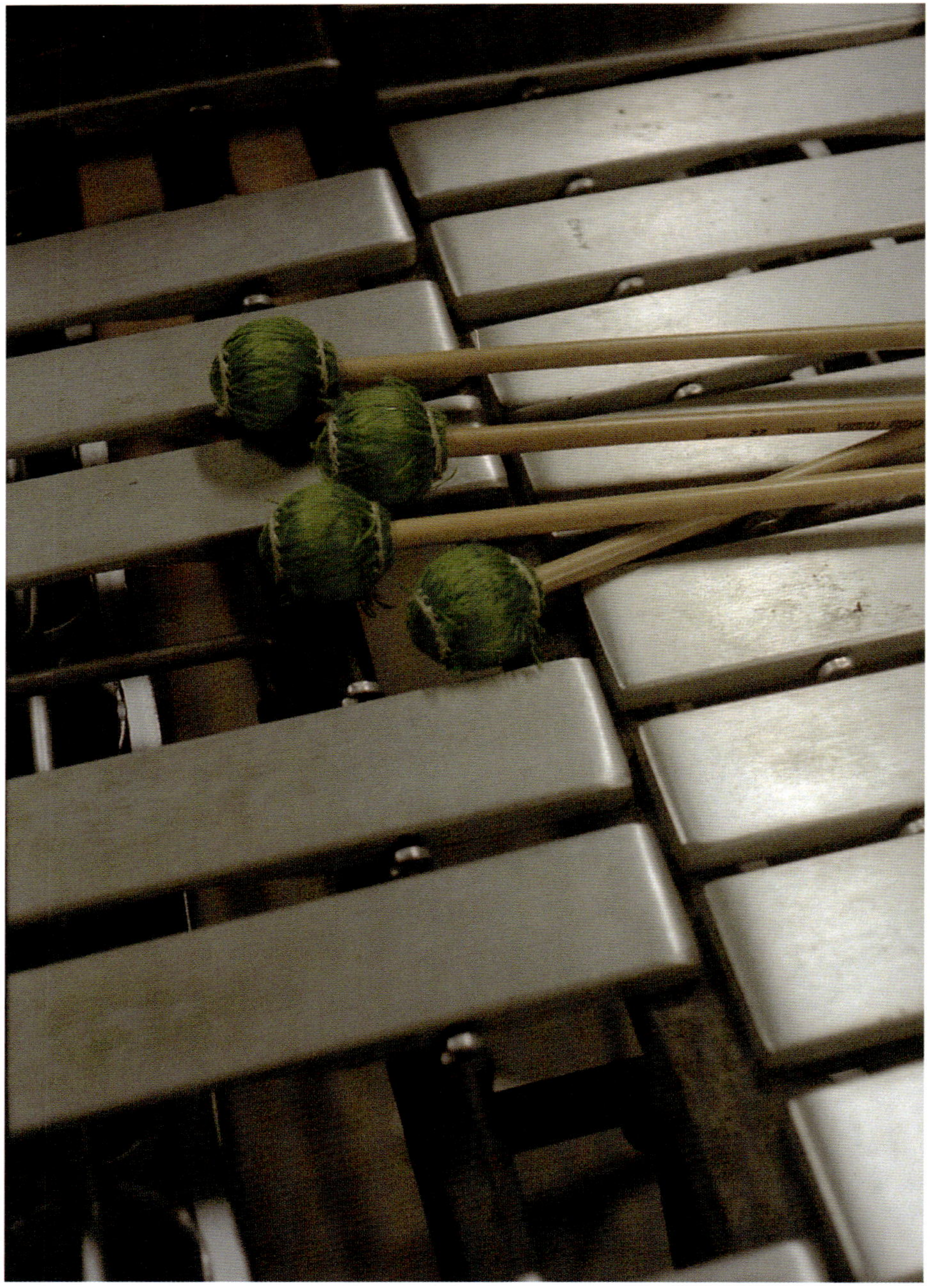

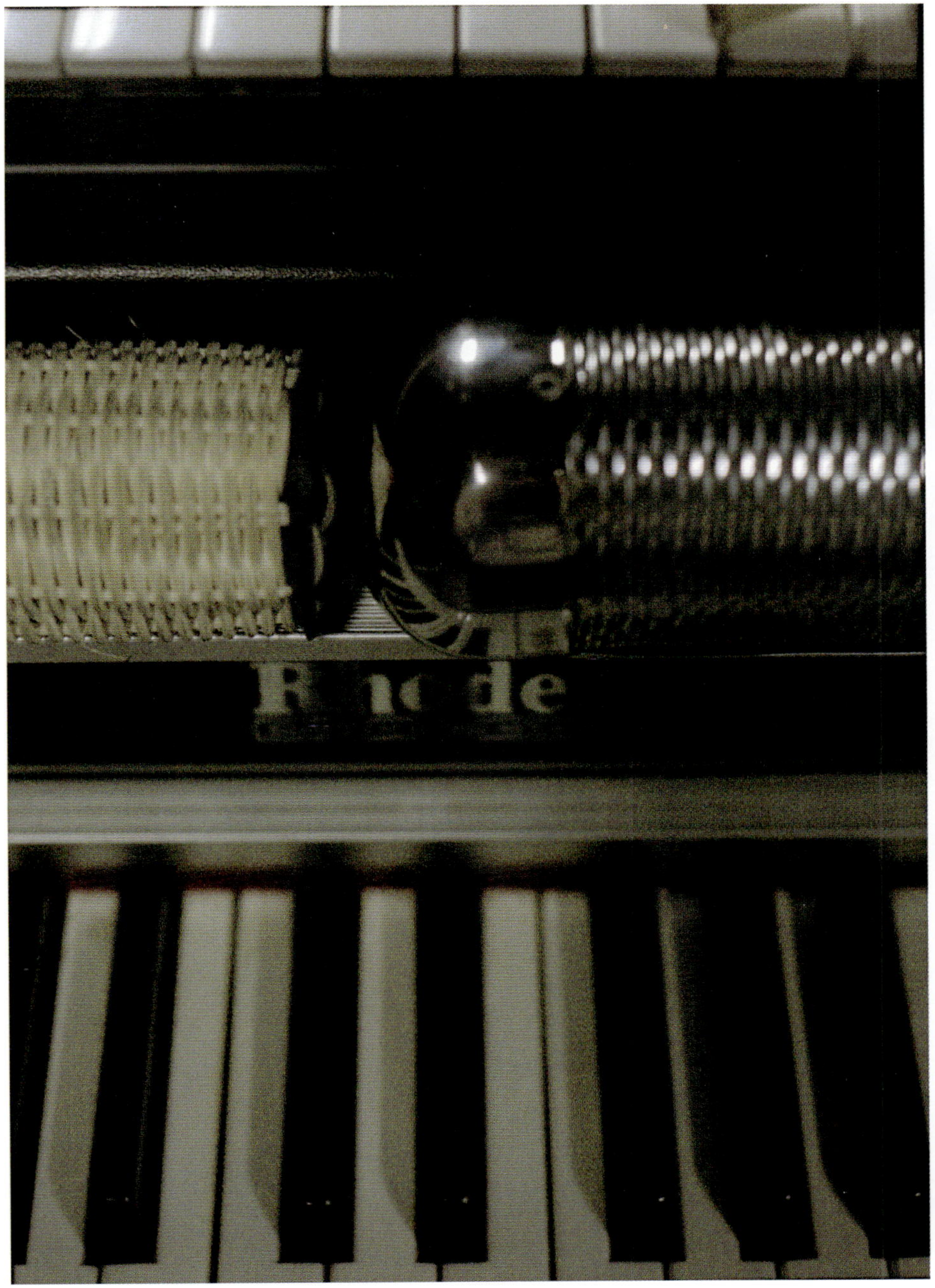

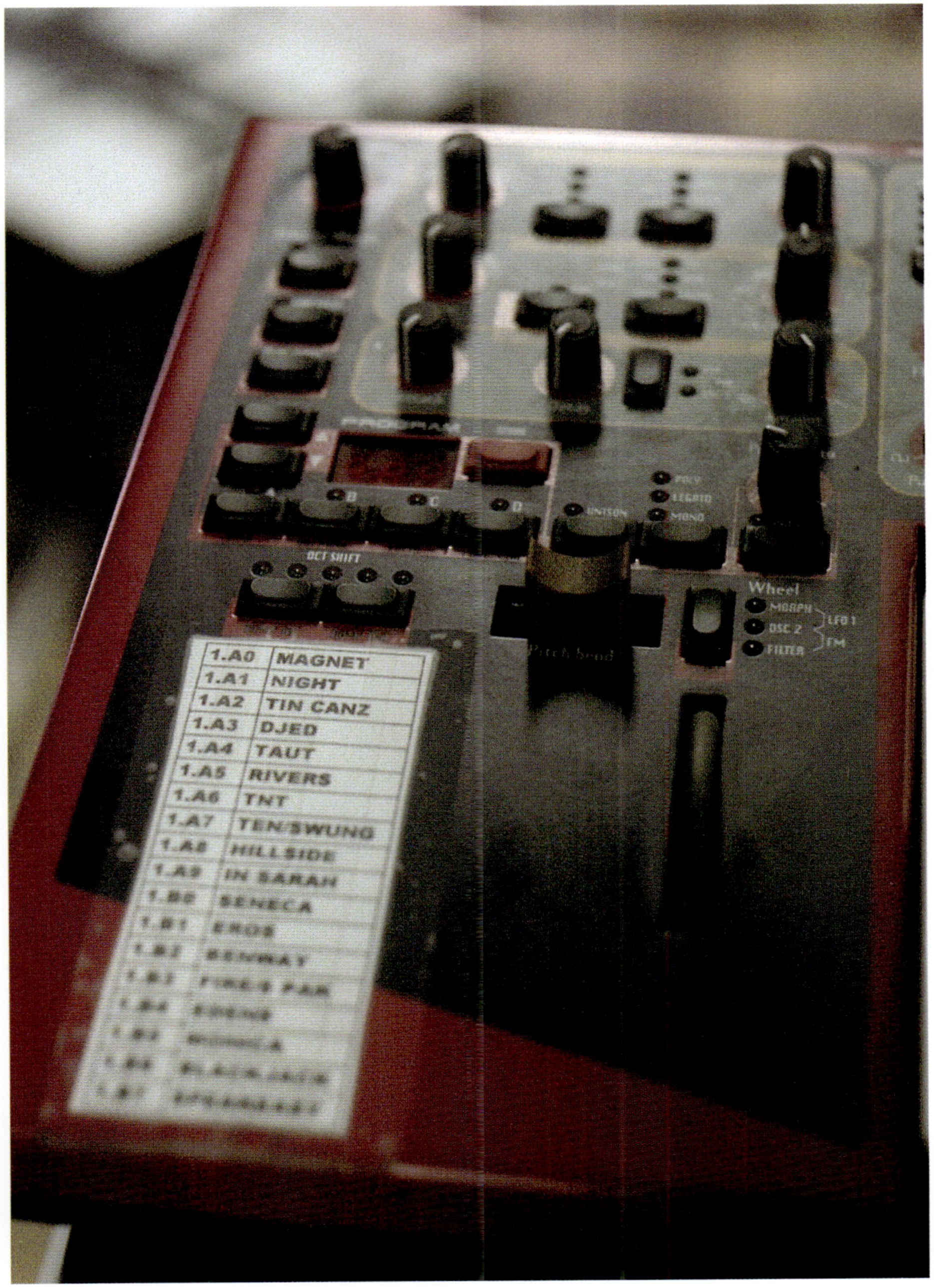
1.A0 MAGNET
1.A1 NIGHT
1.A2 TIN CANZ
1.A3 DJED
1.A4 TAUT
1.A5 RIVERS
1.A6 TNT
1.A7 TEN/SWUNG
1.A8 HILLSIDE
1.A9 IN SARAH
1.B0 SENECA
1.B1 EROS
OCT SHIFT
UNISON
LEGATO
MONO
Wheel
MORPH
OSC 2
FILTER
LFO 1
FM

NELS CLINE

Wilco, The Geraldine Fibbers, Nels Cline Singers, Mike Watt
1959 Fender Jazzmaster guitar

My guitar was purchased in the summer of 1995 from Mike Watt after the first tour by The Crew of the Flying Saucer. I had used my old '66 Jaguar on Watt's first solo record and really didn't know the difference between a Jaguar and a Jazzmaster other than the different pickups and switching configurations. I didn't know then that 1959 is one of the best years for Jazzmasters, and that this would end up being my favorite guitar. I first chose both Jazzmasters and Jaguars for their feel and because they have strings behind the bridge and single-coil pickups. I was copying Sonic Youth and Tom Verlaine, basically. But when I finally played the Jazzmaster, I was smitten with the whole feeling of the neck and body, the sound, and the inherent durability. Watt engraved his name on the base of the neck where it joins the body and on the base of the tremolo assembly. He engraves everything!

This guitar has done more tours and records than I can count: all the Mike Watt tours, the Geraldine Fibbers tours and *Butch* album, later records with the Fibbers' Carla Bozulich and Scarnella, dozens of recordings by various improvised projects, including all my solo records since *The Inkling*, tours with Wilco, and all three records I made with them. This guitar mostly lives in Chicago in the Wilco loft now, and I have a different '59 at home in Los Angeles so that I don't always have to fly back and forth with it. I have been extremely hard on it, as you can see—it was in perfect shape when I got it.

I play hard. There is actually a very deep and ever-deepening gouge above where the strings stretch from the bridge to the tailpiece, where I play a lot and, apparently, with considerable vigor! Admittedly, the finish was delicate. It is easy to scratch the paint, revealing a purplish hue, much like eggplant. I used to wear my keys on my pant loop, and after hopping up and down on stage with Watt, I created an interesting and rather sizable stippling on the back of the guitar. In the Geraldine Fibbers, I would sometimes throw the guitar to our drummer Kevin Fitzgerald and play my effects pedals while he savaged it with drumsticks, sometimes ripping out the strings, which is difficult to do on a Fender guitar, and bleeding on it. I have bled on it plenty. The Geraldine Fibbers' "Dusted" caused some wounds, and these days Wilco's song "A Shot in the Arm" might be another danger, though I am much smarter now about things like fret wear. The body, well . . . I think it looks great. It's a work in progress, just like me.

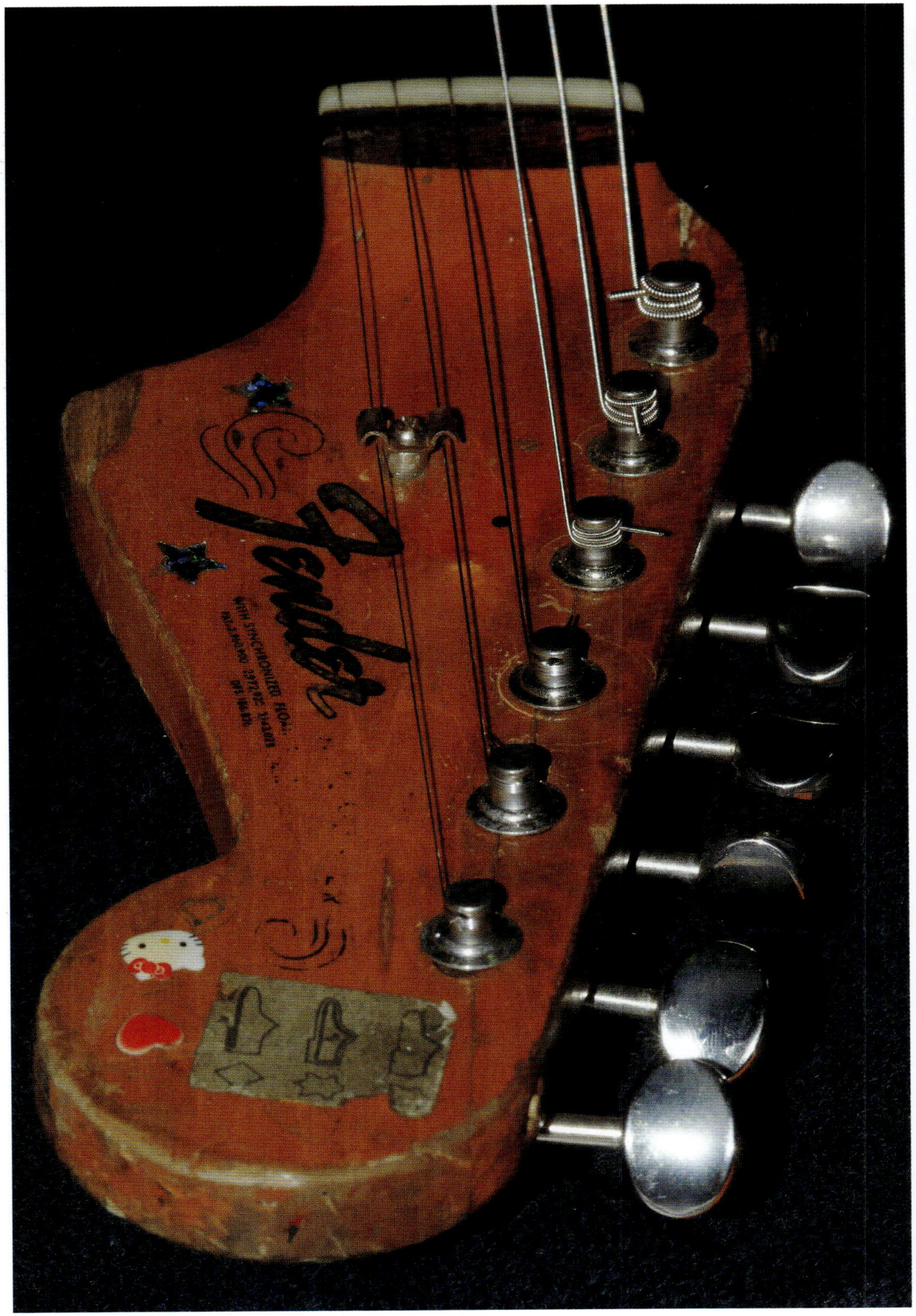
Fender

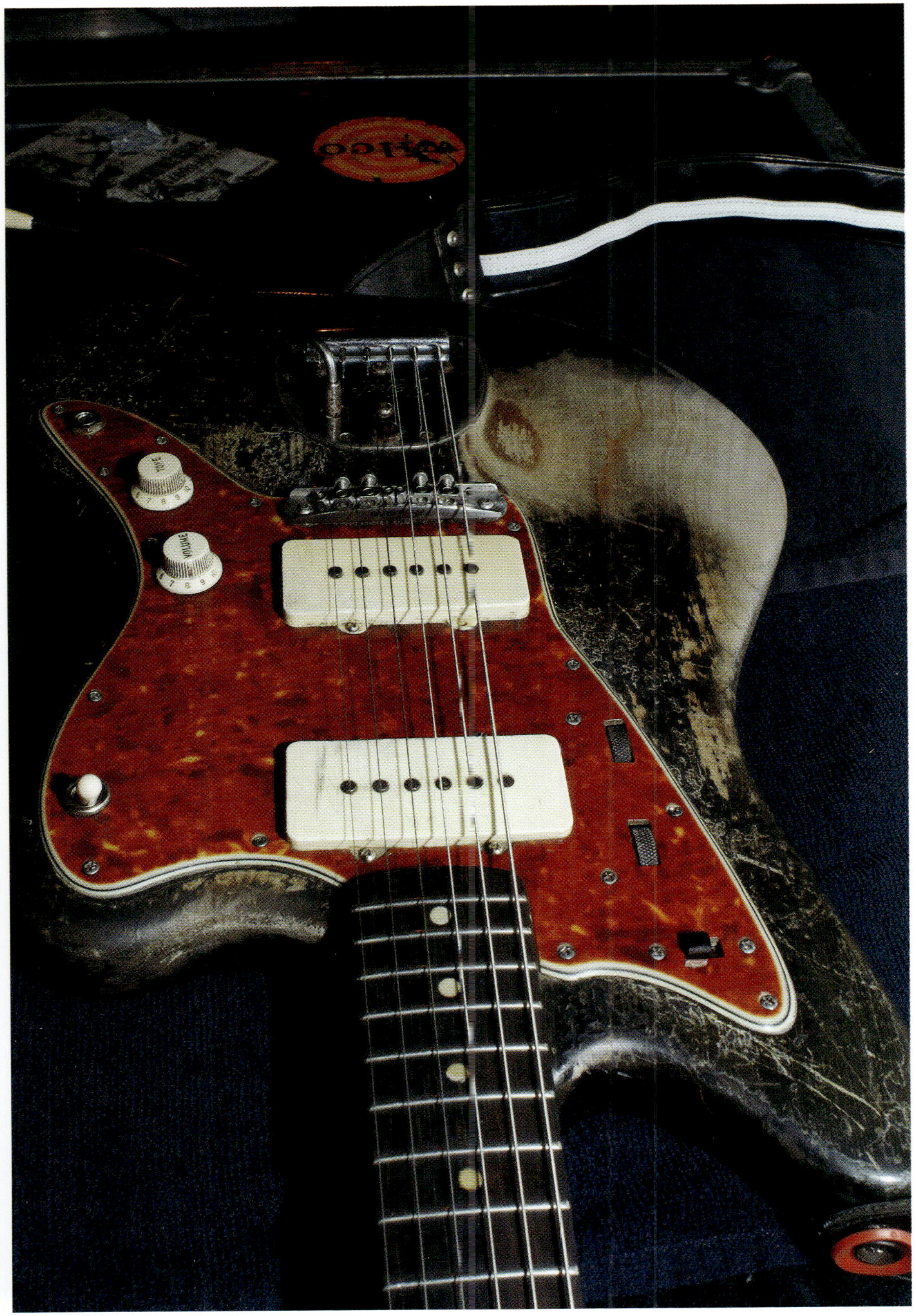
TONE
VOLUME

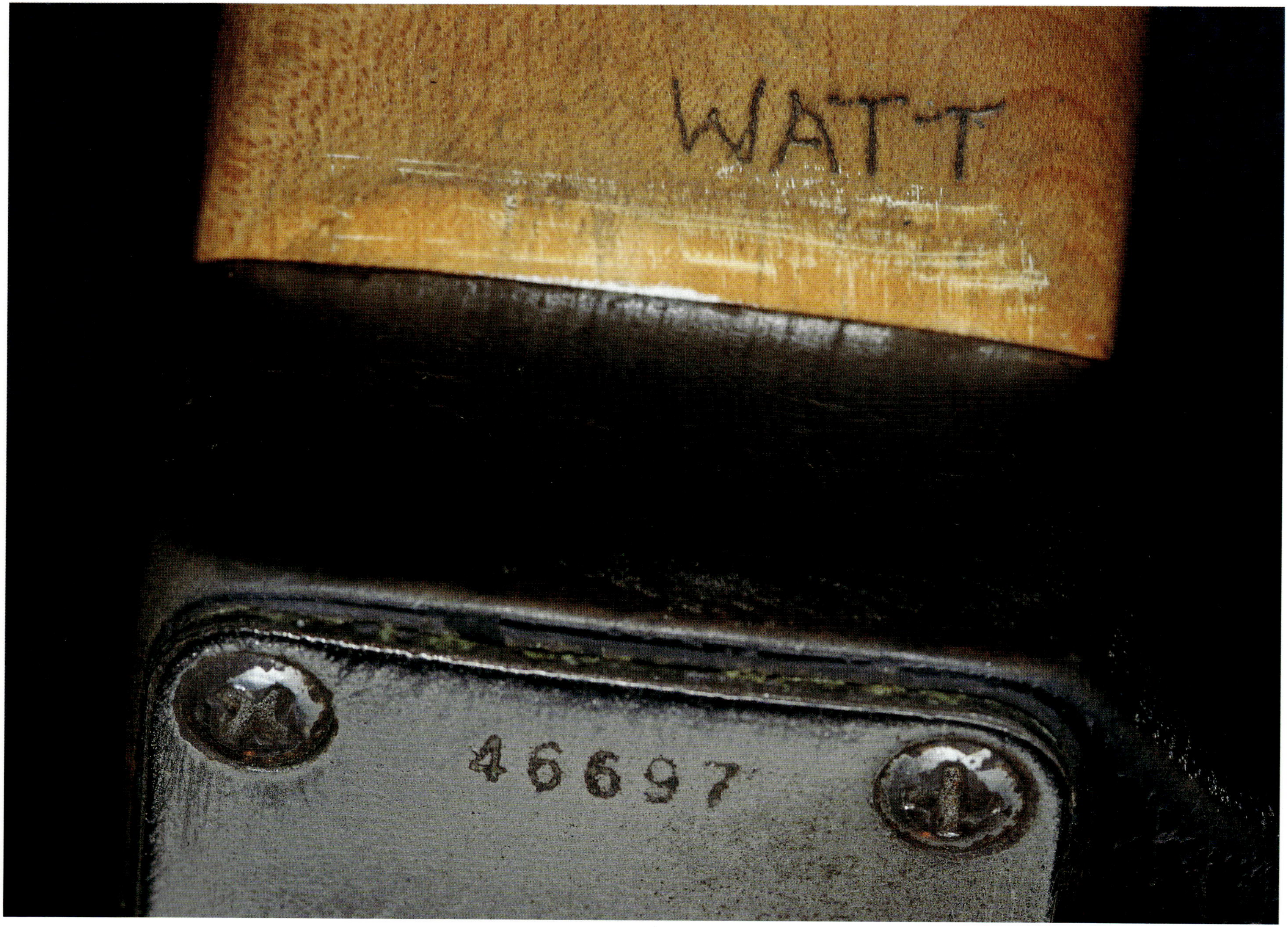
WATT
46697

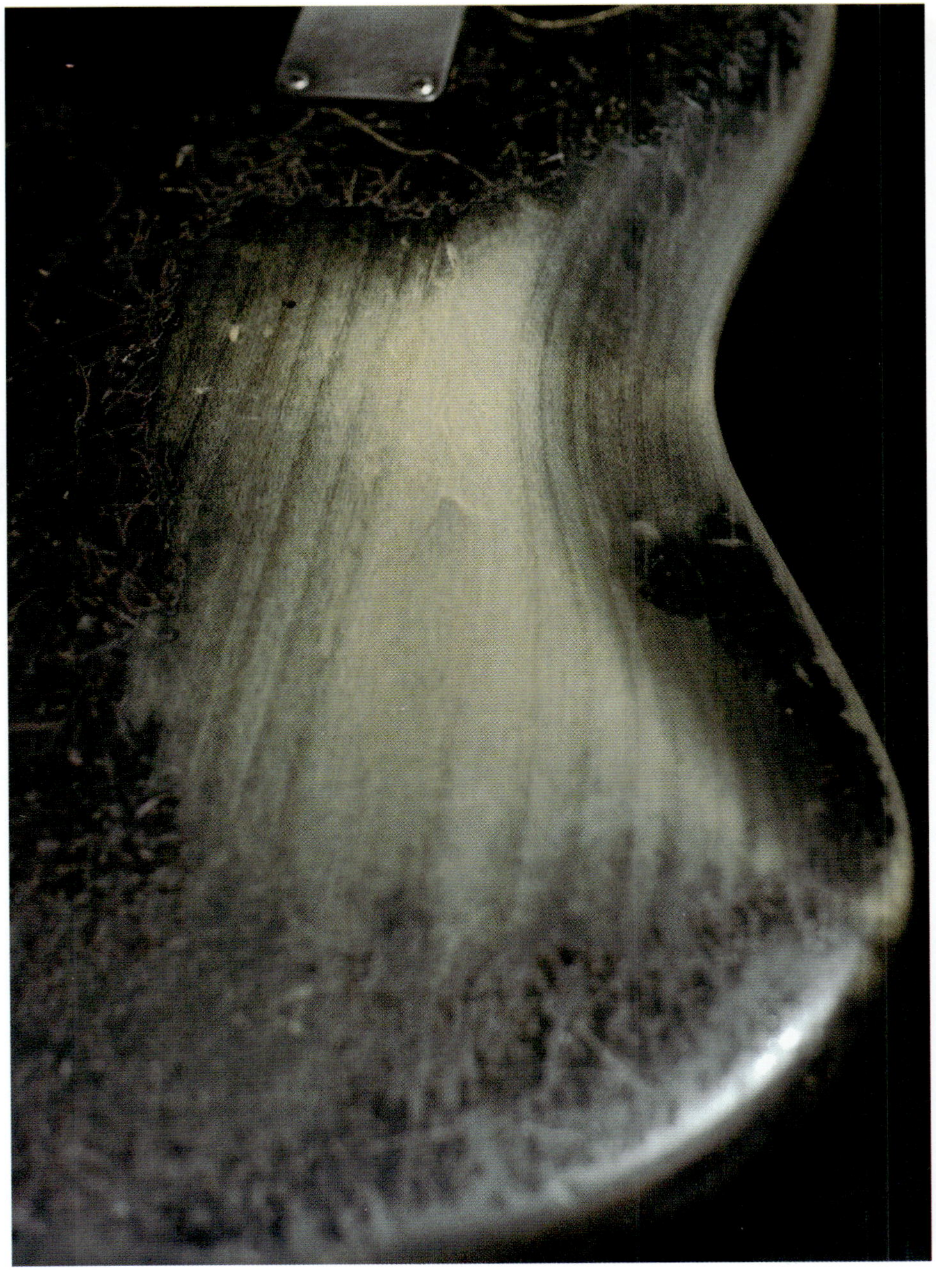

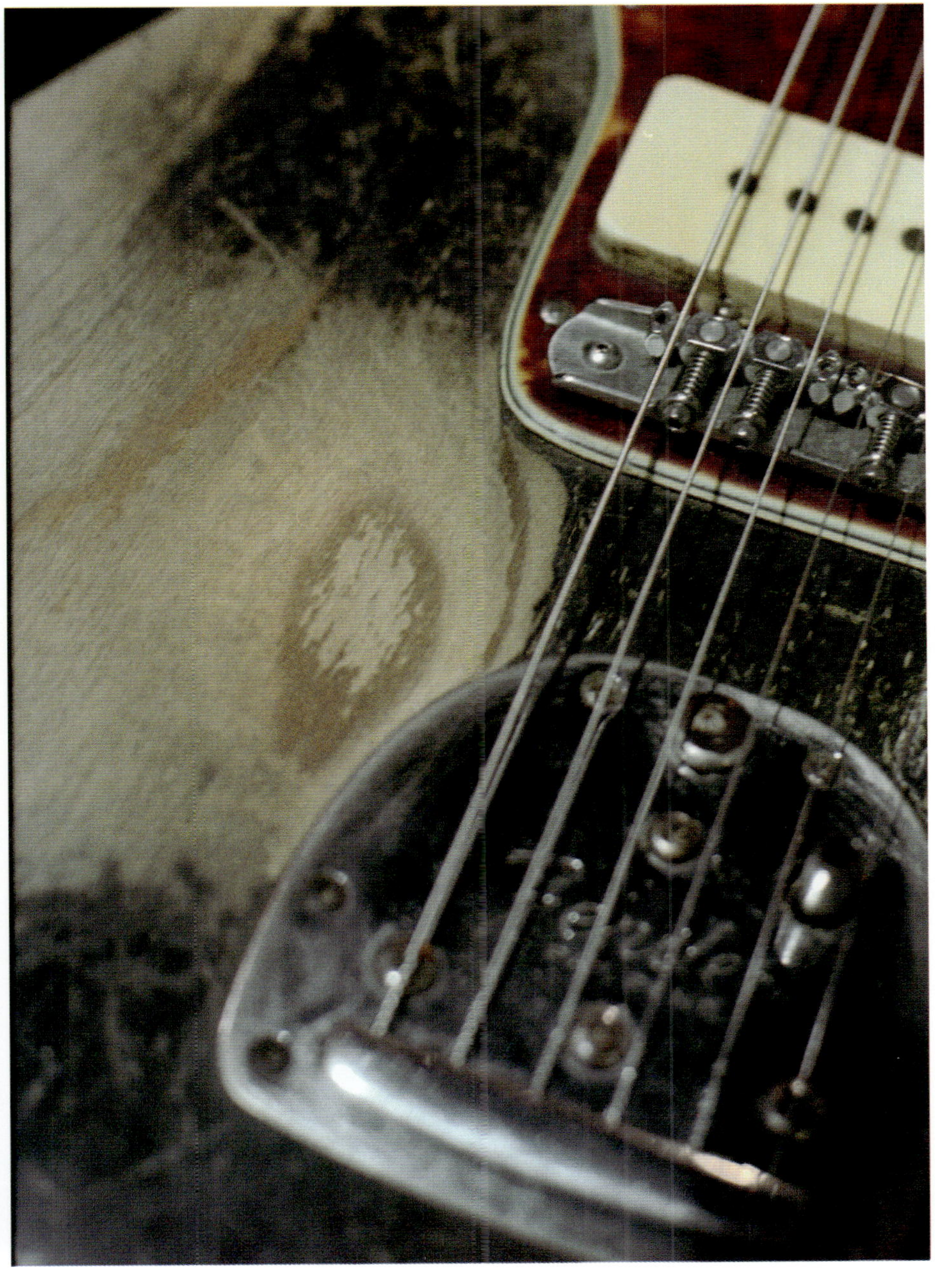

BERNARD SUMNER

Joy Division, New Order, Electronic, Bad Lieutenant
Moog Source synthesizer

This is the first Moog that I ever bought. I got it because it was the first monophonic programmable synth. I bought this synth and a DMX drum machine, and the first thing we wrote with both of those things was "Blue Monday." This was the synth that was used to do the bass line, a whopping great bass sound—I didn't know Moogs had a great reputation for bass. In fact, the bass on that record was created by this synth and nothing else.

In most synthesizers, the sound starts on the left-hand side with the oscillators and works its way across to the right-hand side. You can see the numbers 95, 93, 50, 59—these are oscillator wave shapes for the song at these settings that have been penciled on. The sound moves to the right in the machine to the mixer, where you can control the volume of each oscillator; then it moves to the filter, where you can shape the envelope of the sound. Another section adds modulation to the sound. It's a pretty straightforward synth—not many things you can do with it, but I've found these are the best kind of synths. You can spend all day getting a bass drum with other, larger synths in the studio. Really, what I do is about writing songs. I don't want to spend all day making sound.

In the early days, when we started making dance music, it was a question of linking the synthesizer up with drum machines and synchronizing synthesizers together with a sequencer that could play a very precise bass or soft line. People were only really doing that in the studio. I thought, that's great, because if we take this gear out on the road and we start doing it live, we will be one of the few bands doing it.

I heard "Blue Monday" in a club in Berlin a couple of years ago, and everybody got up, even then. There is something about that song that just makes people dance. And it sounds great even now, it just sounds so powerful.

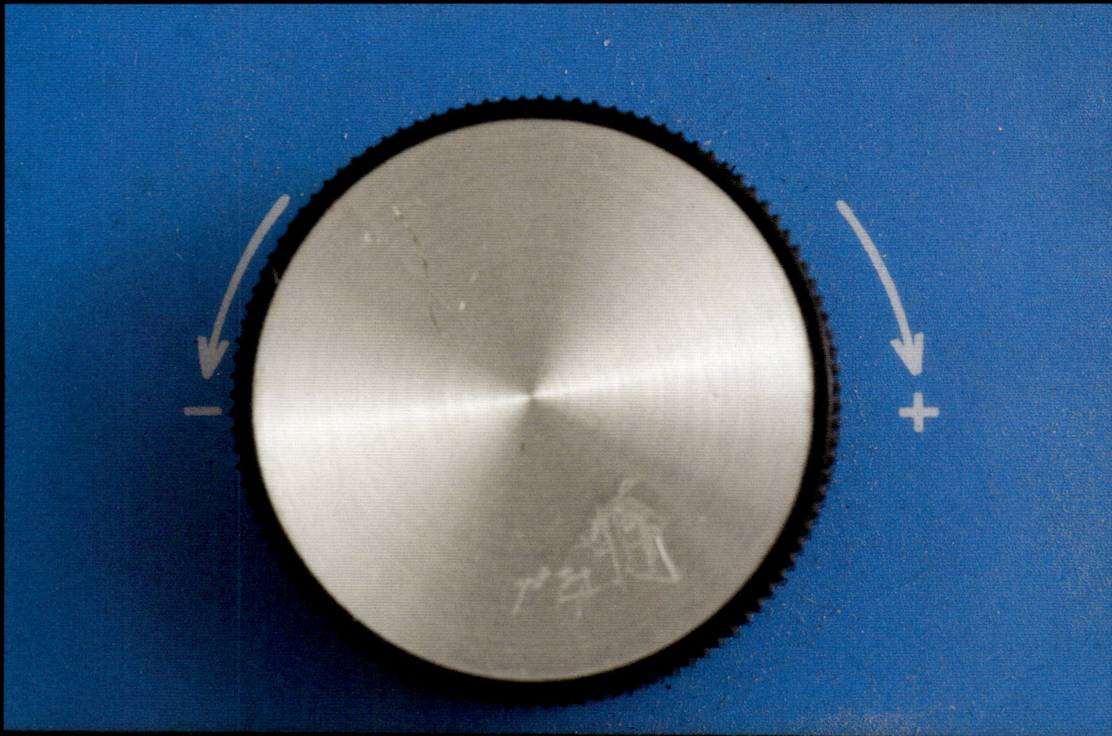

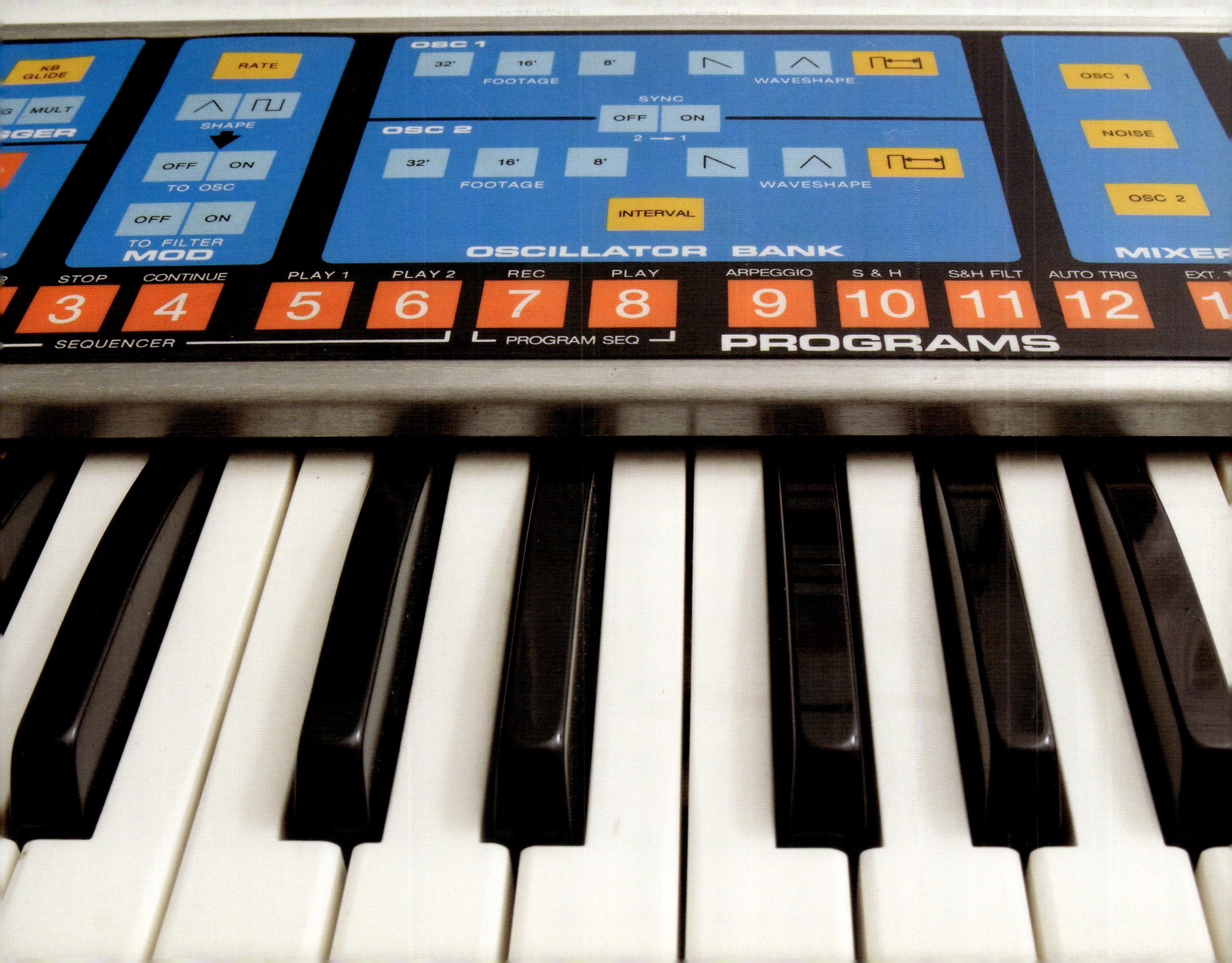
KB GLIDE
MULT
RATE
SHAPE
OFF
ON
TO OSC
OFF
ON
TO FILTER
MOD
OSC 1
32'
16'
8'
FOOTAGE
WAVESHAPE
SYNC
OFF
ON
2 → 1
OSC 2
32'
16'
8'
FOOTAGE
WAVESHAPE
INTERVAL
OSCILLATOR BANK
OSC 1
NOISE
OSC 2
STOP
CONTINUE
PLAY 1
PLAY 2
REC
PLAY
ARPEGGIO
S & H
S&H FILT
AUTO TRIG
3
4
5
6
7
8
9
10
11
12
SEQUENCER
PROGRAM SEQ
PROGRAMS

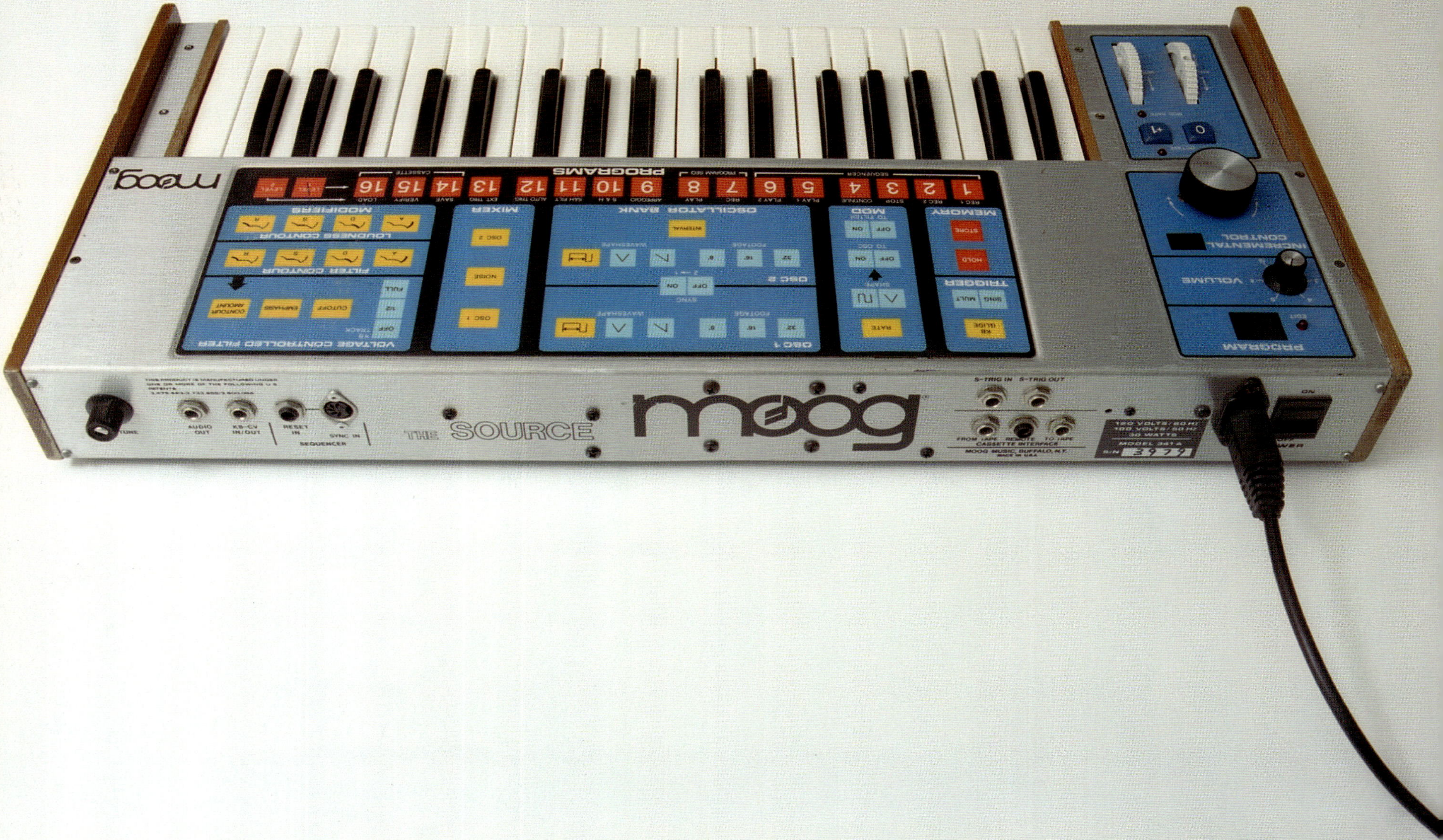
moog
THE SOURCE
AUDIO OUT
KB-CV IN/OUT
RESET IN
SYNC IN
SEQUENCER
S-TRIG IN
S-TRIG OUT
FROM TAPE
REMOTE
TO TAPE
CASSETTE INTERFACE
MOOG MUSIC, BUFFALO, N.Y.
MODEL 341A
S/N 3979

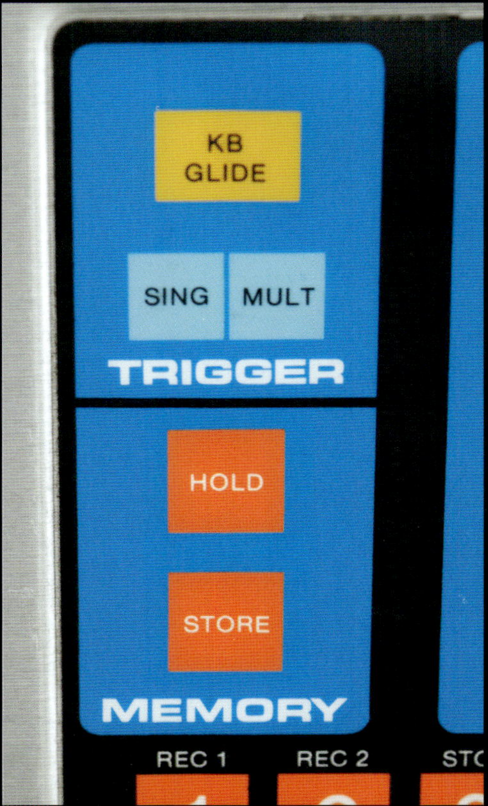
KB GLIDE
SING
MULT
TRIGGER
HOLD
STORE
MEMORY
REC 1
REC 2

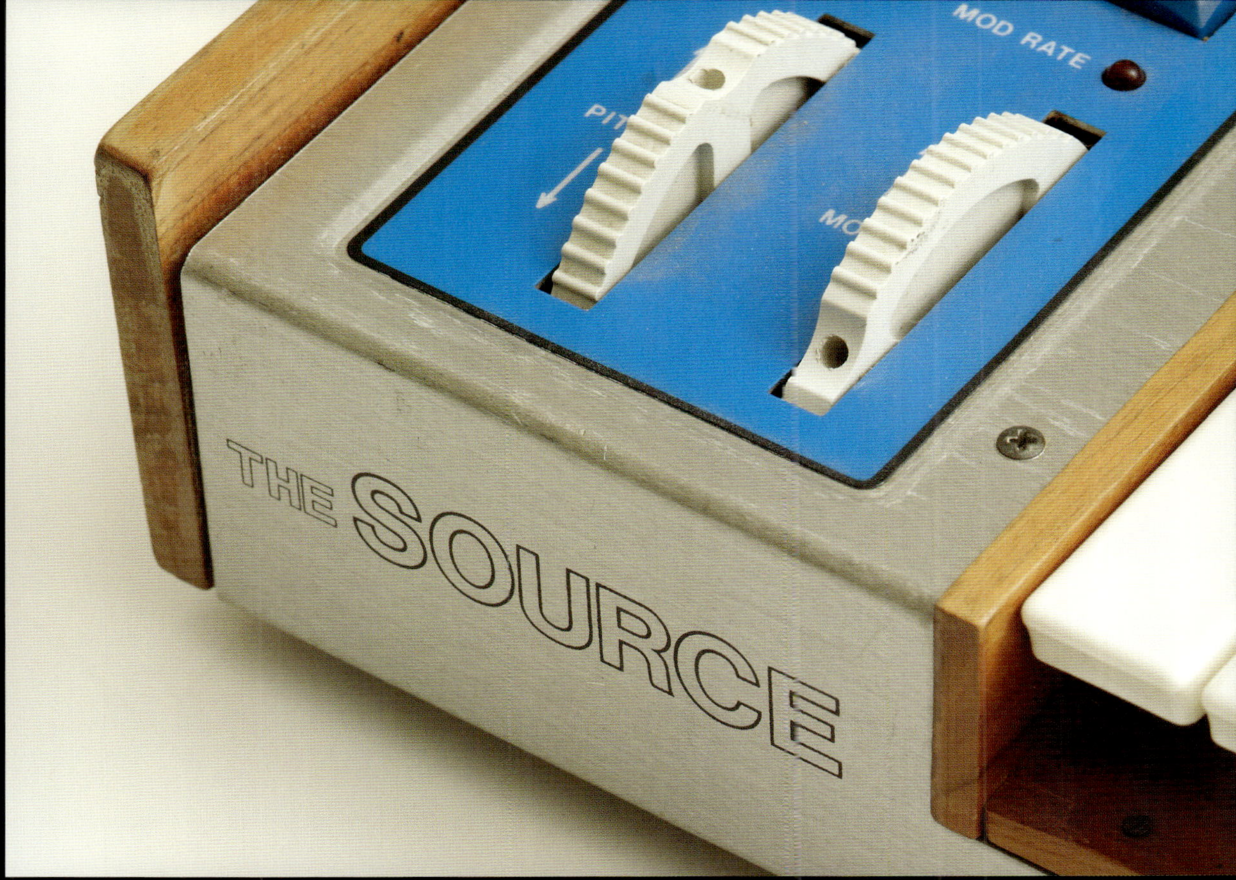
MOD RATE
THE SOURCE

STEVE ALBINI

Big Black, Shellac

Travis Bean TB500 guitar

I was on the lookout for a Travis Bean because I had played one in a shop in the 1970s and remembered liking it. In 1990 or so, a now-departed friend of mine who was a bit of a guitar collector and dealer called me from a guitar show in someplace like Midlothian and said there was a dealer with a TB guitar and bass for sale, and he'd take $900 for the pair of them. I told him to get them. When he came to collect the money, he was a little drunk and there was a poker game running, so he sat down with the guitar money in front of him and lost about $100 of it to the table. I think I won $40 of it. So there was a bit of a discount there.

I have since become very fond of certain aspects of this guitar, in particular the way the neck bends easily for warping the notes but doesn't go out of tune on its own. I often grab the T headstock with my free hand as a handle for bending. I had the tone knob removed because I never used it. I also particularly love the placement of the toggle switch, which allows me to wibble it in lieu of playing the guitar conventionally, one of my favorite things. I have had to replace the toggle switch maybe ten times because I wibble it so much.

It's the guitar I play in Shellac, and except for one or two oddities, it's on everything we've ever done.

I use metal picks, which tear into the wood, strings, pickup covers, and pickguard over time. They are terribly destructive, but I'm so used to them now that anything else feels wrong. The photos were taken with the most recent pickup covers, made from hardened aluminum by Kevin Burkett of the Electrical Guitar Company. At the time of the photo, I'd had them about a week, and you can already see the beginnings of wear.

When Bob [Weston, Shellac bass player] and I decided to paint the guitar and bass to match, we used a really hard epoxy-based coating normally used on boats and marine equipment. It is really hard, but I chopped through it almost instantly. At one time, I tried making a patch of a very hard resin, the remains of which you can still see on the exposed wood area, but the resin just broke and made the guitar even uglier. The guitar shop that does all my repairs is the one I've been going to since I moved to Chicago, called The Guitar Works, and they generally have good instruments there, which they treat reverently. Over time they've gotten used to my odd instruments and requests. Usually I need them to make the guitars more bulletproof in the face of the abuse they get onstage. There are a few moments in our shows where I encourage Todd [Trainer, Shellac drummer] to whack the guitar with his drumsticks, and over time this has knocked pretty big chunks out of the fingerboard. Terry at The Guitar Works has come up with a patch formula for those chunks that is almost invisible, and by now the fingerboard is probably 40 percent resin patch.

The only time I ever broke my guitar, I was acting like an asshole, swatting my amp with it at the end of a set. We were playing with Fugazi at the State Theatre in Detroit, and at the end of the set there was a noisy part, so I was whacking my amp with the guitar and it was howling and I felt really cool. Until I whacked it hard enough to break the neck right out of the body, which also tipped the amp far enough that it fell over, and the big heavy head punched a hole about the size of my foot in the stage. I felt pretty stupid after that.

I appreciate my guitar as the means of my expression, and I see part of my job as learning to use it for its innate characteristics, not taming it to my expectations. I definitely feel like I have a relationship with this guitar, and I am gradually learning what it can do. I hear other musicians say they feel limited by certain instruments, and I think they have it completely backward. They should be cooperating with the instrument, not demanding things of it.

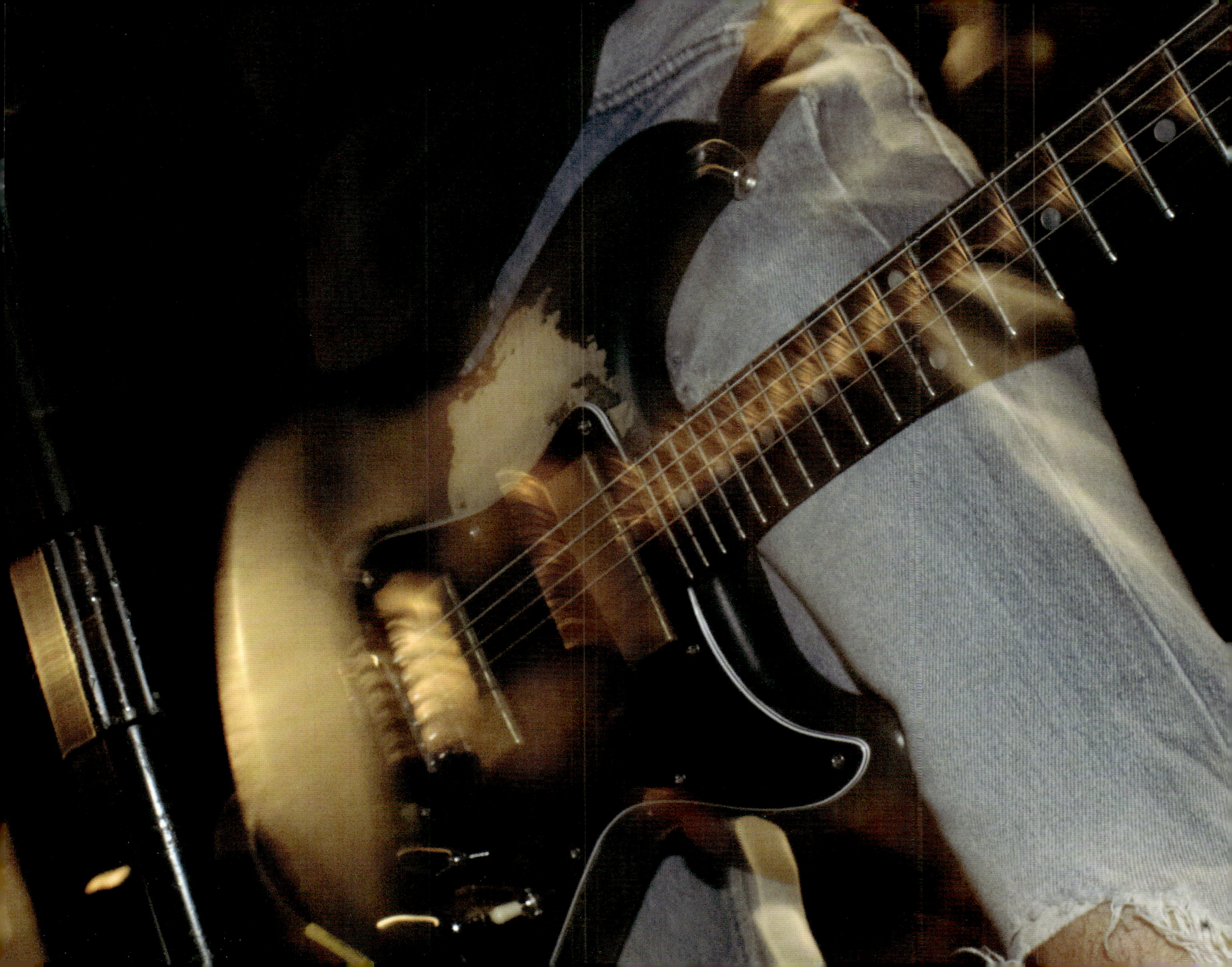

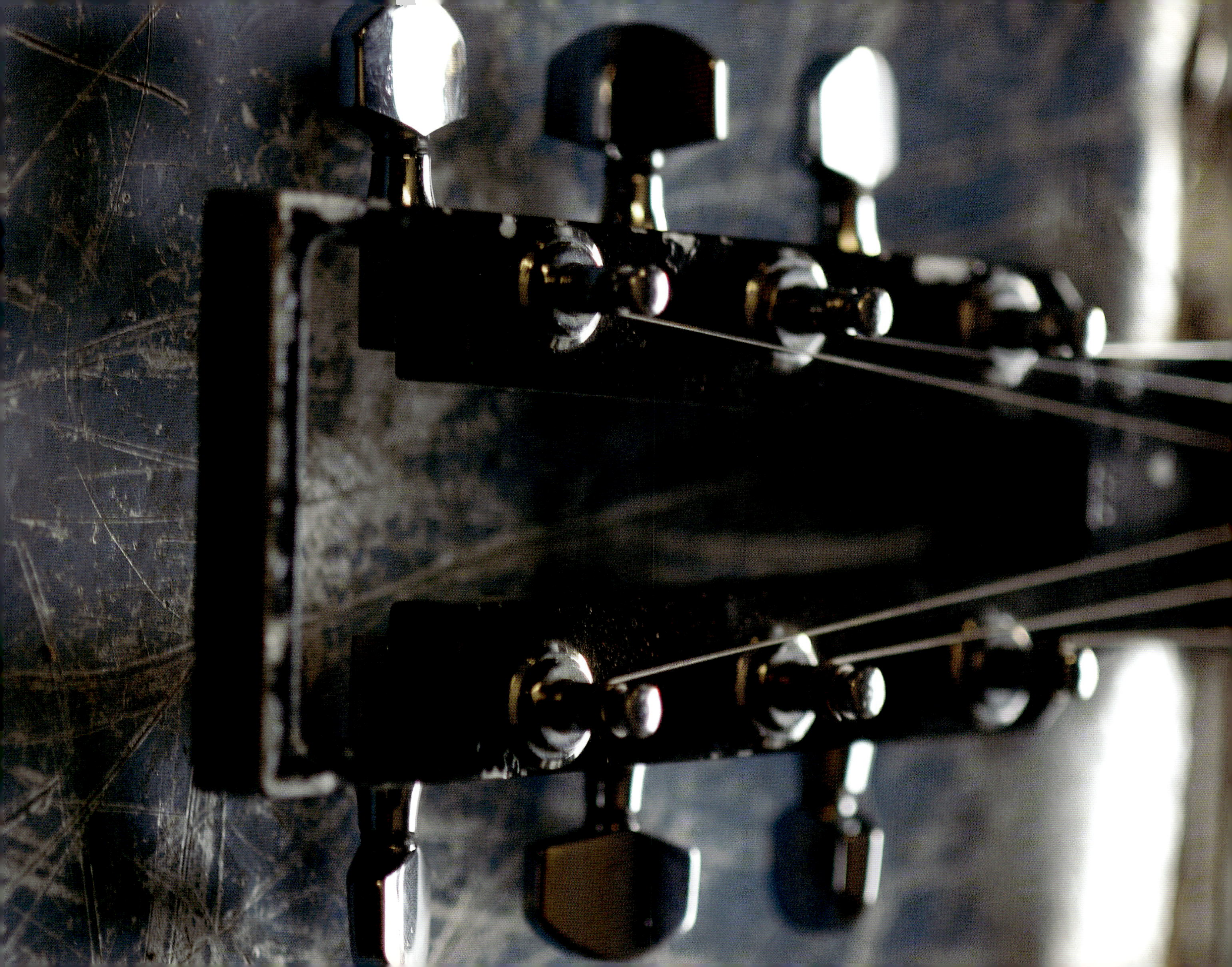

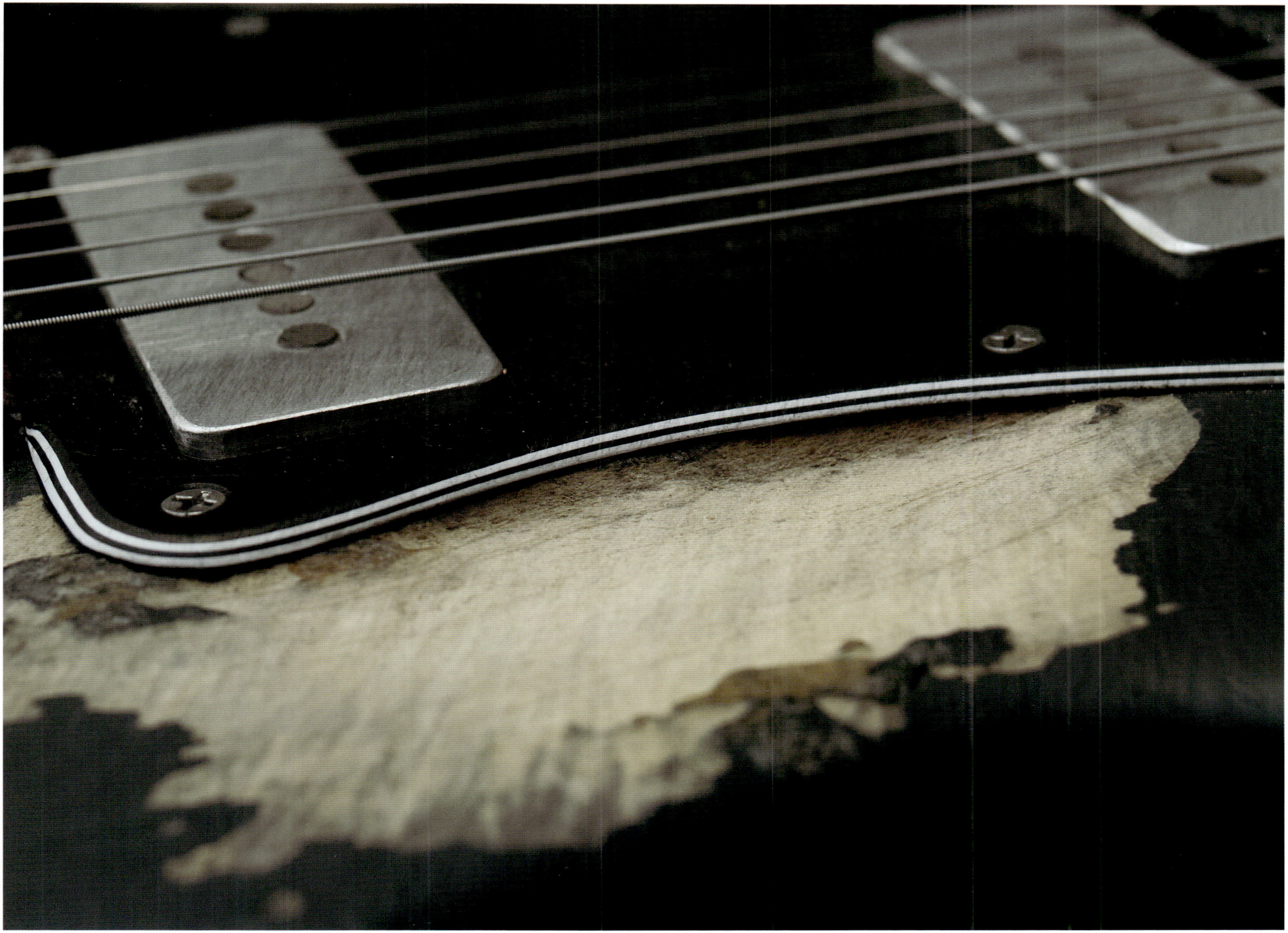

BOB WESTON

Shellac
Travis Bean TB2000 bass

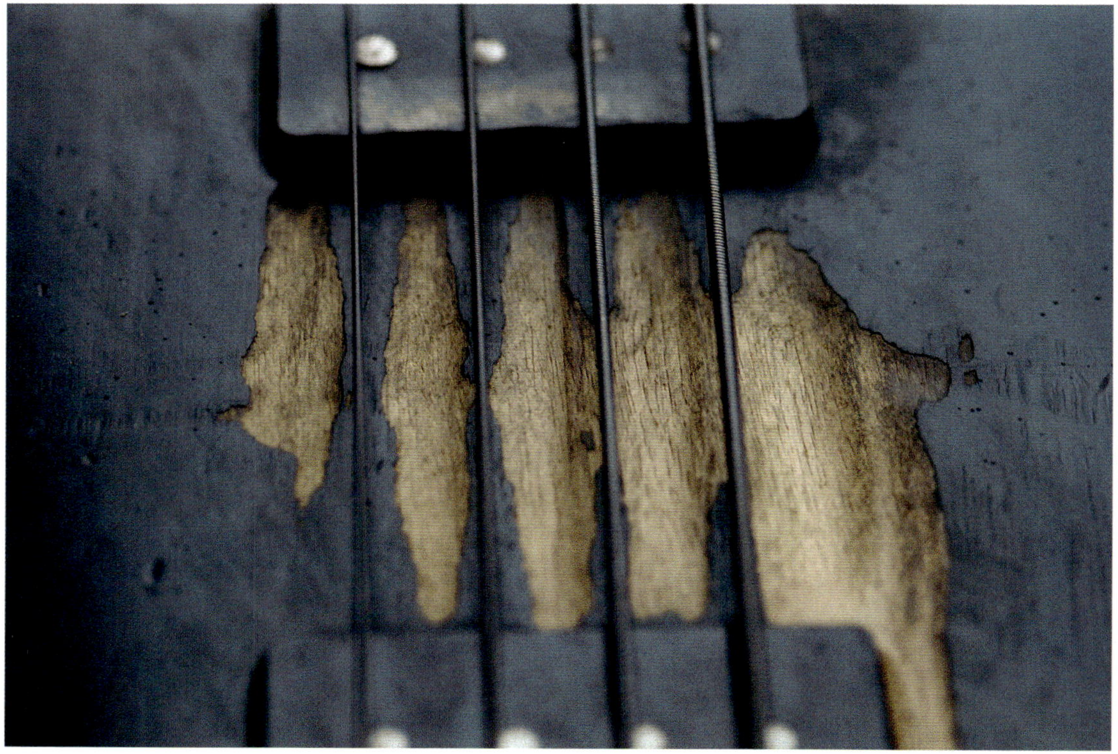

Steve [Albini] owns the bass. When I started playing with him and Todd [Trainer] in the early 1990s, I was using my Rickenbacker 4005. Early on, we decided to have matching and symmetrical gear onstage on either side of Todd's kit. I tried playing the TB bass and liked it. Steve and I built matching speaker cabinets. We painted the cabinets and the guitars with a marine epoxy coating that was custom mixed to be a sort of battleship/filing-cabinet green-gray, dubbed "Shellac Green" by Hi-Grade Paint Co. in Chicago. Neither of us was about to learn how to play left-handed, but we're pretty close to being matching and symmetrical.

The bass sounds like a gigantic, overdriven piano. I love the sound. And it matches Steve's guitar. I play the bass in a sort of flailing manner at times, often strumming chords, and I tend to play hard with my picking/strumming hand. The bass does not have a pickguard, and so my "style" has allowed the pick, a yellow Tortex pick, to slowly gouge out those trenches over almost twenty years.

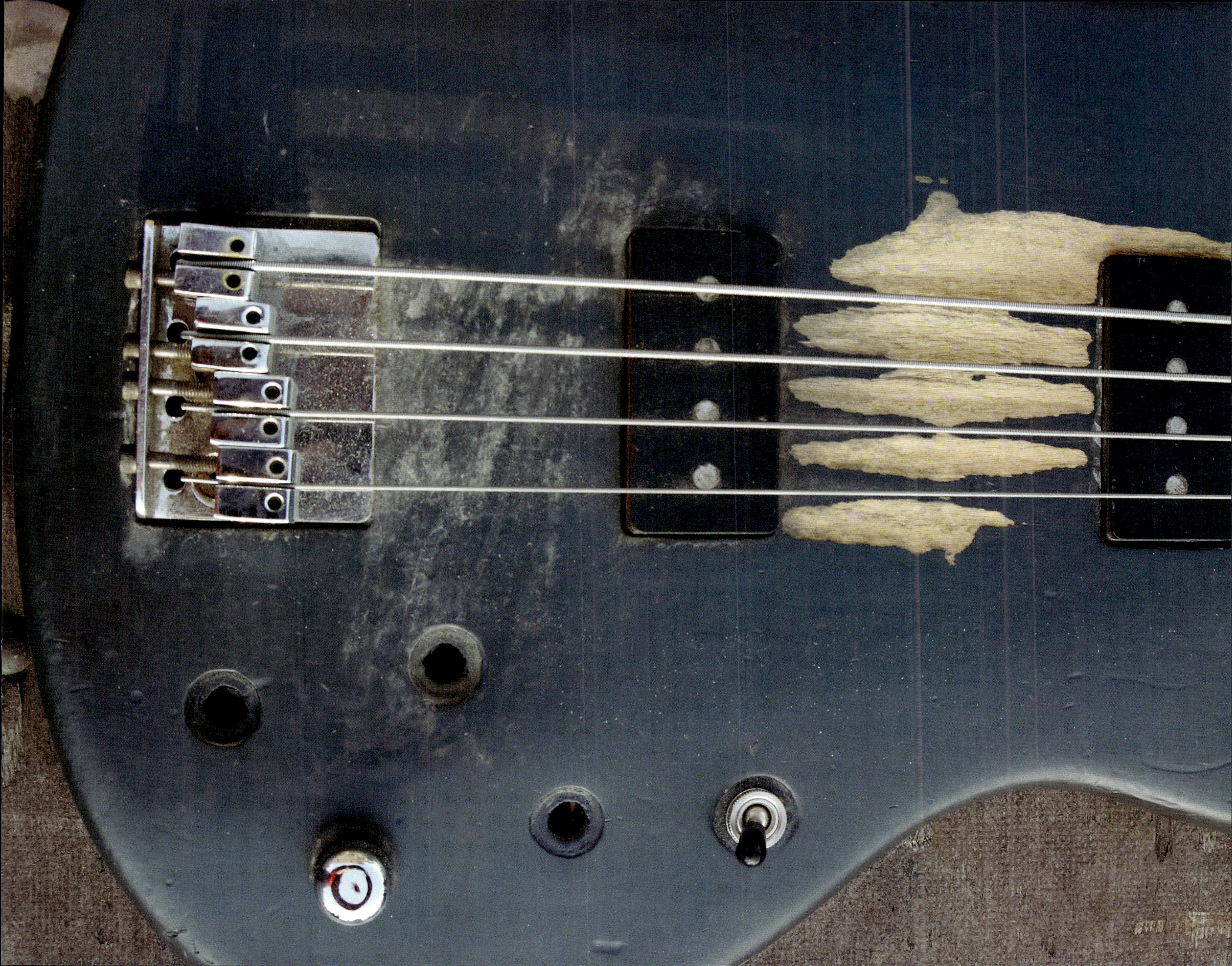

RYAN JARMAN

The Cribs
1976 Fender Mustang guitar

I got this guitar after my original Mustang got nicked after a gig in Leeds. It was the first and only thing I bought immediately after getting signed. I spent ages looking around for the "perfect" Mustang, and it really was a beautiful guitar when I first got it: a 1976 model that had sat in some guy's closet ever since he bought it, immaculate, with all the original hanging tags. The color was a really pale blond, almost white.

It took me about a year to almost completely destroy it.

One of the best things about these guitars is that if you set them up properly, they are so solid that they can really withstand anything; but the amount of touring we did took its toll really fast. I snapped the neck and superglued it back together four times, but eventually I had to replace it with the current neck.

The different-colored mark is where I had stuck some chewing gum on it when we were recording *The New Fellas*, and it stuck really hard. It finally came off when Sonic Youth's guitar tech set it up for me. Before that, I never used to let it get cleaned or polished. It was so disgusting. Covered in blood. Our tech hated it.

I don't use it live anymore. Out of all my guitars, it is the one I love most, yet the one I've fucked up most, too. I'm sure you could psychoanalyze that.

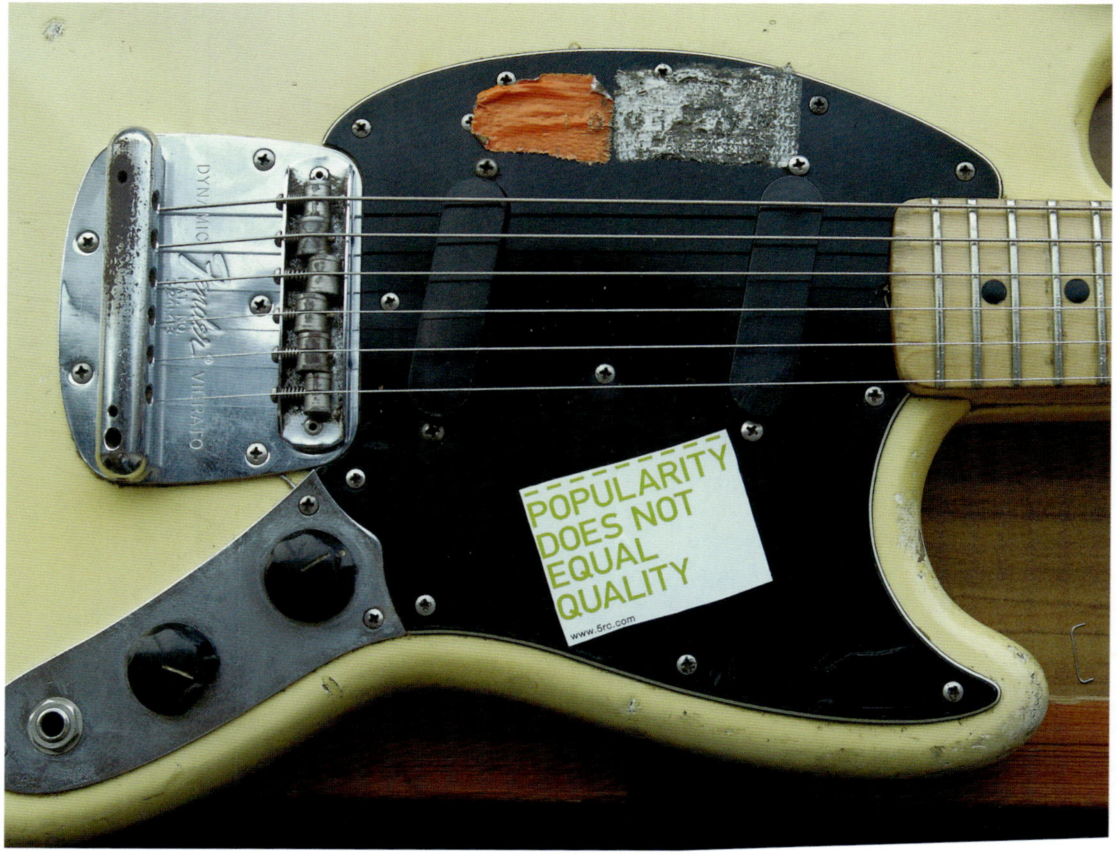

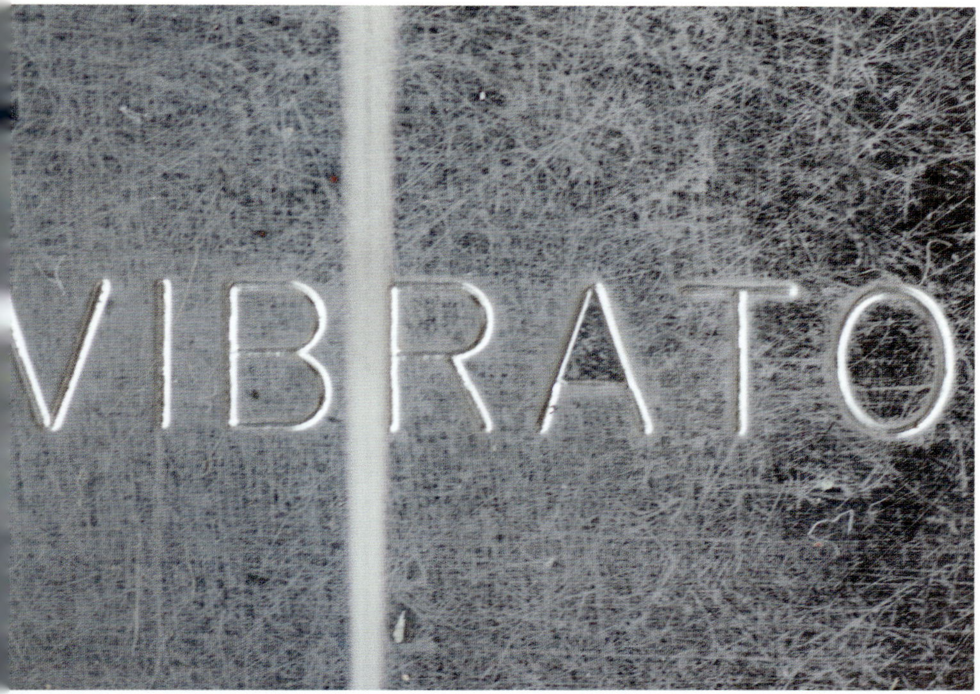
VIBRATO

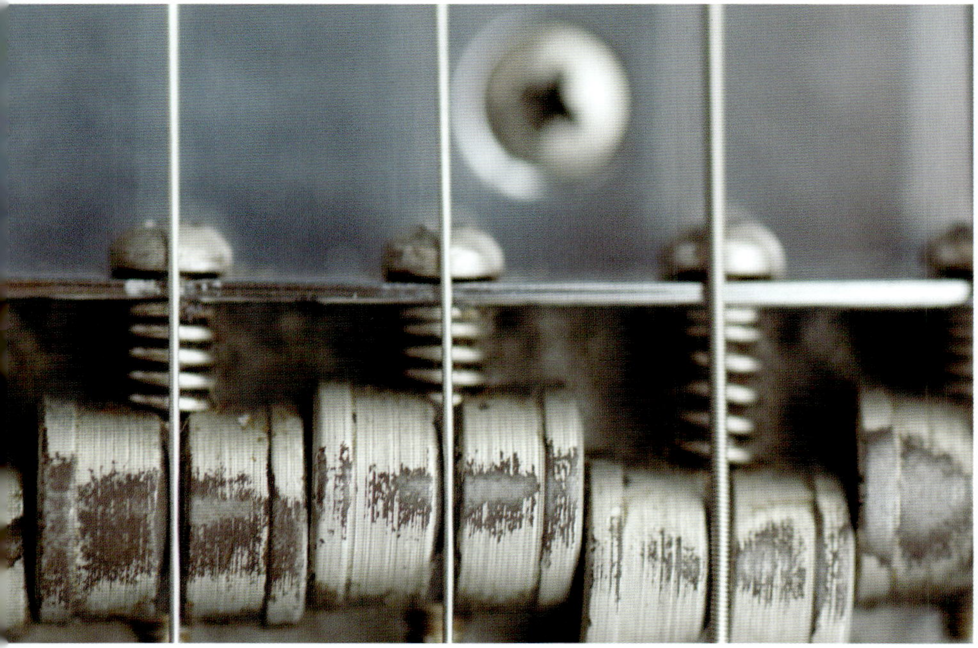

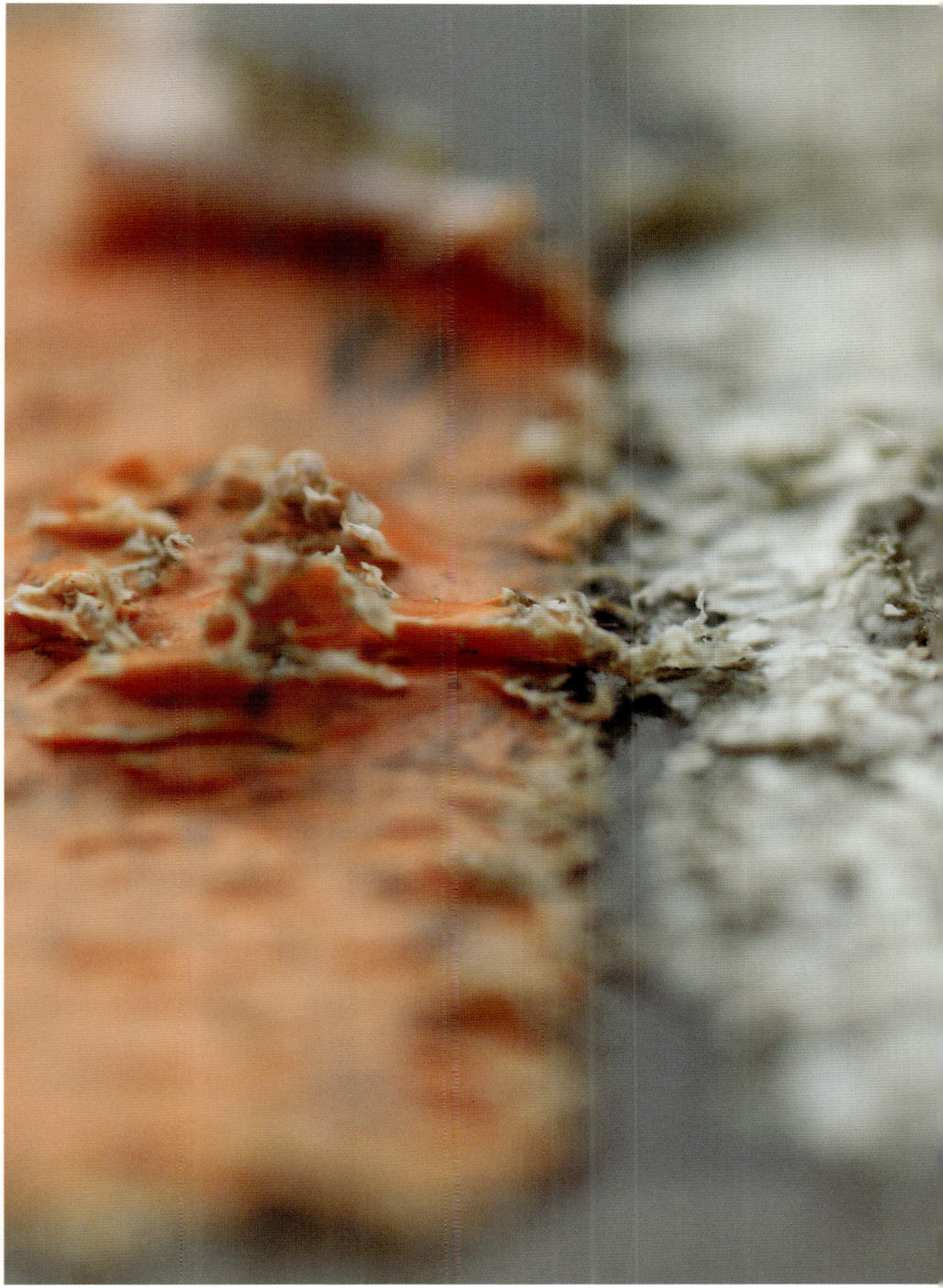

GARY JARMAN

The Cribs

1970s Fender Precision bass

About eight years ago I went into this horrible music shop in Leeds, and they had this incredibly ugly 1970s p-bass. I always loved the early '70s Fenders, even though that is considered to be Fender's worst era, so I was mortified to see that someone had obviously "updated" it in the 1980s, adding active pickups, a heavy duty bridge, and a terrible fluorescent paint job. I used to take pleasure in telling everyone that it was the worst example of the ruining of a 1970s Precision I had ever seen.

Then a few years later I was on tour in Germany . . . and I realised that I had to have it. It had evoked such strong feelings in me that, over time, that fine line between love and hate had become confused. Maybe I loved it all along, and that is why I was so preoccupied with it. Anyway, it was long gone, so I embarked upon a mission to build my own, as accurately as I could. I have to admit it pained me buying some of those parts, such as the active pickups, but it had to be authentic.

Since then it has been my main bass, touring with us for basically four years straight and hundreds of shows. It is pretty beat up now. The headstock has been super glued on four or five times in different places, and the body has a split running its entire length (again repaired by super glue), but it still feels solid as a rock. The PDX was added on the day I returned to the U.K. from Portland after my first visit there. We were playing an MTV special and it was kind of like sending a message back to the Northwest and my new life.

I am really proud that the bass I built around such an ugly subject could produce such beautiful photos, and I have to admit, I'm relieved that it has been immortalised in such a way, as I am not sure how much longer it will last.

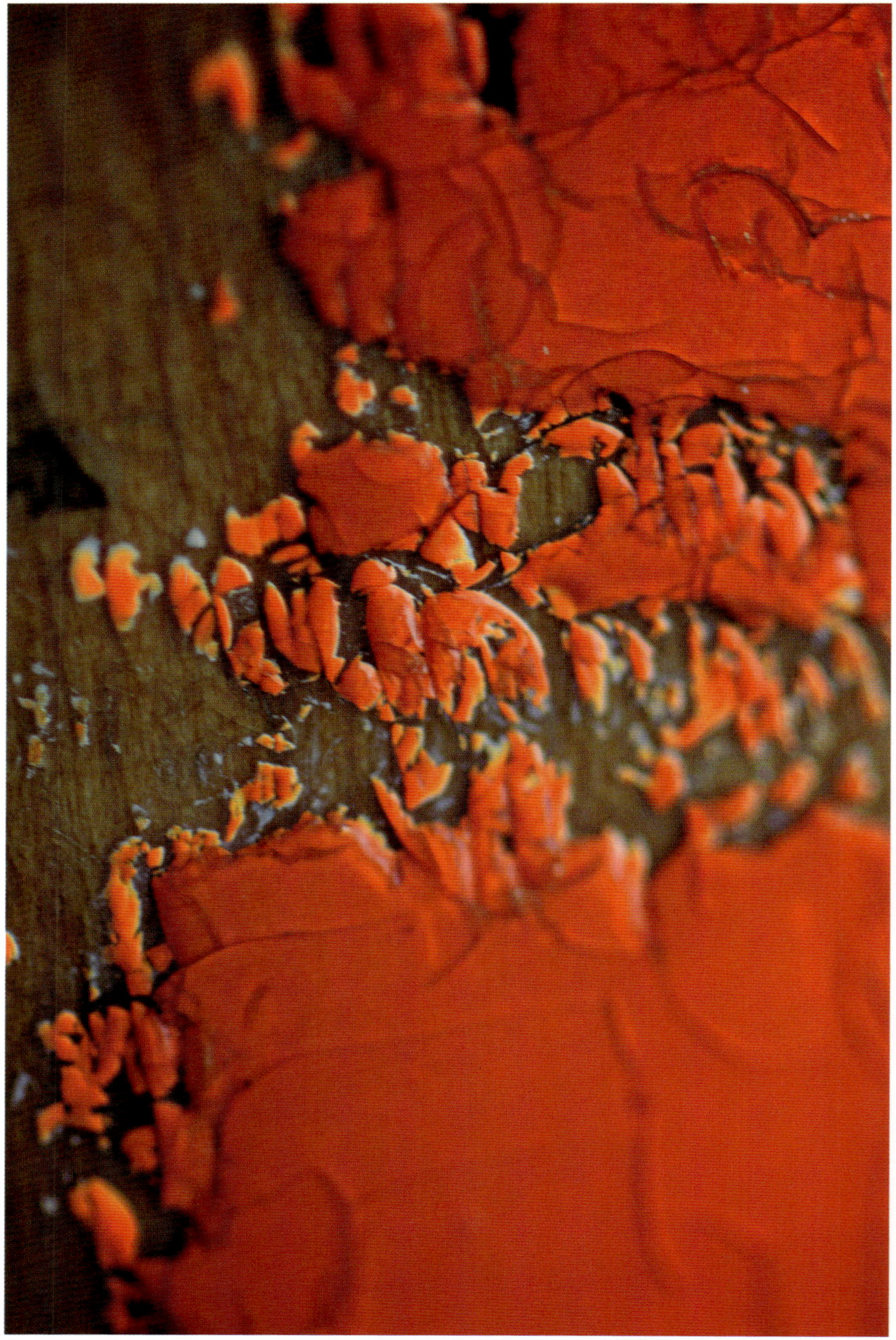

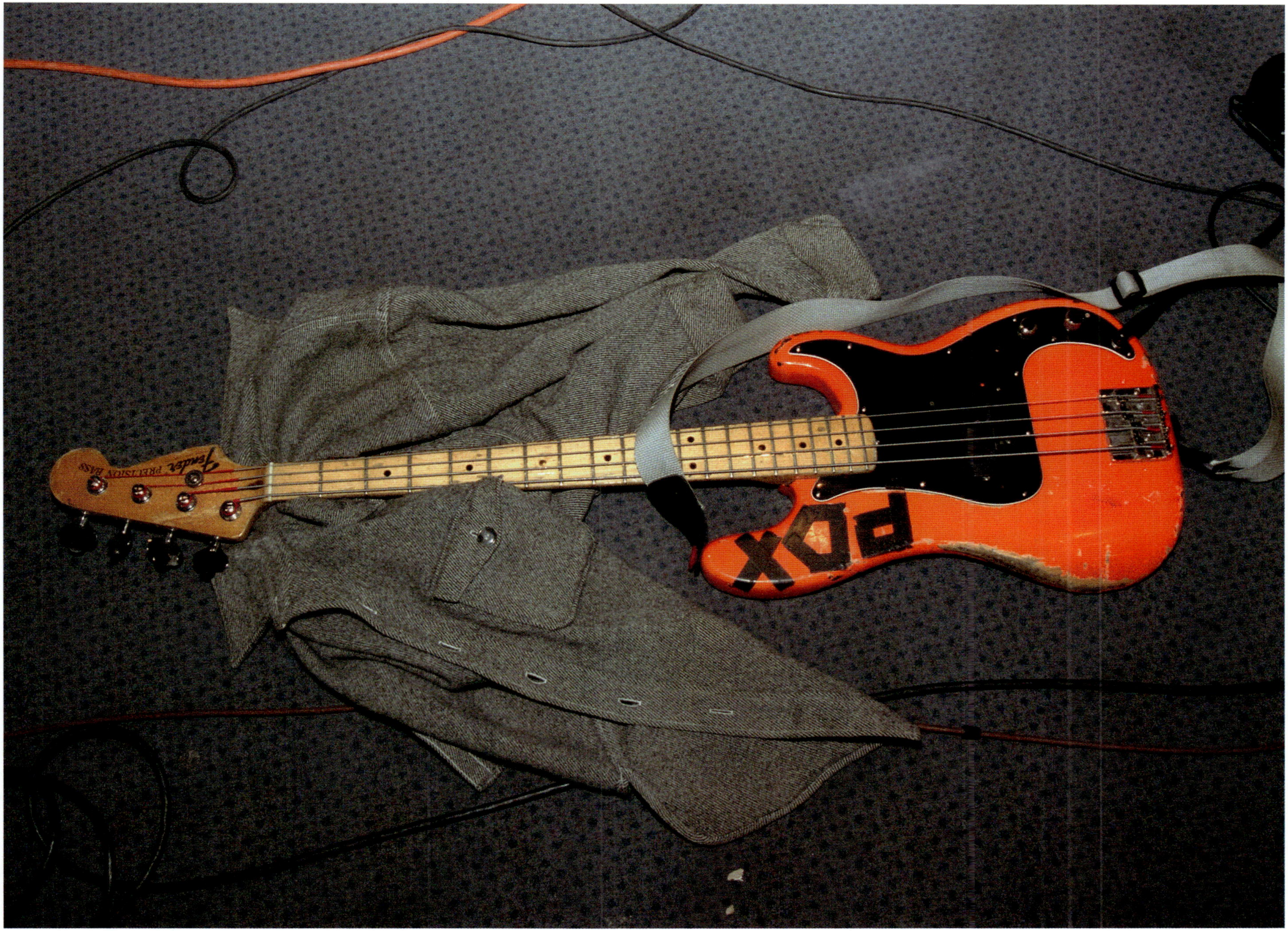
Fender PRECISION BASS
POX

KATE NASH

2004 Taylor guitar
1960s Epiphone Coronet guitar
1983 Granados guitar

The acoustic Taylor was the first guitar I bought once I had a publishing deal. It was the prettiest, and felt the best to play, and had a small body, which was what I was looking for. It really is so nice to play—everyone who has a go says so. I do a lot of writing on this guitar. I played it on all the first tours, and used it to record some songs on *Made of Bricks*. As far as recordings, you can hear it on "Birds," "Kiss That Grrrl," and "Early Christmas Present" and live on "Foundations."

Ryan bought me this Coronet Epiphone for my twenty-second birthday. I loved his. We both have one that matches our hair color. I wrote a bunch of songs for the new record on this because I wanted to do more on electric. I feel really comfortable with it and always use it live. This is on "Take Me to a Higher Plane," "Don't You Want to Share the Guilt?," "I Just Love You More," "I Hate Seagulls," and "You Are My Best Friend."

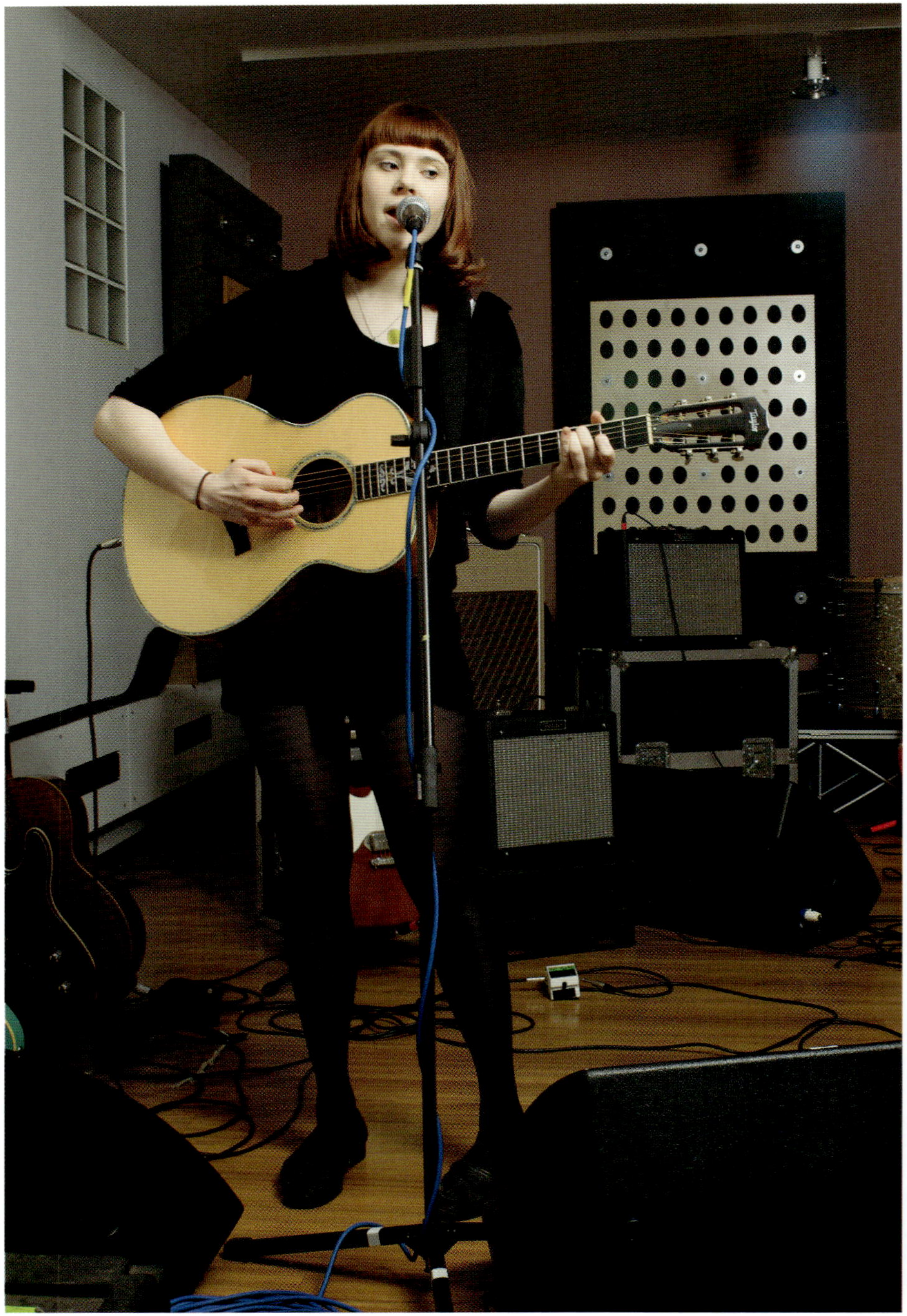

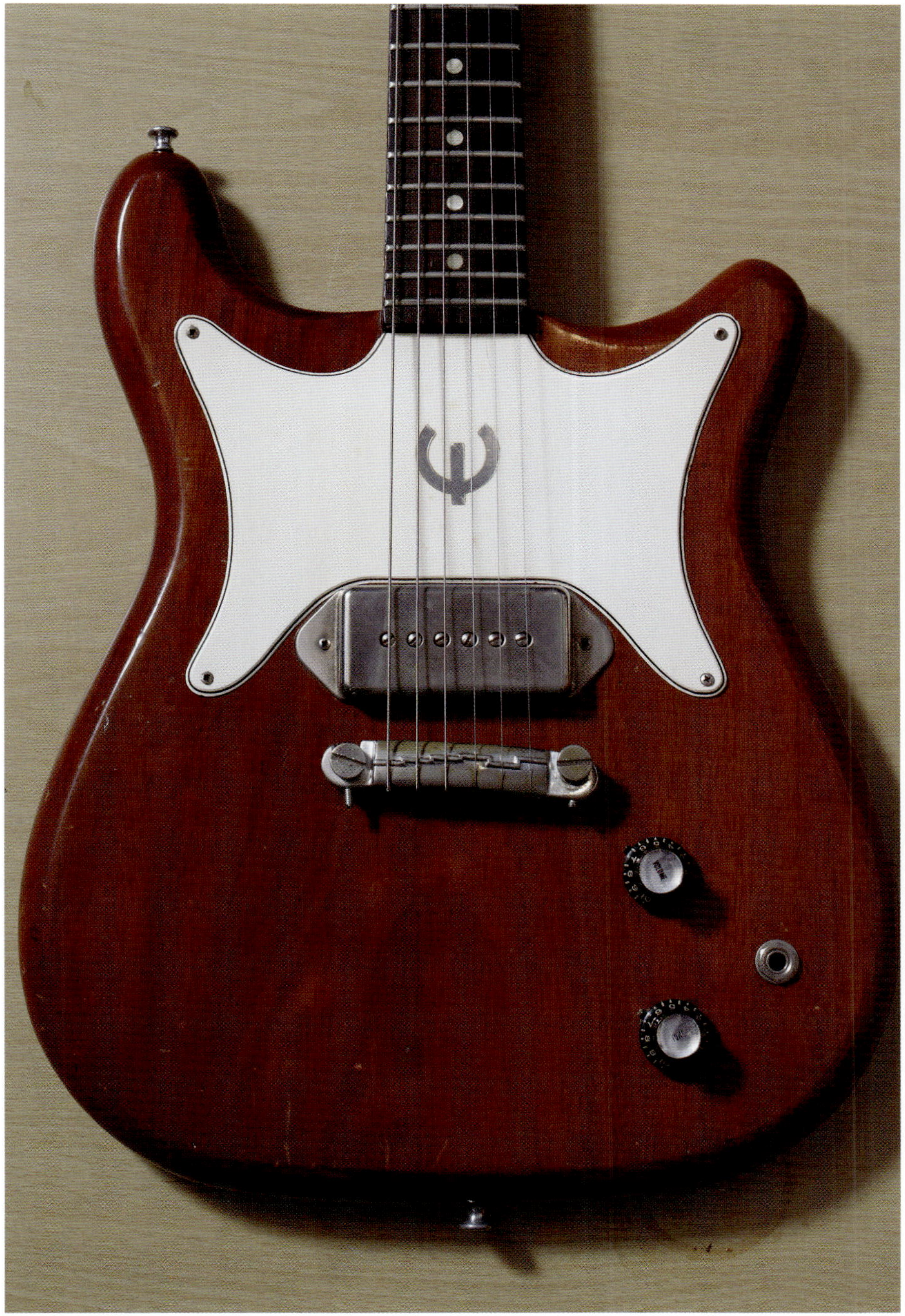

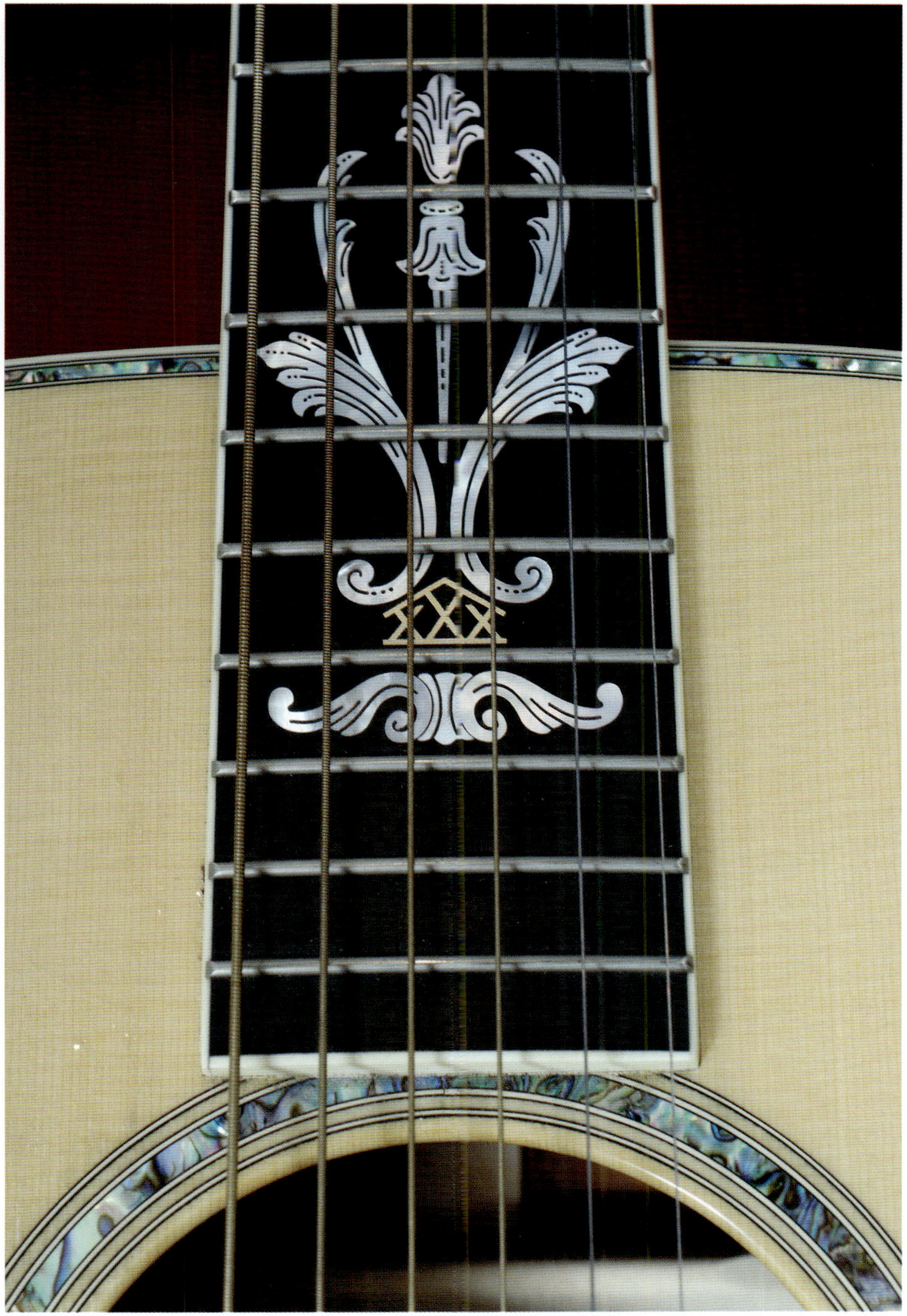

JIM FAIRCHILD

Grandaddy, Modest Mouse, All Smiles

Yamaha acoustic guitar

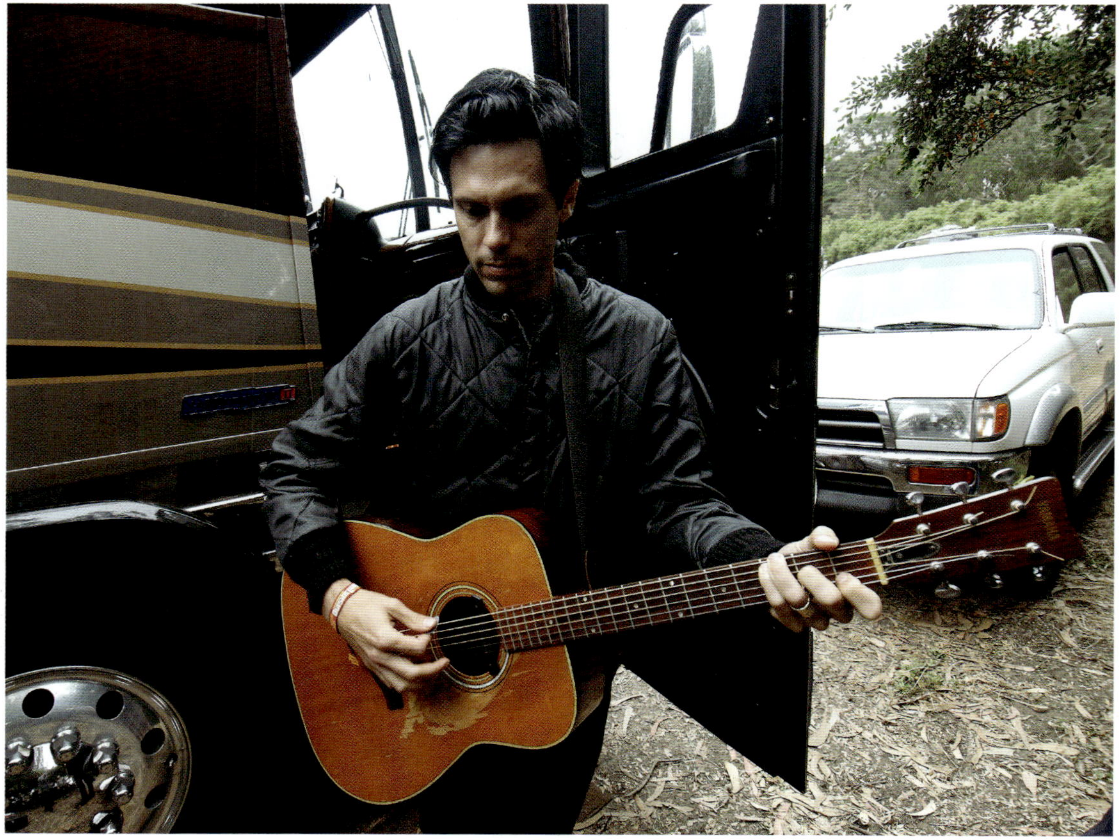

I bought this particular guitar with the money from my advance for the first All Smiles album. It was my luxury purchase. The rest went to living and paying down debt. I got it off eBay—which is not advisable for guitars, since you can't try 'em—for $275. More people were getting turned on to these at that time because of the Elliott Smith connection, but no one was bidding on this one because of its cosmetic wear. It's the same model guitar that Elliott used on his early recordings, I think up through *Either/Or*. He was my buddy and I loved him a lot. I think of that every time I pick it up, the quasiconnection to him, how much he means to me, what I learned from being his friend.

When Natasha [Wheat] and I started dating, she had another of these, same model and general age, sitting in her closet. I started playing it and loved it. She said her dad had bought it new in Greenwich Village in 1968 or '69. He was and is a very interesting and sweet hippie freak, and that made me like it even more. I recorded the first All Smiles album on that one, but I can't take it on tour because of its heirloom status. You can hear this guitar any time you hear acoustic guitar on the All Smiles *Oh for the Getting and Not Letting Go* album or *Fall Never Fell* EP, and it's played every All Smiles show. It has also become Isaac Brock's live acoustic. He likes the way it sounds.

While writing the songs for the last All Smiles album, I had few friends in Chicago, and Natasha was away. I sat for three weeks in our storefront/home and played that thing all day, every day. It's really easy to sing with. I would make a pot of beans every few days and eat that with some rice until it was gone. That food, the guitar, and a few glasses of wine each night were my only companions during that time. I didn't feel very lonely.

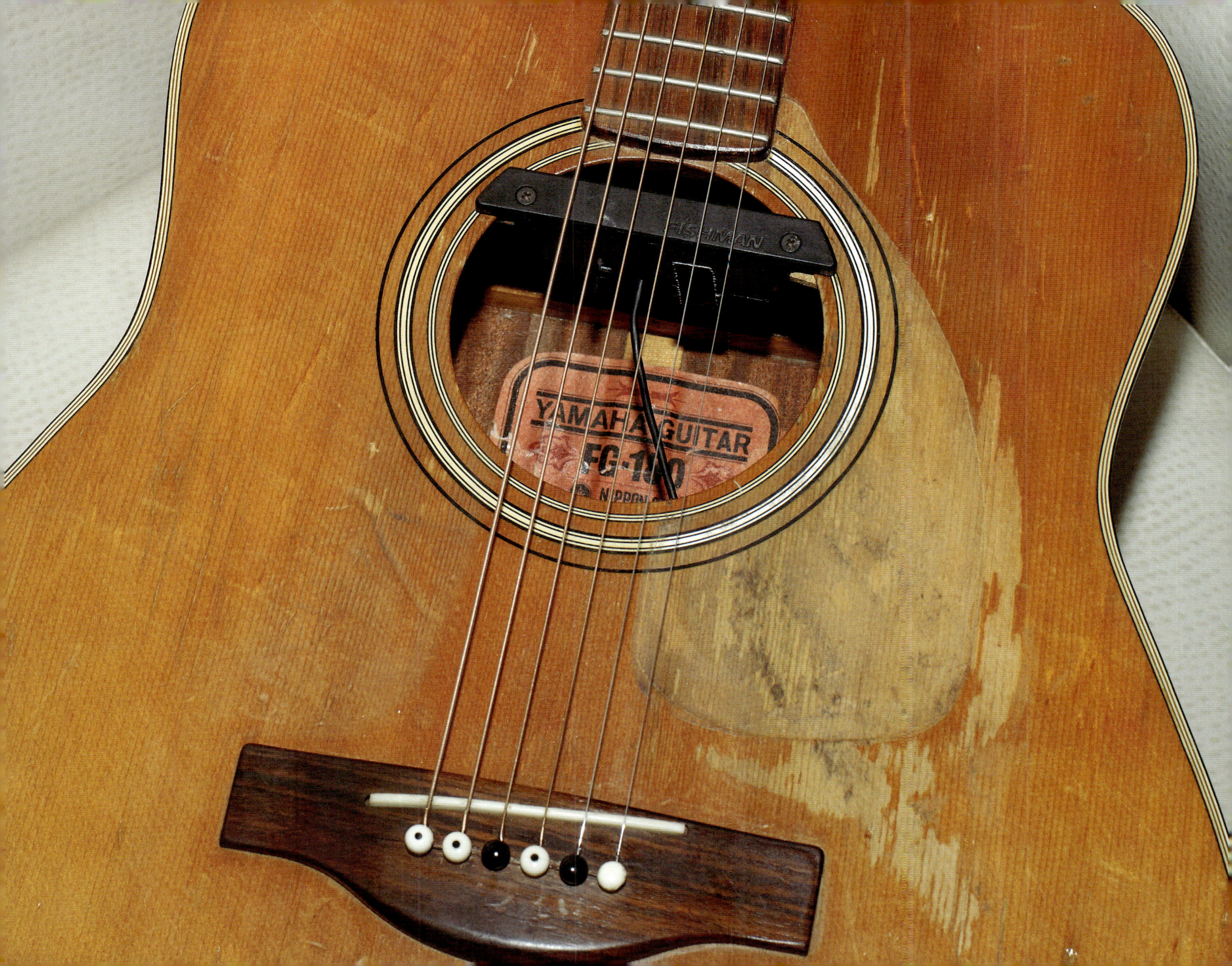
FISHMAN
YAMAHA GUITAR

JANET WEISS

Sleater-Kinney, Quasi, Wild Flag

Craviotto snare drum

I bought it the morning of February 15, 2003, before our Sleater-Kinney show at the Roseland in New York. Tom Cruise was on Letterman that day. I remember walking to the venue for the sound check with my new snare and seeing a large crowd around the Letterman back door. A limo pulled up, and a very smiley Cruise stepped out. He gestured and waved wildly to the fans. I took a picture of him on my phone, like a good American.

While recording a band for a compilation, I fell in love with the drummer's snare drum. He had borrowed it from the owner of a local shop, Trade Up Music. The kind owner let me use the drum to record a few times. I started looking for my own Craviotto, and found one in New York at a place called Drummer World. We have been inseparable ever since. I call this snare my snare mate. I like the sound and feel of a maple drum. It's the closest thing to what I hear in my head when I imagine myself playing.

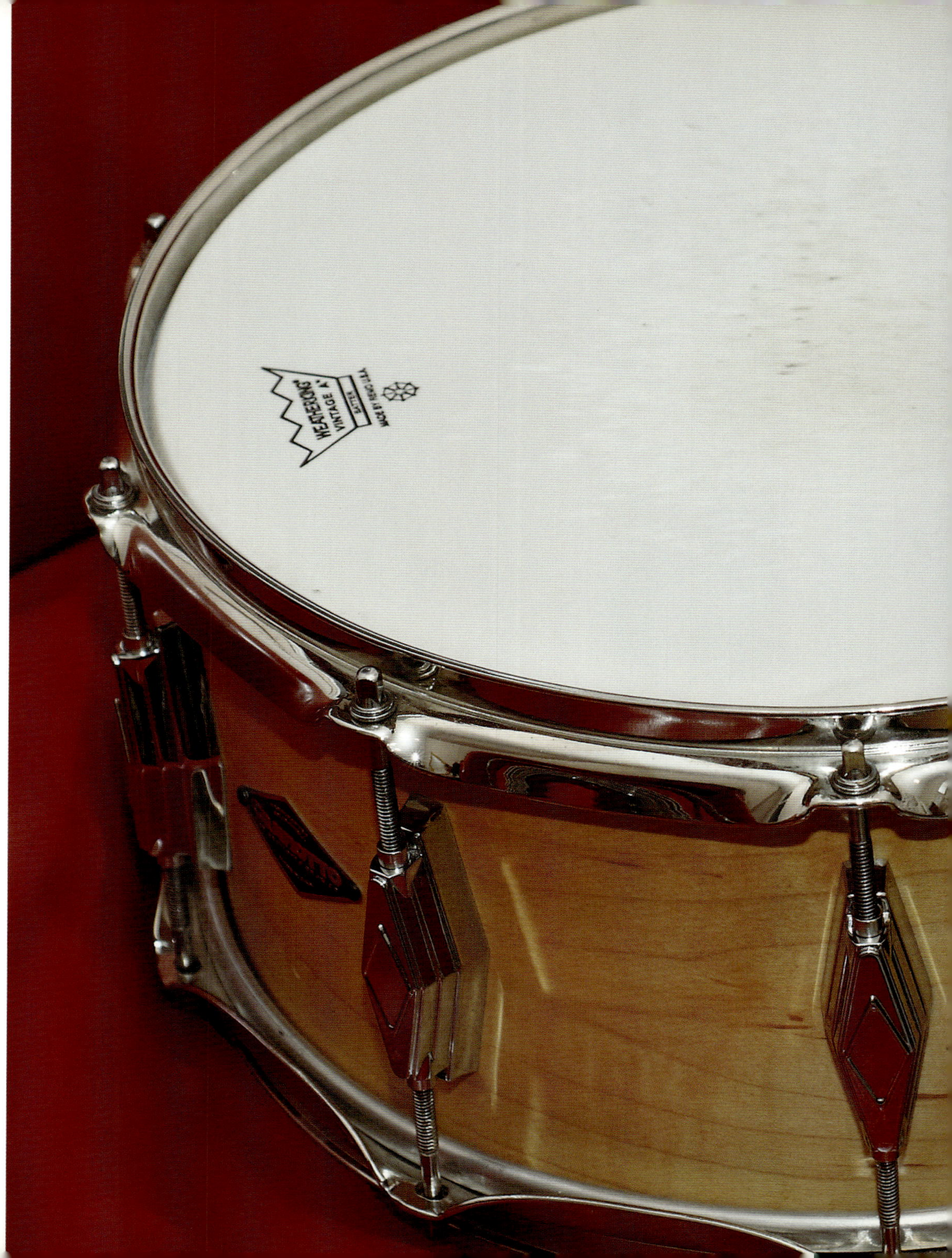

JOANNA BOLME

Jicks, The Minders, Quasi
Fender Jazz bass

It's a Fender Jazz bass, though the headstock says Precision, so it's a sort of Frankenstein bass. I play this bass on the Jicks albums *Real Emotional Trash* and *Face the Truth* and the Quasi album *American Gong*. I got it in 2002. I mentioned in passing to Eli Johnson from the Heavy Johnson Trio that I wanted to get a new bass, and he called me the next day and said there was a Jazz bass down at Old Town Music that I should check out that was probably cheaper because it had an ugly paint job. He was right, it was amazing. I traded in a crappy heavy metal bass I had for $300 and got the Jazz for $400. Best deal I ever got. It came with the original case, and had apparently belonged to someone in Ohio who played in The Little Big Band. Inside there were lyrics to several boogie rock songs, including "Old Time Rock and Roll."

It sounds great. It's really heavy, literally, heavier than any other bass I've played. My back is kinda fucked from it. Once I was watching the luggage being unloaded from the plane, and I saw my case come off. The luggage guy picked it up, held it vertically, and slammed it against the edge of the cart really hard. Just for fun, I guess. I don't have a proper road case, not that this would be acceptable if I did, but it survived.

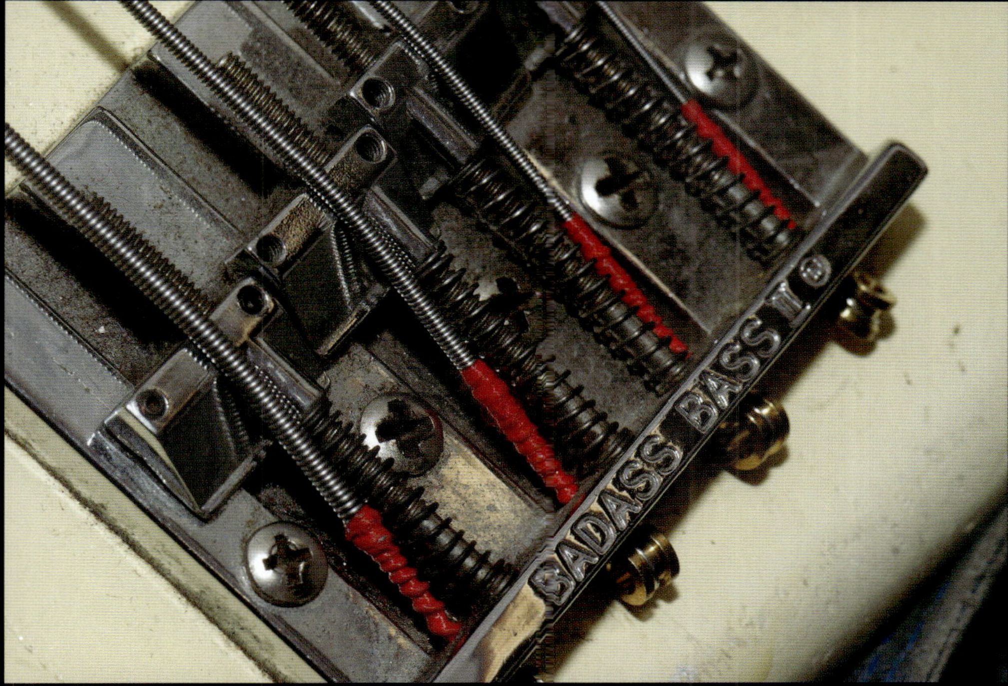

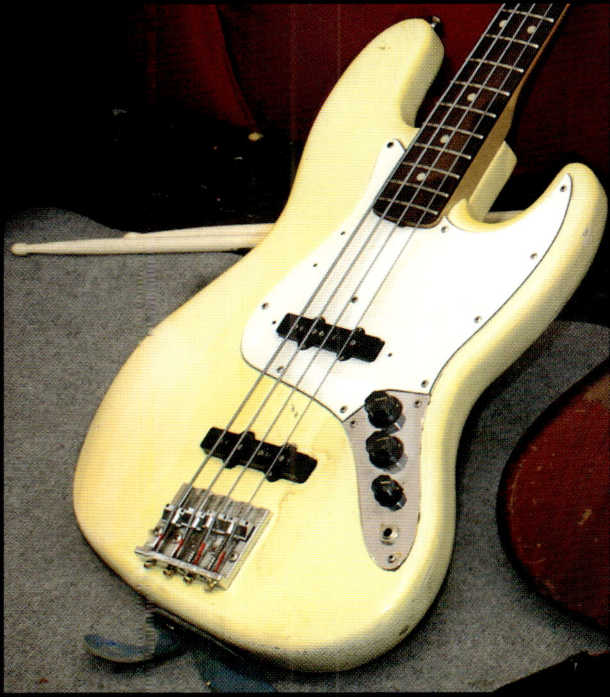

CORIN TUCKER

Sleater-Kinney, Cadallaca
1964 Fender Showman head amp
Electro-Harmonix Bass Micro synthesizer
1957 Danelectro Silver Sparkle reissue guitar
Ibanez Roadstar II Series guitar

Danelectro started reissuing their guitars in the 1990s. They're fun to play, and are not heavy, either! This one has eight pickups on it, some fun and funky sounds to play with. I think I used it on the Cadallaca album *Out West*. It was all about the sparkly guitar and the wigs.

I think Dave Fridmann, who produced Sleater-Kinney's *The Woods*, said something like, "You should get some guitar pedals to play with." His studio has quite a few fun boxes to play with. I think Janet [Weiss] pointed out this pedal at Trade Up Music and thought it might be cool to try with my guitar. It's almost like having an old '60s synthesizer hooked up to your guitar. We ended up using it on "Steep Air" and "What's Mine Is Yours" on that record.

This gorgeous amp originally belonged to Janet, and she generously let me adopt it eventually. We used it on every S-K record since *The Hot Rock*, and schlepped it all over the world. It's held up beautifully. Someone once told me that 1964 was the last truly great year for Fender before they were bought out or changed production or something and that's why this particular amp sounds so fabulous. It really helped me find my sound in a two-guitar band.

I bought this Ibanez Roadstar guitar in about 1996 from Paul Schuster in Olympia. We wrote and recorded *Dig Me Out* with it, so I've kept it, although it is not a particularly great guitar. It has been good to me.

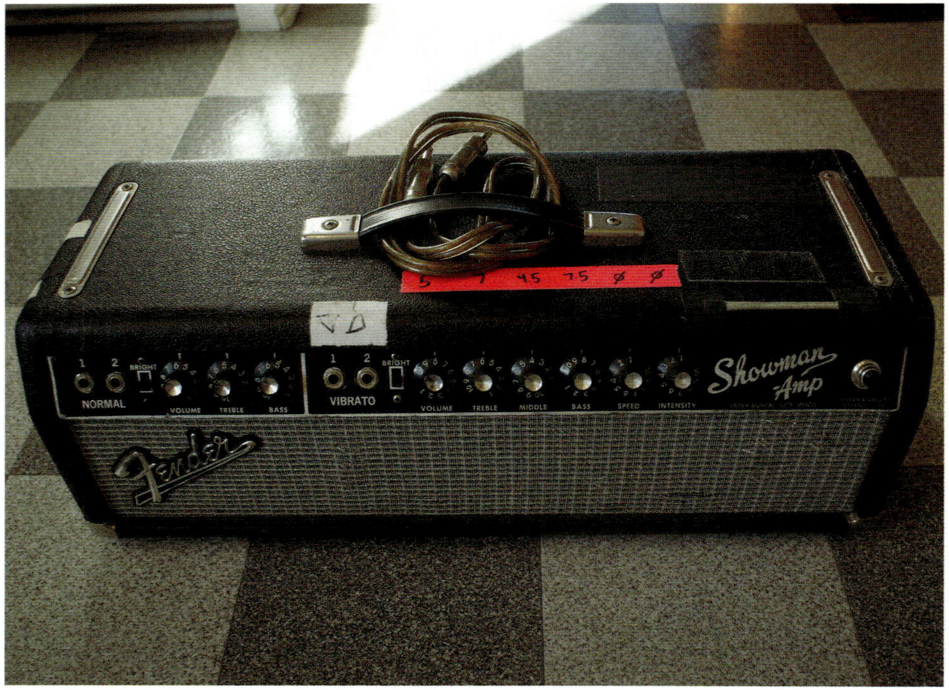

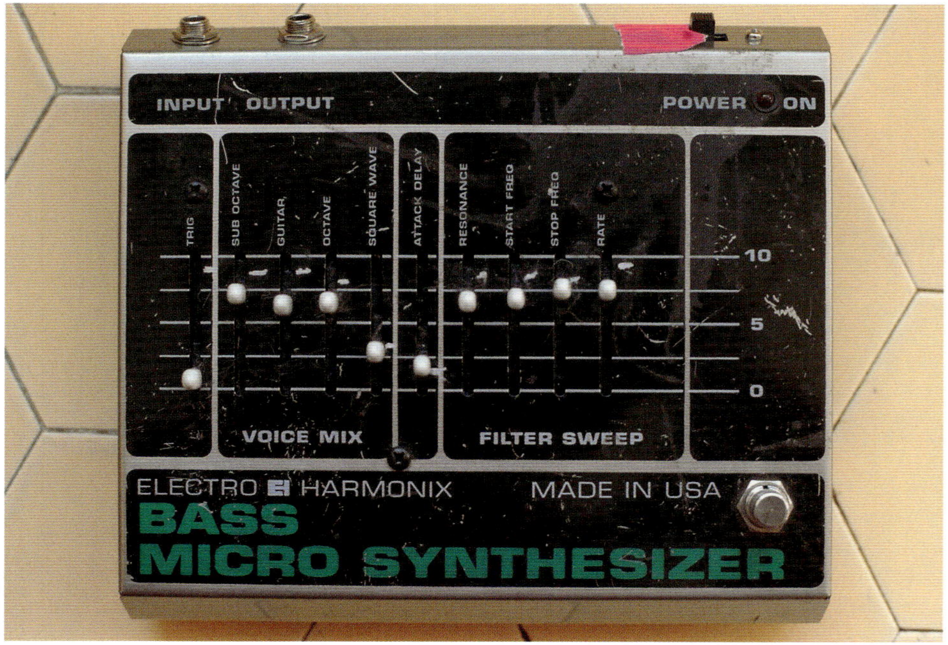

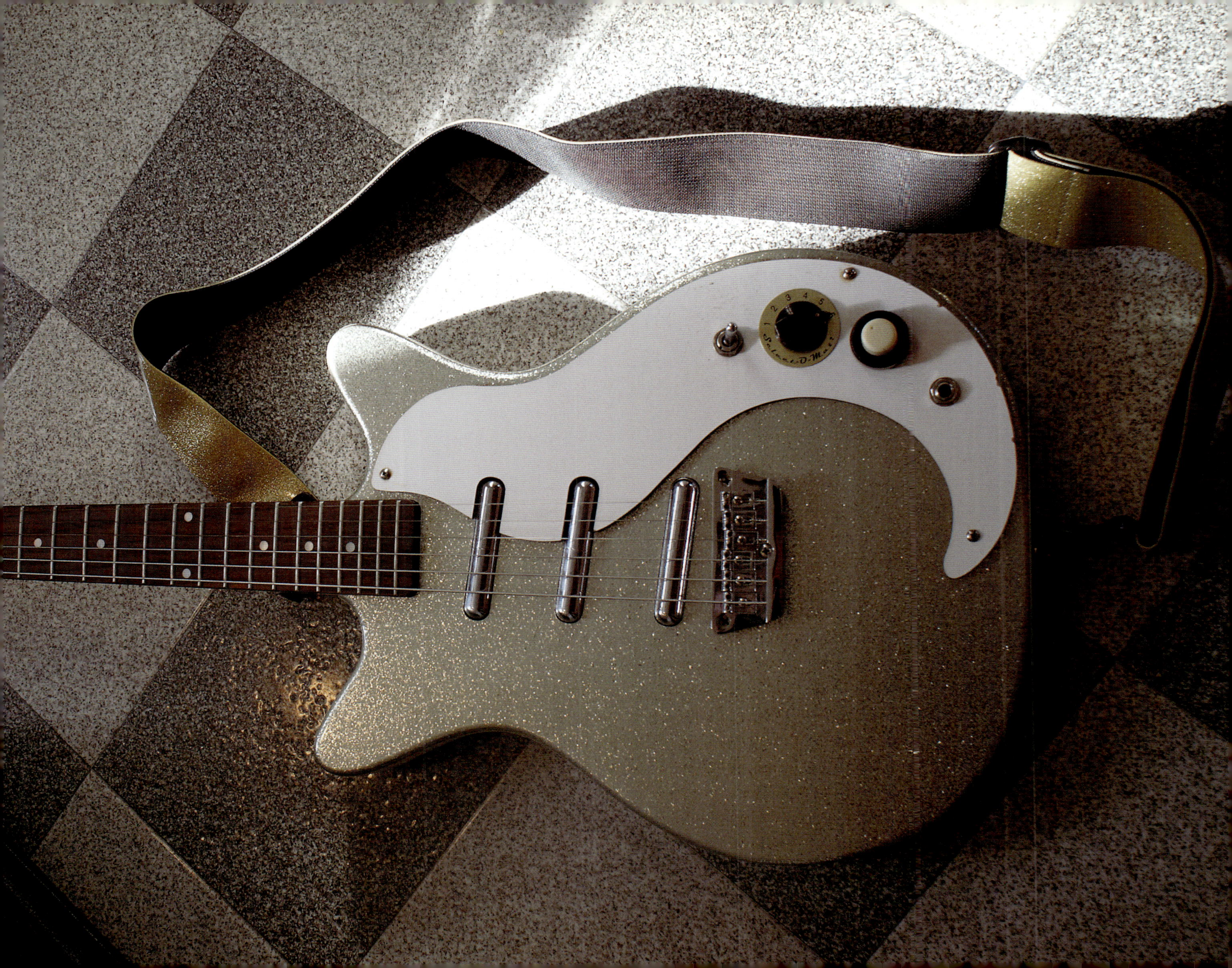
1 2 3 4 5

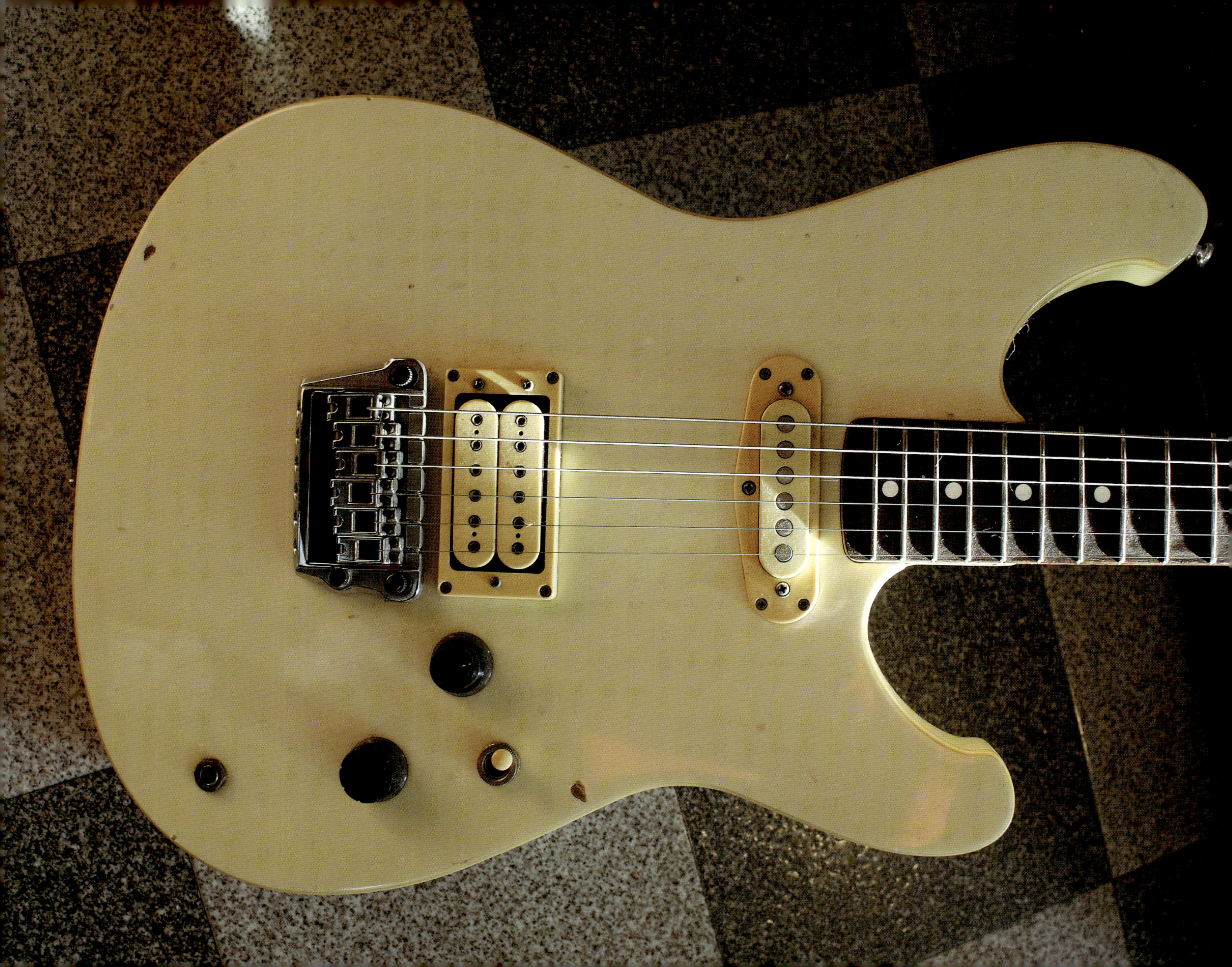

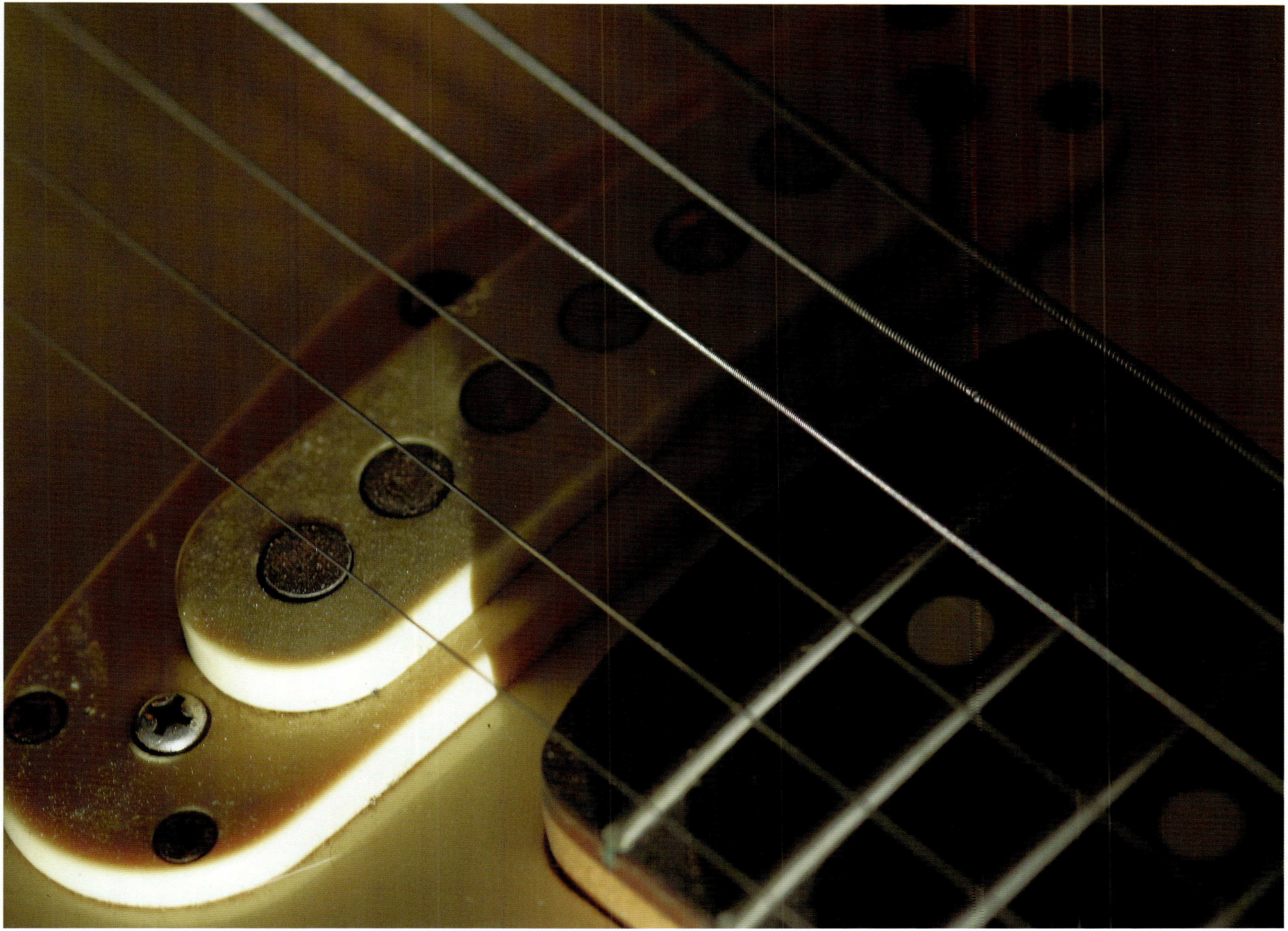

DAVID PAJO

Slint, Tortoise, Palace Brothers, Bonnie 'Prince' Billy, Zwan, The For Carnation

Fender Precision bass

I bought this at Guitar Emporium in Louisville, Kentucky, in the early 1990s. Grunge was trendy at the time, and suddenly the price of beat-up Fenders took off. That wasn't the case in the '80s! The salesman said that the bass was purchased from a church in Atlanta, Georgia, and had been played every Sunday since 1964 and was worn from sweat. I bought it for $350. I just wanted a cheap P bass. I knew the difference in feel between a Precision and a Jazz bass, and I just felt this was more suited for rock.

I've used it for every recording I've played bass on: Tortoise, Palace Brothers, Bonnie 'Prince' Billy, and all my solo stuff, and I used it on all the tours where I played bass: Yeah Yeah Yeahs, Tortoise, Stereolab, Royal Trux, and the rest. The crack is water damage—my basement flooded when I was on tour. I always thought it was a $300 bass, so I treated it like shit, and continue to treat it like shit. It's always sounded and played amazing though. I never think about it. It's like an arm or something. It's just always there; you only think about it if it gets broken.

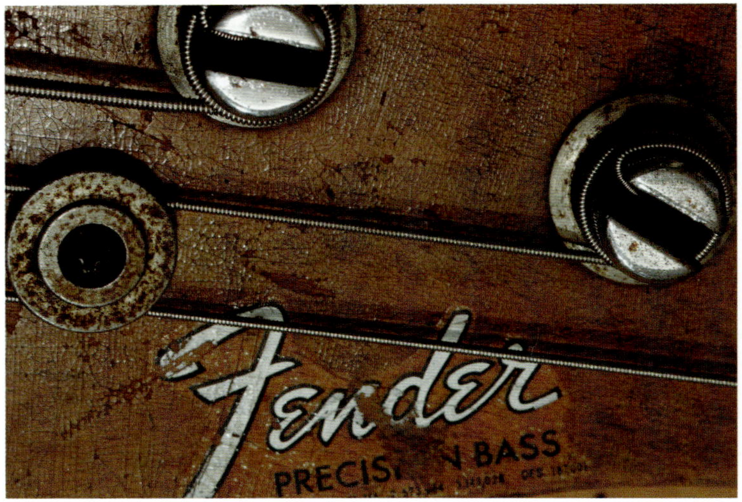

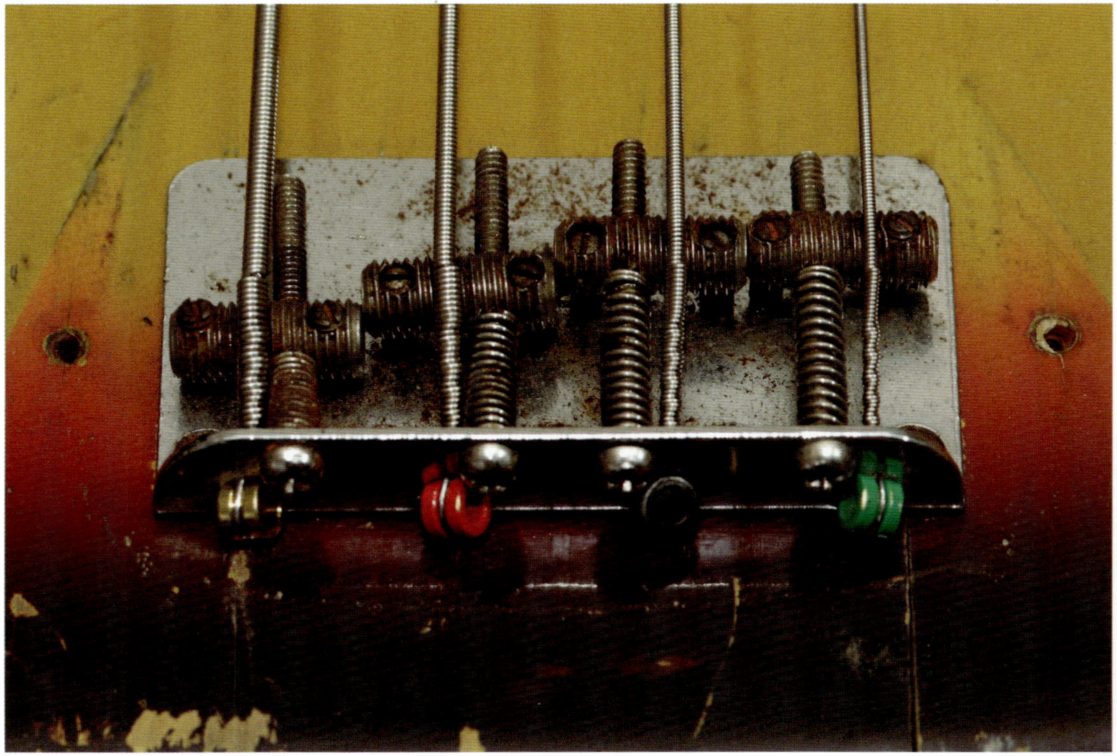

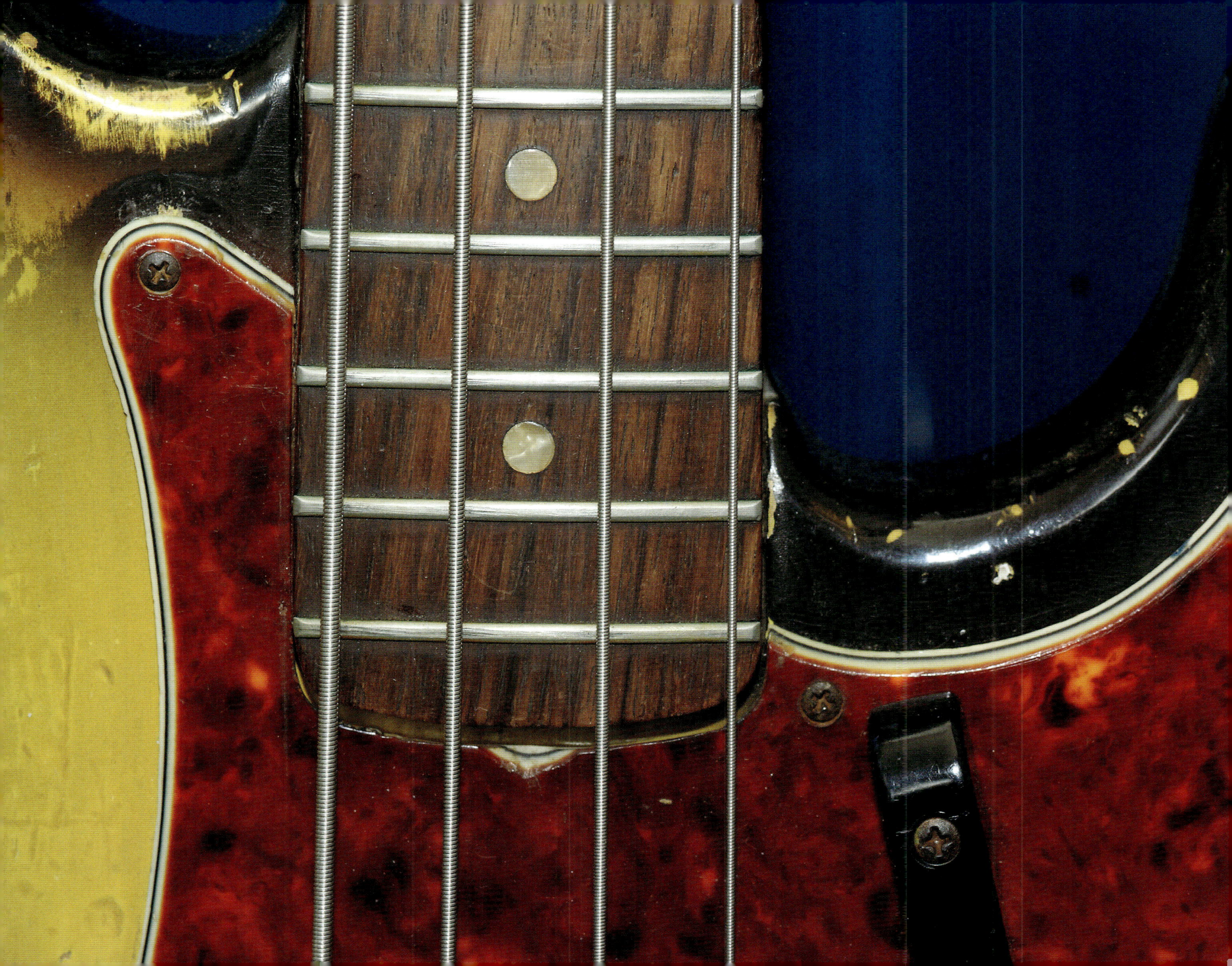

JERRY DAMMERS

The Specials, Spatial A.K.A. Orchestra
Clavichord
Polyvox synthesizer
Jennings amplifier
Yamaha organ

My theory is that all the best music is made on brown instruments, and the very best is on fawn or beige equipment. If you study it carefully, the most creative moments in rock's history have been on fawn or beige equipment. The early computers were fawn and cream.

In the orchestra, we do a lot of music by Sun Ra, and he said he was into tones, not notes, so it's about the sound of the different keyboards, rather than the actual notes that you play.

I like this clavichord because it's so quiet you can barely hear it at all. People have to listen really hard to hear it. It's really nice to hear something quiet in this day and age. It's my favorite of them all.

This Polyvox is my favorite synthesizer. It was built on a Russian military base, and it's one of the heaviest-sounding synths ever, a very industrial, Stalinist-style sound. I love that every key squeaks and the nice nicotine stains. I hope that it was used in some bar in Siberia or something. There are quite a few dodgy switches on it. My Russian isn't very good, so I can't be totally sure what these buttons do. One switch says *danger*. If you get past the idea that it says *danger*, it's about five times as loud as the entire orchestra put together. It leaps out and deafens the entire audience and band for about a week. I love the Russian technology—it's like emulating the West but in a low-tech, broken way.

The Jennings amplifier is probably from the 1950s. I like the instructions on it, and the fake crocodile skin. It also has a good tone, and when I say "good," I mean awful.

The Yamaha organ is the one you hear on the Specials' "Ghost Town." The famous clarinet sound that you hear on the record—it's like from another planet. Nobody's ever come up with a sound like that . . . a strange Japanese imitation of Western culture.

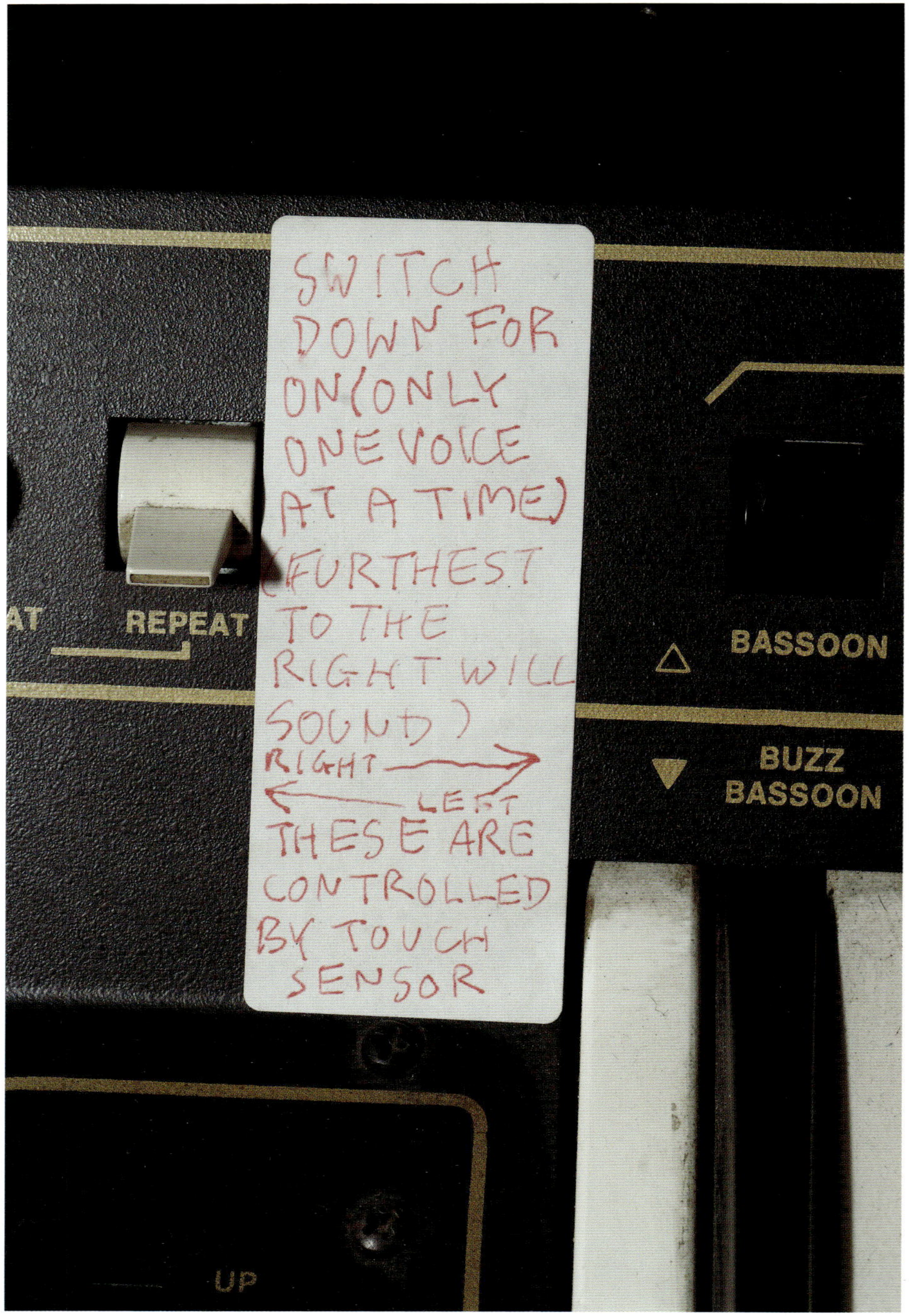

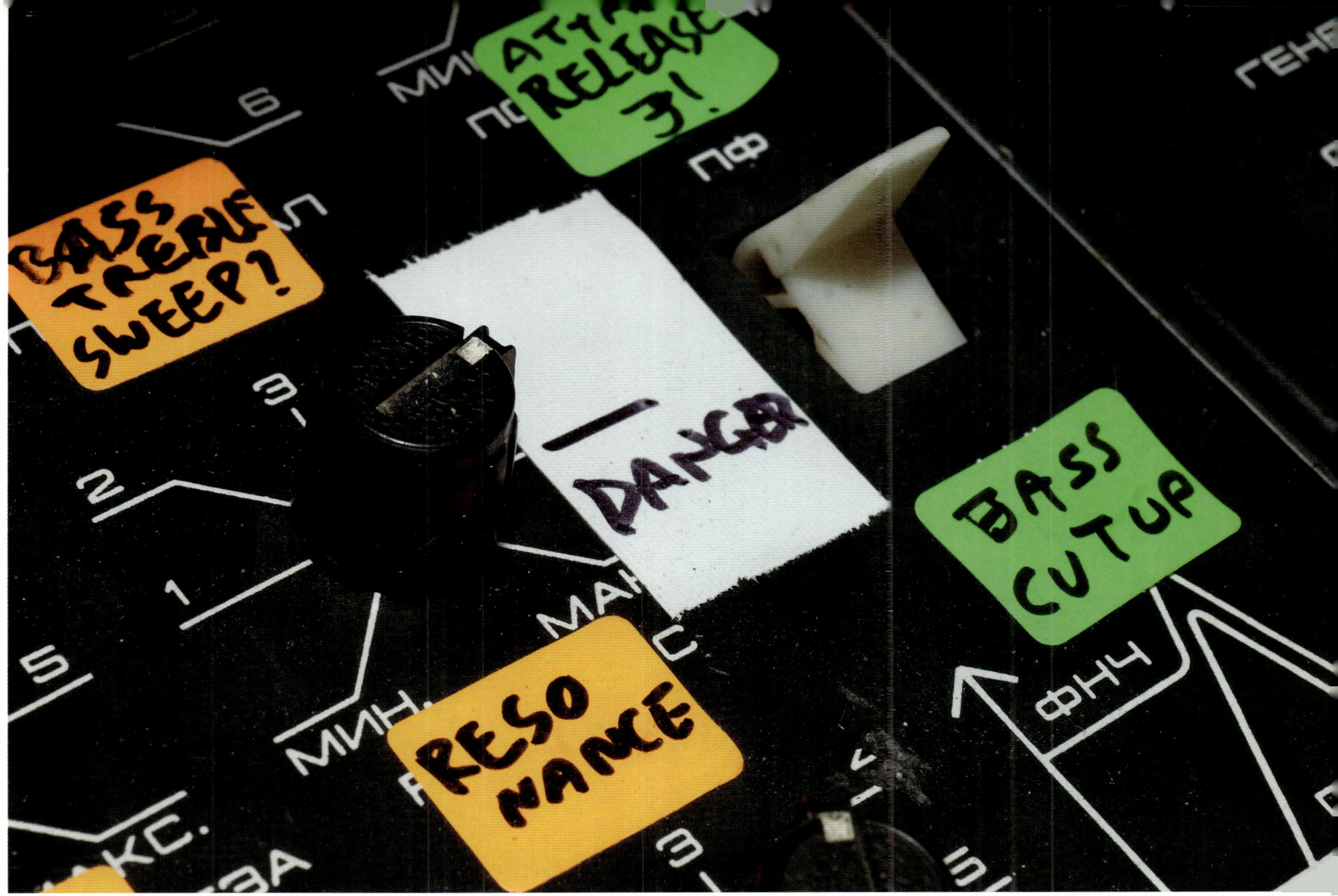
BASS TREBLE SWEEP?!
DANGER
BASS CUTUP
RESO NANCE
ПФ
ФНЧ
МИН.
МАКС.

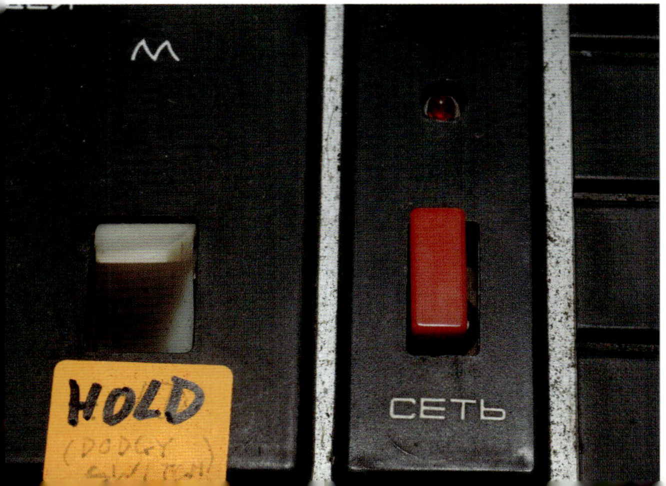
HOLD
СЕТЬ

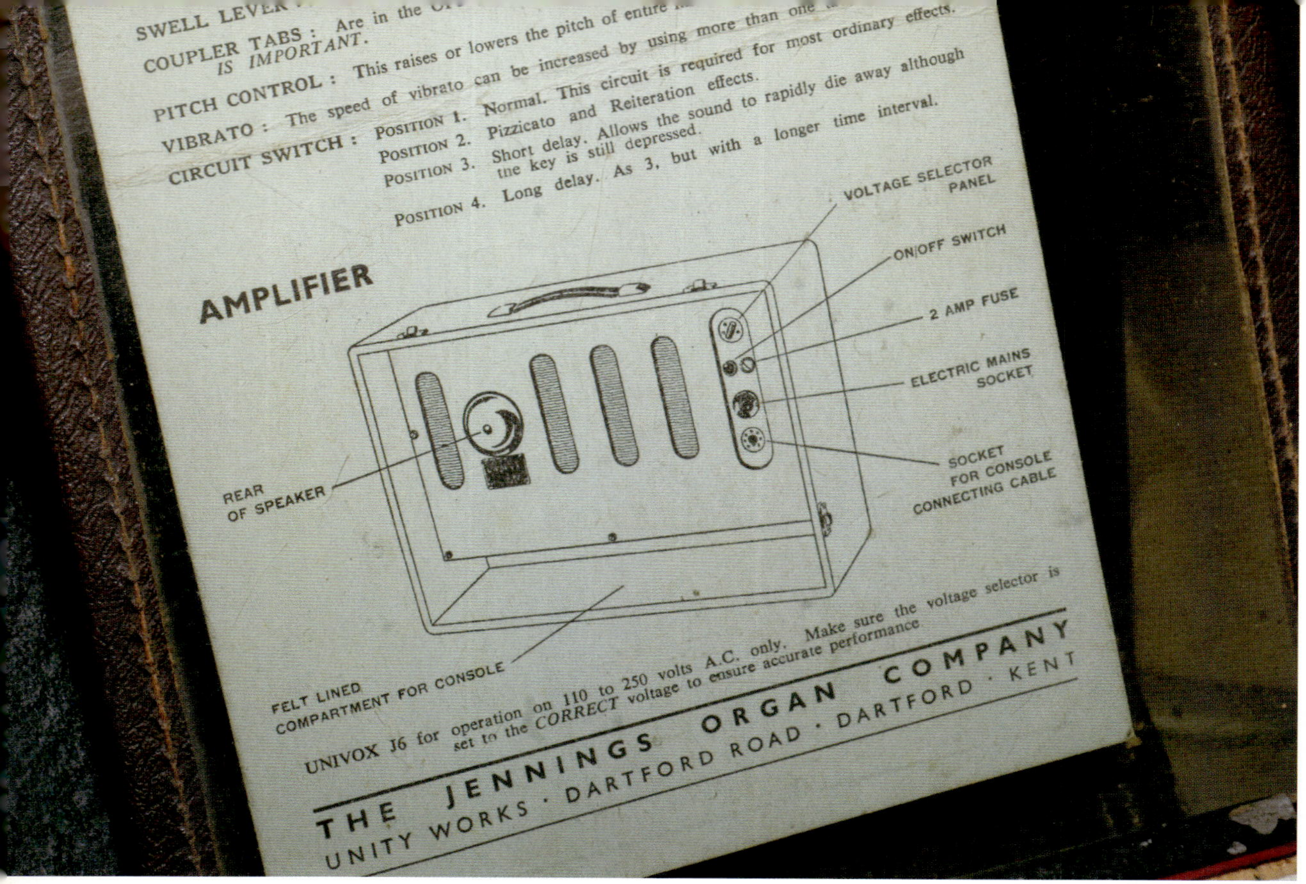
COUPLER TABS : Are in the
IS IMPORTANT.
PITCH CONTROL : This raises or lowers the pitch of entire
VIBRATO : The speed of vibrato can be increased by using more than one
CIRCUIT SWITCH : POSITION 1. Normal. This circuit is required for most ordinary effects.
POSITION 2. Pizzicato and Reiteration effects.
POSITION 3. Short delay. Allows the sound to rapidly die away although the key is still depressed.
POSITION 4. Long delay. As 3, but with a longer time interval.
AMPLIFIER
VOLTAGE SELECTOR PANEL
ON/OFF SWITCH
2 AMP FUSE
ELECTRIC MAINS SOCKET
SOCKET FOR CONSOLE CONNECTING CABLE
REAR OF SPEAKER
FELT LINED COMPARTMENT FOR CONSOLE
UNIVOX J6 for operation on 110 to 250 volts A.C. only. Make sure the voltage selector is set to the CORRECT voltage to ensure accurate performance
THE JENNINGS ORGAN COMPANY
UNITY WORKS · DARTFORD ROAD · DARTFORD · KENT

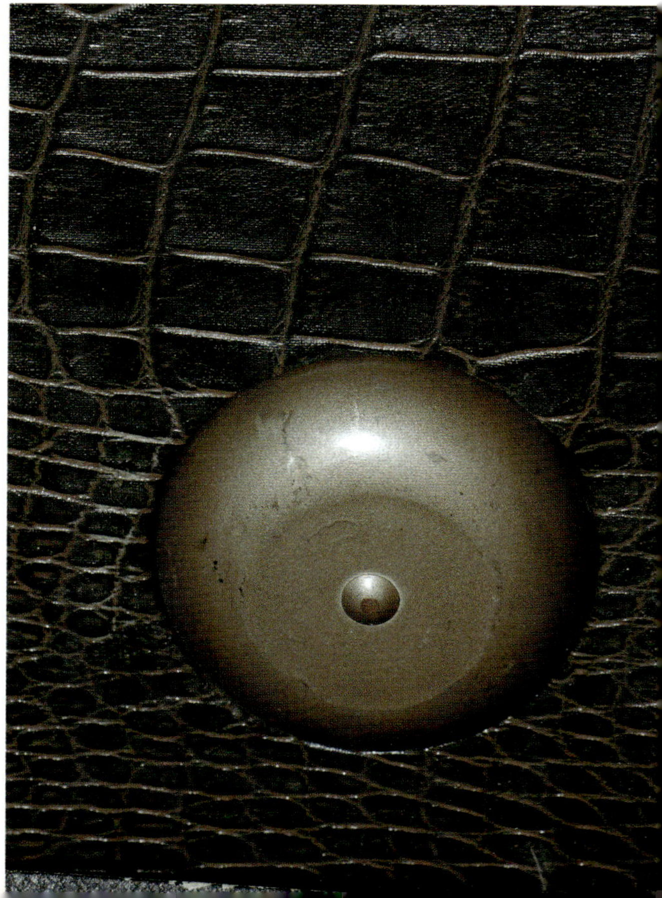

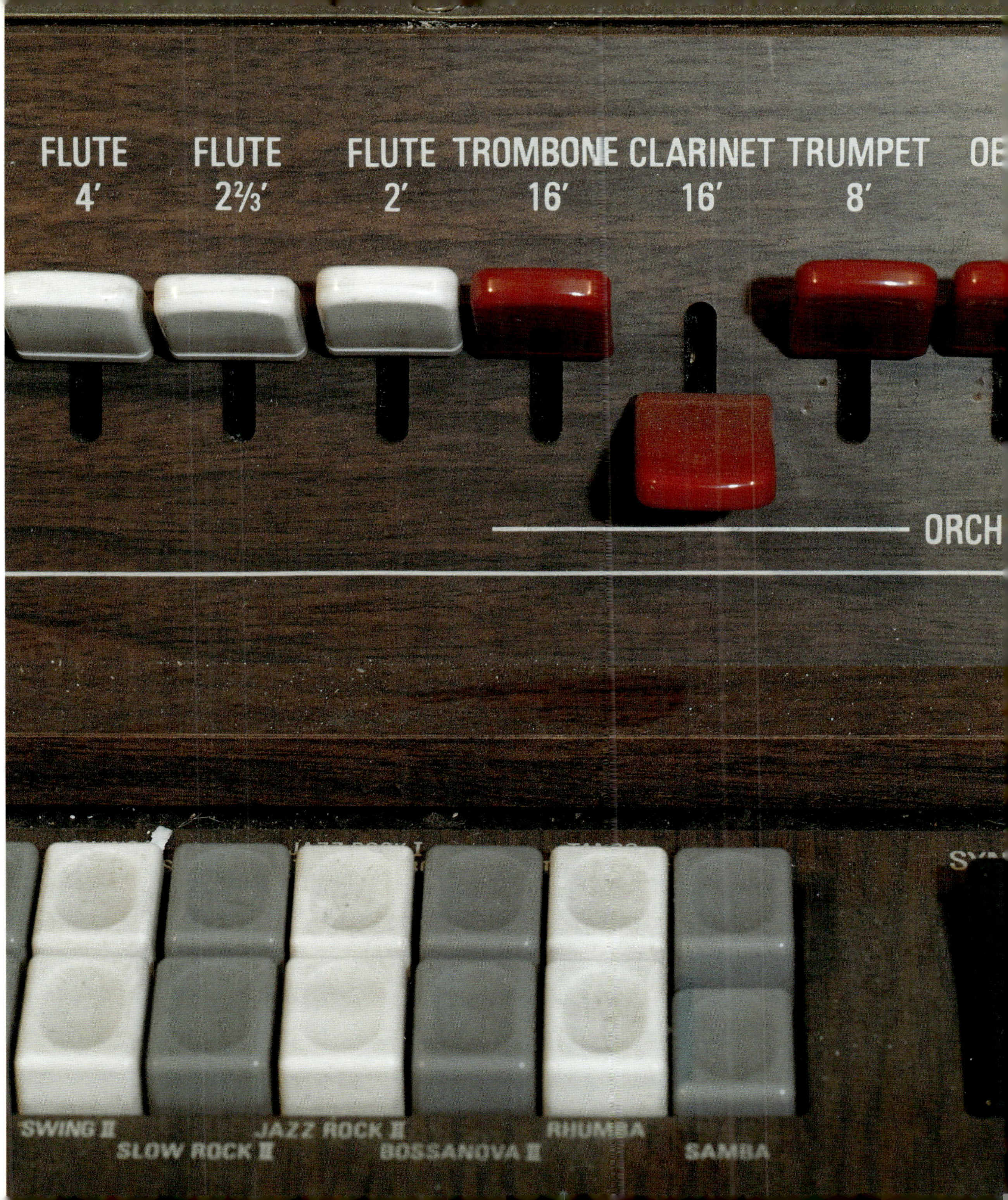
FLUTE
4′
FLUTE
2⅔′
FLUTE
2′
TROMBONE
16′
CLARINET
16′
TRUMPET
8′
ORCH
SWING II
SLOW ROCK II
JAZZ ROCK II
BOSSANOVA II
RHUMBA
SAMBA

nent, The Jicks

r Jazzmaster guitar

his guitar from some friends in the band Silkworm in
It has big frets and is kind of dull-sounding, which I
really keeps on working, with the original electronics.
cool.

ably need to get another guitar, but this one keeps on
ating itself into the equation. Once you're comfortable
certain guitar, it's hard to make a move.

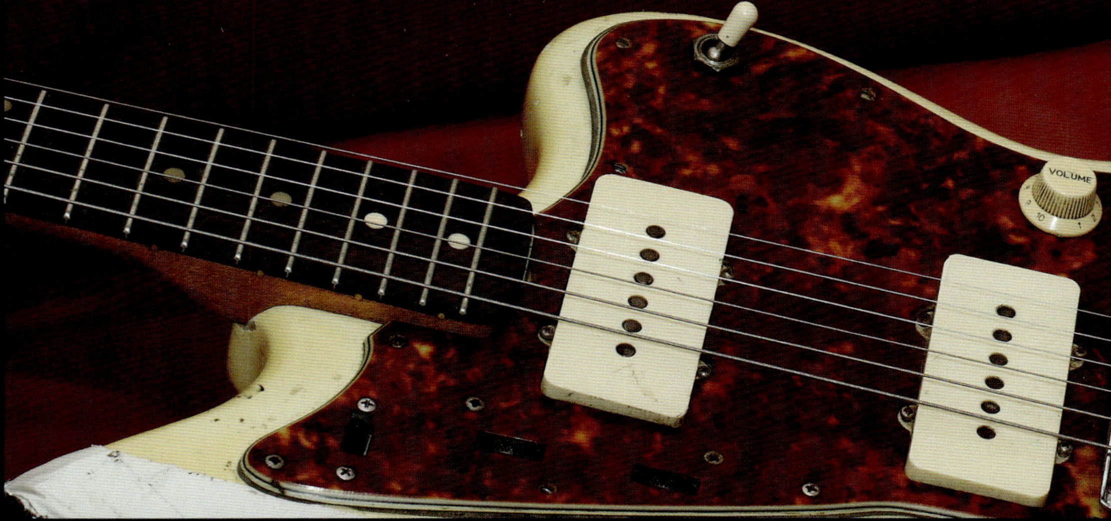

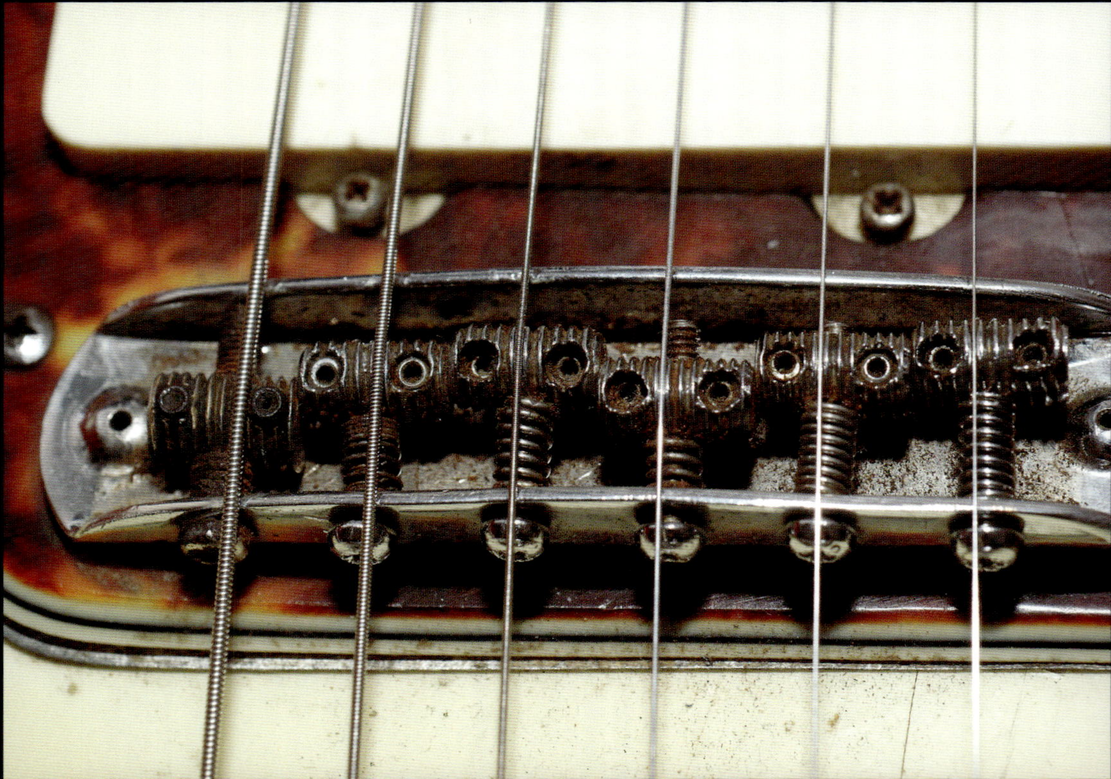

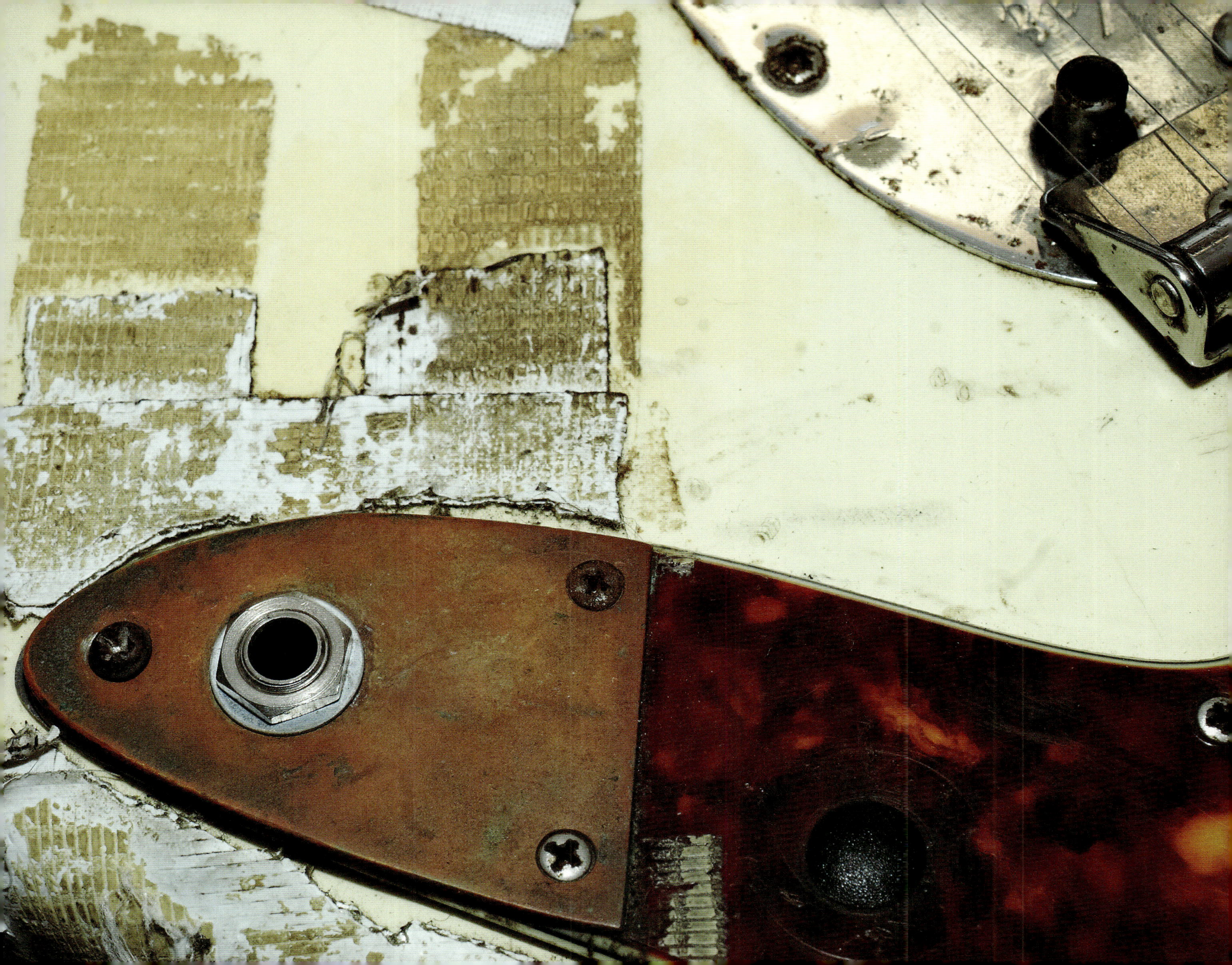

PETER BUCK

R.E.M.
Rickenbacker 360 JetGlo guitar
Kay Kraft mandolin

I bought my first Rickenbacker in about 1980, from a little shop right next door to where we rehearse now in Athens called Chick Pianos. They had five guitars, and one of them was this beautiful blond Rickenbacker, for, I think, $200, which was a world of money to me at the time. I loved it. I love the tone, I love the way it sounds. I love the history, knowing that Roger McGuinn and George Harrison and Pete Townshend played Rickenbackers—that's kind of the trifecta. They have a very nice distinctive shape. The other thing I like, having visited the factory, is that Rickenbacker is the only major guitar company in the world that makes guitars the same way they did fifty years ago. It's a bunch of folks in a room passing pieces around, sanding them, and passing them to the next guy. That makes the new ones just as good as the old ones, but all a little different.

That blond one got stolen eventually, I think in '81, when I was in Hartford, Connecticut, doing a show for $100. I think it was stolen out of the van or someone's apartment or something. So we went to a tiny little guitar shop and pulled a Rickenbacker out of a box. It was in tune. I played it, it sounded great, and it's the one I've used on every single record I've ever made. I've played it on stage my entire adult life and on every R.E.M. record except the "Radio Free Europe" single, because I didn't have it at that point.

This one got stolen, too, in Finland in 2008, and I had to ransom it back. We were in the middle of a tour, and my entire rig, which I have been using for years, is designed for this guitar and maybe one other. I was having trouble getting any kind of real tone without it. So it was nice to get the Rickenbacker back and just not have to think about it. We have a lot of fans who come regularly to a lot of shows, and like fifty of them were holding up signs that said "Welcome back Rickenbacker." It was really sweet.

—Exerpt from an interview by Tony Bacon, *Rickenbacker Electric 12-string*

I was shopping for a Kay Kraft Venetian archtop guitar for Peter, and during my search, I found a matching Kay Kraft mandolin. I had two auctions running concurrently trying to purchase the two instruments. Alas, I lost out on the guitar, but did win the mandolin. It cost thirty dollars, plus shipping.

Upon arrival to our shop I found the instrument to be in a sad state. The headstock was cracked, the neck was loose and the frets were worn. At the time, I was preparing an extremely old Gretsch ukulele to be shipped to a luthier I know in St. Louis, and decided to send the mandolin as well, to see if it was worth salvaging.

The luthier, Jimmy Gravity, proprietor of J. Gravity Strings, had restored numerous old, not-so-pricey, vintage instruments for Jay Farrar and Jeff Tweedy during the days of their band, Uncle Tupelo, and I have used Jimmy's services over the years. He repaired the headstock, re-set the neck, re-fretted it, re-glued the braces, and customized a bridge out of a Fishman archtop mandolin piezo pickup. The job he did was amazing.

I subsequently made it Peter's back up touring mandolin. His number one is a Flatiron F-5 Artist made by Bruce Weber. The Kay Kraft with its thicker, archtop body has a more mellow, deeper bass tone. Though it isn't as punchy or as loud as the Flatiron, it is a beautiful sounding instrument nonetheless, and provides a nice, tonal compliment to the Flatiron. Peter can be heard playing it on "It Happened Today" on *Collapse Into Now*.

Regarding the R.E.M. painted on the top: When I got the instrument, a previous owner had painted their or someone's or something's initials on it. They were R. L. M. My wife, Jackie Burton, changed the L to an E and *voila*.

—DeWitt Burton

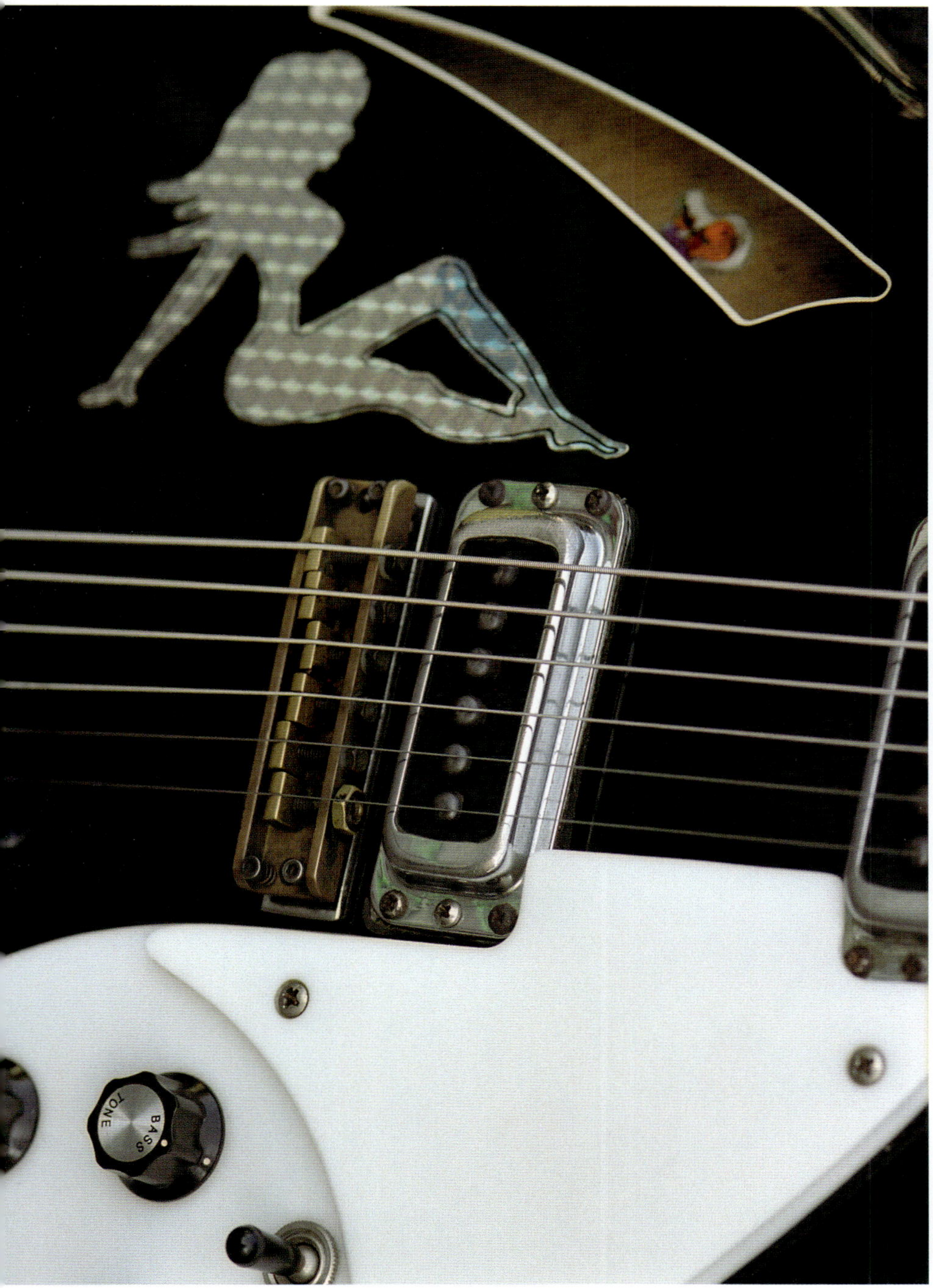
BASS
TONE
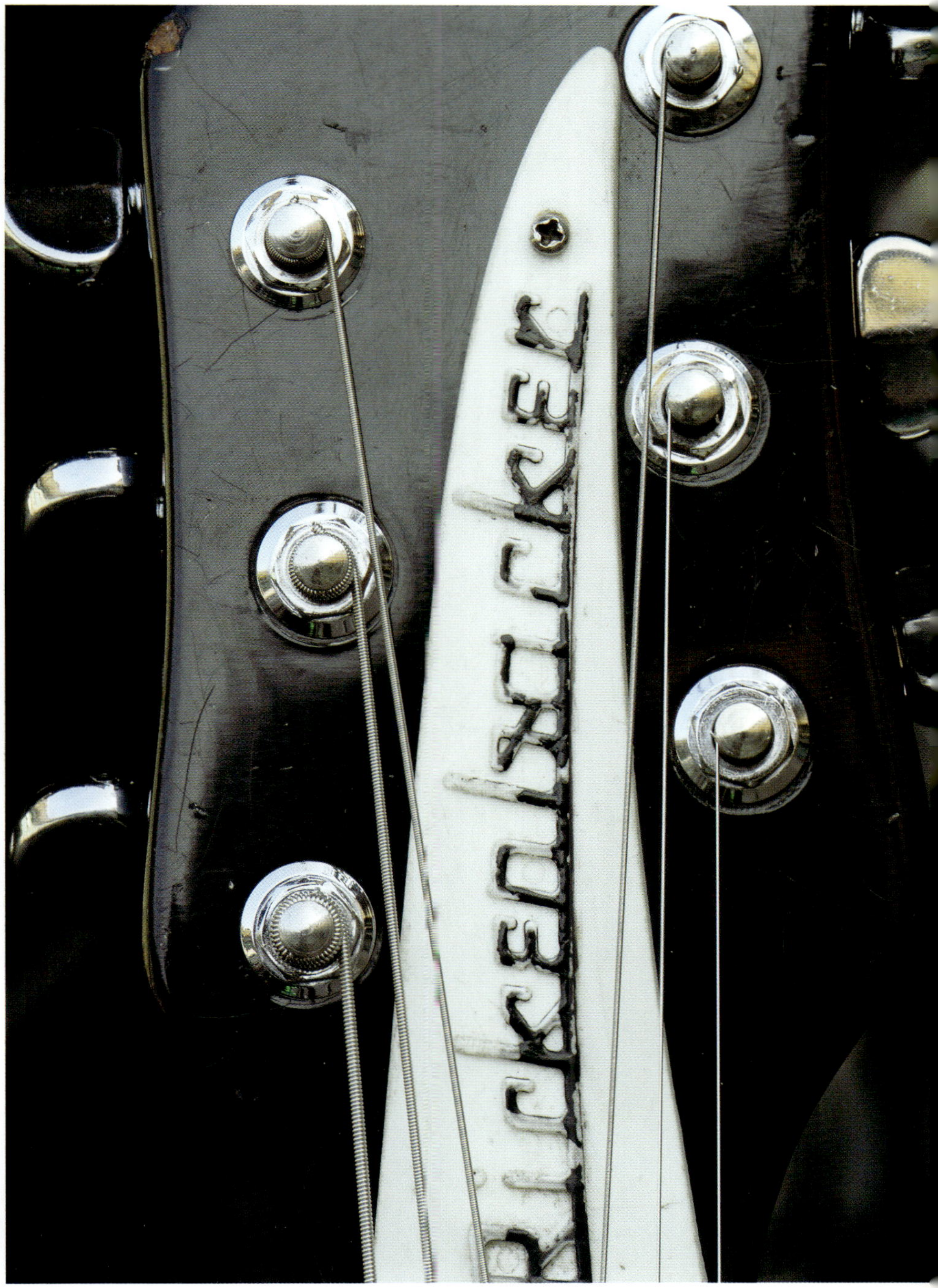
Rickenbacker

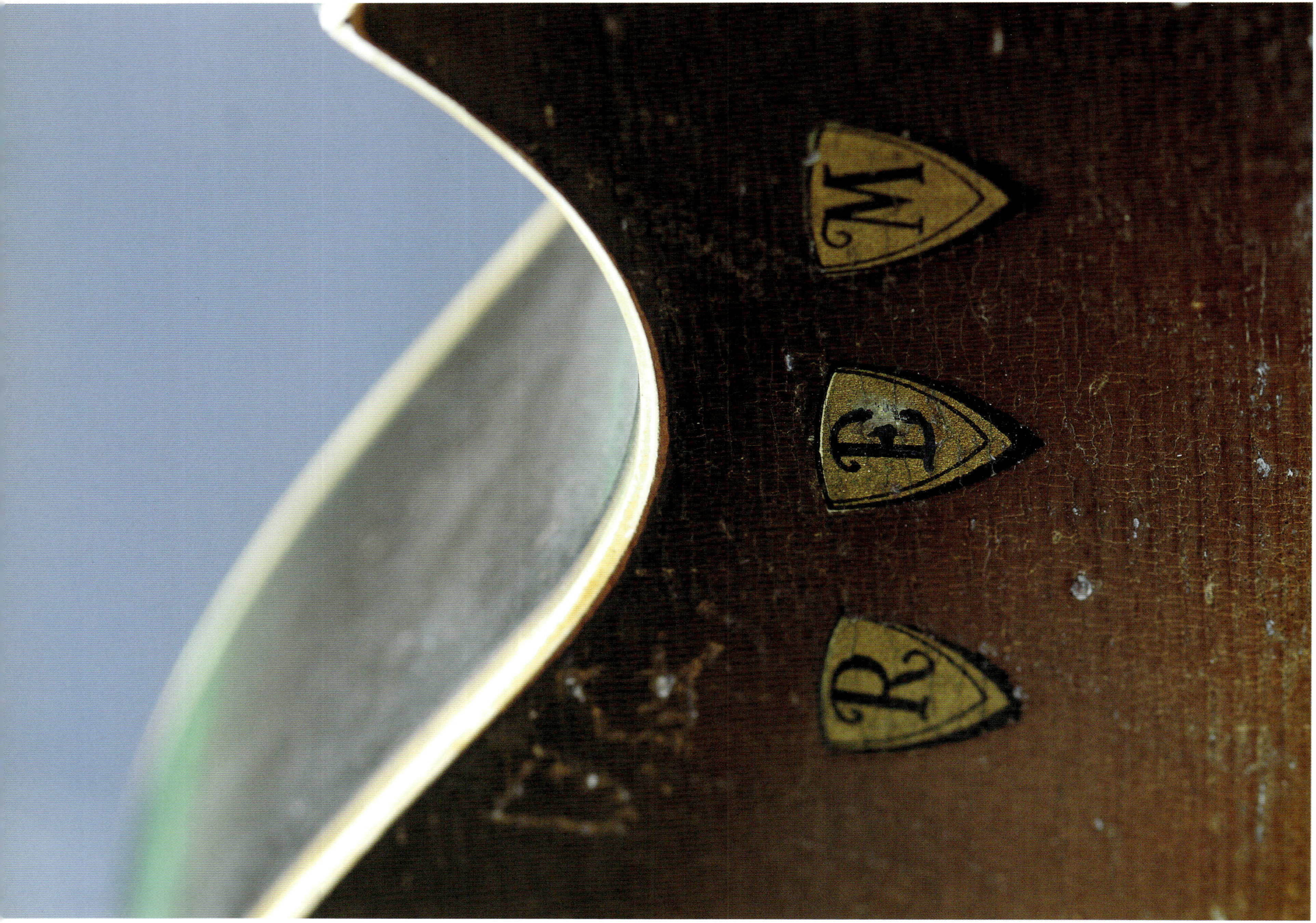
M
E
R

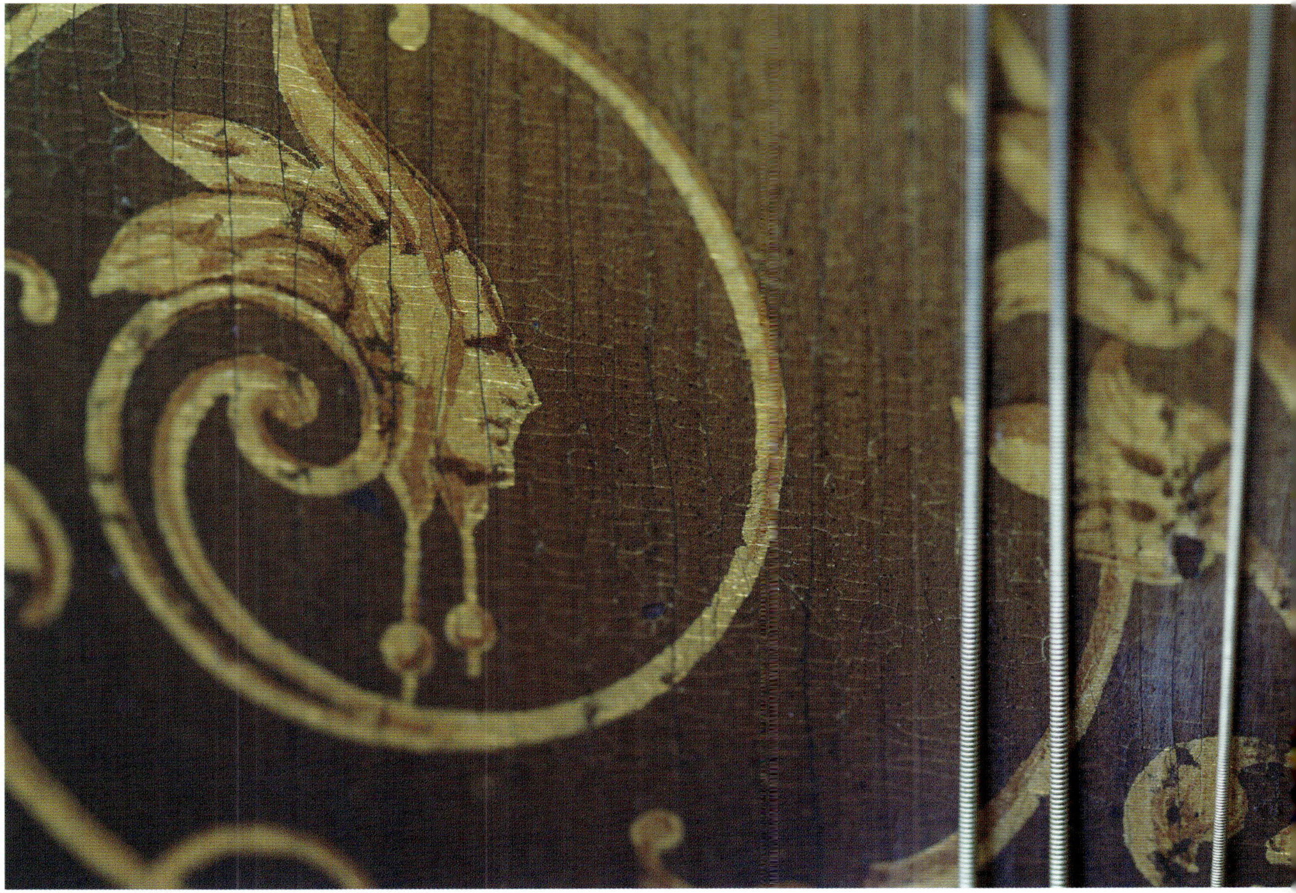

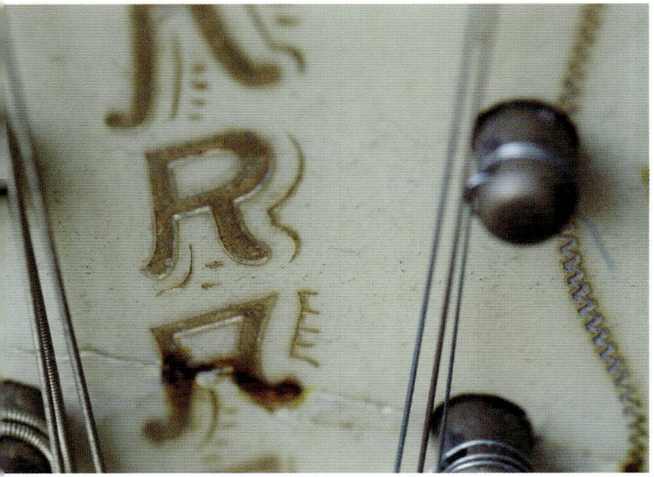

HAL BLAINE

Elvis Presley, The Beach Boys, The Ronettes, Nancy Sinatra

Various percussion instruments

As a percussionist and session musician, Hal Blaine played on dozens of hit records in the 1960s and '70s, including records by Elvis, the Ronettes, the Beach Boys, the Carpenters, Sonny and Cher, and many other artists. He often made instruments himself. He would look at the situation and think: *I'm in a three-piece band and I need to do finger cymbals here, I can't set my drumsticks down, grab the finger cymbals in each hand, then clang them together and set them down.* So for instance, he would mount the finger cymbals on this giant safety-pin-looking thing so that he could hit them and not even miss a stroke. He played the bottom of a giant water bottle on the Beach Boys' "Caroline, No."

These sleigh bells were used on everything from the Ronettes' "Be My Baby" to the Beach Boys' "Good Vibrations" and "God Only Knows" to the Captain & Tennille's "Love Will Keep Us Together."

Behind Phil Spector's "Wall of Sound" was Hal Blaine standing at the door of a recording session, handing out percussion to everyone in the studio, be it musicians, celebrities, or secretaries. That meant having ten to twenty tambourines around. He also labeled all his instruments, because he was doing at least five separate engagements a day, running from one place to another, and he just didn't want that stuff to go away after it was handed out. If it was just a tambourine, you might take it with you to the next gig, but not with "Hal Blaine" written over the top of it.

As your ear becomes familiar with these items, you can start to pick them out and hear them all over '60s and '70s music.

—Rick King

I had been inventing sounds and instruments since the late 1940s. Working with duos and trios and larger groups with dancers, I used many Latin percussion sounds, which I also later used with all the great percussionists in the studio.

The sounds that I had heard since childhood, listening to the big bands of the day with their great drummers, and practically living in movie theaters and paying close attention to the soundtracks, led me to sounds I would later use on records and soundtracks myself.

Every "toy" that I had I either built or had seen other drummers or percussionists use when working on scores or records. We all learn from watching and listening to others who were doing stuff before us. I found that filling an empty 35mm film can about halfway with glass beads found at a craft store printed so much better than any actual shaker can generally used in that period.

I enjoyed every minute of every session I was ever fortunate enough to work on. Remember, when you love what you're doing, it's not work!

When we used castanets with Phil Spector, everyone said, "This is not a Latin tune." The same thing happened with the sleigh bells: "This is not a Christmas record." But Phil loved the unusual sounds and wanted them on all his records. The great percussionist and drummer Frankie Capp was on all the Phil Spector, including the sleigh bells.

That black case on wheels was duplicated for sessions in the early 1960s so that I always had my toys with me. Anything that felt good on any track and helped the feel of the song always worked. Sometimes I could use something that was just sitting around. For the Dean Martin song "Houston" I overdubbed a triangle beater on a glass ashtray. In those years everyone smoked, including Dean and the Rat Pack.

—Hal Blaine

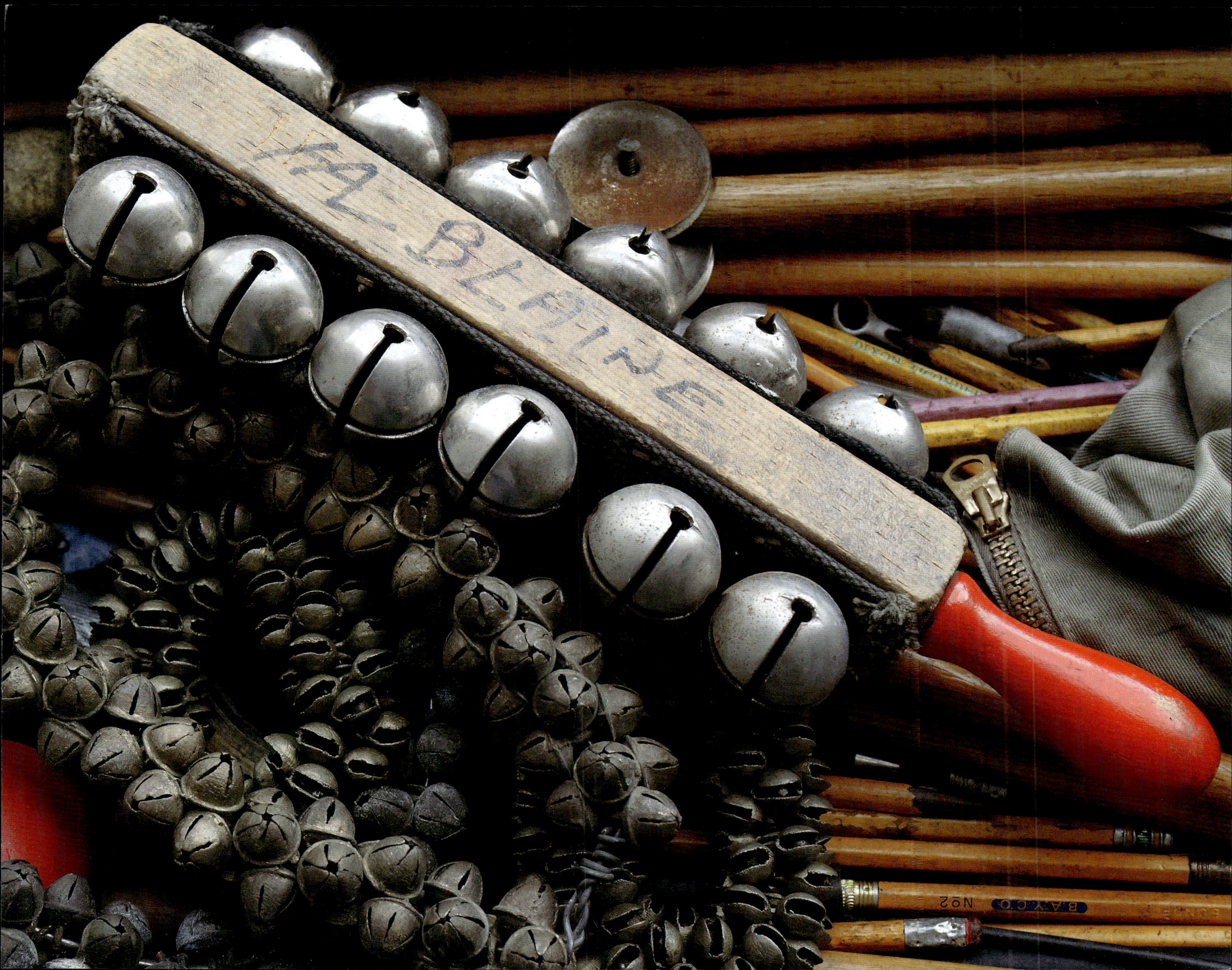
B·A·Y·C·O
No2

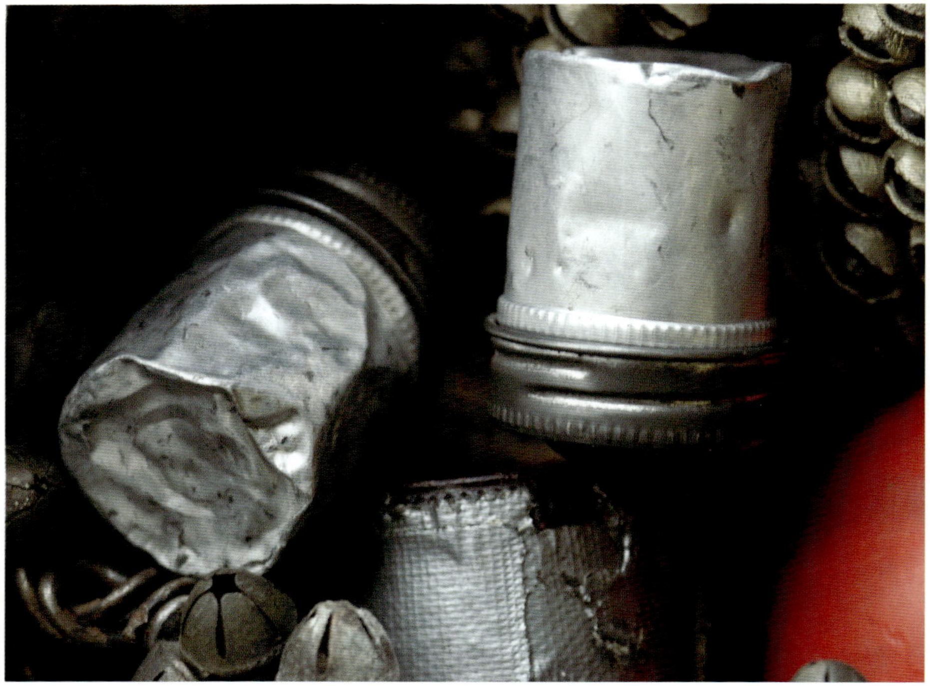
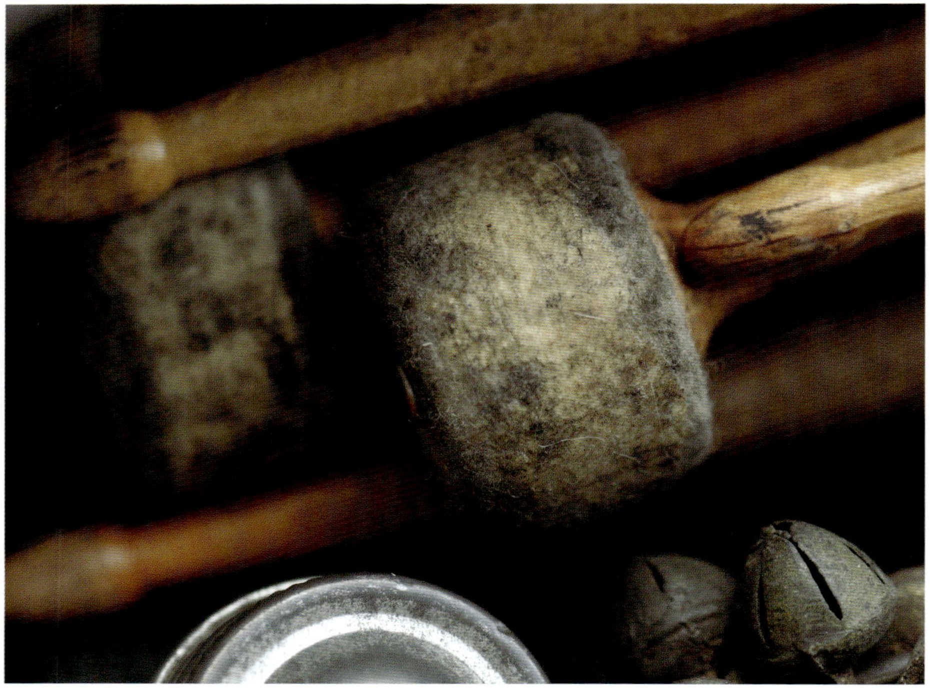
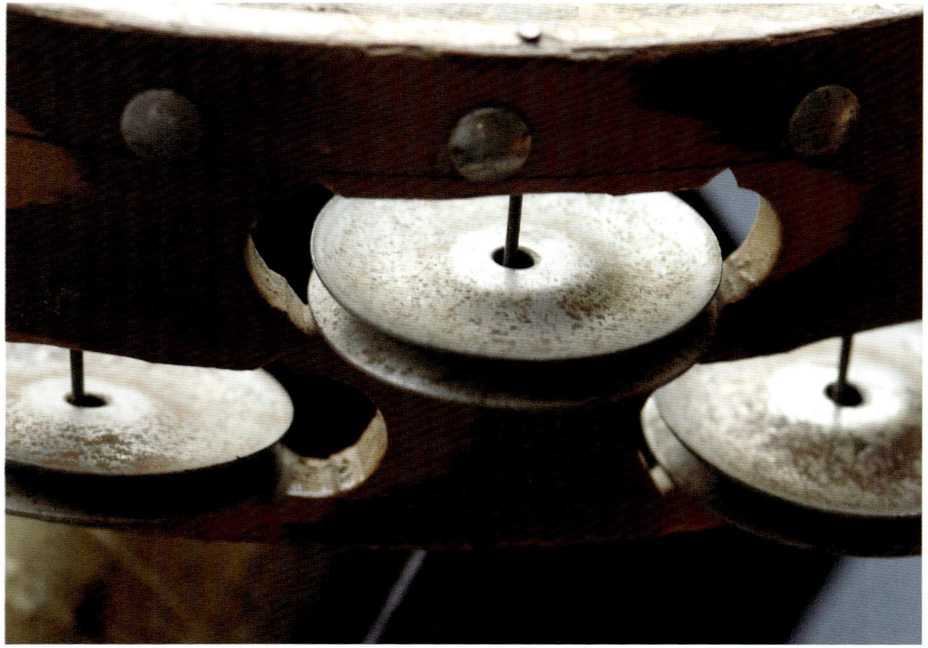
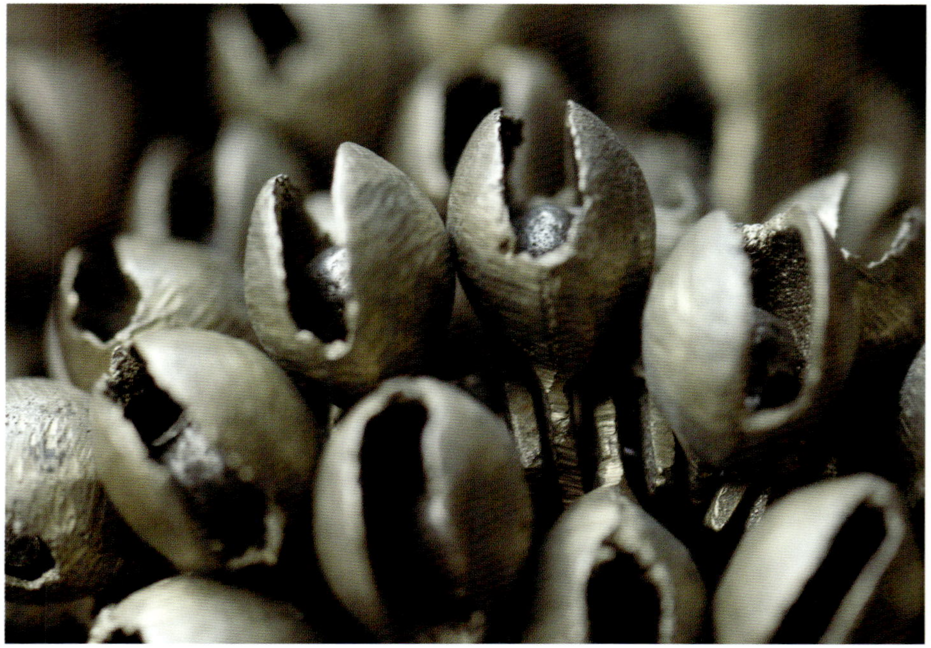

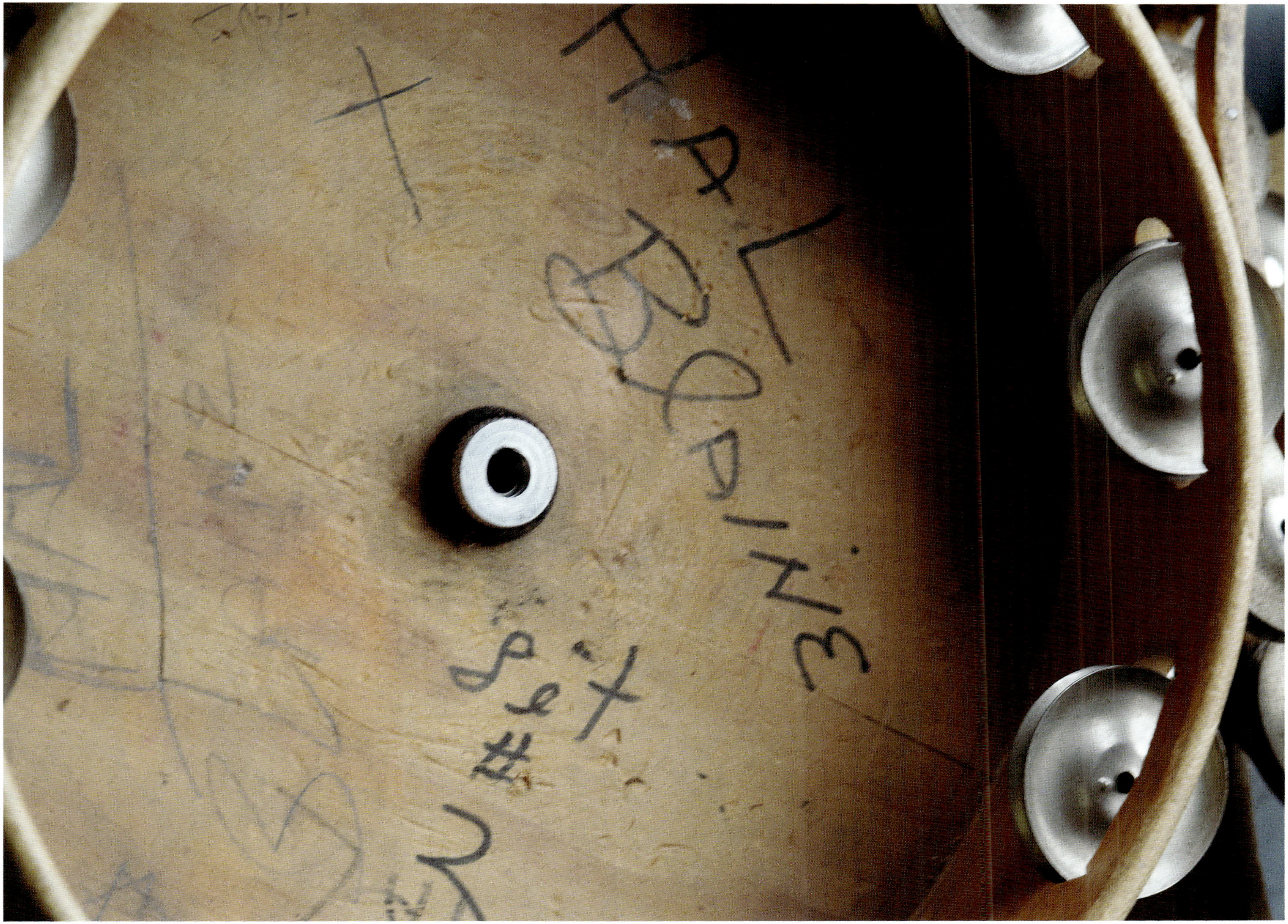
HAL BLAINE
set #2

NICK ZINNER

Yeah Yeah Yeahs

Fender Stratocaster guitar

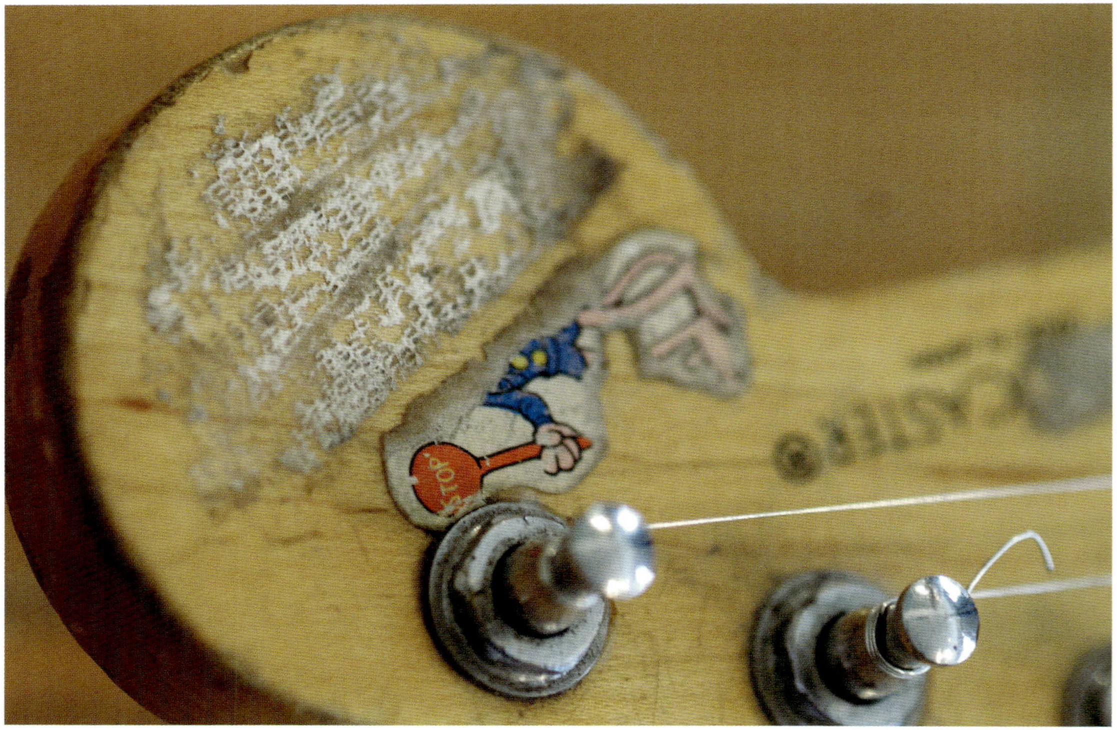

This was my second guitar. I got it from my best friend, Scott Burg, in the seventh grade. I can't remember if he sold it to me so he could buy more comic books or if I traded him half of my comic book collection for it, but I remember really wanting it, being impressed by the floating whammy bar and the sophisticated locking nuts at the top of the neck. (Though I took off and lost the whammy bar and the locking components when I was in high school because it seemed too heavy metal—I'd briefly stopped listening to heavy metal.) After I got it, I spent the majority of my adolescent years locked in my room playing it, learning it. Today, it's probably the guitar I've written, toured, and recorded with the most. It's not the greatest sounding or most desirable Stratocaster, but all of its weaknesses have been ultimately responsible for how I play the thing now. It's a pretty thin-sounding guitar, so when we started the band without a bass player, I started looking for effects and secret tricks that would make it sound bigger, and now I'm overwhelmed by pedals.

Like a body with tattoos, I have lots of little stickers on it from different periods of my life, most meaningful only for the time and people they mark. The big circle sticker with the 50 on it is from Indonesia; I got it for 25 cents in Sulawesi when I was traveling there before I was in a band. It's celebrating fifty years of Indonesian independence. A lot of kids there write us about it, which is pretty great. When the band was in Singapore a few months ago, a girl from Jakarta gave me a new sticker; it's been sixty-four years of independence now.

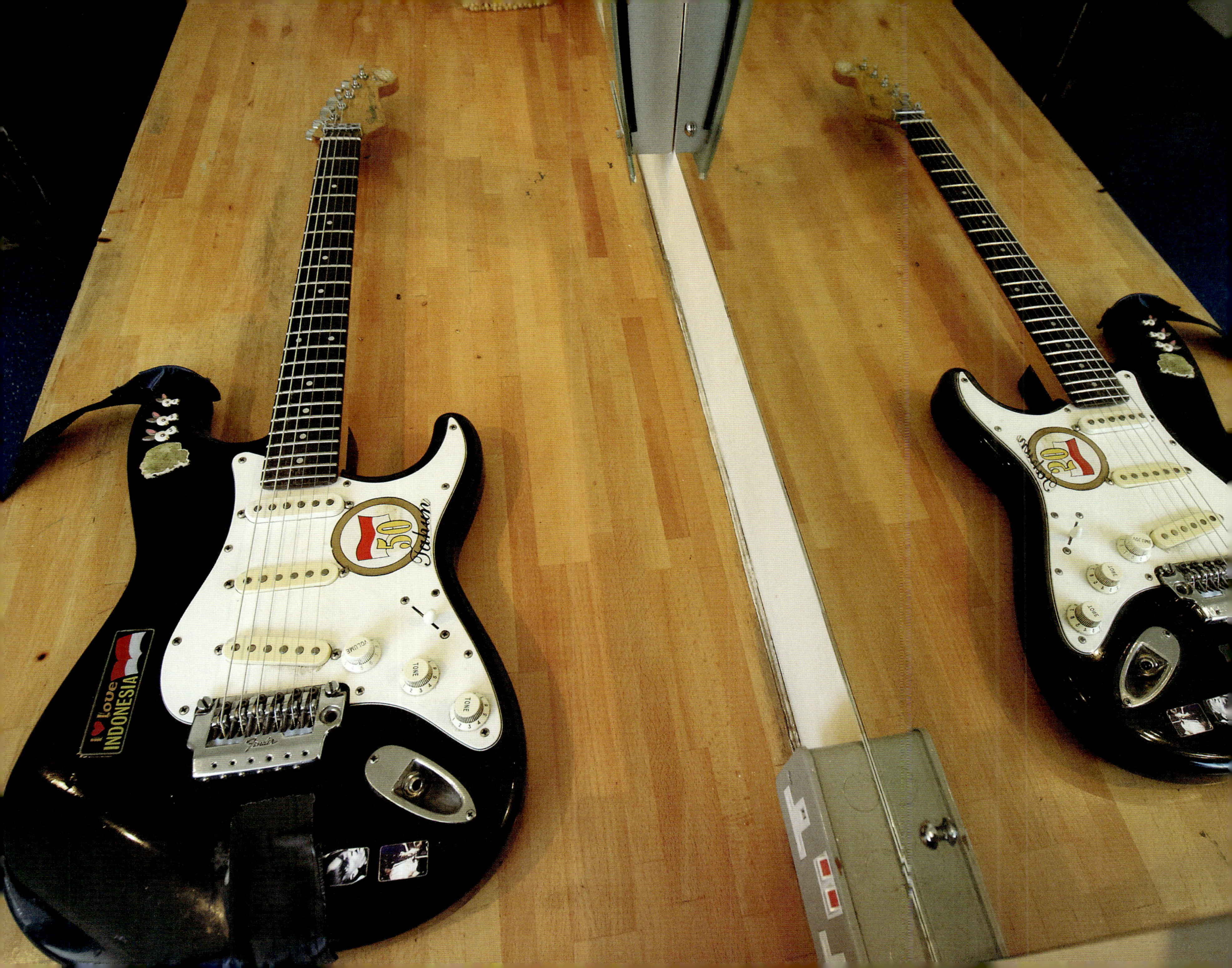

I ♥ love
INDONESIA
50
VOLUME
TONE
TONE

KURT COBAIN

Nirvana
Broken guitar head
Electro–Harmonix Clone pedal

The first thing I can remember Kurt buying from the store was an Electro-Harmonix Clone [pedal].

After that he bought every one that came in, and he bought five of them. I thought it was weird that he wanted this lush chorus pedal when none of the music that he had played prior to that had any kind of inflection. I asked Krist Novoselic, [bass player for Nirvana], "What's up with Kurt and these pedals?" He just said, "Oh, you'll see." Then, "Smells Like Teen Spirit," "Come as You Are," and songs like that came out.

Kurt's guitar tech on the *Nevermind* tour was Ernie Bailey. He got the job because he could take apart broken guitars and put them back together, and being conscious about money, the band would recycle guitars out of parts and pieces that Kurt would break during performances. I knew Ernie before he started working with Nirvana. He gave me this piece of headstock and neck from a guitar Kurt broke during the tour.

–Rick King

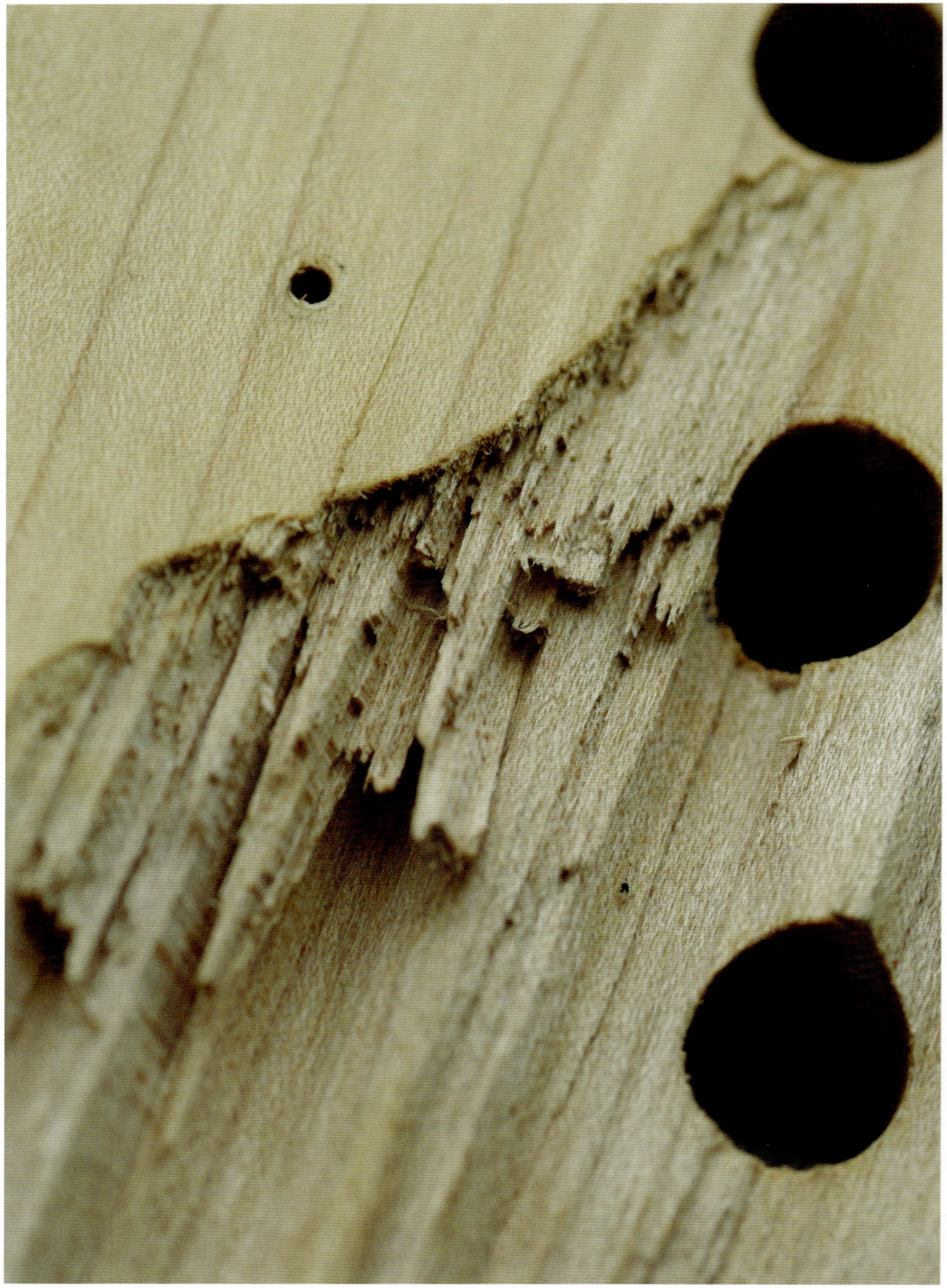

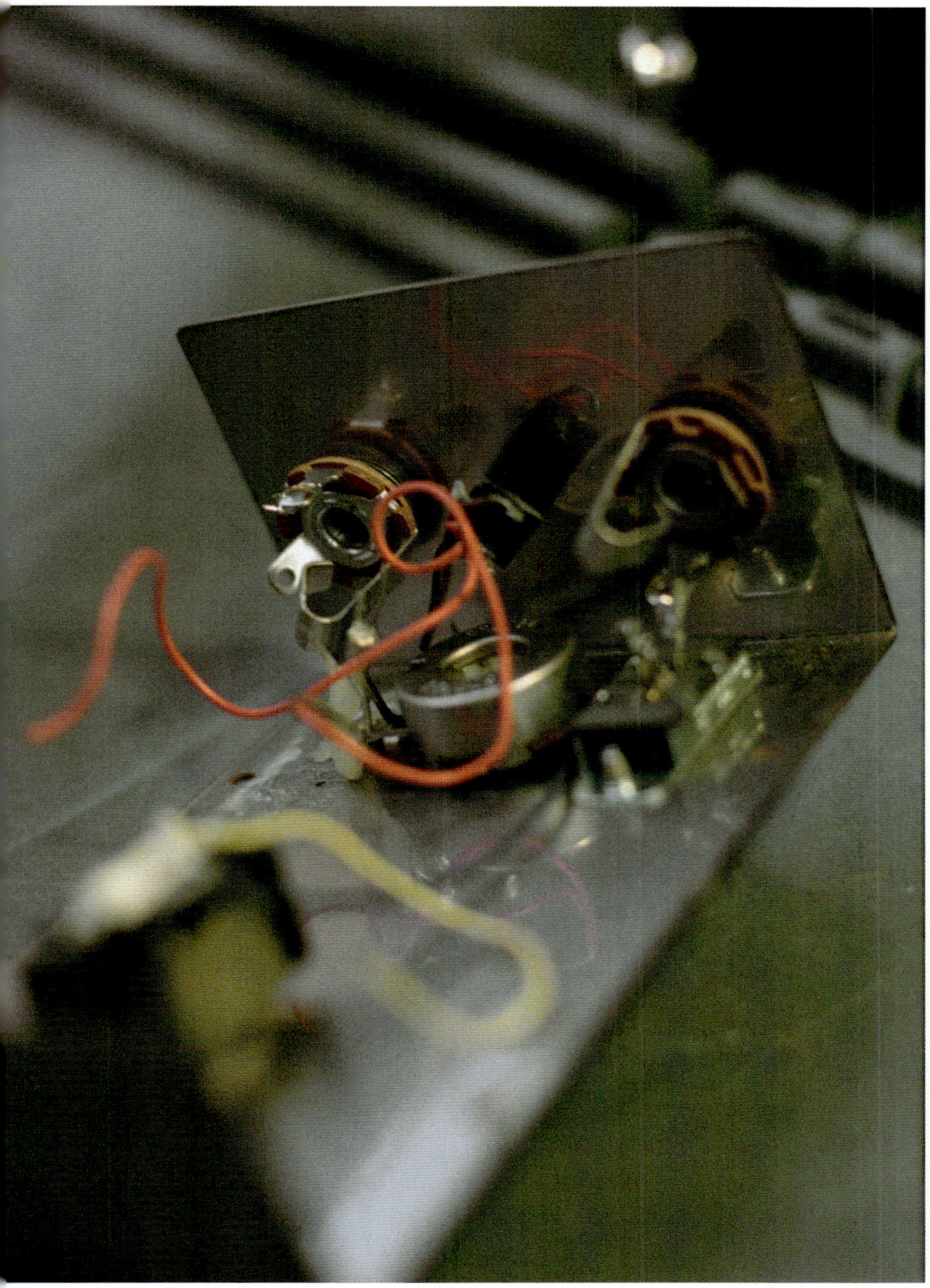

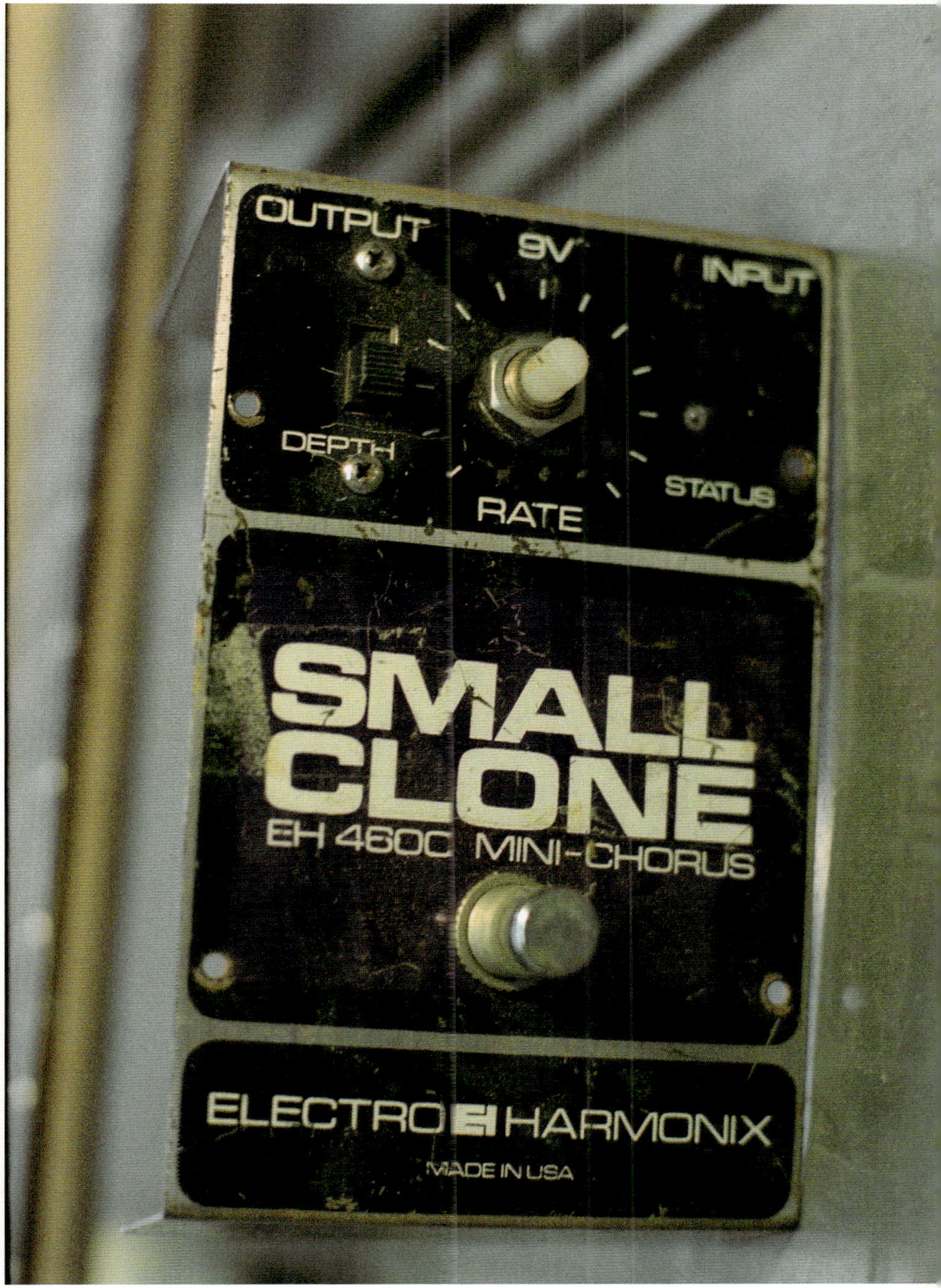
OUTPUT
9V
INPUT
DEPTH
RATE
STATUS
SMALL
CLONE
EH 4600 MINI-CHORUS
ELECTRO HARMONIX
MADE IN USA

ALEX KAPRANOS

Franz Ferdinand
1973 Fender Telecaster Deluxe guitar

I bought this guitar on April 17, 2003: the first time I used eBay. It was the most expensive object I'd bought in my life. I'd been after a Telecaster for years—I'd seen one in a guitar shop when I was a teenager and had never seen another. Then I heard about this Web site where you could buy stuff, and I figured I might find one there. I couldn't believe how cheap it seemed at first—just over a hundred quid. I didn't realize that there would be a flurry of bids at the last minute until I watched the seconds counting away as the guitar quickly doubled, tripled, quadrupled, and quintupled in value. "Ah, fuck you all," I thought, and typed in my second and last bid of £666 with seconds to go. There. I'd won. Bollocks. How could I afford that? It was fine. I just didn't pay my rent that month. I've played the guitar ever since.

The things I like about it are its sound, the way it is to play, and the way it looks, in that order. The sound is shaped by the broad, chrome Seth Lover pickups, which are a sort of humbucker with offset CuNiFe magnets set as screws that produce an extremely clear sound with a presence that surrounds the notes like a halo. The guitar has a long-scale neck, which suits my long, twisted fingers, and which is worn away to the wood—way more pleasant to hold than a piece of varnished plastic. Unusually for a Tele, it has a contoured cutaway body, like a Stratocaster or Jazzmaster (the back is carved to fit the curve of your hip), so that it feels very natural to hold. Finally, it looks both mean and fair: the square shape, smashed finish, and scratched chrome.

I've jumped into audiences quite a few times when I've been carried away. Sometimes guys in the audience will try and nick it, but they'd have to break my fingers or pull my arms from their sockets before I'd see it go. If I see someone behaving like a prick in the audience, I'll hold the guitar against my arm like a Sten gun and spray the person with riffs, like Billy Liar mowing down Shadrack.

It's an early model, '73 I think, a year younger than I am. I have a later one that I use as a spare, but it's heavier and doesn't feel or sound as good. These guitars were scorned by musos for years, because they were considered ugly mutations, impure. In recent years they have come into vogue, which kind of pisses me off—what was my wee secret was appearing in the hands of every cack-handed nob in an indie band. But there you go. If I was looking for my first proper guitar now, I wouldn't buy one, as due to fashion they are overpriced. I've seen them on Denmark Street for more than four grand, which is ridiculous. I'd look for the ugliest, least fashionable guitar—probably from the late '80s—that is scorned by the musos, but actually sounds fantastic.

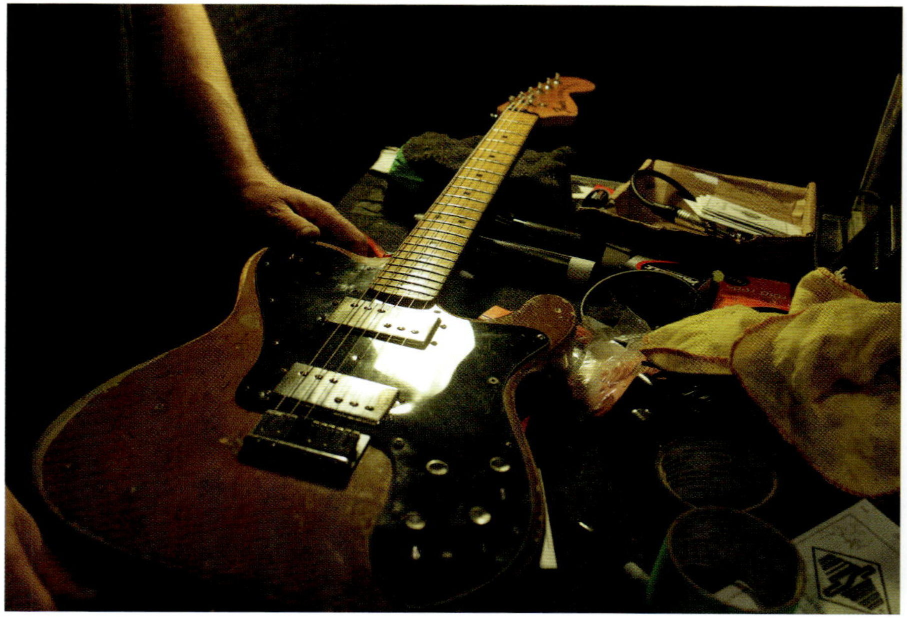

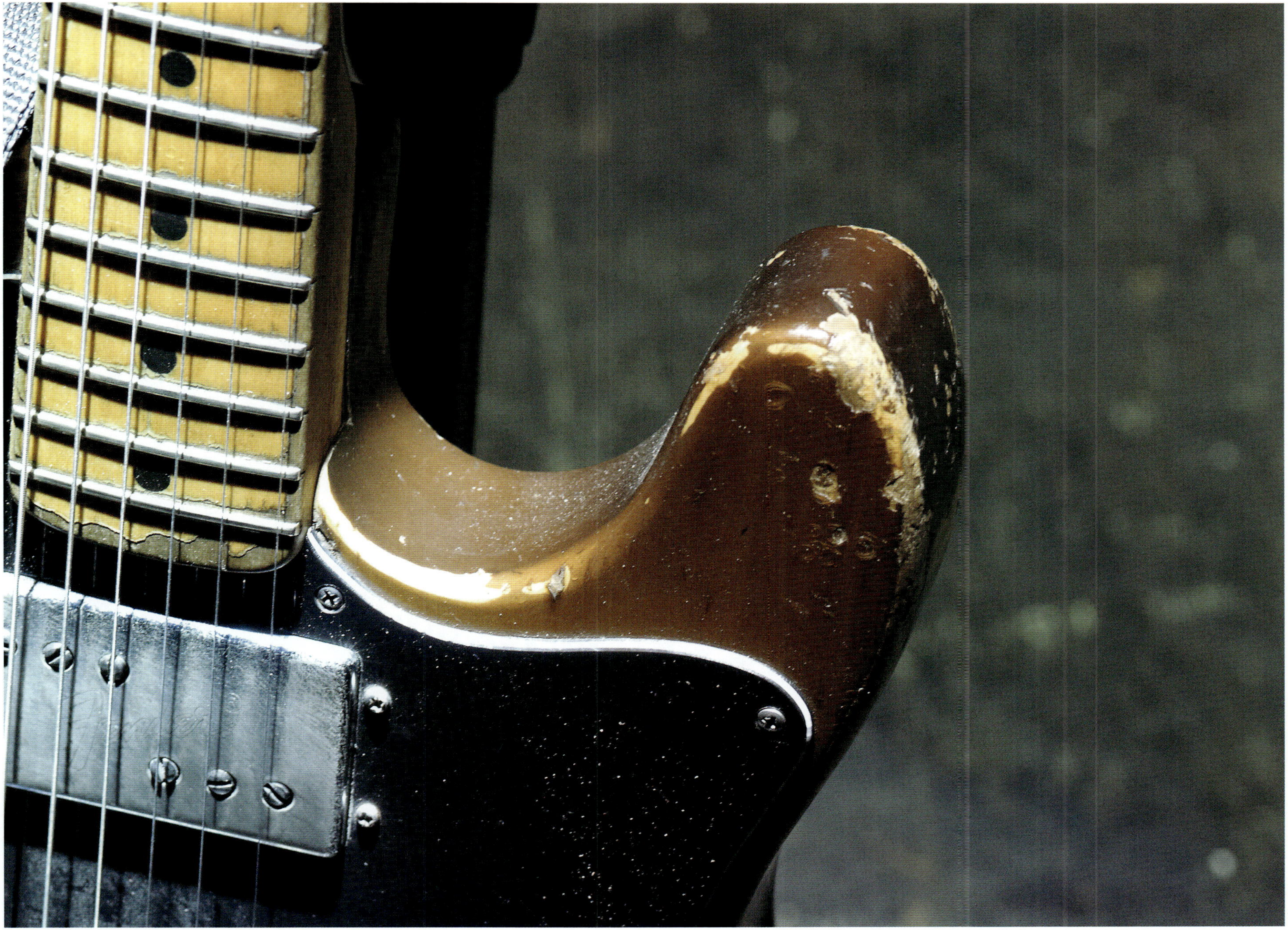

TREVOR KAMPMANN

hollAnd

Casio SK-1 keyboard

I bought this SK-1 at a local used music shop and quickly figured out that if I sang a sustained note into the sampler, it would produce one never-ending "oooooh" or "aaaah," and with that, I could make chords reminiscent of the impossibly expensive Mellotron.

One of my favorite songs I used it on was "The Garden," with Bridget Cross of Unrest and Kathy Wilcox of Bikini Kill for their band Panax. We tried for ages to get the hum out of the sampled drumbeat, and finally just accepted it as part of the tune. I saw Bridget at the recent Unrest reunion and she mentioned the session, and we actually talked about recording another record with the SK-1.

I've played this keyboard on nearly every hollAnd record, and have used it on records I produced. It conjures thoughts of all the lovely people who have played it on their recordings.

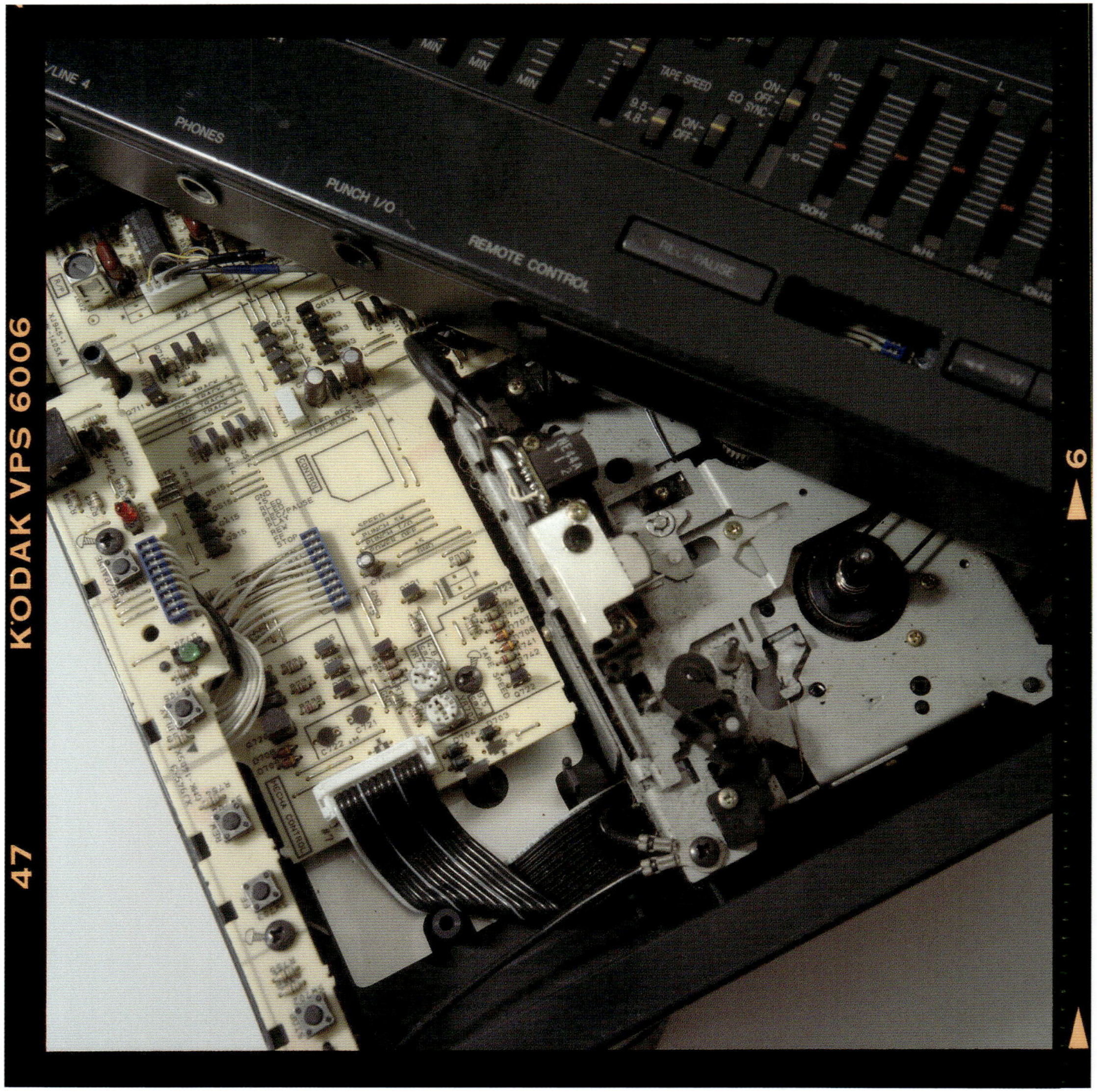

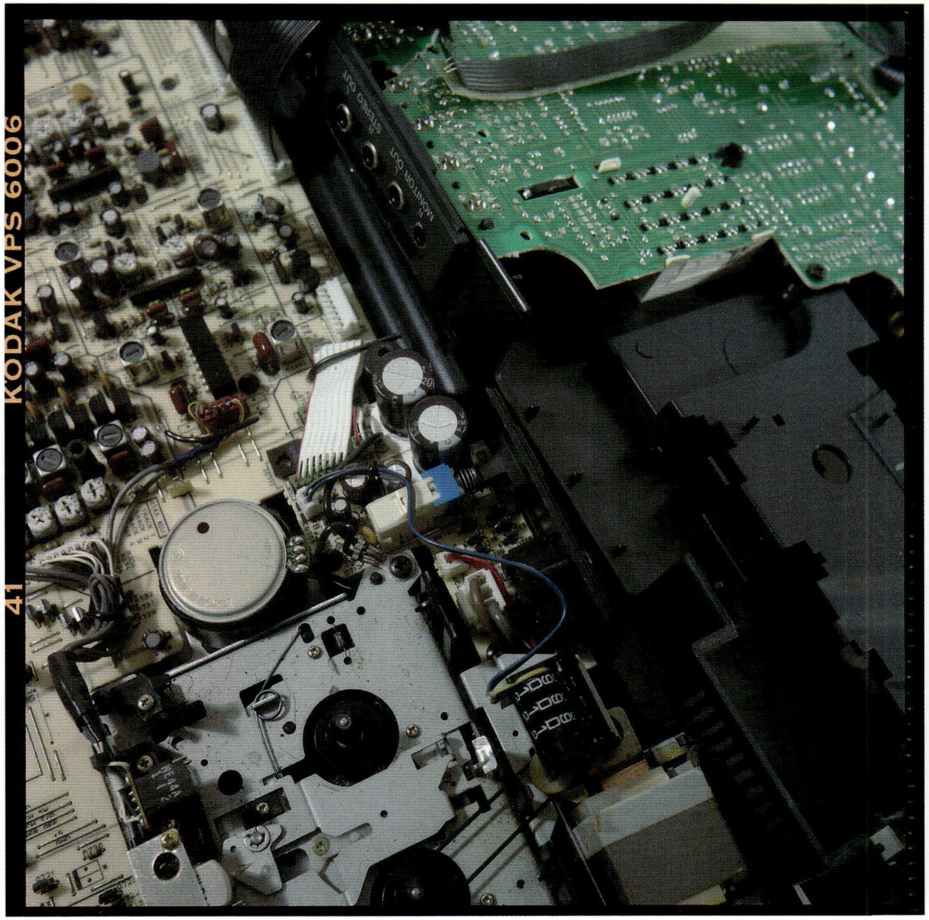
KODAK VPS 6006
41

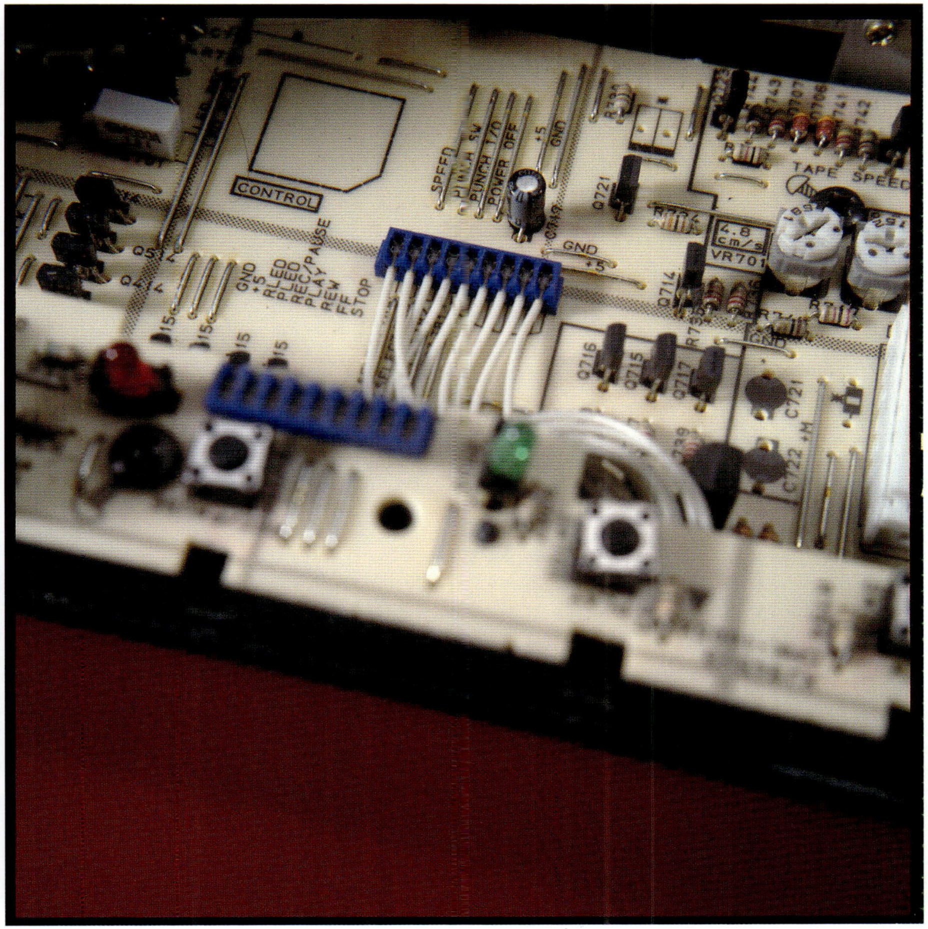
CONTROL
TAPE SPEED
POWER OFF
PLAY
REW
FF
STOP

TOM PELOSO

Modest Mouse
Carl Fischer cornet

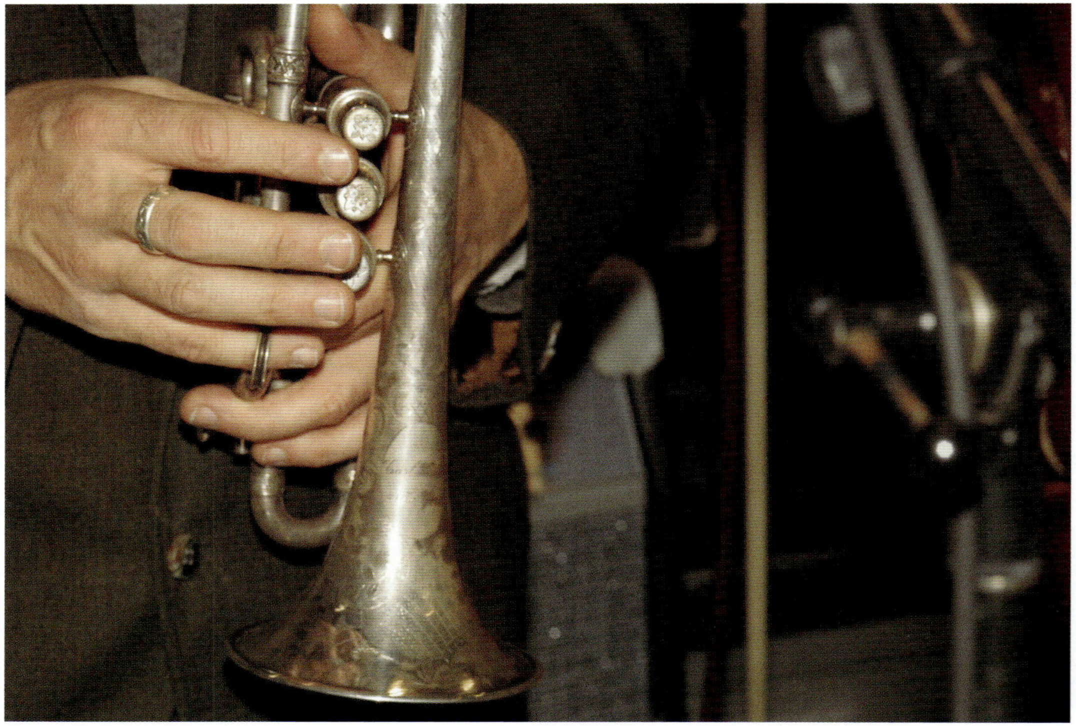

This is a Carl Fischer. Fischer was an instrument maker who started business in 1872 in New York City. I'm not sure of the model or year, as no one has serial number listings for these instruments. I was in Portland with Isaac [Brock] and the rest of the guys, and we found it in a local music shop called Artichoke Music. We were gearing up to do the record that wound up being *We Were Dead. . . .* (I played it on "Dashboard" and "Spitting Venom" on the album, as well as on "King Rat.") For as old as it was, it was in very good condition when I got it, but two or three years of travel have weathered it a good bit.

It really doesn't even work as it should with today's tuned instruments because at the time it was made there was no set standard pitch. It is called a "low C" cornet. I had to come up with different fingering positions to make it work with today's standard pitch. Although it's not my strongest asset, I have been playing the horn (not this particular one, of course) longer than any other instrument, and I thought I could incorporate that into Modest Mouse. My music teacher from fifth grade through high school, Mr. Taylor, taught me how to play the cornet and clean it. I learned a lot from him.

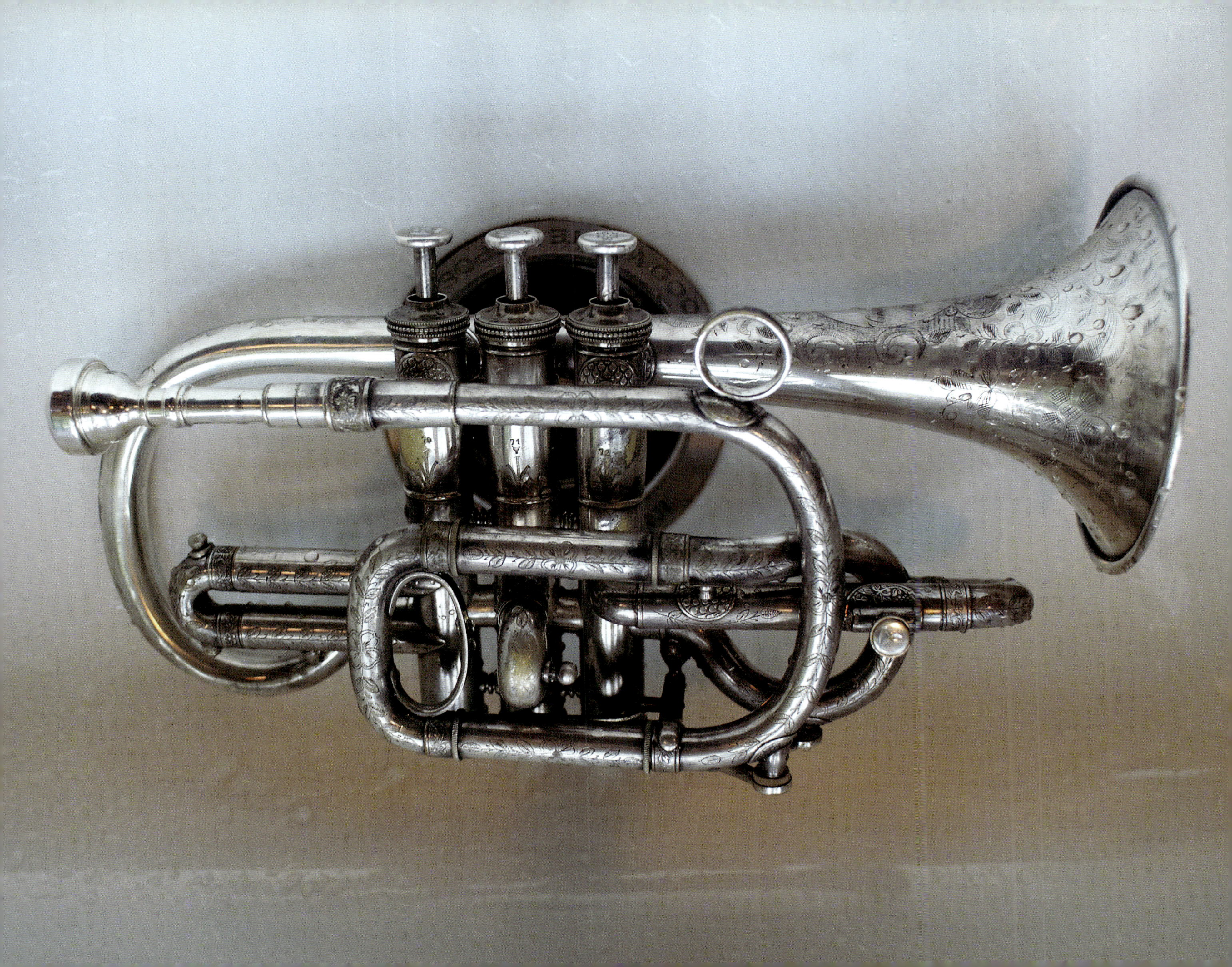

DAVID STONE

The Melvins, The Sads, LCD Soundsystem
MOTM analog modular synthesizer

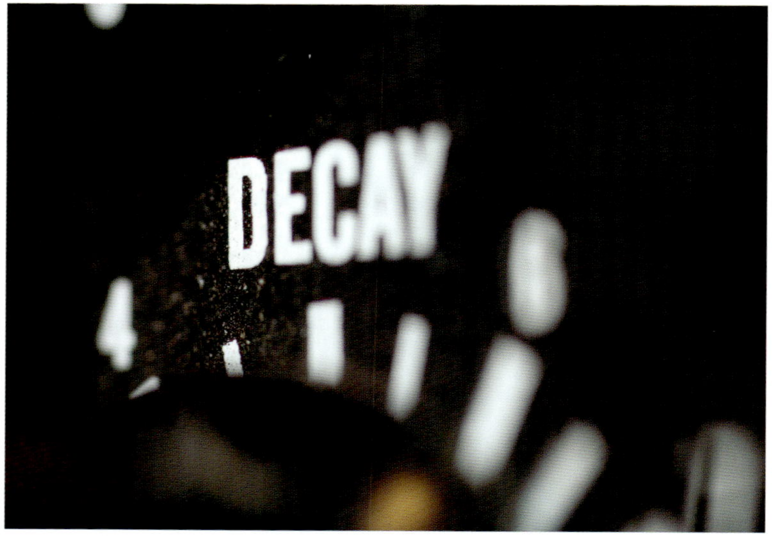

This is my self-built MOTM–based modular synthesizer system, which I started building in 2002. I've sourced parts, soldered the components to the circuit board, and wired up all the jacks and pots on my own. What you see here is only part of my full system. . . . It's never ending, and I'm always thinking about new modules and the sonic spaces I want to go with it.

I wanted to build a system that was super-roadworthy so I could tour with it. I also loved that so many of the pioneering artists of electronic music built or modified their own synthesizers: Suicide, Silver Apples, Throbbing Gristle, Cabaret Voltaire, Kraftwerk, Richard D. James, The Normal, Cluster, Stockhausen, Black Dice. . . . Plus, I can afford to have a lot of modules by building them myself, and it's so much better big and bold!

Working with it and learning its ways led me to make a record called *Plays the Modular Synthesizer*, where I explored lots of the composing and recording ideas from the '60s and '70s I loved so much: abstract textures, pulse as rhythm, raw waveform drone, power ambience, and even trying to sing a duet with a gal in French.

I love the seeking, and the unexpected surprises my system gives me all the time. It's closer to playing with another person than other instruments, because you have the action > reaction > action dialog with the synth that you'd have playing with a friend. I'll get an idea and try to get a particular sound or sequence going by building a patch that I think will take me there. I'll plug in a cable, or a knob will not be set to where it should be, and all of a sudden I have some sound that I couldn't have imagined. From there, I'll throw my original idea out and start working with the new one. It's all and all an excellent practice for staying in the present!

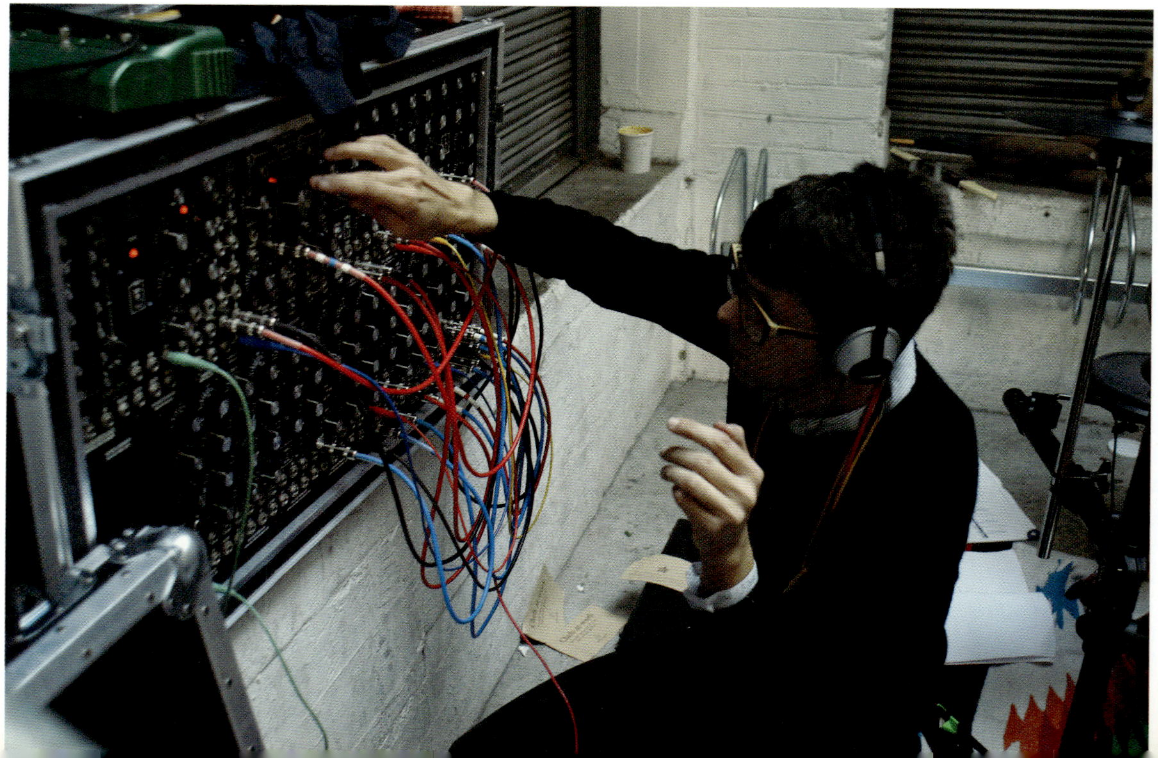

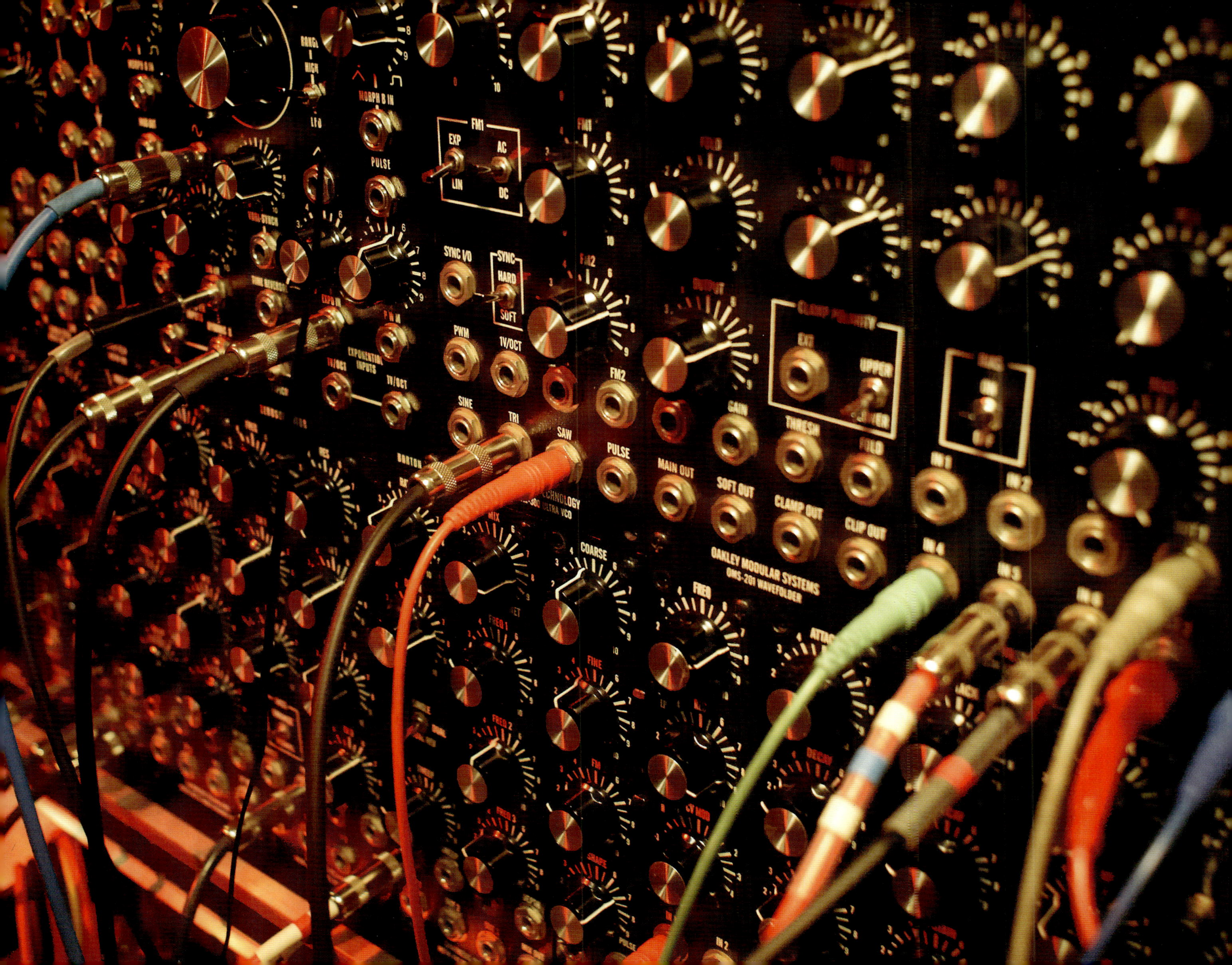
FM1
EXP
LIN
AC
DC
SYNC I/O
SYNC
HARD
SOFT
PWM
1V/OCT
SINE
TRI
SAW
PULSE
FM2
FM2
PULSE
CLAMP POLARITY
EXT
UPPER
GAIN
THRESH
FOLD
MAIN OUT
SOFT OUT
CLAMP OUT
CLIP OUT
OAKLEY MODULAR SYSTEMS
OMS-201 WAVEFOLDER
COARSE
FREQ
IN 1
IN 2

BEN BRIDWELL

Band of Horses
Wine Red Les Paul Custom guitar
Univox Hi-Flier guitar
1978 Les Paul Custom guitar

The wine red Les Paul Custom is a '77 or '79 model, and I think I got it through our original drummer, Tim, but I can't remember how. This one wrote my most successful song, "The Funeral," and has been the most consistent piece of gear I've had since I started the band. The belt rash on it is all me, and I'm quite proud of that. It just shows how many hours I've dry-humped the thing. A lot of sweat has seeped into that guitar as well. It's probably been at every show we've ever played, and you can hear it on "The Funeral," "Laredo," "Wicked Gil," "Ode to LRC," and many other songs I can't remember right now.

The Univox Hi-Flier was traded to me by an old friend. I gave him a Squire Strat in return. That still doesn't feel quite right, but he needed the Strat for a birthday present. This one wrote "No One's Gonna Love You" for me. I always keep flat-wound strings on it, which seems to make the already soft tone even smoother. It's pretty fragile, but I've taken it everywhere regardless. The neck has bowed a bit from so much flying, but otherwise it's had good luck. Since I got it, I've been collecting Univox products and I've formed a decent collection of other guitars, effects pedals, amps, posters, and so on. This guitar might only be on "No One's Gonna Love You." I bring it on every tour though, just to play that one song. The Annabelle dedication to my two-year-old daughter was written on the guitar before I played it for the filming of the *Yo Gabba Gabba* TV show. I wrote her name pretty small because I was afraid they'd make me use another guitar if it was too obvious, but actually the producers really liked it and focused in on her name. It's always nice to see her name there now when I'm so far from home.

The 1978 Les Paul custom was a thirty-first birthday present from the band and crew. I'd always wanted a Les Paul from my birth year, and had been obsessed with this one forever. I could not believe my eyes when they presented it to me. I also couldn't believe how heavy it is. I adore that guitar and my friends. I always just seem to connect with the Les Paul Custom guitars. I love the heaviness of the wood and the dark tones from the neck pickups. Somehow it's just become my guitar sound. This one hasn't left my side since April 2009. You can hear it on "Compliments," "Bartles & Jaymes," and on lots of the *Infinite Arms* record. I've never been much for black guitars with gold hardware, but the rusting on this one is also gorgeous to me.

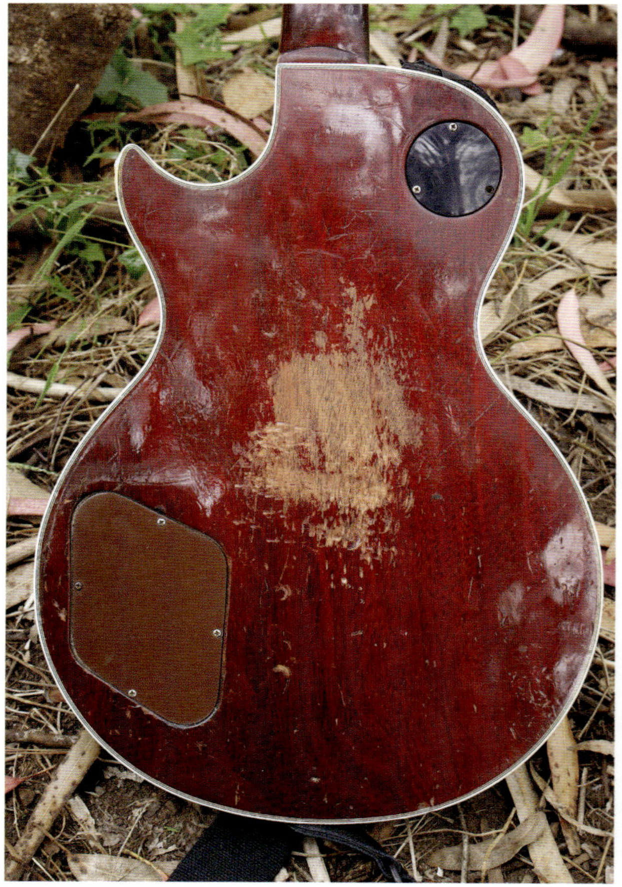

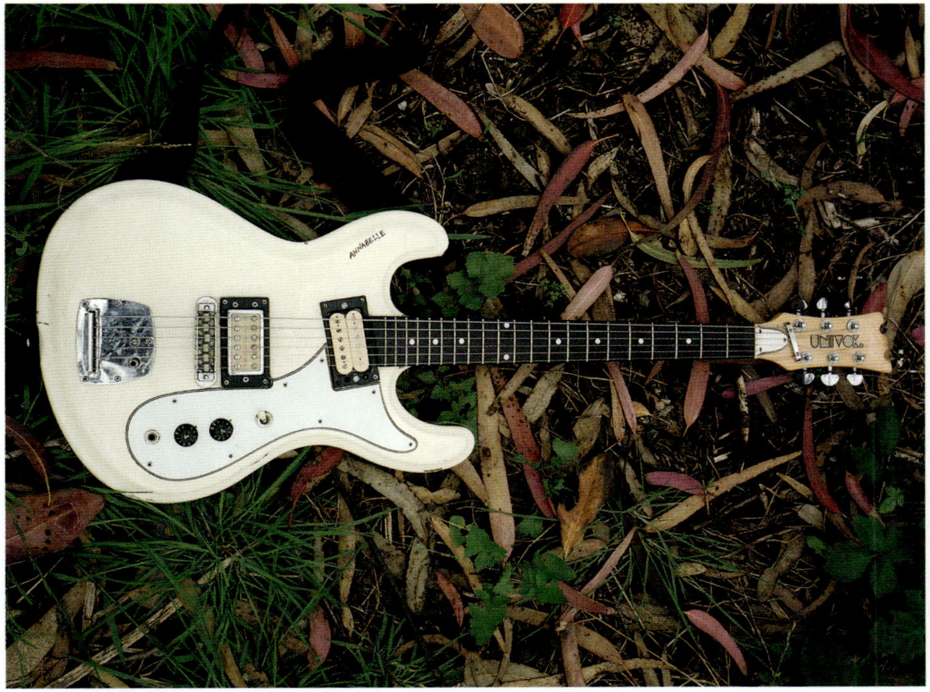

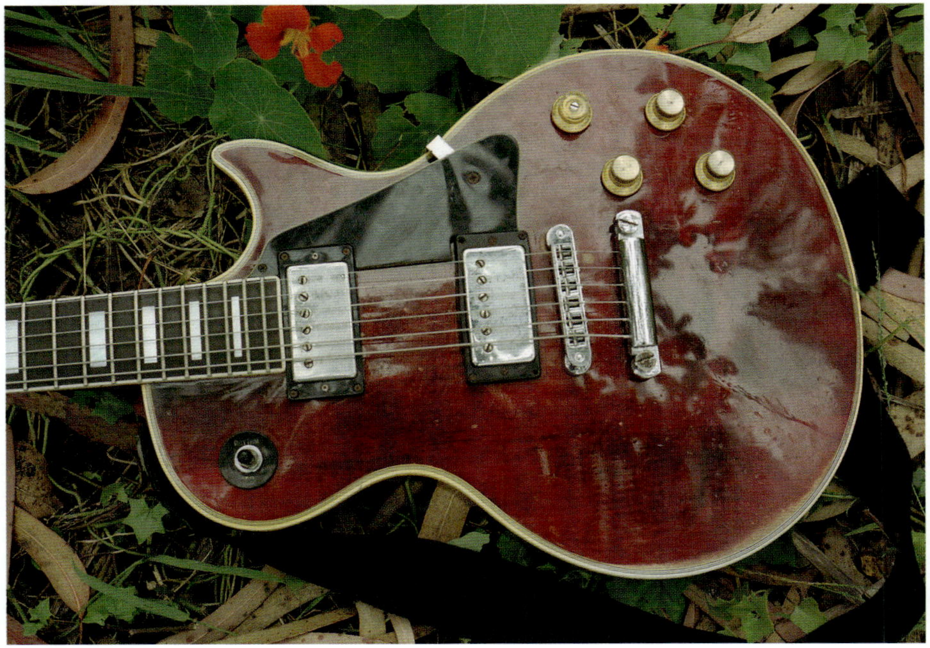

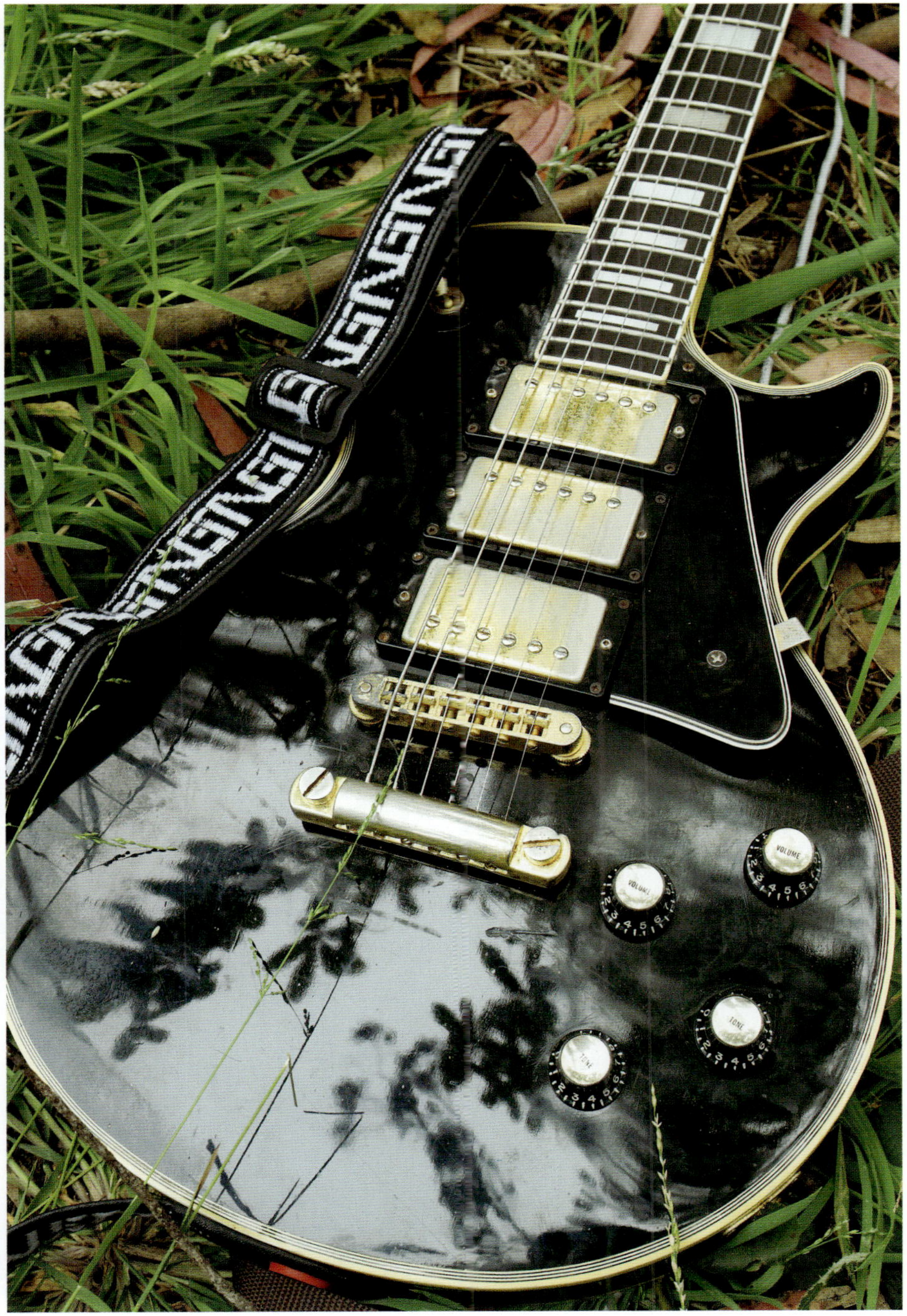
VOLUME
TONE

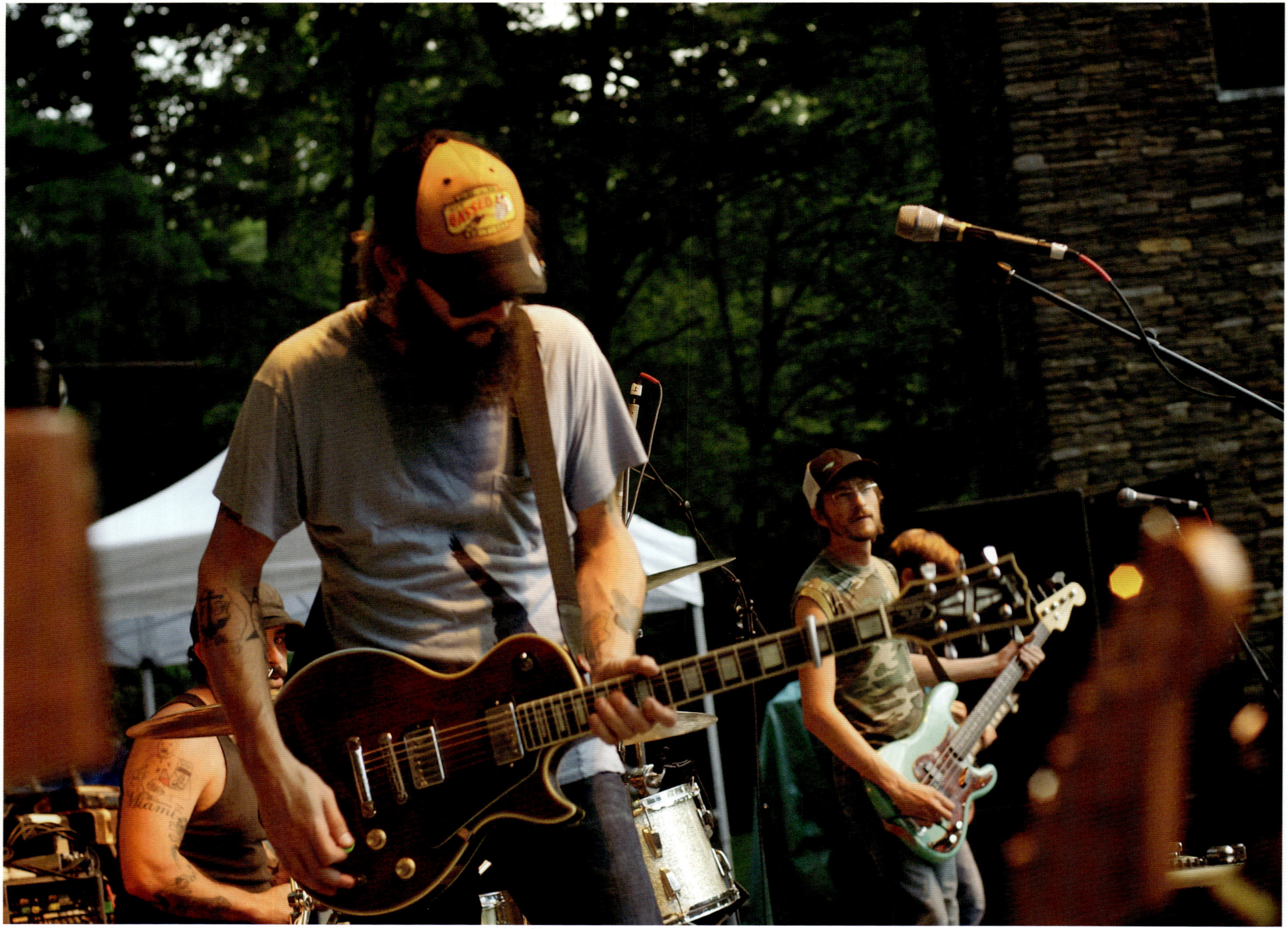

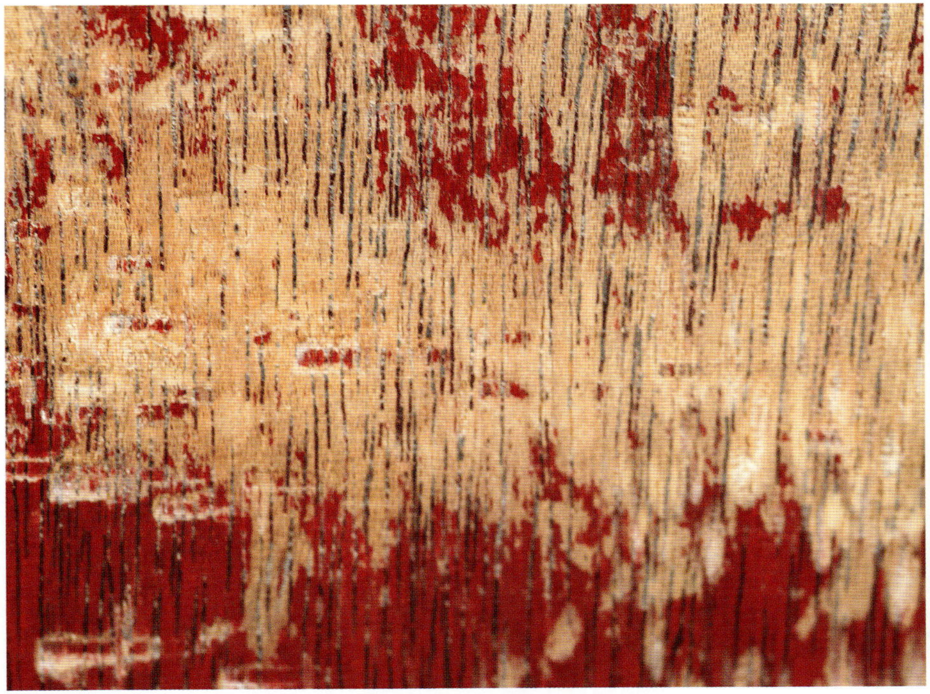

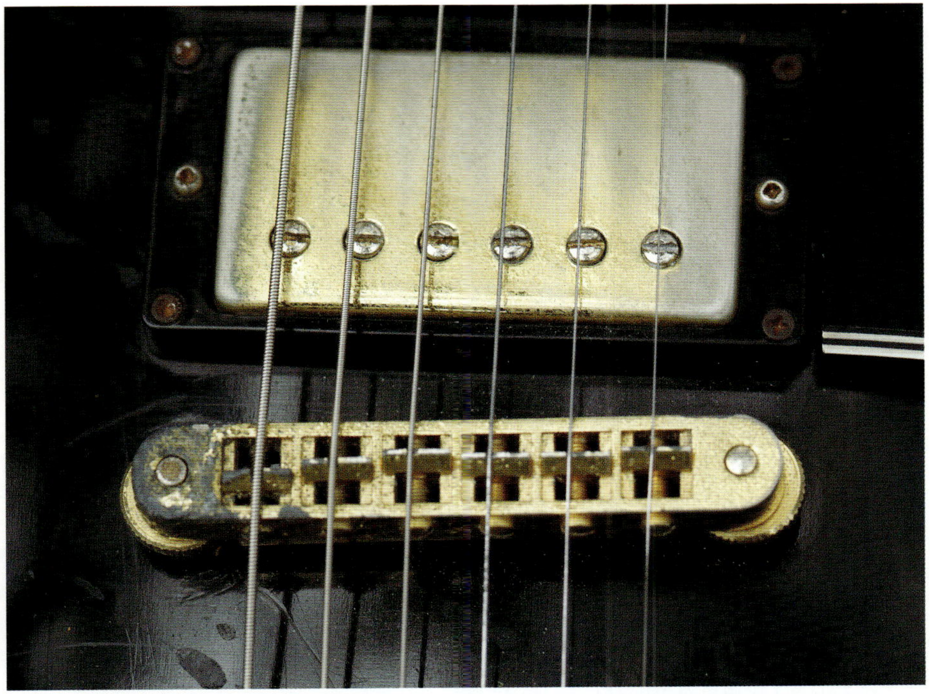

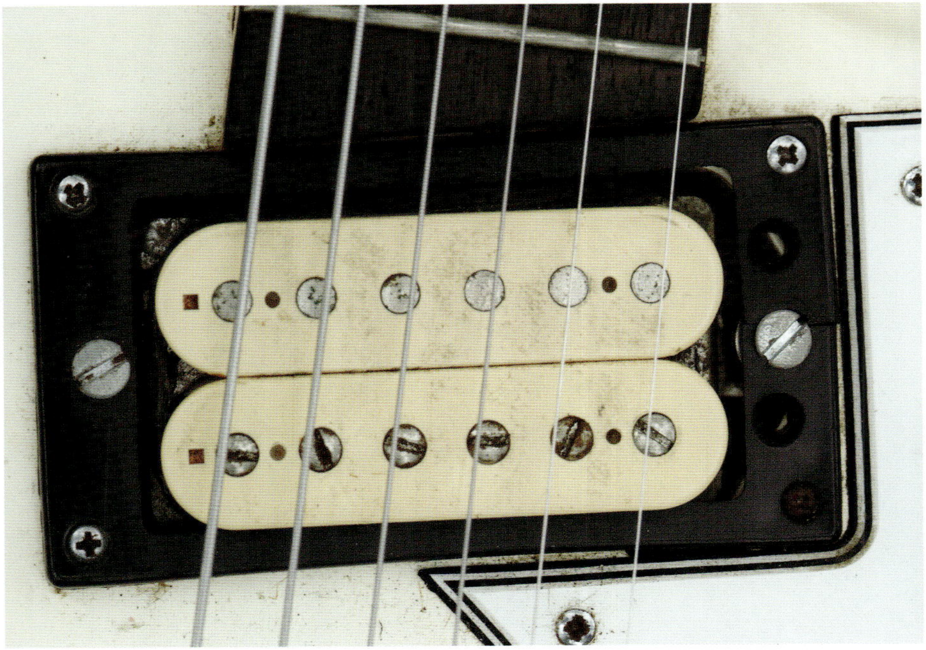

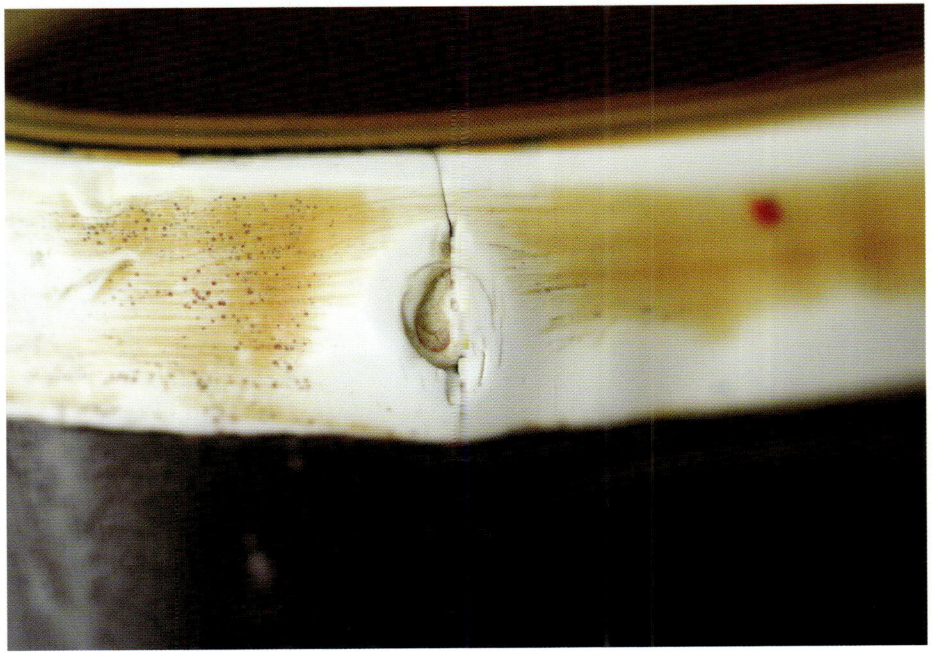

JEFF TWEEDY

Wilco
Gibson SG guitar

1. What's your history with the guitar?
2. Why this model?
3. What if any recordings/songs/tours has it been on?
4. Any war stories relating to the gear?
5. What song caused all those deep wounds or markings?
6. How does it feel to play it?

1. Picked it up at a store in '98 and it just felt right
2. That style of guitar has always felt comfortable
3. On all tours and too many songs to list
4. Normal wear and tear
5. "Spiders"
6. Effortless

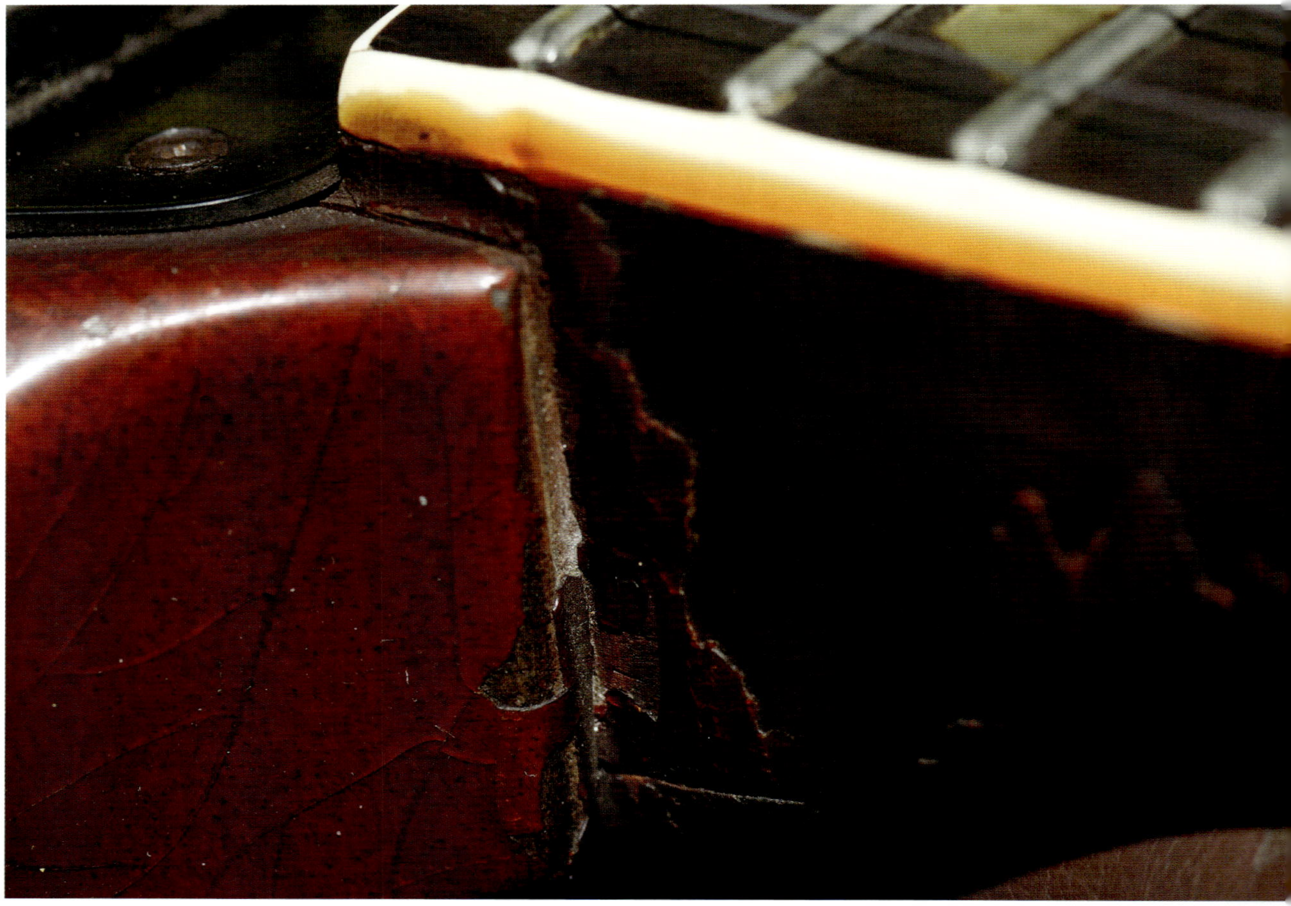

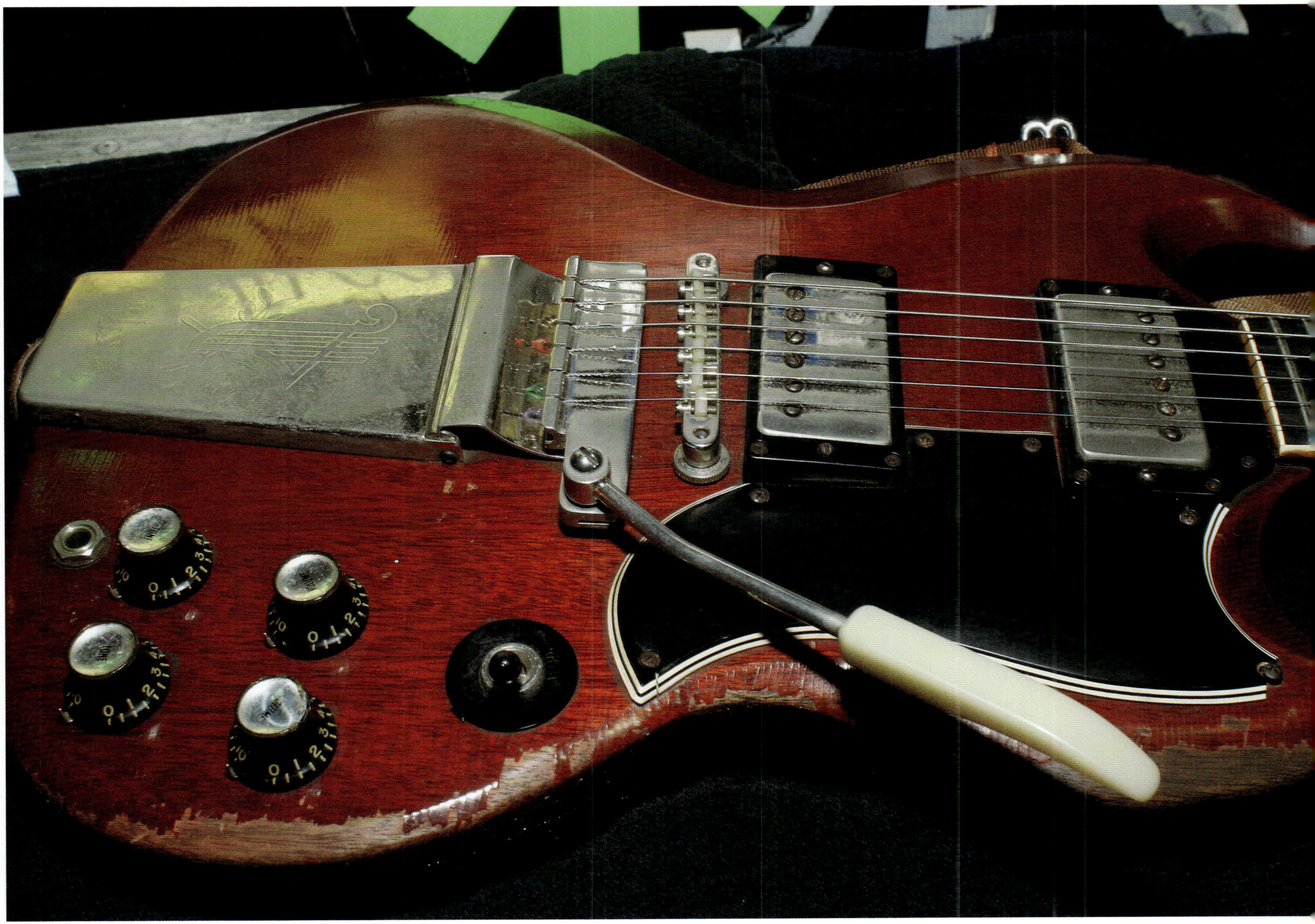

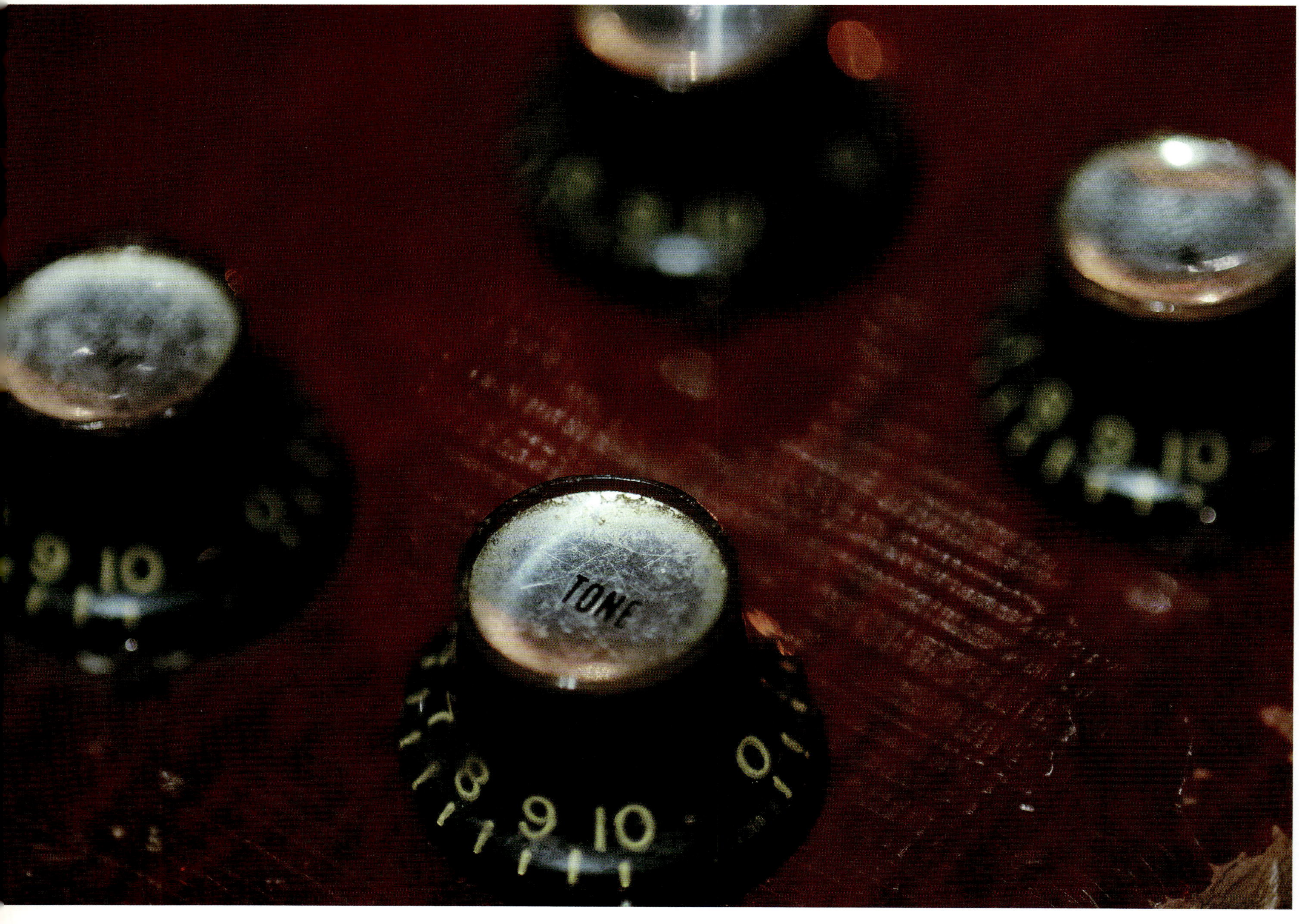
TONE

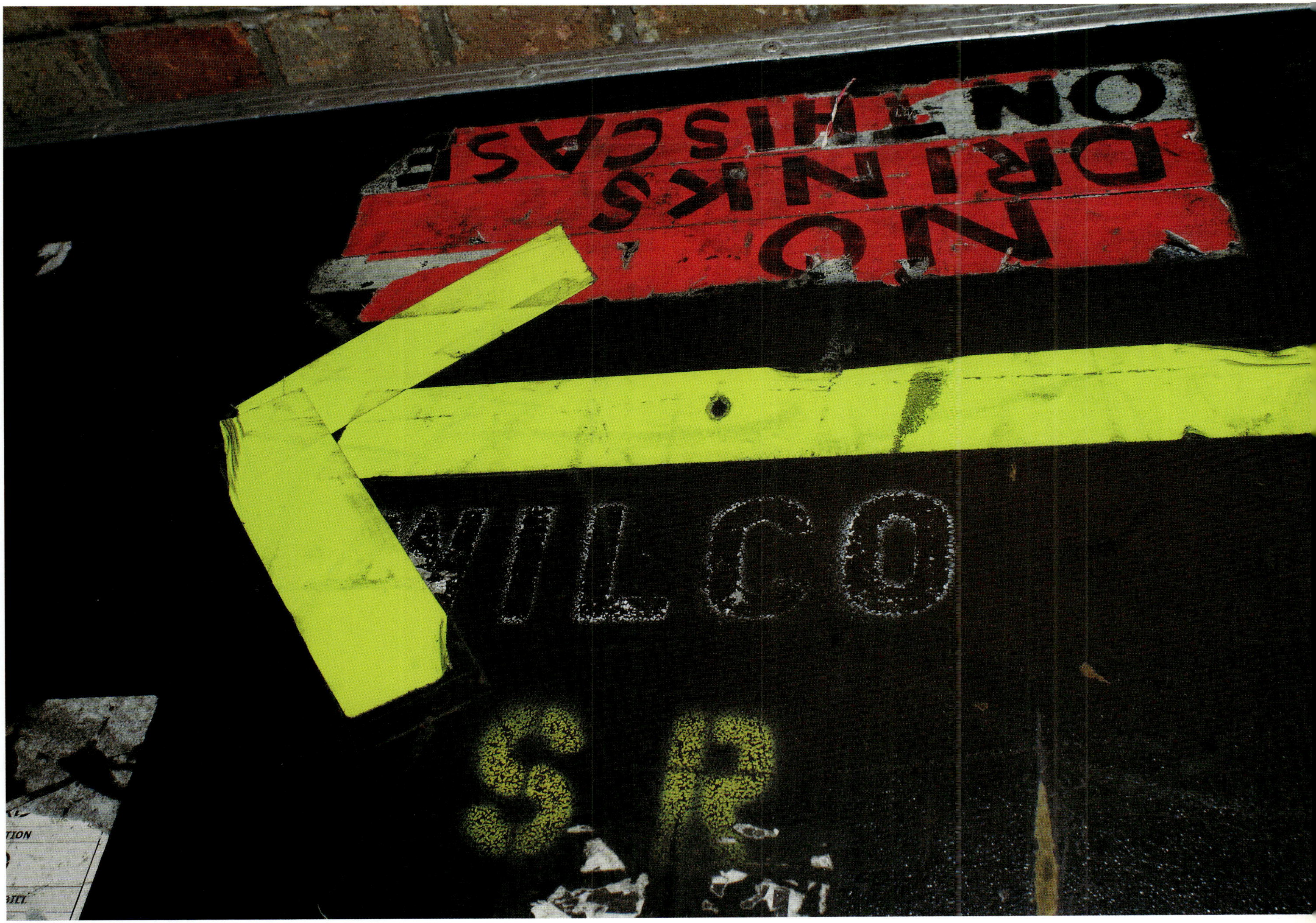
NO
DRINKS
ON THIS CAS
WILCO
SR

TIM KERR

Big Boys, Poison 13, Monkeywrench, Lord High Fixers
1960s Gretsch Rally guitar

A good friend of mine wanted to trade this guitar to me for an old red Silvertone/Danelectro that I had. I thought it wasn't a very fair deal for him, but he *really* wanted that red guitar.

At first I thought the Rally looked cool, but wasn't all that into playing it, so it just sat around the house. When we started Lord High Fixers, I decided to play a guitar that I hadn't been playing and I picked it up. The combination of listening to lots of free jazz at that point in my life and the realization that I could actually control the feedback that was coming out of that guitar played a huge role in the way I was approaching the music I was playing, then and now.

When an instrument becomes an extension of your body/yourself, as opposed to a "tool" and you are armed with the knowledge that all sound is valid, it lifts all the rules. The guitar becomes something to express yourself with that now has no rules or boundaries. It's not a guitar anymore; it's something to use to find and get sounds from. It gets used 360 degrees, from the headstock to the tail piece, which means that yes . . . things get modified. The electrics were changed to either on or off with everything wide open. The spring in the whammy bar was "bolted" in so that it would not pop out, and parts of the body were reinforced because I would really push/pull and force the sound out.

The guitar is signed by Bobby Seale and Eldridge Cleaver. They came to the university where I worked to do a book signing, and when I heard that they were coming, I commented to friends that *they* should be the ones signing guitars. When the day came I waited in line with my paint pen and they signed it. Mr. Cleaver said, "I've never signed a guitar before."

You can hear it on the Lord High Fixer records, my favorites being *Is Your Club a Secret Weapon?* and *The Beginning of the End . . . the End of the Beginning!* Playing this guitar feels like celebrating life with an old friend.

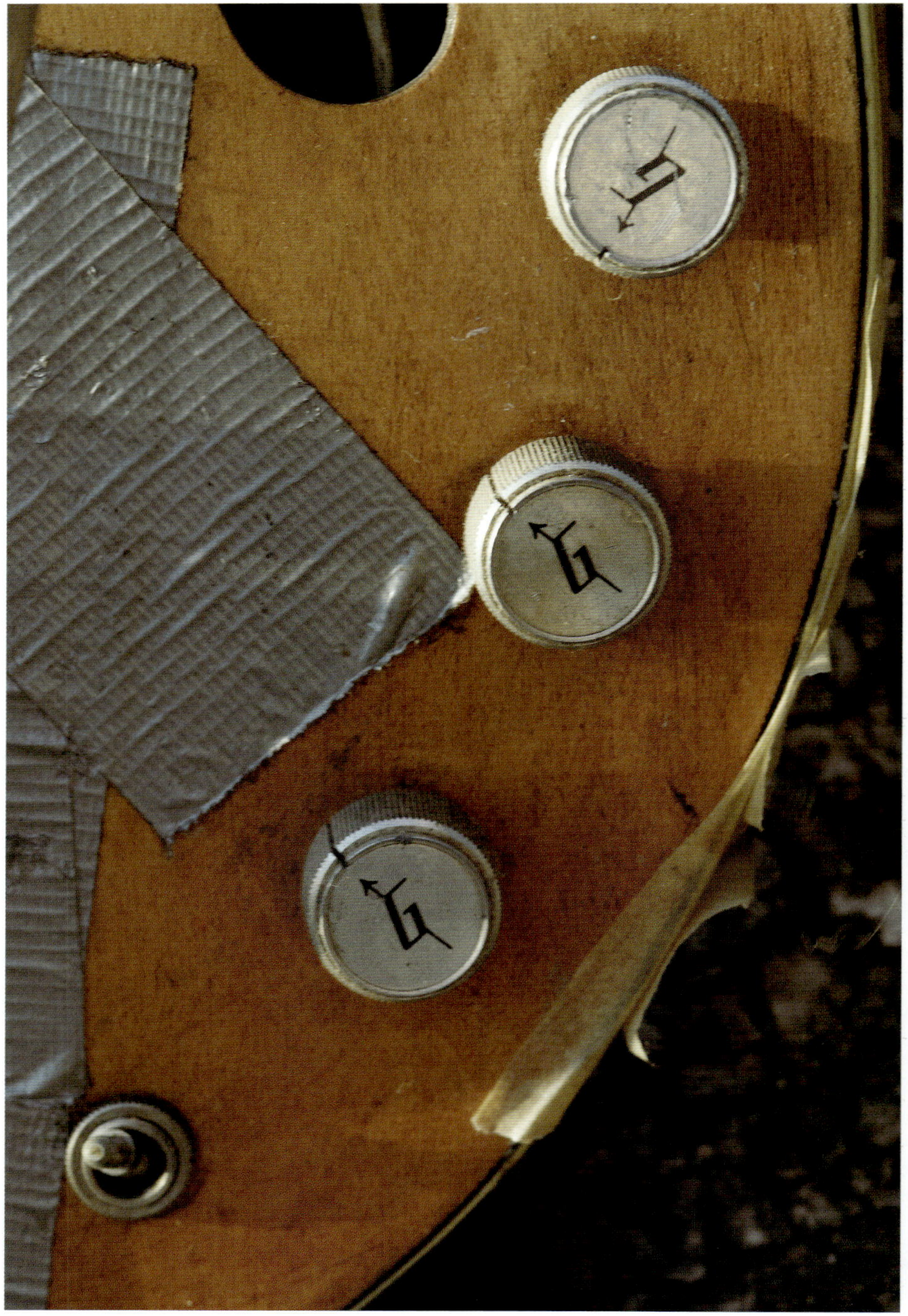

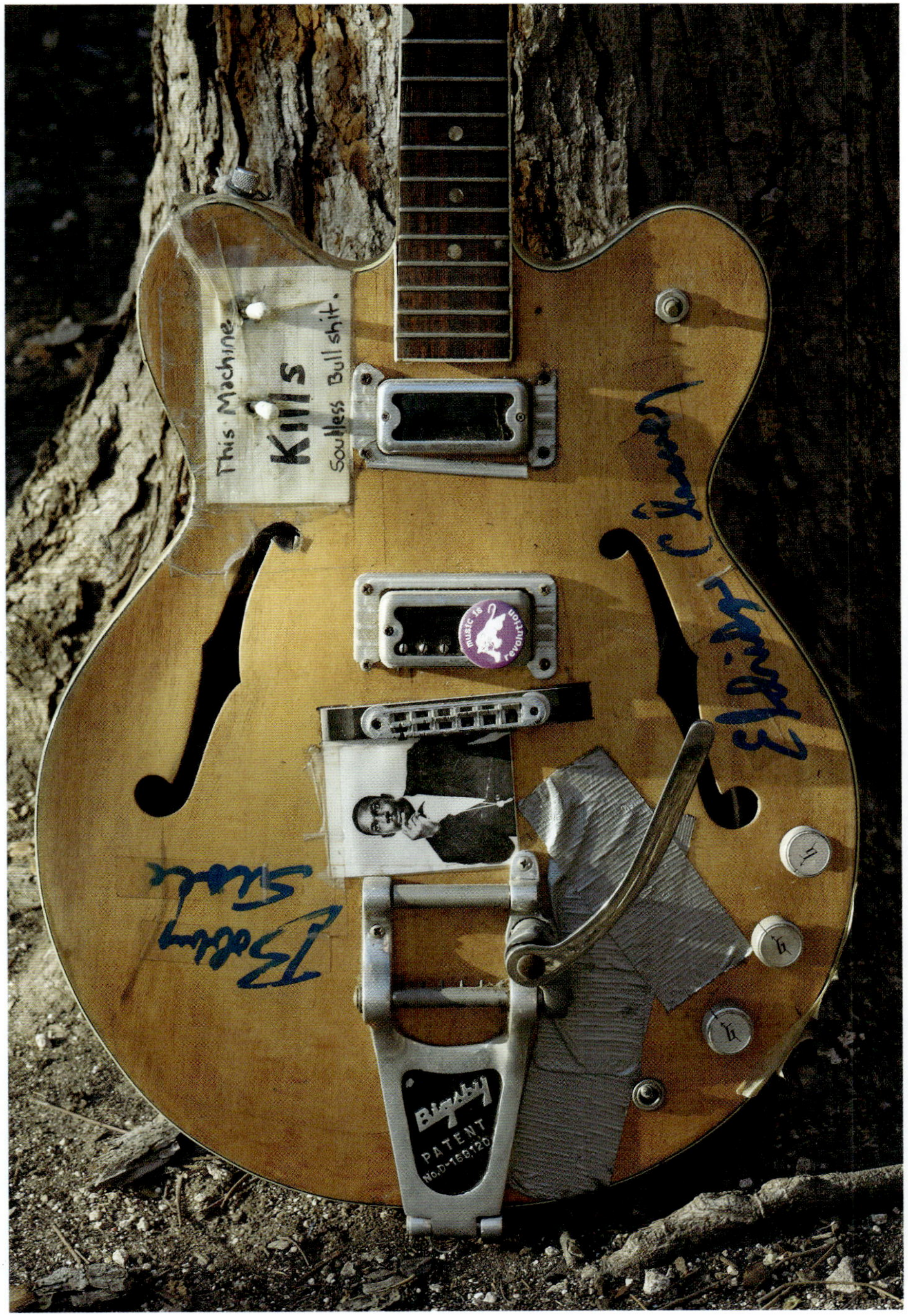
This Machine
Kills
Soulless Bull shit.
PATENT

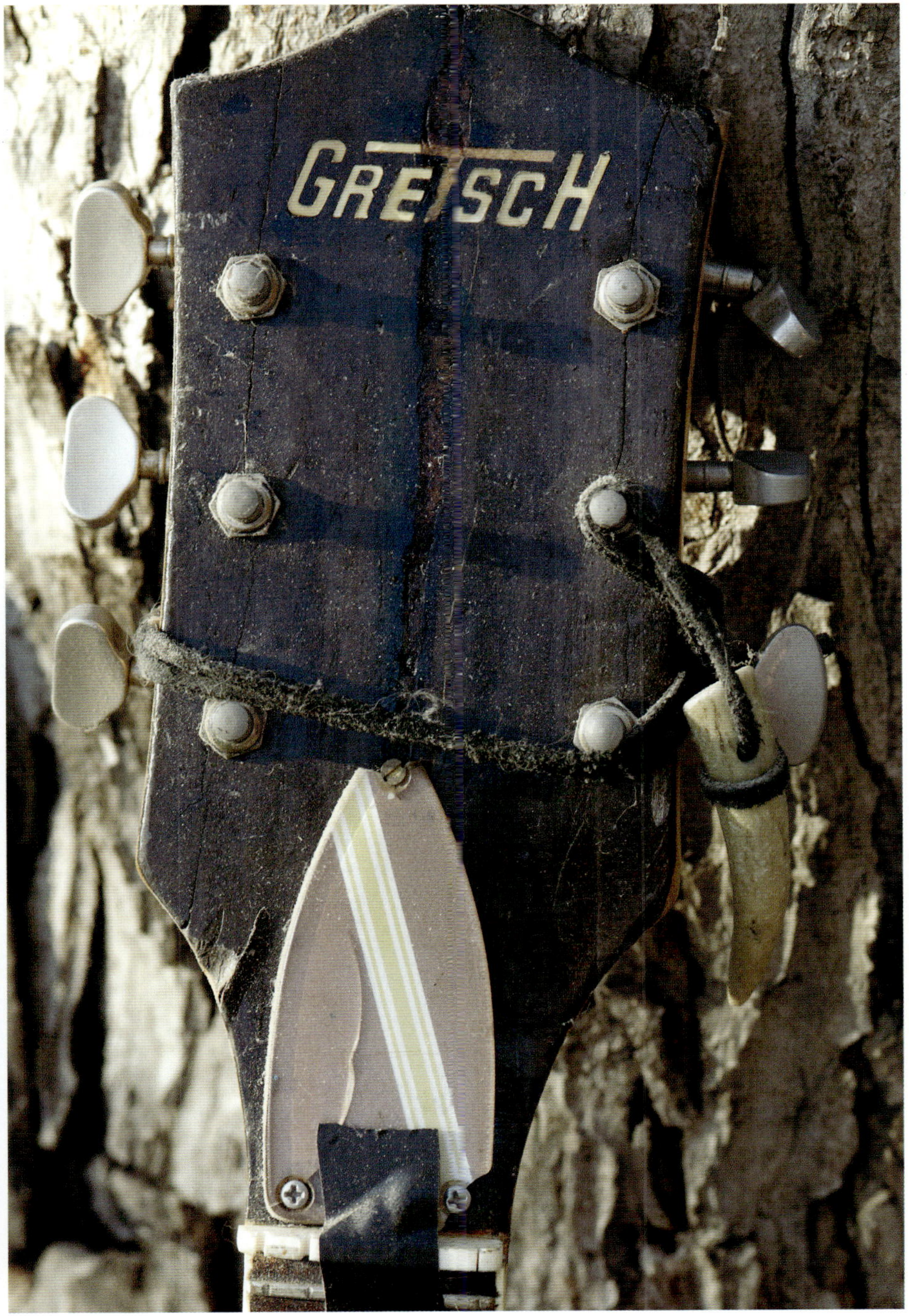
GRETSCH

THURSTON MOORE AND KIM GORDON

Sonic Youth

1959 Fender Jazzmaster guitar
1961 Fender Jazzmaster guitar
1965 Fender Jazzmaster guitar
1966 Fender Jaguar guitar
1980s Gibson Sonex guitar
1970s Epiphone Thunderbird bass

The gold 1959 Jazzmaster was a gift to Thurston from Patti Smith after the big gear theft of 1999. [The band's touring equipment was stolen from a Ryder truck in Orange County, California, in 1999. Only four pieces of equipment have been recovered to date.] I gave Thurston the stickers with various phrases in the Japanese Osaka dialect. In the last few years, this guitar has been used mainly to play the song "Express-way to yr Skull."

The seafoam green Jazzmaster that Thurston is playing is one I bult for him in 2007 for the *Daydream Nation* concerts. It's a vintage 1965 rack on a new Warmoth body.

The black Jazzmaster is a '61 and has been around since about '99 and is Thurston's main axe for Sonic and side projects. It goes where he goes, and is subject to all manner of abuse (files, knitting needles, etc.) so if I haven't seen it for a while, it's often a bit "broken." When we start a Sonic tour, I usually need to give it some special attention to get it show-worthy again.

The blue 1965 is one of my favorites, and was also a post-gear-theft donation. This one's suffered the most onstage abuse of any Thurston guitar. It's most notably used for the anything-can-happen feedback freakout at the end of "Pattern Recognition." It would often end up stuck high in some lighting truss and once dropped about 12 feet off the stage in Dublin. Fortunately, one of the security guys found and returned the big chunk of headstock that broke off, so we were able to glue it up and get it back into rock action.

Probably the most unique guitar to get stolen in '99 was a four-string beast called "The Drifter." It was a Gibson Sonex that had all the frets pulled out, and had just four thick strings tuned to pretty high tension, played with drumsticks by Thurston for the song "Eric's Trip." I had this neck and body around and got the idea to re-create The Drifter so they could play "Eric's Trip" again. This was the first guitar I built for Sonic Youth. Since then, I've done a couple more that are a little nicer.

The red 1966 Jaguar is one of the few original Sonic guitars that didn't get ripped off in '99, and it has a lot of the classic Sonic modifications. In my opinion, it's the best surviving historical example of their original batch of axes. Back in the '90s it was mainly played by Thurston on songs like "Silver Rocket." Since then, Thurston has gone on to almost exclusively Jazzmasters, and this has become one of Kim's main jams.

This early 1970s Thunderbird bass also thankfully didn't get ripped off in '99. It was Kim's main bass during the *Daydream Nation* era and came in handy when they revised those songs in 2007. She had it inscribed, most of it still intact, by John Brannon, the singer of Laughing Hyenas (and ex-Negative Approach), who toured with Sonic Youth in the late '80s. When Sonic supported Neil Young in San Francisco, the local union crew broke off the headstock while pushing a rack of guitars through a too low doorway. Whoops! Careful guys! It has been nicely repaired and is one of the most rockin' basses around.

—Eric Baecht

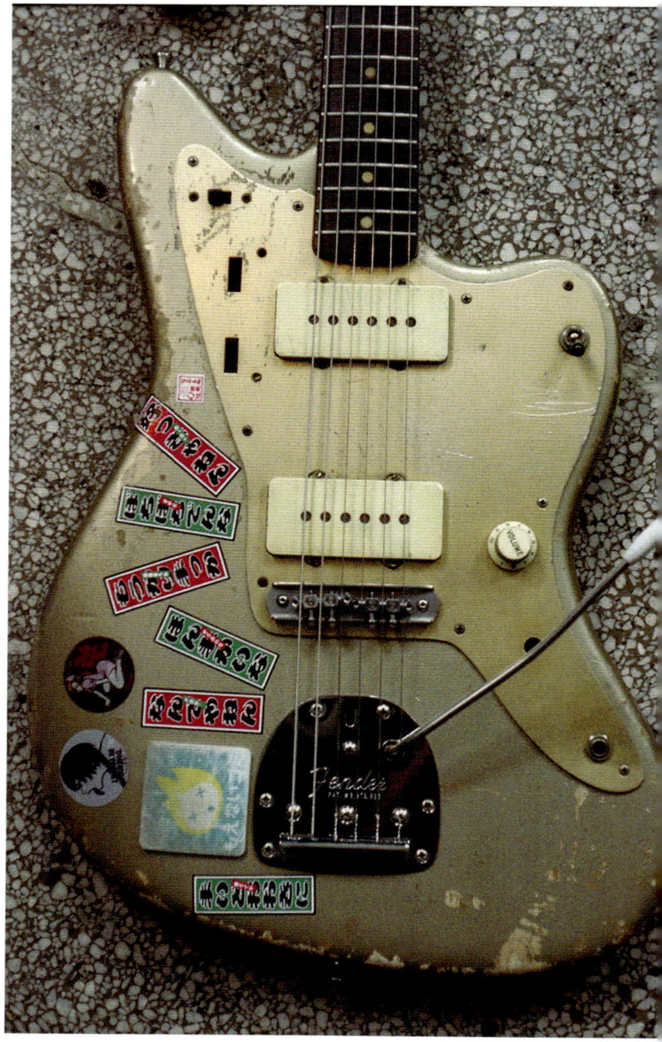

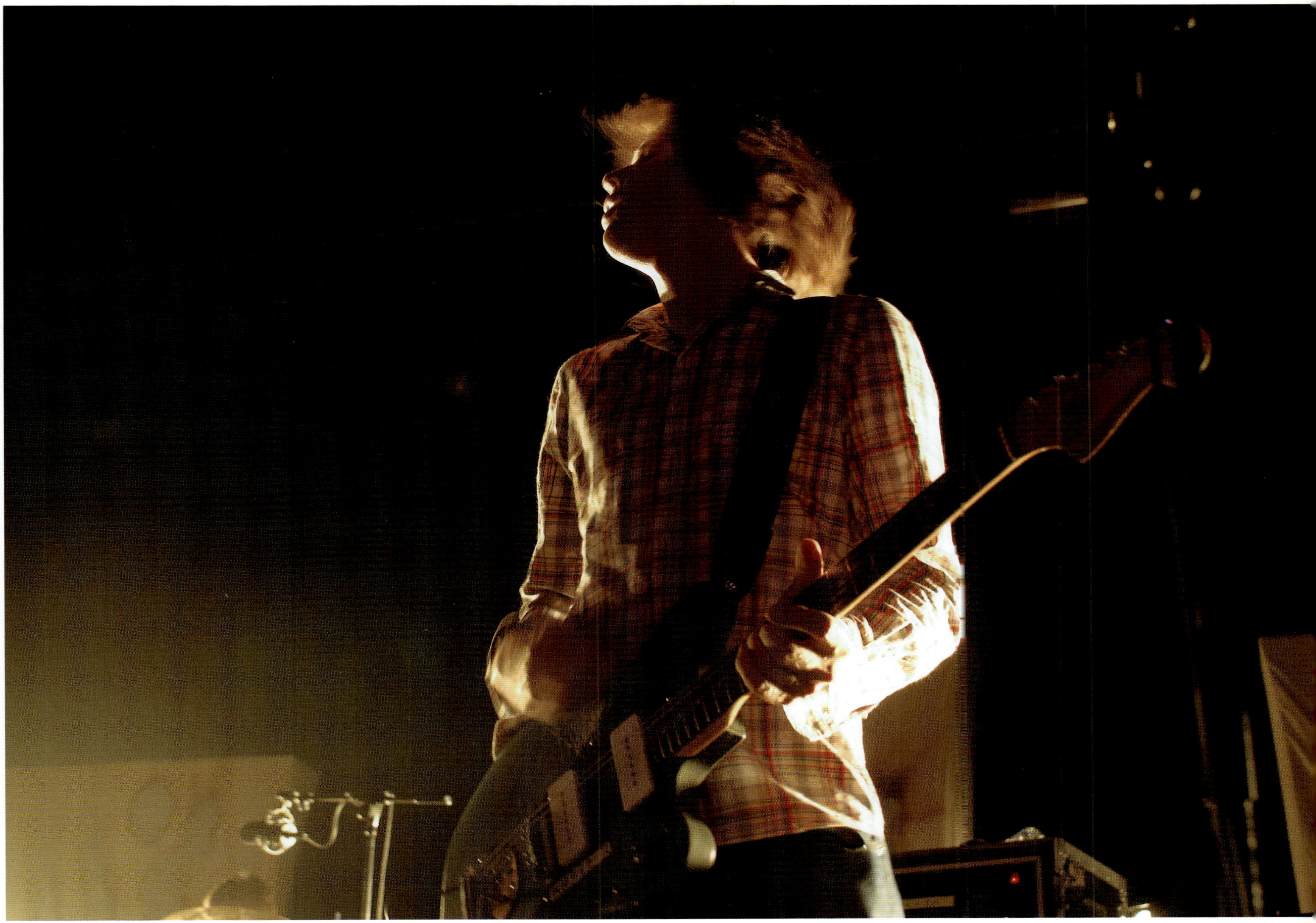

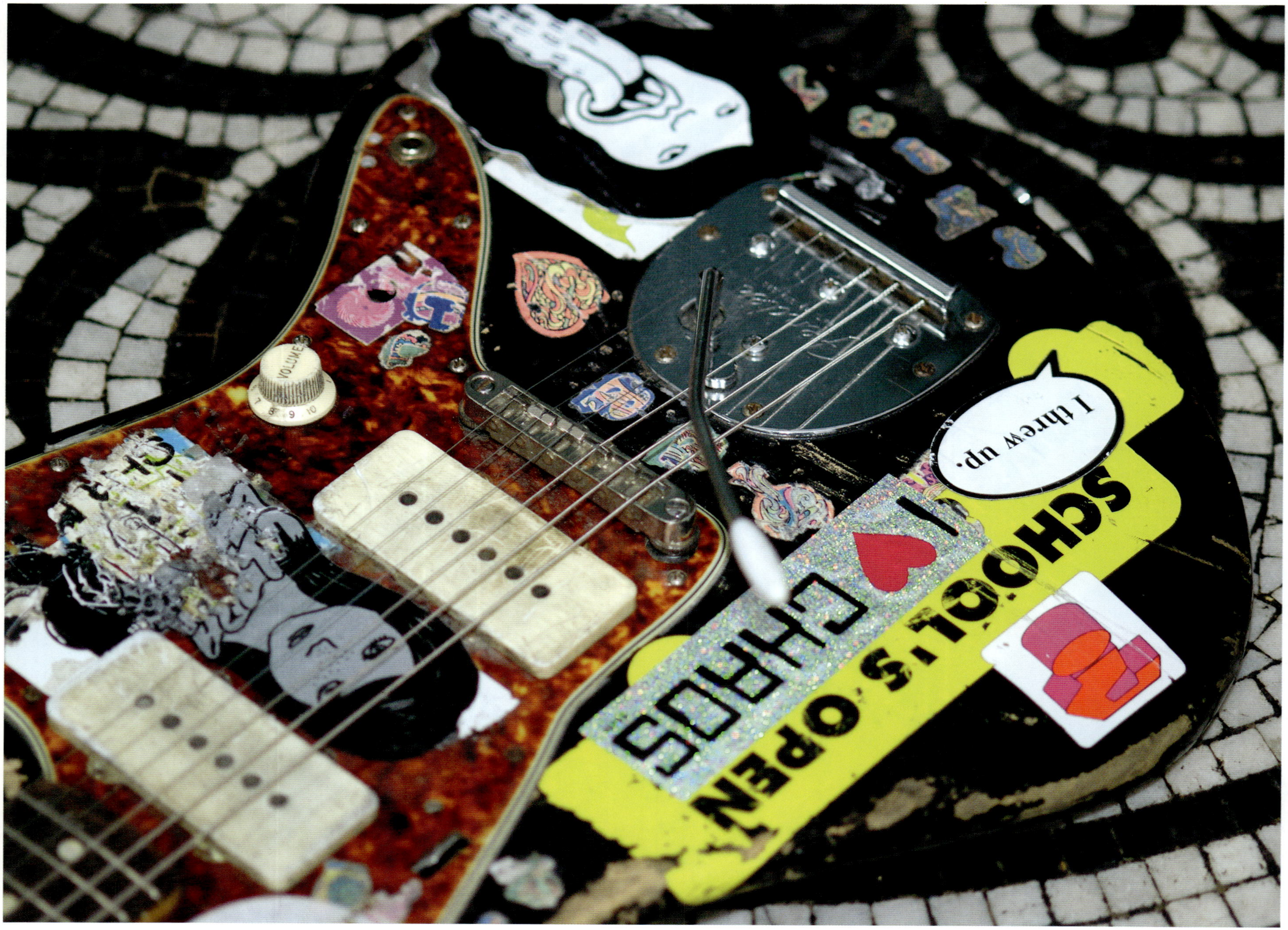
VOLUME
I threw up.
SCHOOL'S OPEN
I ♥ CHAOS

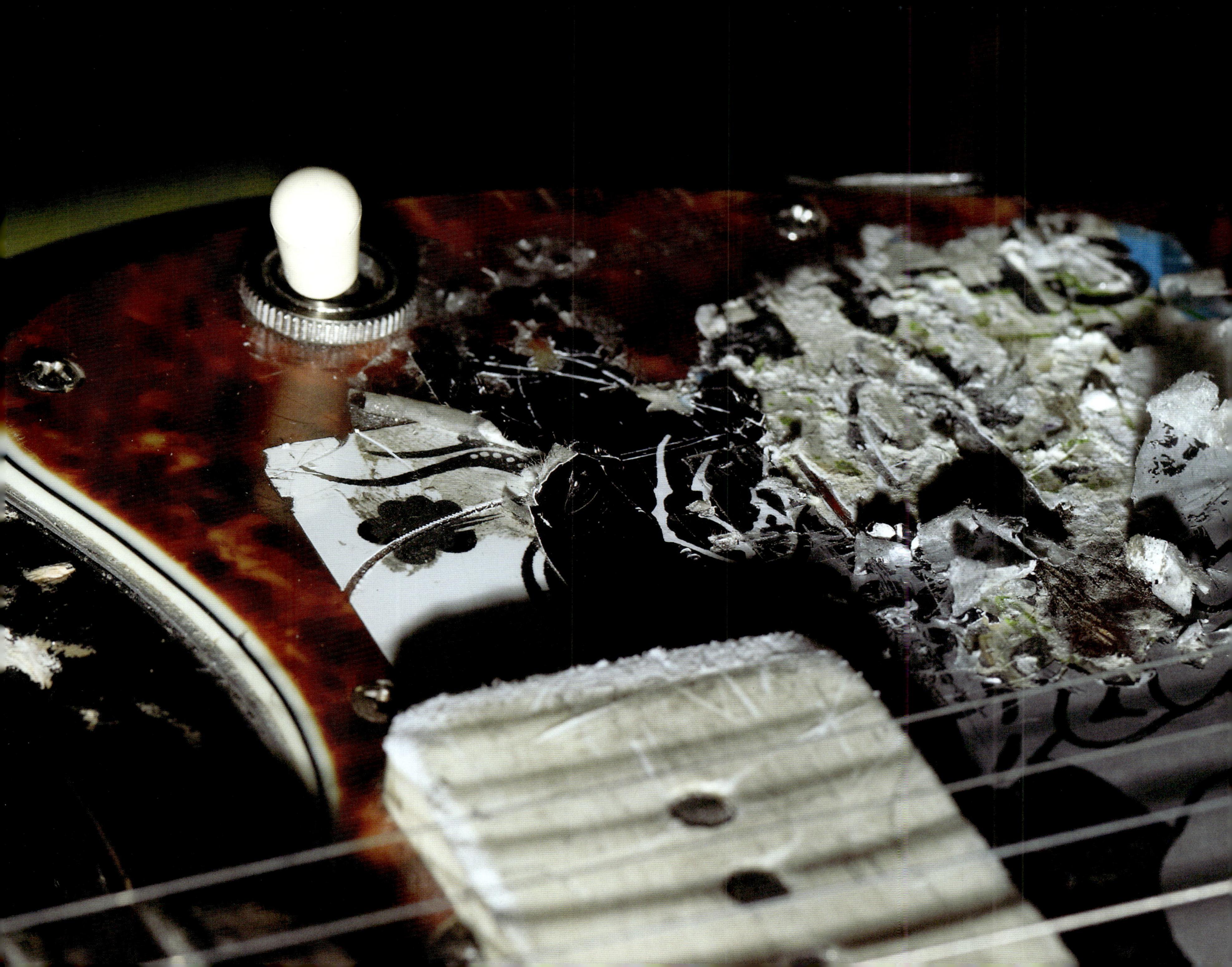

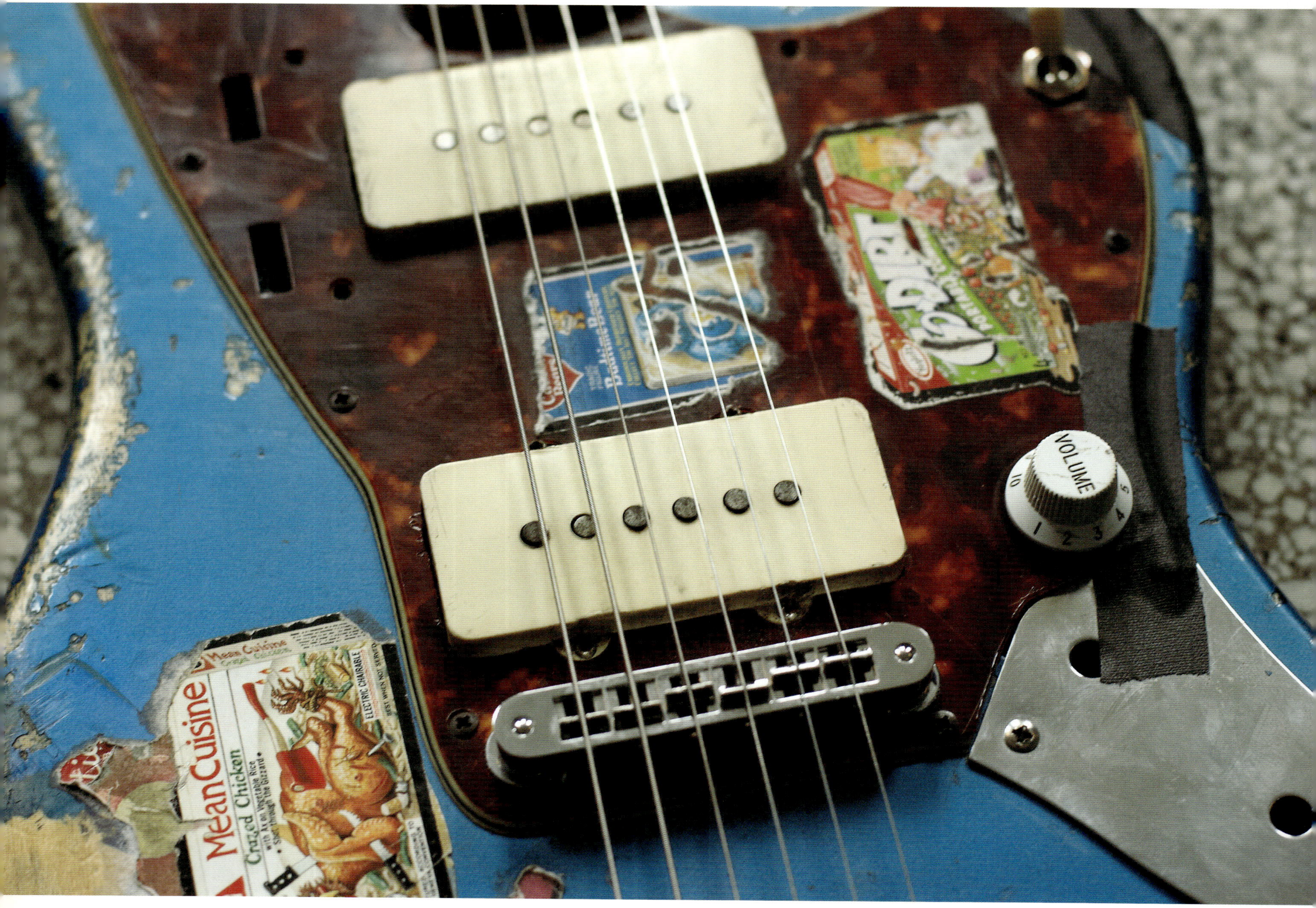
VOLUME
MeanCuisine
Crazed Chicken
ELECTRIC CHAIRABLE

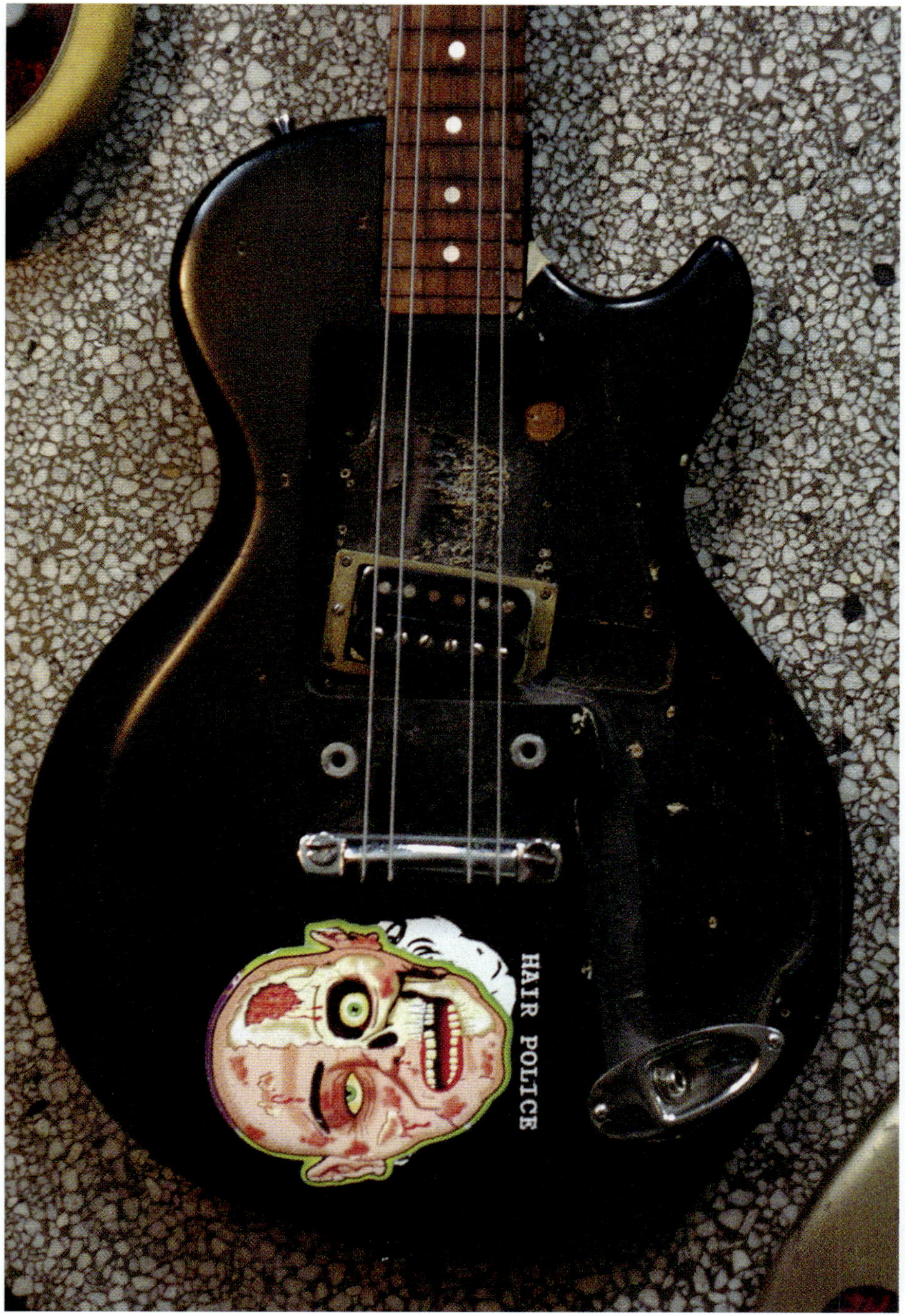
HAIR POLICE

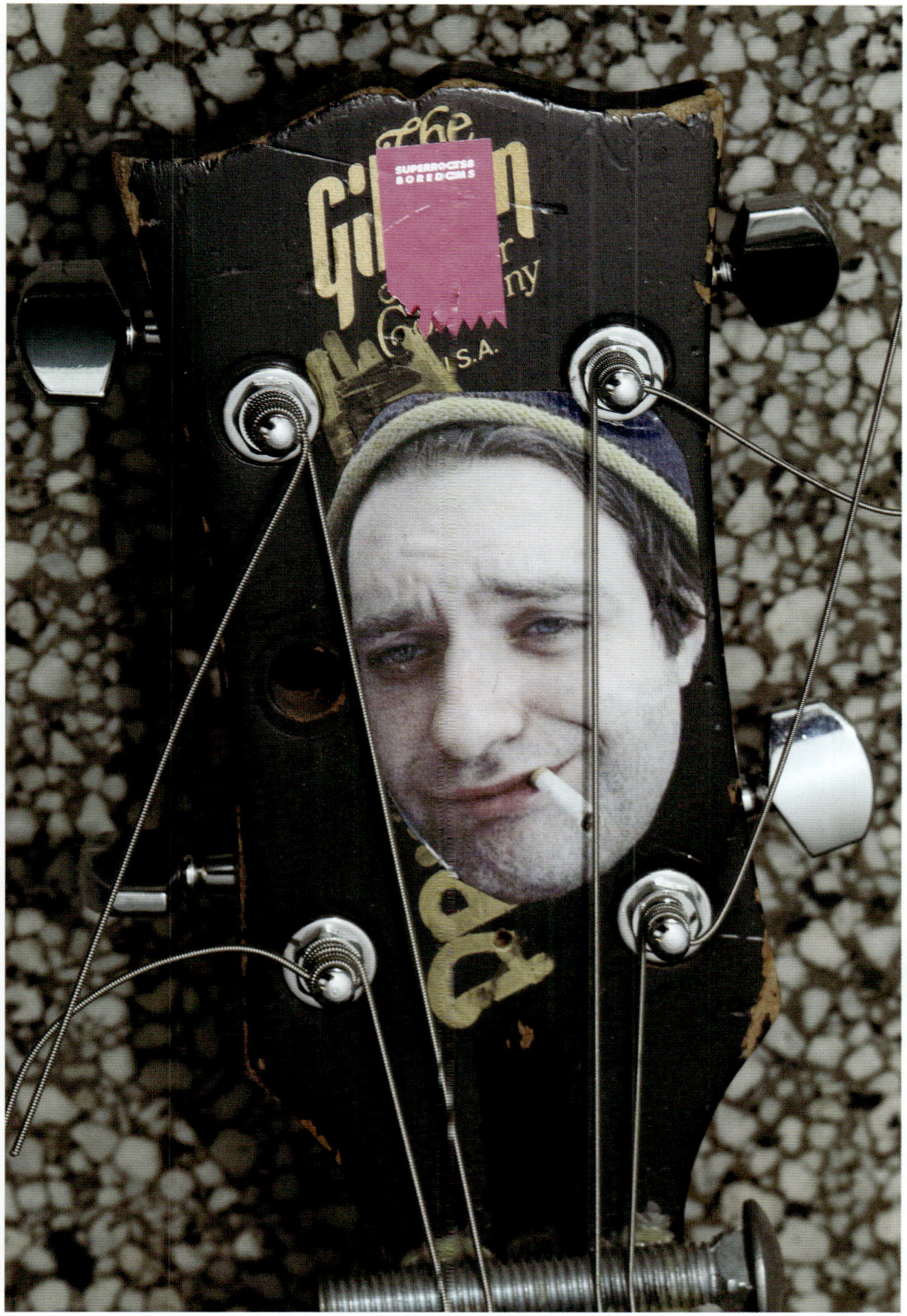

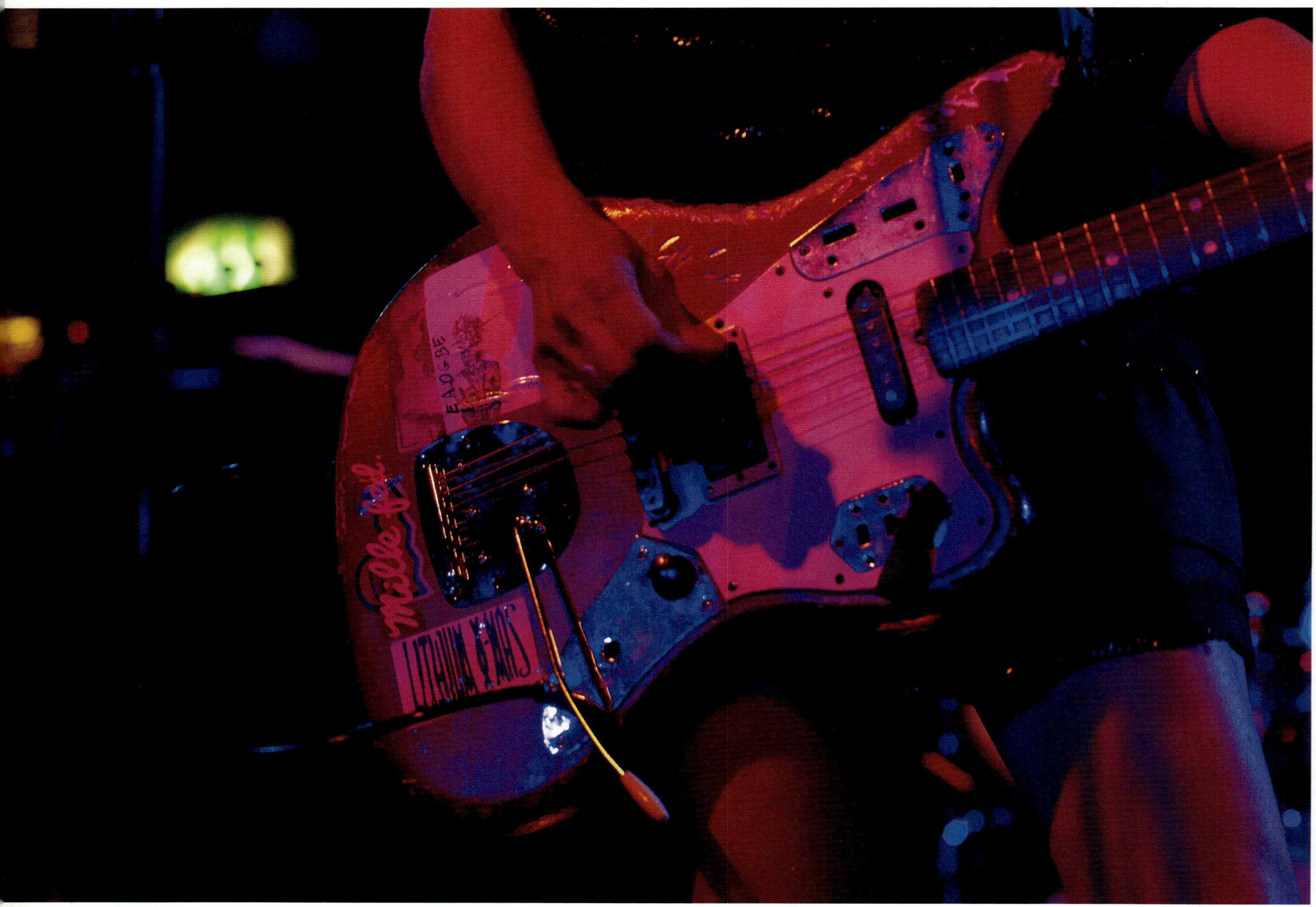
EADGBE
LITHIUM X-MAS

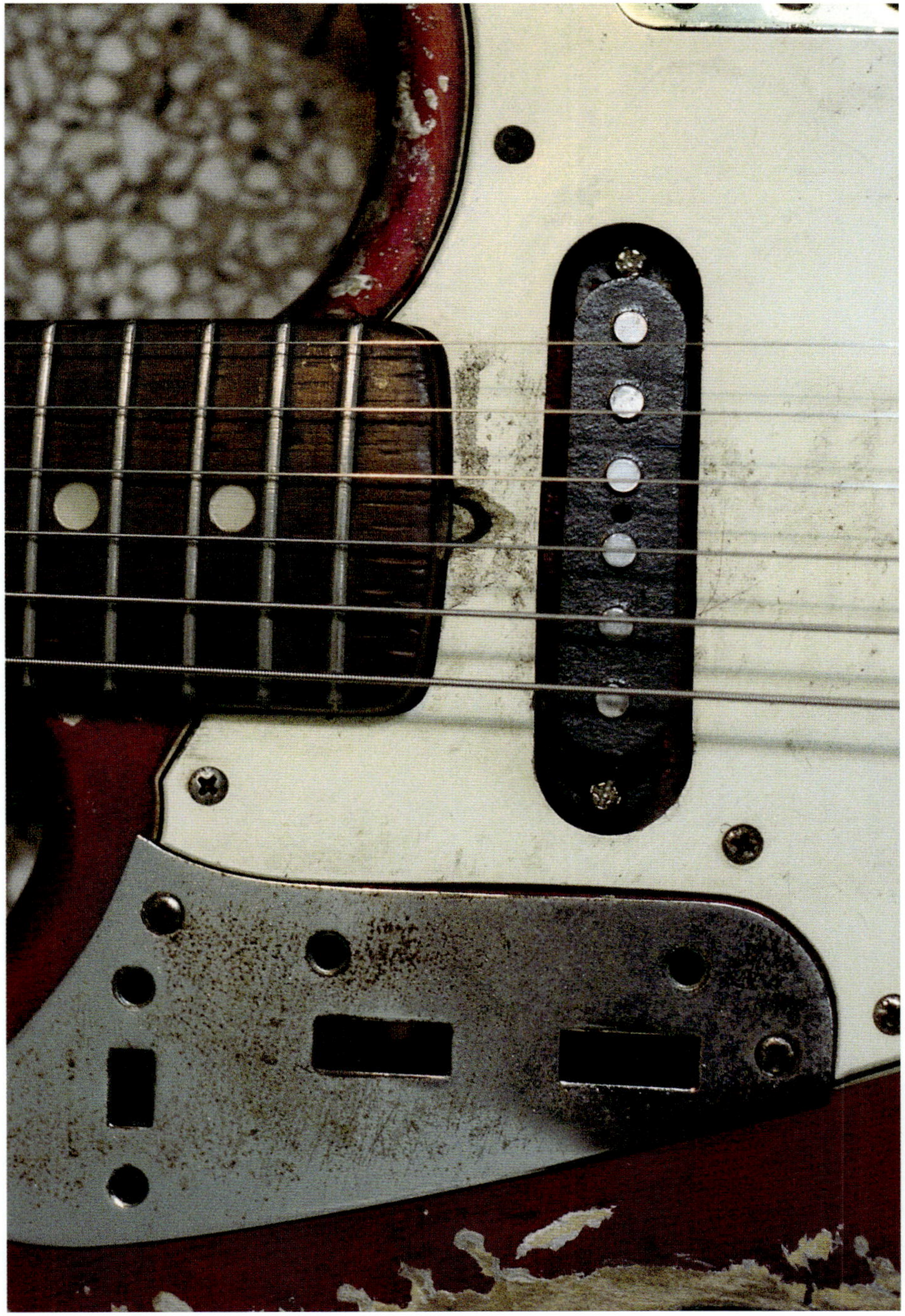

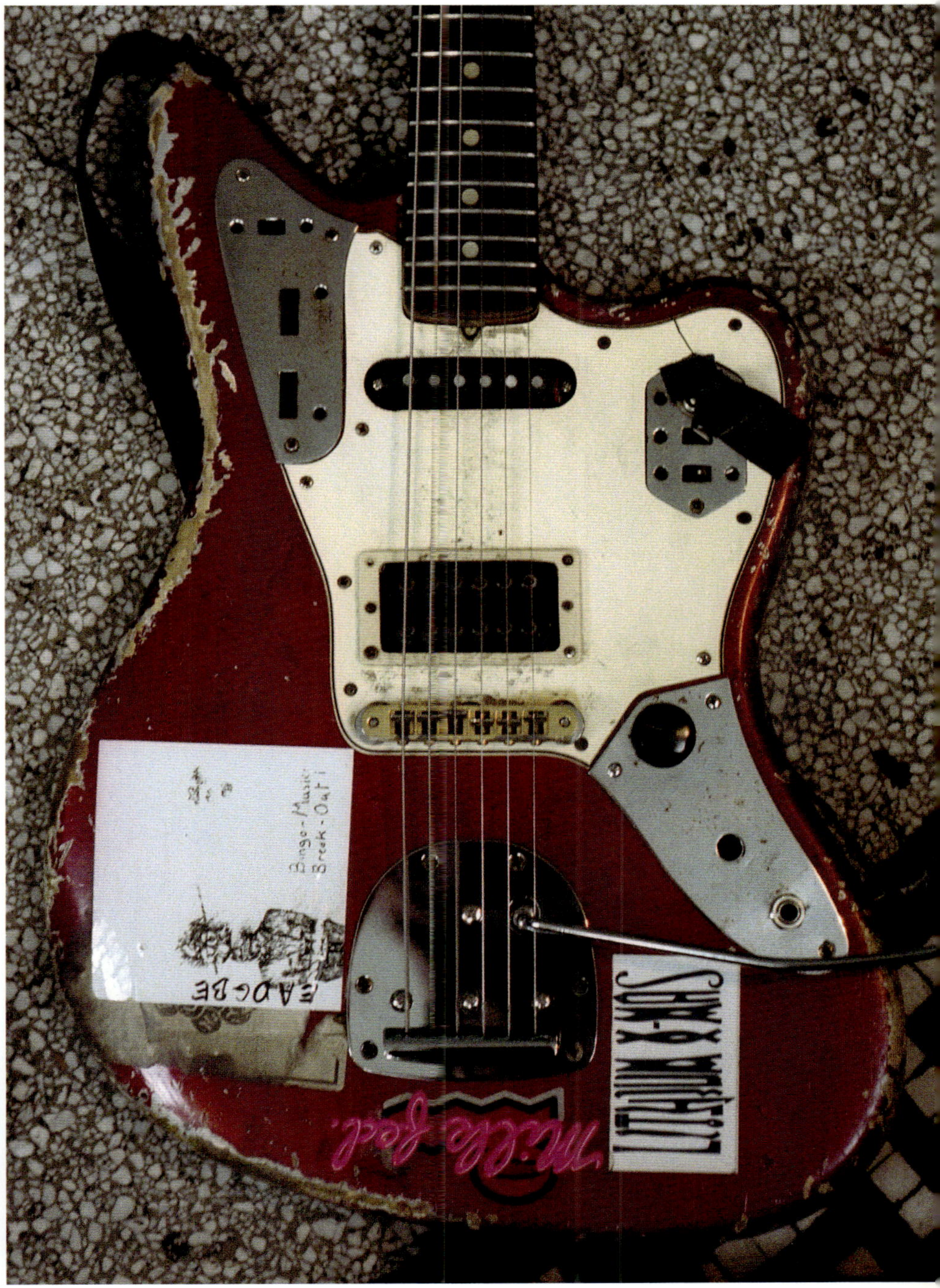
EADGBE

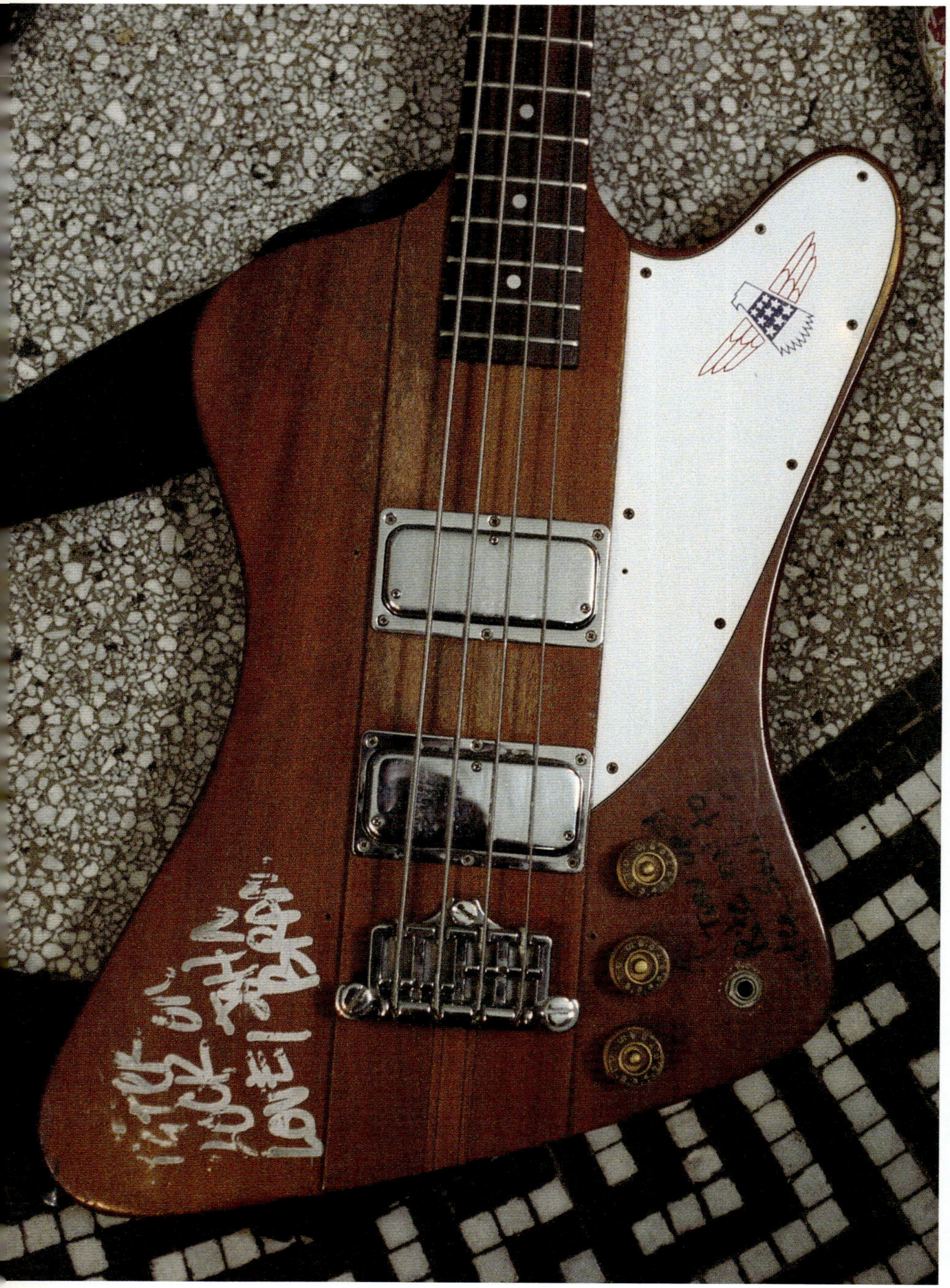

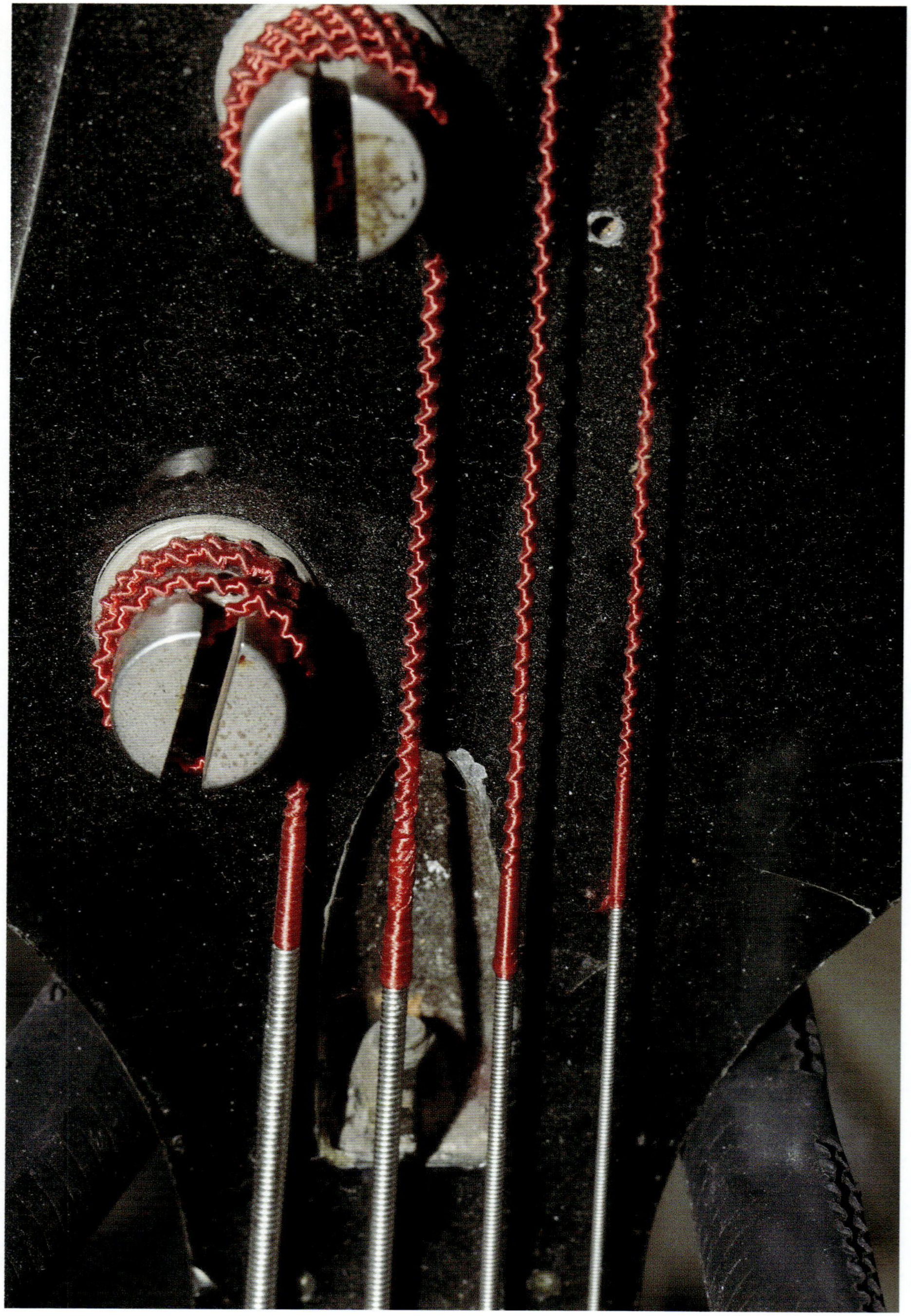

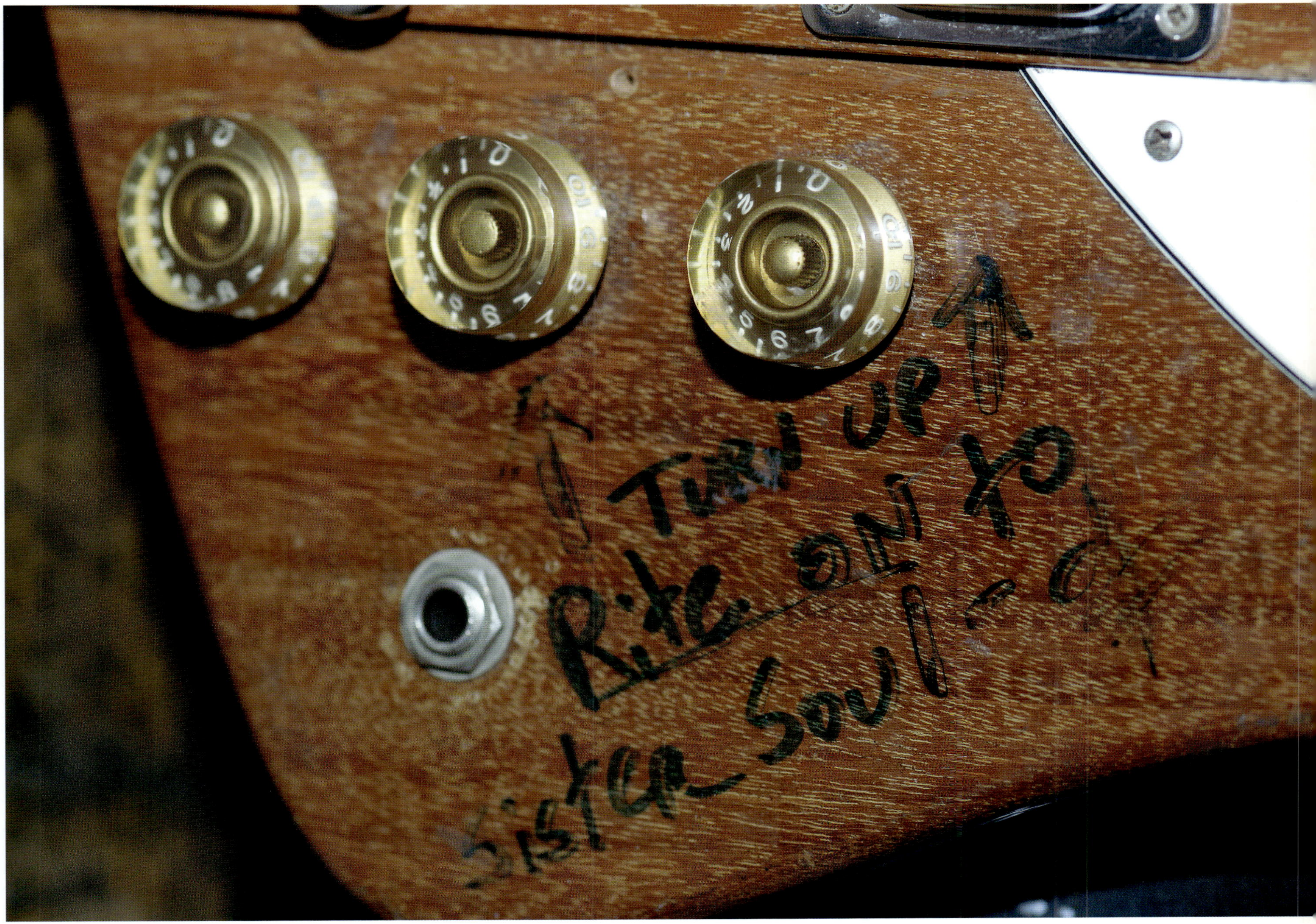
TURN UP
RiTe ON TO
SiSTER SOUL

LEE RANALDO

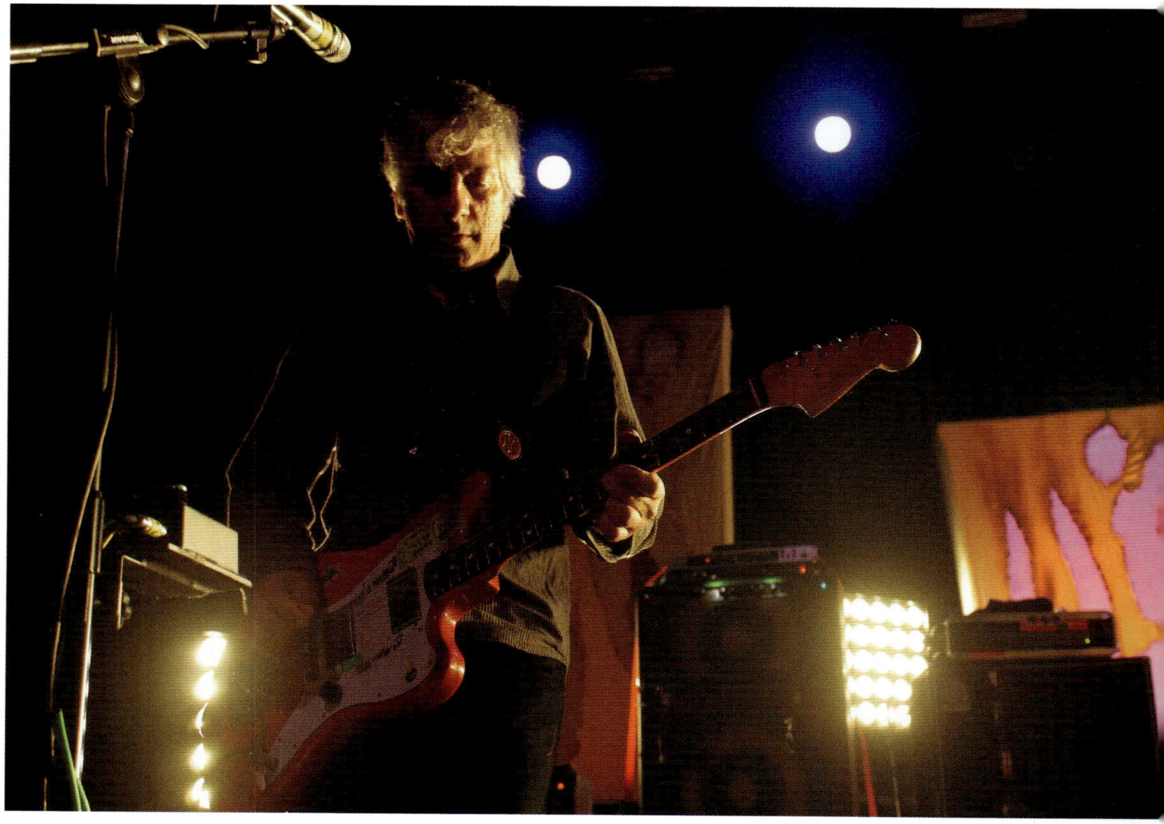

Sonic Youth

1999 Fender Jazzmaster guitar
1974 Fender Telecaster Deluxe guitar
1978 Travis Bean Standard guitar

The coral-colored U.S. Vintage Series Jazzmaster was purchased after the gear theft in 1999. It's heavily modified, with mid-'70s Fender wide-range humbuckers and straightforward wiring (pickups, toggle, volume, output). A Mustang bridge usually rounds out the Sonic Youth mod, "Jazzblaster" designation, but this guitar, like all Sonic's floating tremolo guitars, has since been modified with a newer design of bridge. This Jazzmaster is definitely a guitar in constant evolution. A lot of the seemingly cryptic writing on this guitar is various notes for some of Lee's solo guitar stuff. You can hear the guitar on "Rain on Tin," "Pattern Recognition," and "What We Know."

The Telecaster Deluxe with simplified wiring is one of the few Lee "pre-theft" instruments still around. It started in the Dirty era, and you can hear it on "Sugar Kane." According to Lee, "It was the sound of the Fender-designed humbucking pickups in the Tele Deluxe guitars of this era that first gave me the idea to install some in a Jazzmaster, thus creating the Sonic 'Jazzblaster' that I prefer today."

Lee has had this aluminum "Imron" neck Travis Bean Standard for about ten years. As with all of Sonic's guitars, it has had the simplified wiring mod done. It's on "Skip Tracer" and "Death Valley '69." Its headstock can often be seen being dragged around the stage surface for a droning sustain, as well as being attacked with a pair of Steve's bucket beaters.

—Matt Zivich

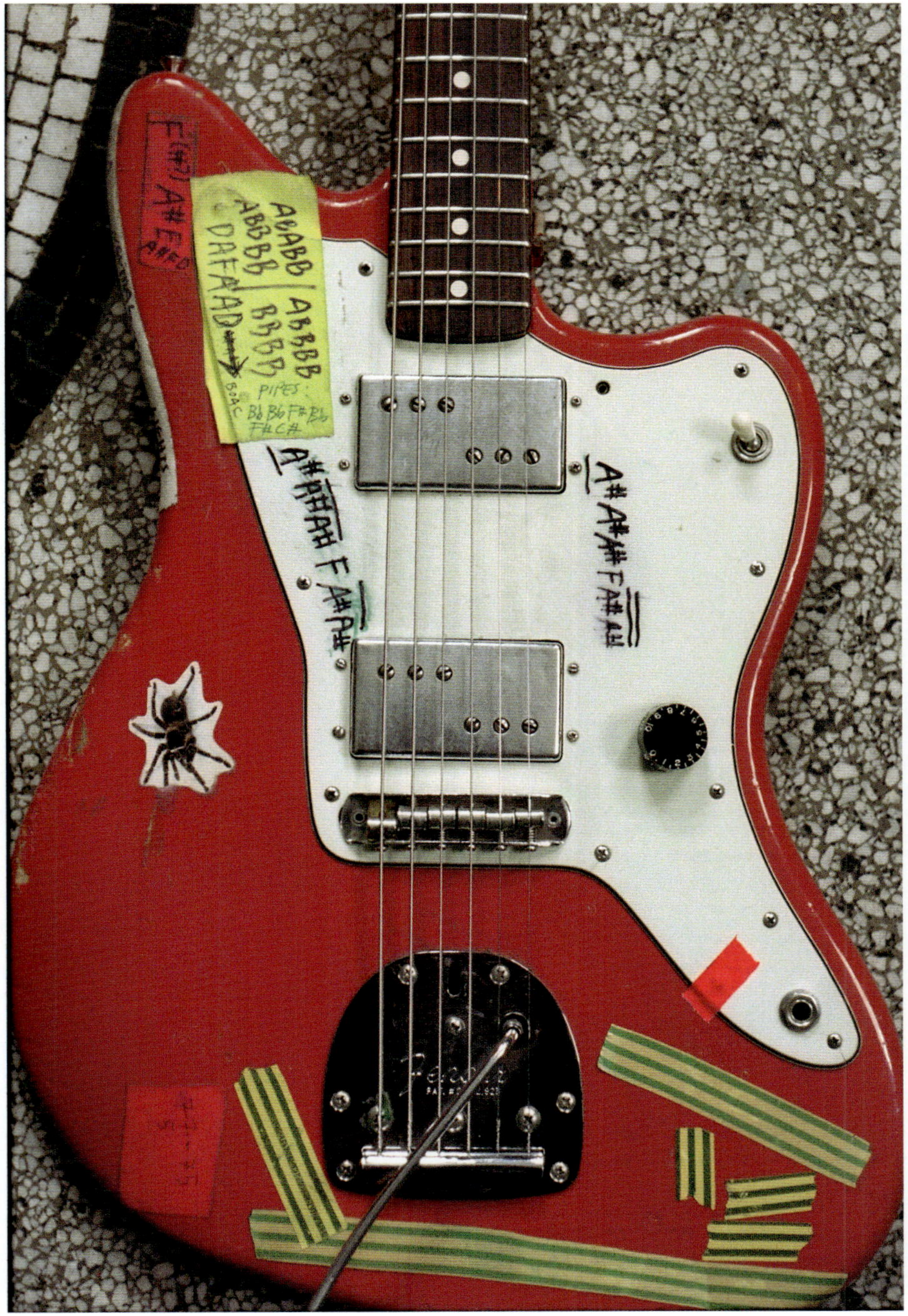

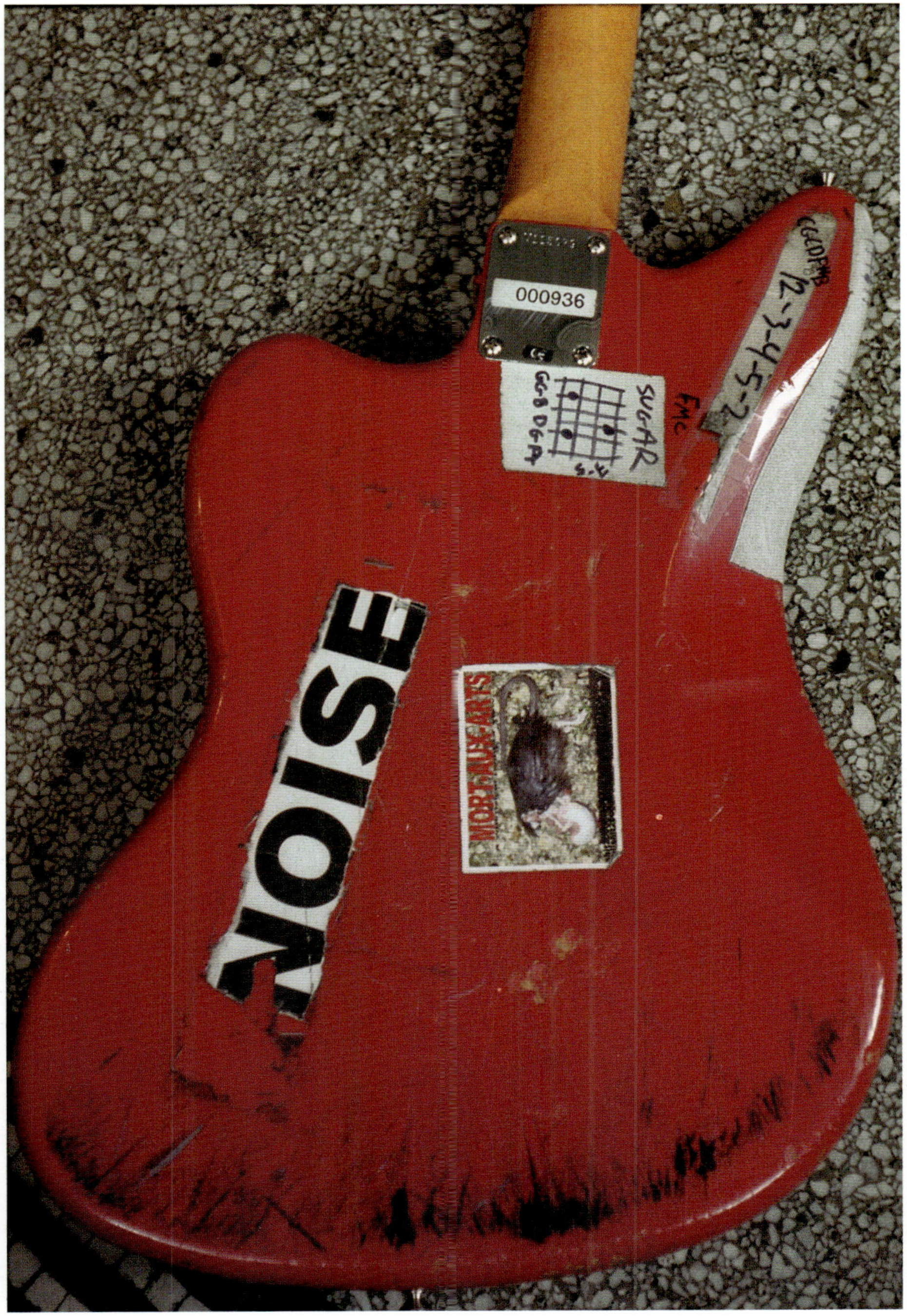
000936
SUGAR
NOISE

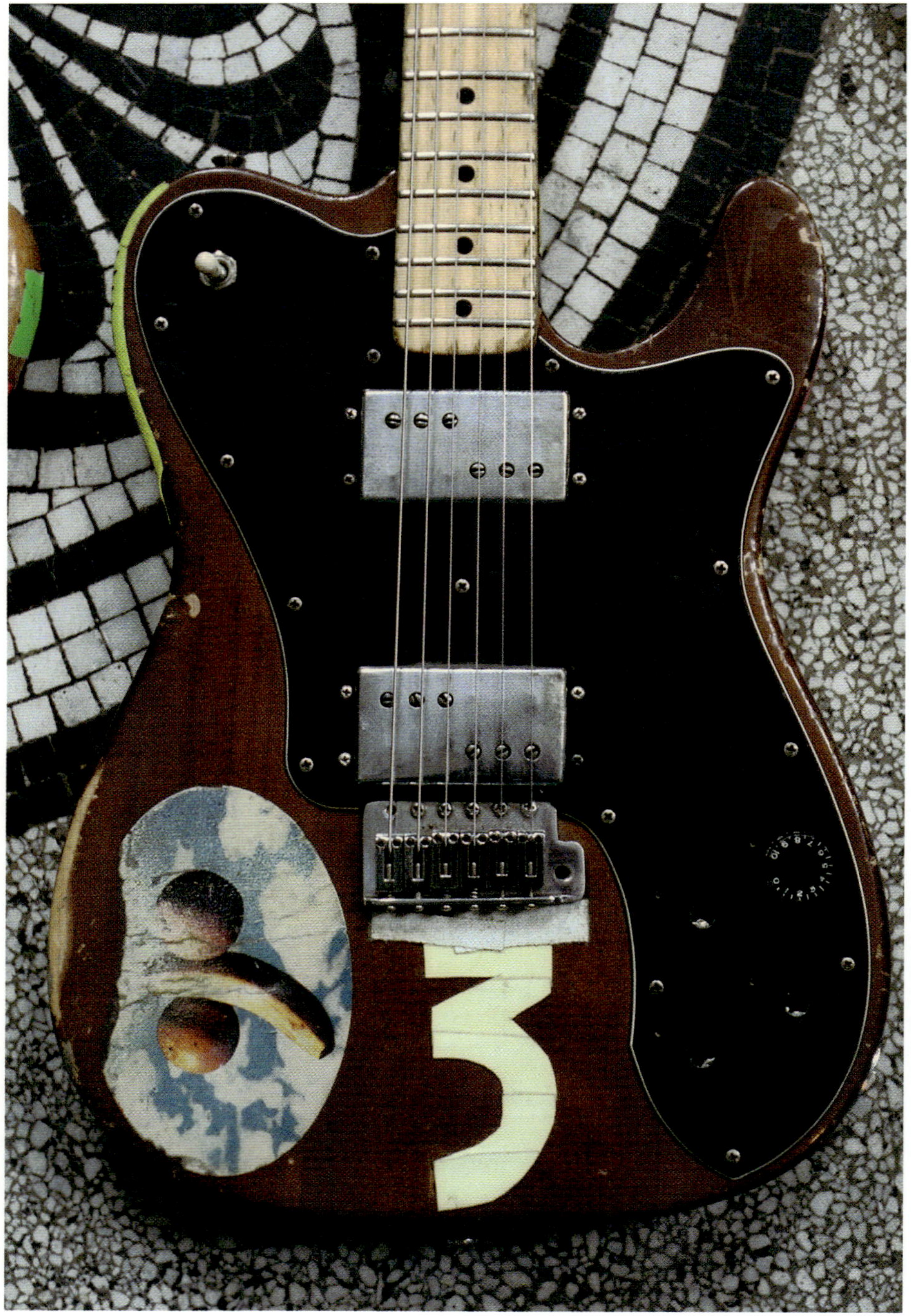
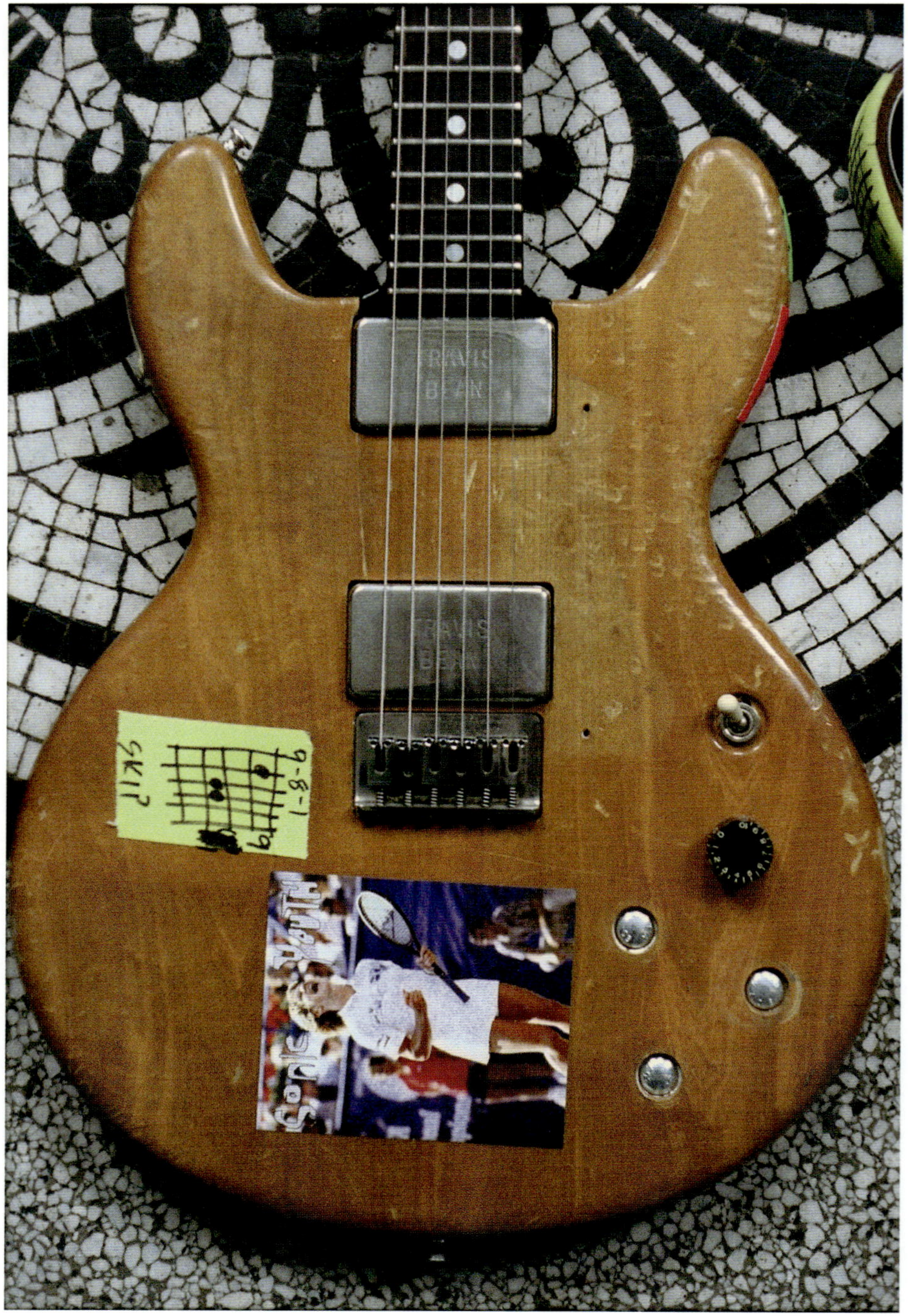

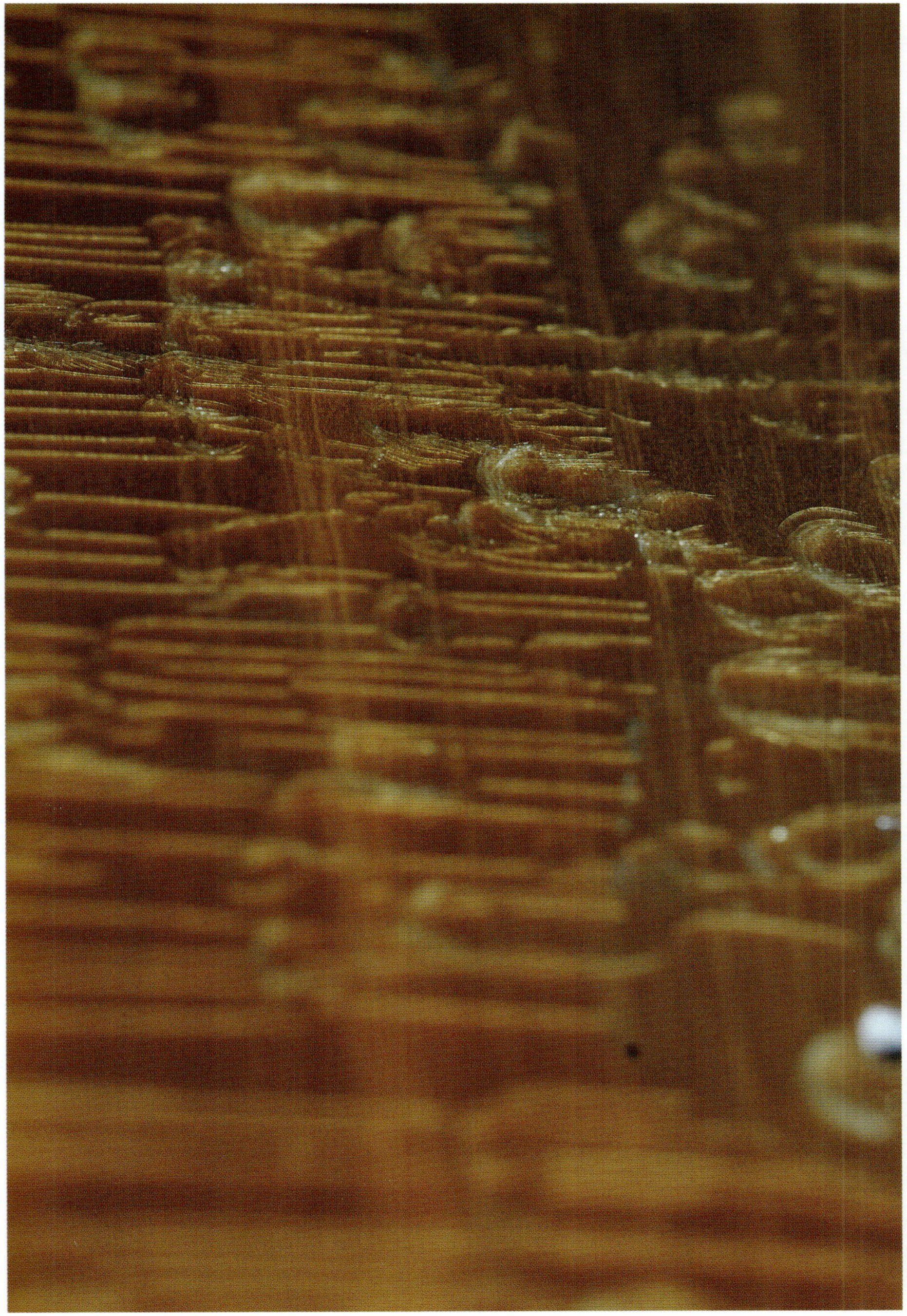
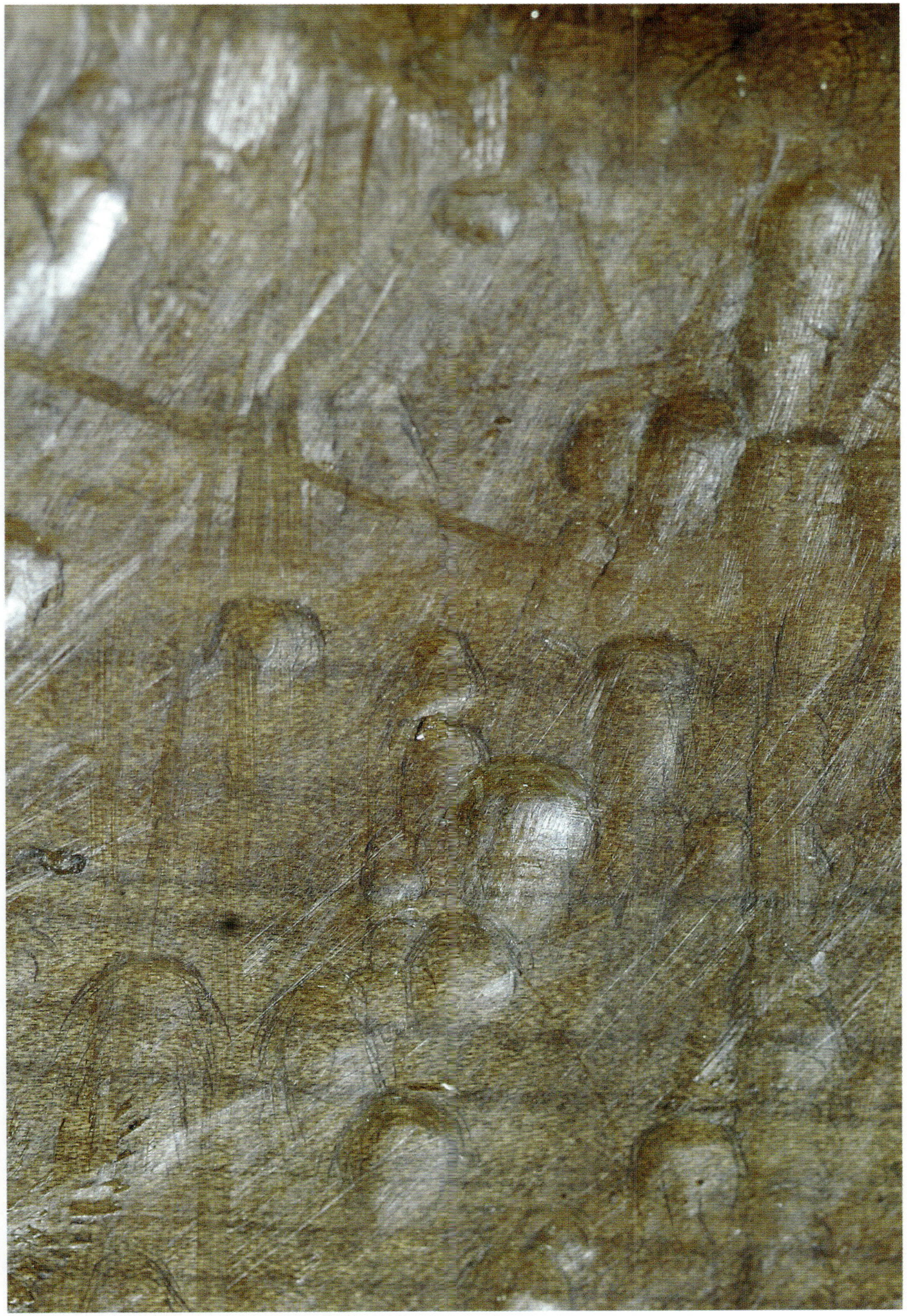

STEVE SHELLEY

Sonic Youth
1968 Ludwig bass drum

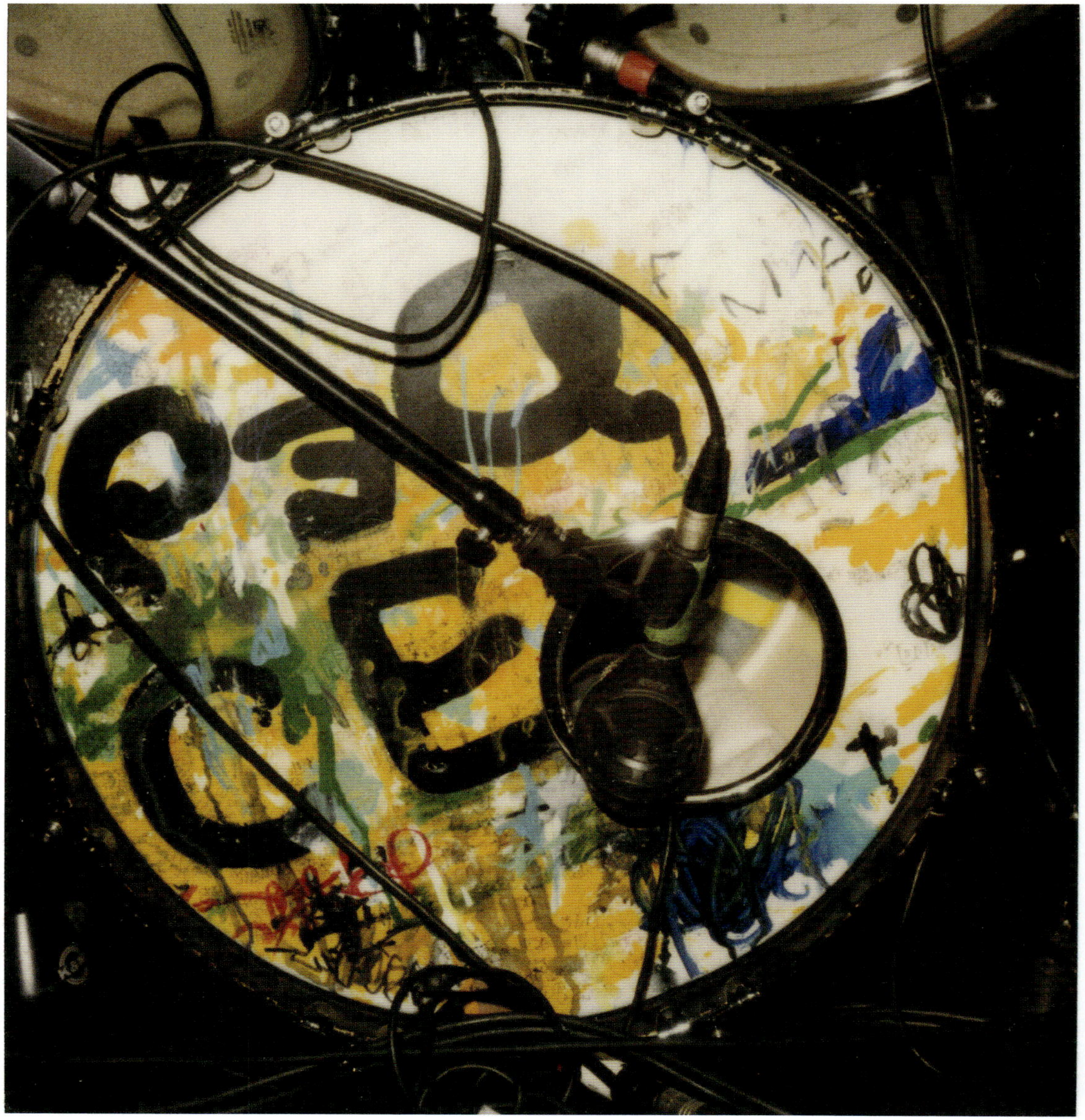

At the end of an SY Japan tour in March 2005, Steve and I went out to Kyoto and hung out with a friend, Harufumi Fujimura, for a day. We saw some temples, hit the Philosopher's Walk, and ended up at a restaurant that the Japanese artist Shinya Yamamoto was running at the time called Yamamoto 844 Shouten. I think there is some pun in the name on pot smoking if you speak Japanese.

Shinya's art was all over the walls of the restaurant and we ended up talking to him about it, and I think it was Steve who suggested that he do a painting on a kick drum head. Steve went back to Osaka that night and I stayed on at Harufumi's place. The day I departed we made a side trip to a drum shop, purchased a blank kick drum head, and I left it with Harufumi to hand off to Shinya.

The bass drum head in this photo, the second head Shinya painted for Steve, came about on another SY Japan tour, in April of 2007. A bunch of us went to Shinya's house on the very outskirts of Kyoto, and Steve and Shinya hatched the idea for this one over dinner—a collaboration between Shinya and Steve.

—Nic Close

KIM DEAL

The Pixies, The Breeders

Fender American Vintage 1962 Precision bass

It was 1988, and I needed a bass guitar. I was a six-string player and didn't own a bass. Joe [Santiago, Pixies guitarist] was borrowing my beautiful gold-top Les Paul, and I was borrowing my sister's Aria Pro II Cardinal Series bass. When the Pixies played some shows with My Bloody Valentine, I noticed Debbie played the same bass. But the Pixies released two records already, and I needed to get a bass of my own.

I bought it at some music store in Boston, Massachusetts. The store might have even been on Mass Ave. I was looking for a cooler color, like black, or red, or even some wood sunburst, but there was only a white P-bass and this one. I think Fender calls the color "Fiesta Red," but it's really an orangey coral. I didn't like the look of the white pick guard so I took it off and exposed the silver metal shielding underneath. Then I was cutting my hand on the edges of the shielding, so I attached a molded black rubber piece running all the way around the metal.

This bass always sounds good. It sounds good DI'ed. It sounds good with or without a pick. It just sounds like a good bass guitar.

And, of course, now I love the color.

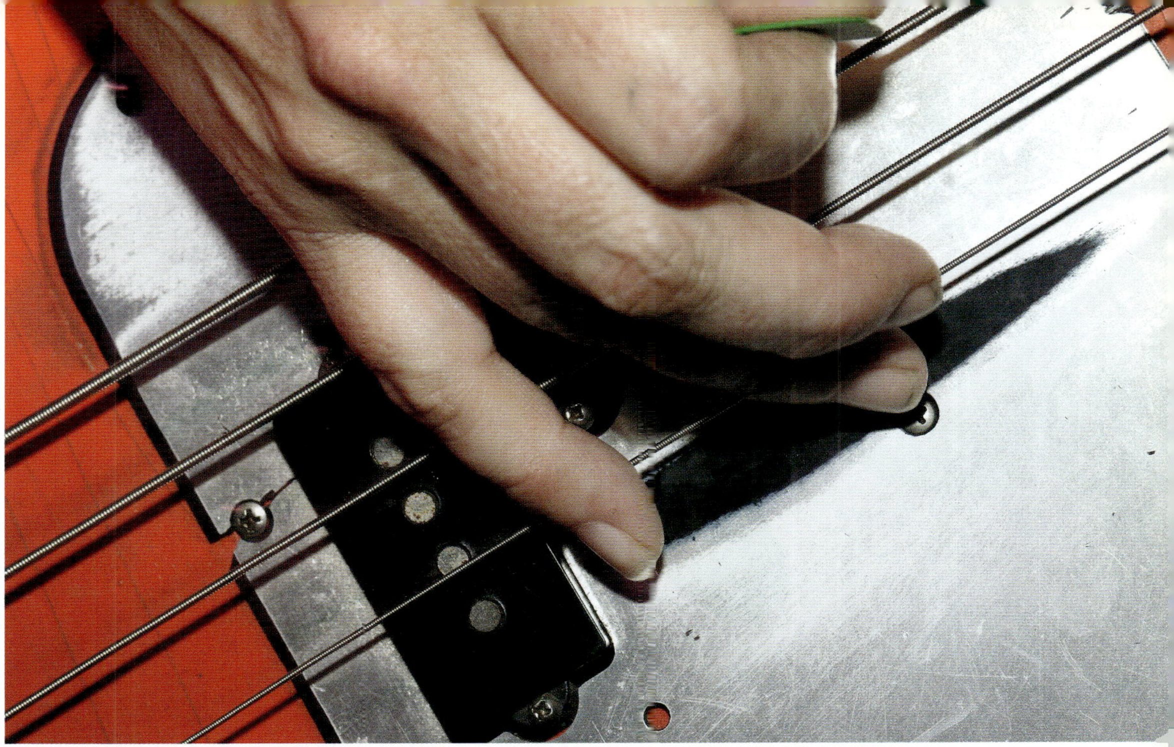

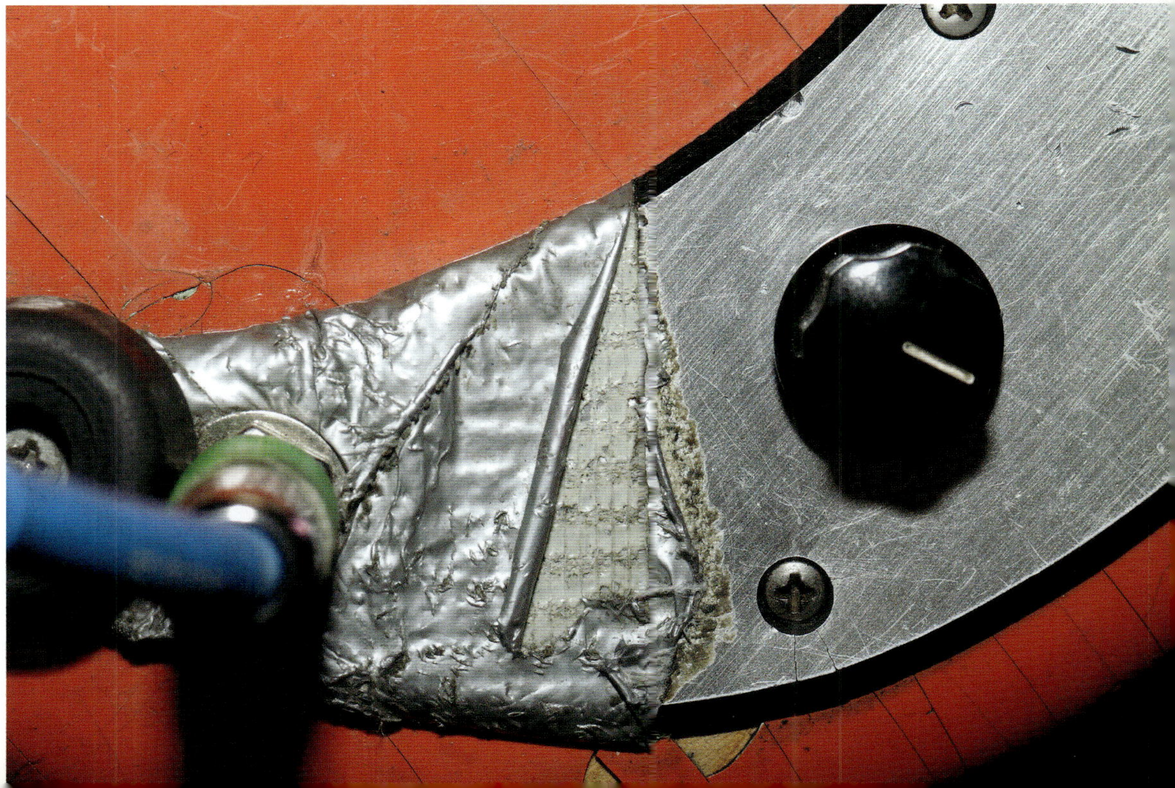

ERIC JUDY

Modest Mouse
Mid-1960s Fender Precision bass

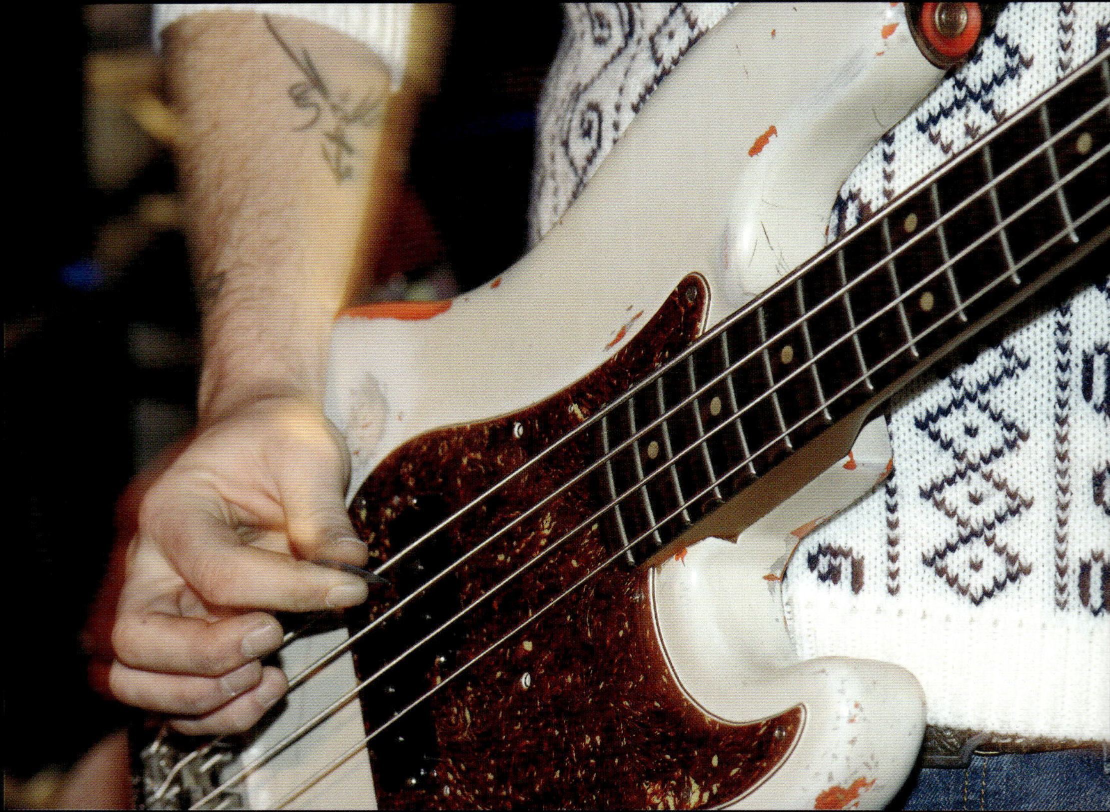

I had seen this bass at the guitar shop down the street from my old house. I'd held it on occasion, and played some notes, wondered about ownership. I didn't need a new bass, but it also didn't take too long to think of a bunch of reasons why I needed a new bass.

You can see orange paint through the chips in the white coat of paint. The shop owner, who also counted this as one of his personal instruments, said that these particular instruments were painted orange at the factory and then rejected by someone who was in a position to reject orange bass guitars and have them returned—the stores who were selling them, I guess?—and then sent back to Fender, who repainted them white.

I like it because it just feels like the bass that fits best in my hands. It is light, it seems like a big piece of dry cedar, but literally, the wood must be alder or ash.

Its sound has been altered over its long life. When I bought it there were some battery-powered pickups installed, and I had grown to appreciate their sound, but a few years later I listened to some other pickups, more similar to the 1960s originals, and had them swapped.

I have been so happy to have owned and played this bass over the years, and barring any unfortunate departure from my life (lost? stolen?) I don't believe I'd ever want to play something different. Although I had held similar thoughts about a Rickenbacker before the Fender, so anything can happen.

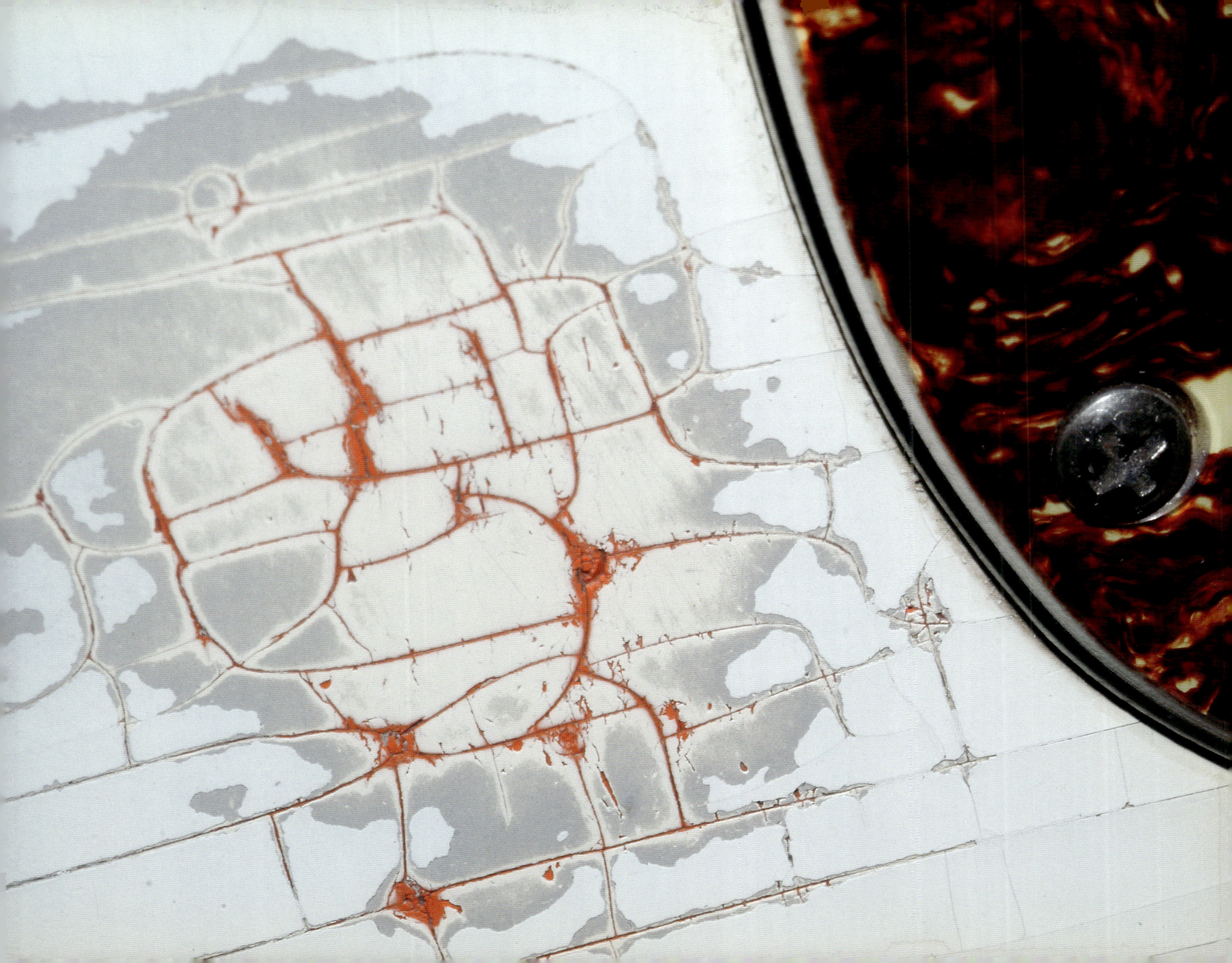

STEVEN DROZD

The Flaming Lips

1967 Fender Jazzmaster guitar

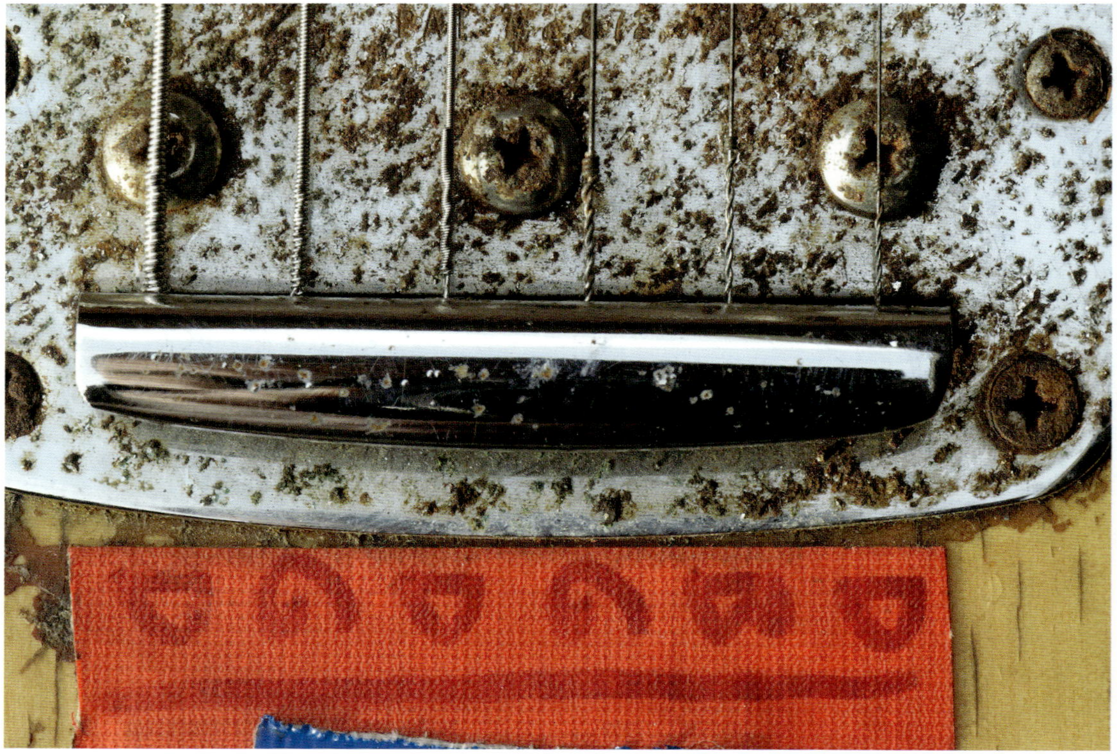

The first time I really got a lot of money from the Lips, in 1993, I decided I needed to go out and buy a real guitar. There's this place in Oklahoma City called Horn Trader that sold all this vintage gear, and the moment I walked in the store that 1967 Jazzmaster just called to me. It's weird to say, but there are times when you walk into a store and it just hits you—that urge or voice that says, "This is the one." Just to make sure I wasn't nuts, I picked it up and played it for a minute and all that did was confirm my subconscious urge. It is just one of those guitars that anyone who picked it up would comment on the neck and just how easy it is to play.

I was still the drummer when I bought that guitar, so I had left it over at Wayne's for a few days and he tinkered with it. I think he got the idea he was going to use it for touring so he dropped a Seymour Duncan Hot Rails pickup in it. I came over later and I was pissed because I had this idea of keeping it original and pristine. But the fact of the matter is that the Hot Rails was a saving grace. The original setup with P-90s would have just howled with all of our fuzz boxes.

—Excerpt from an interview by Chris Kies, *Premier Guitar*

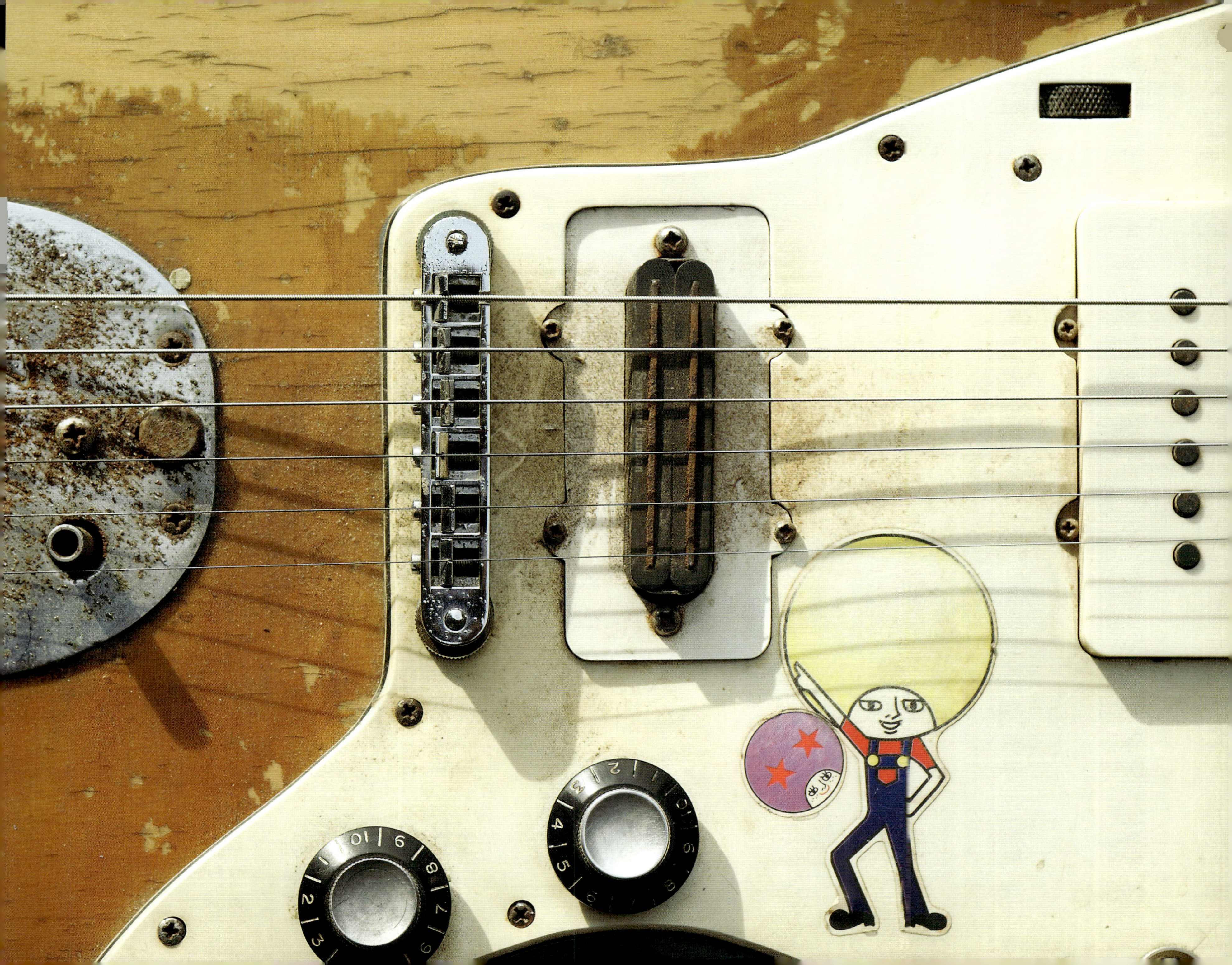

WAYNE COYNE

The Flaming Lips
Alvarez 12-string acoustic guitar
Ibanez double-neck guitar

I stuck a Theremin-like DJ device—a great little thing called an Alesis AirSynth—inside this acoustic guitar body. I've had it in there since 2002 and have used it on recordings and traveling around the world and everything. It makes a lot of great, weird drum tracks. I act like I'm playing the guitar, but I'm really playing the front of the synthesizer—your hand goes on top of it to activate it. The fact that it perfectly fits in the hole of that guitar is a stunning serendipity.

The confetti you see in there . . . we used to use this very small confetti that I would throw out into the audience and it would get into everything. Everything on the FL stage is holding confetti.

The cell phone that's on there is so old that people actually think its some new gadget. It's probably been about five years since I taped it on there, and everybody knew it was a cell phone then. Now they're like, "What is that?" It's funny how technology just flies around so quickly that something that seemed to be an obviously new invention is now so archaic. People think it's some futuristic guitar pedal, which is the fun of it, and why it's on there.

A long time ago I acquired one of these giant double-neck guitars, mostly because John McLaughlin and Jimmy Page play them, and I thought, "What is this cool looking, giant guitar?" At that point everybody was talking about the Guitar Hero guitars and handing them to us all the time. So I took one and taped it to the bottom neck. The Guitar Hero part doesn't actually work—I have a Kaoss pad hooked up to it that really makes the noise—but it looks cool. I get a lot a mileage out it; you put a battery in and it lasts for months! It has pitch change, so you can really do some wacky, unheard-of, bendable notes. The whole thing is like a big machine.

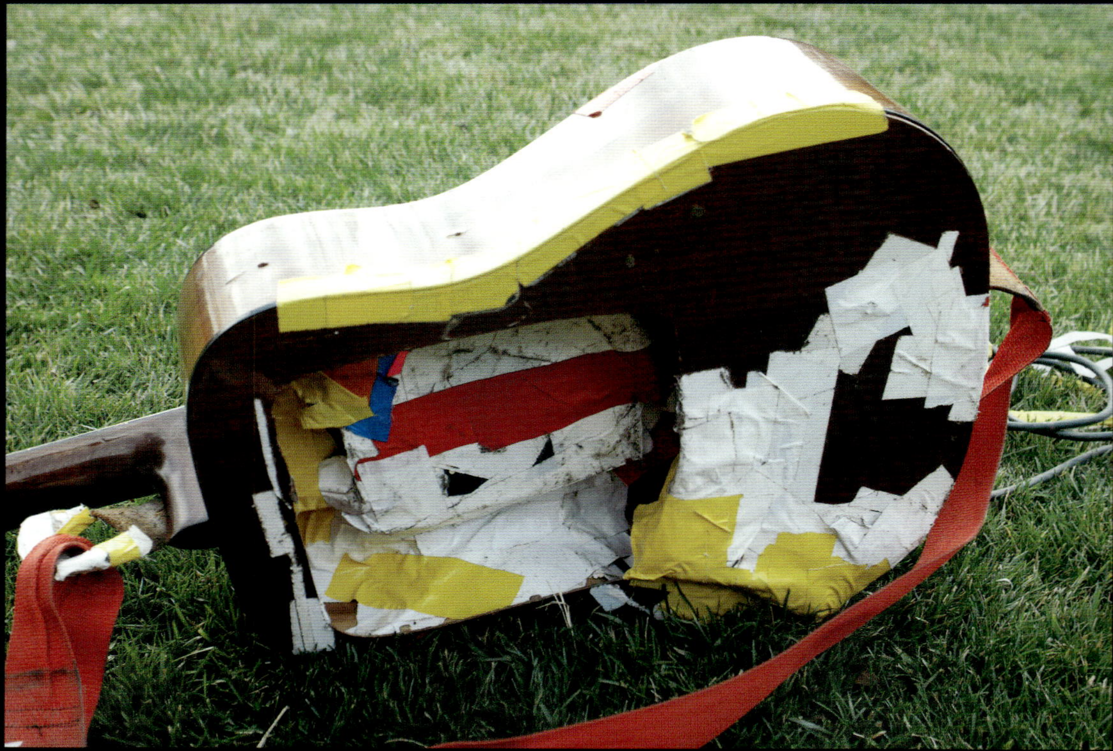

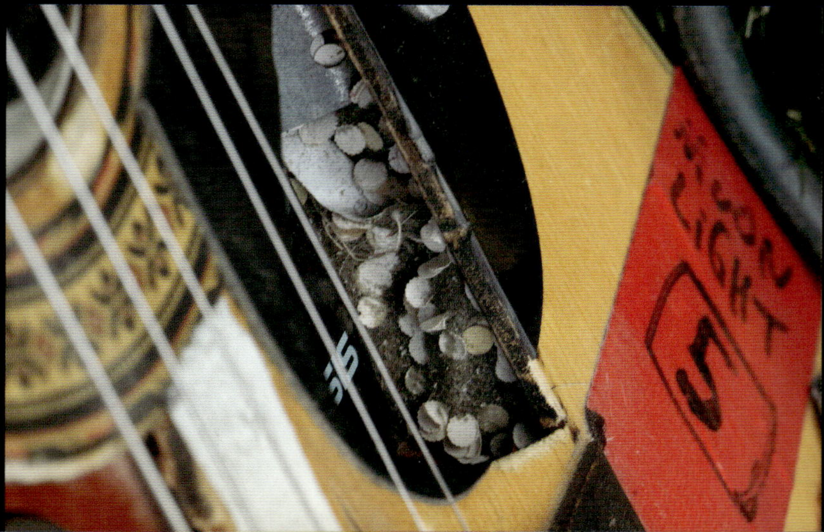

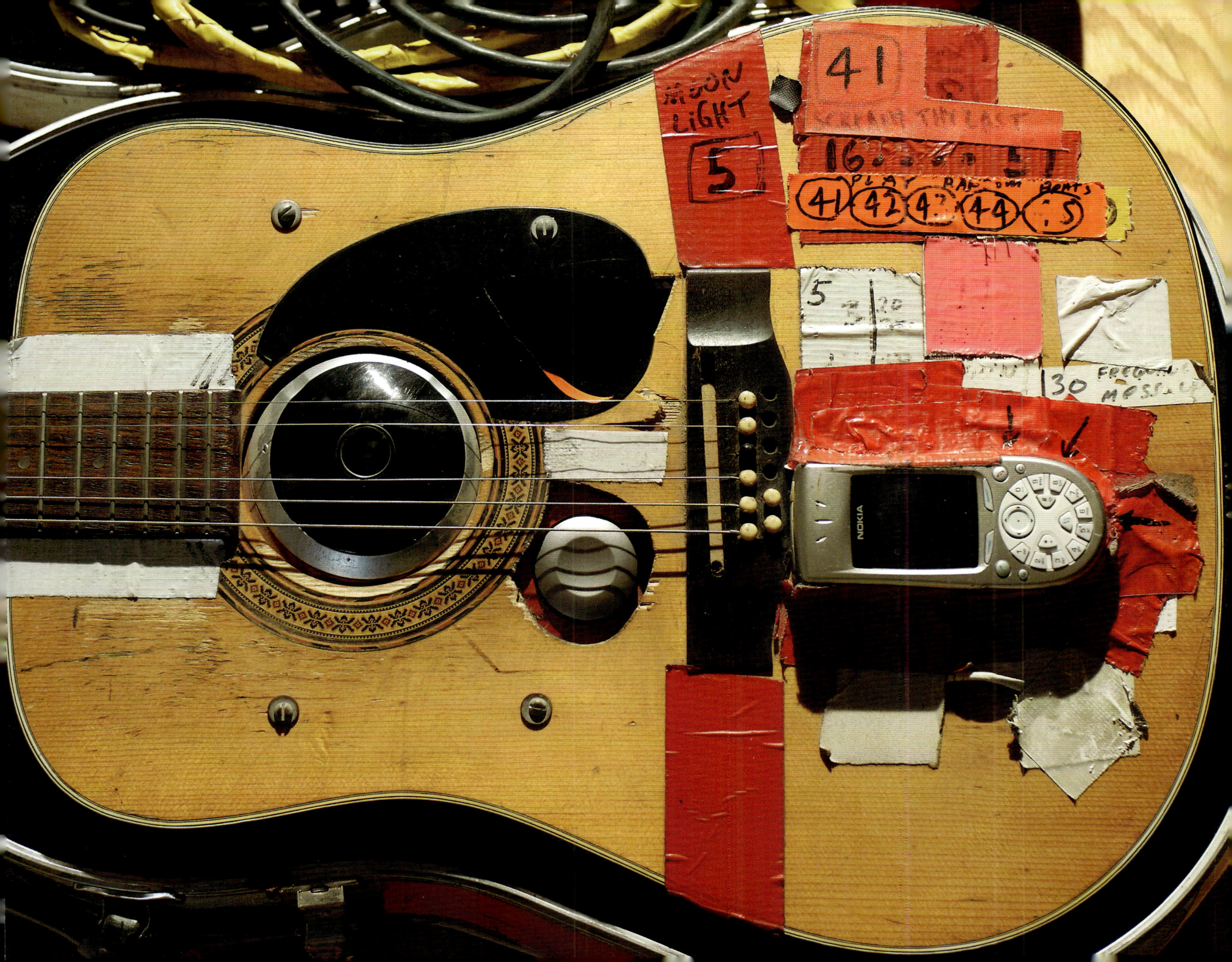
MOON LIGHT
5
41
NOKIA

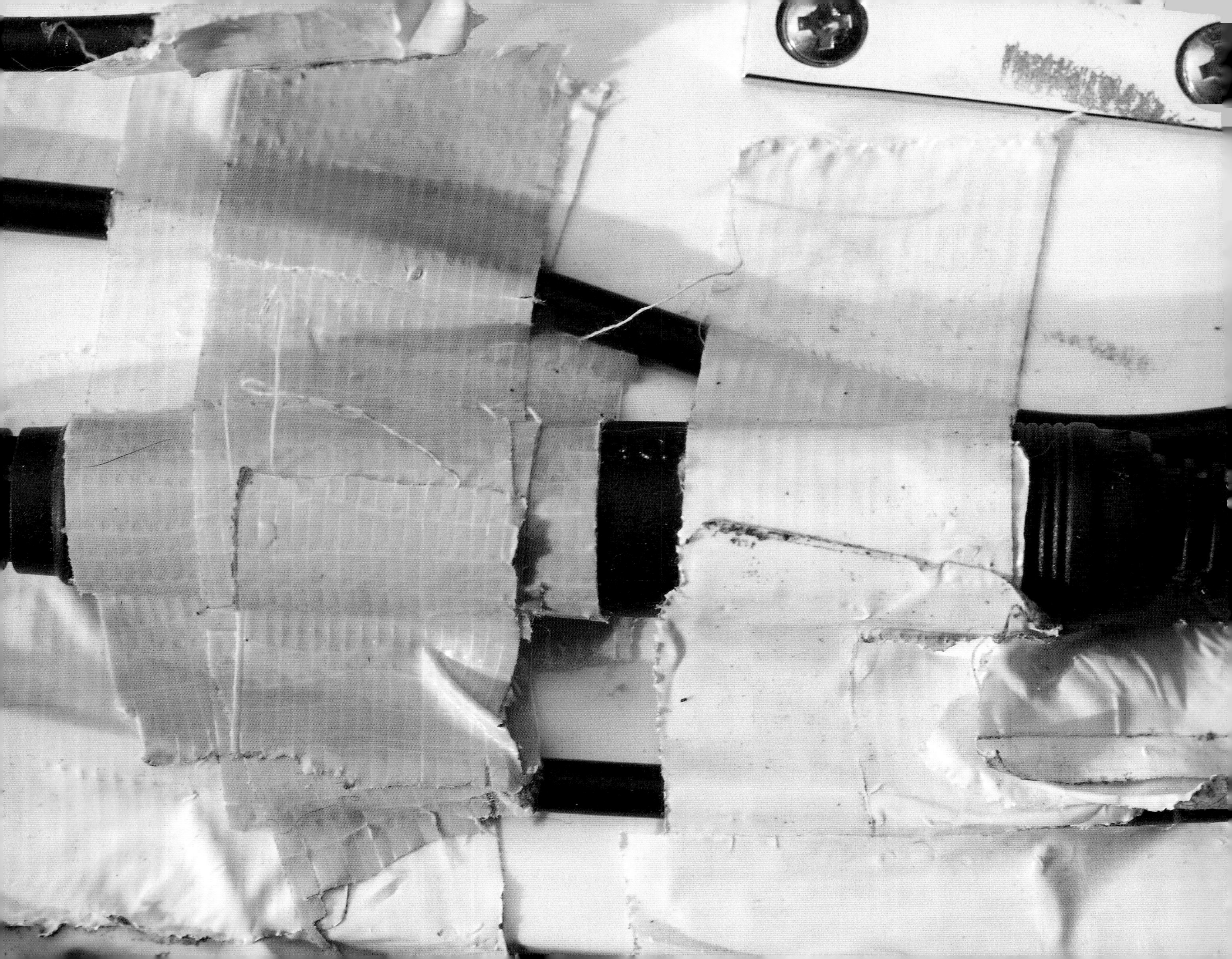

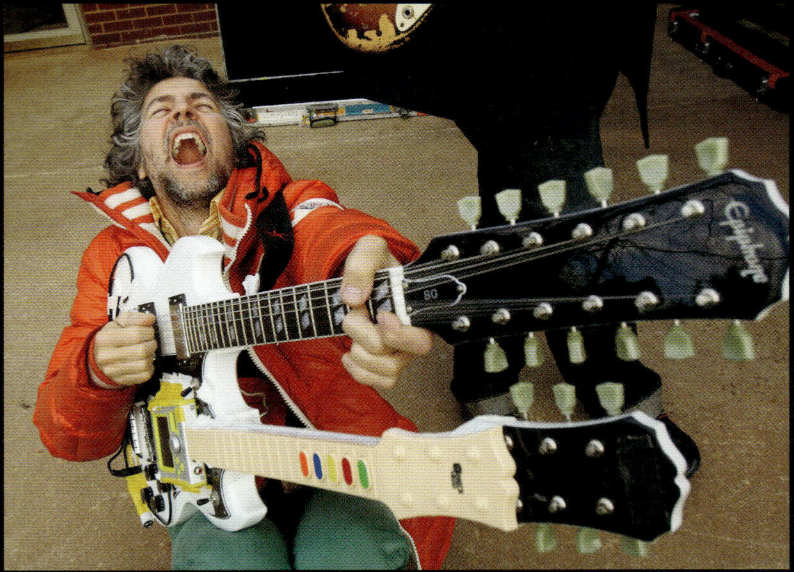
Epiphone
SG

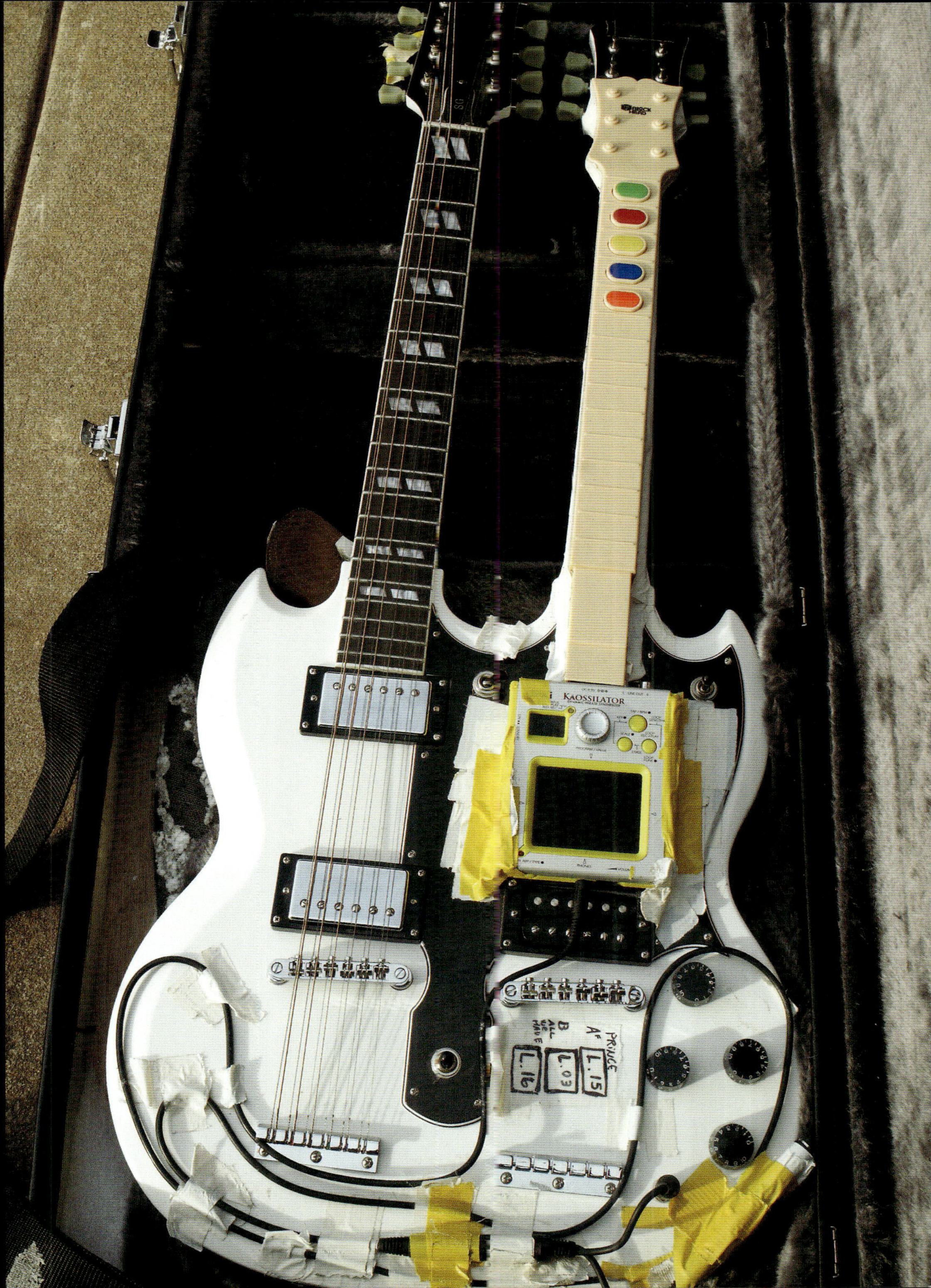
SG
KAOSSILATOR
PRINCE
A#
L.15
B
ALL WE MADE
L.03
L.16

TOM CULLINAN

Th' Faith Healers, Quickspace

Vox Stroller guitar

I'm told these guitars were sold mail order by Sears Roebuck in the '60s. Makes sense, as the neck is fixed to the body with four screws. Handy for getting it on planes. I chose it because it screamed "Fucking buy me!" from a friend of mine's dad's market stall. It also helped that it was made of plywood, and had Vox written on the chrome pickup. It was an absolute rip-off, as he wouldn't budge from his thirty pounds sterling asking price. This is the "Gibson" model; I later acquired the "Strat" for a much more reasonable seven quid. I took this one home and plugged it in, and that made me happy.

The first modification was to tear the knobs off and hard-wire the pickup to the jack socket. That stopped me from hitting them and losing volume constantly—losing volume is not cool, in case you thought it was. I love the simplicity, the small size, and precarious yet deceptively solid construction (you can bend a note by bending the actual guitar). It did get knocked around a bit, but I assure you that it was out of respect. The hacked hole is from field surgery; had to keep her in service.

To play this instrument feels like so many things I wouldn't know where to start and end. It feels like caring for a loved one, yet also like torturing a child. You realize that so much of the playing is two-way. If you don't play this guitar in conjunction with this guitar, you are entering into a battle. I'm not saying you won't win it, after some effort, I'm just saying go back to your Jaguar, you tart.

You can hear this on *Lido* and most other period Faith Healers records.

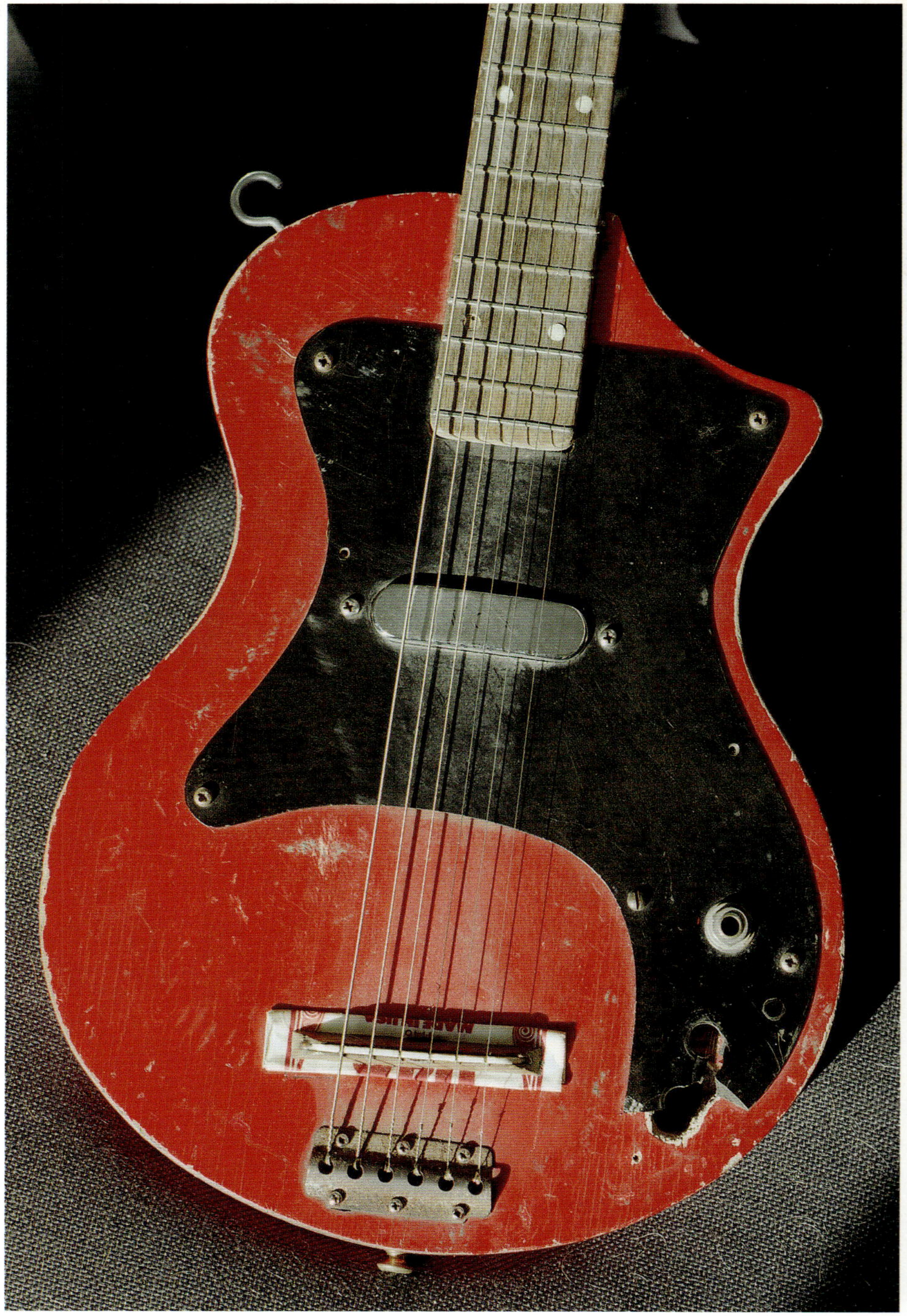

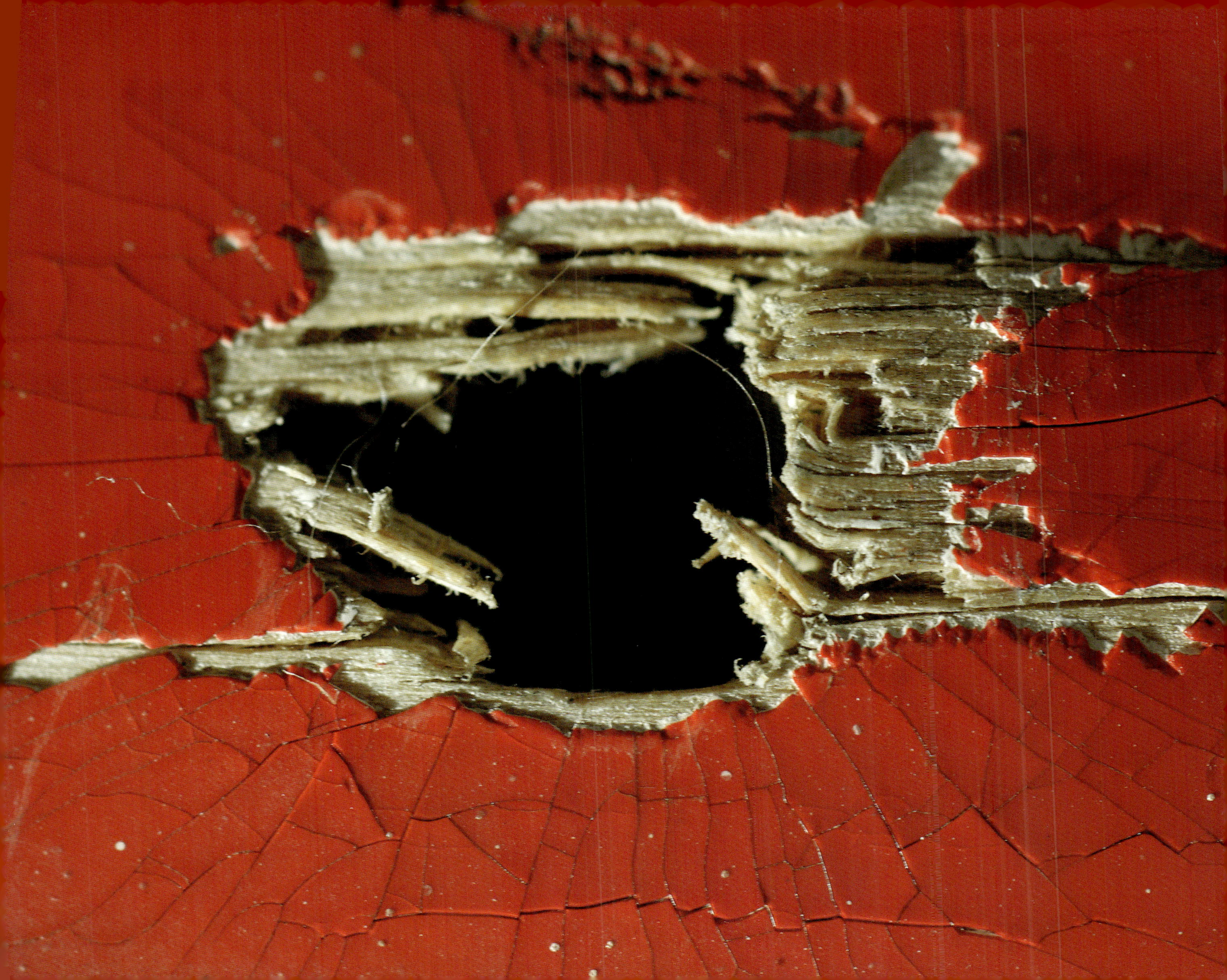

ACKNOWLEDGMENTS

Many thanks for the extraordinary help and encouragement from Melanie Standage, Johnny Marr, and Isaac Brock.

A very special thanks to all the musicians who opened their cases for me and my cameras backstage and at home. Without your kindness and willingness to share, this book would not exist.

Thank you for all the practical support from Sue and Bill Graham, Angela and Kevin Standage, Modest Mouse, Juan Carrera, Sean Hurley, Owen Richards, Ben Norton, Patrick Pendergast, Jessie Quitslund, Rick King, Eric Baecht, Nic Close, Matt Zivich, Dan Mapp, Bob Weston, Chris Chandler, Jason Tobias, Rich Walker, Heidi Ellen Robinson Fitzgerald, Kevin Oberlin, Rick Gershon, Steve Barnett, Trevor Keen, Gary Jarman, Chris Roseneau, Bertis Downs, Steve Lowe, Natalie Curtis, Marie Billegrav Bryant, Jason Kourkounis, and Justin Heit.

A special thanks to my literary agents, Jen Jenkins and William Clark.

Thanks to all at Chronicle Books, in particular my editor Steve Mockus, editorial assistant Emilie Sandoz, assistant managing editor Becca Cohen, designer Suzanne LaGasa, and production coordinator Erin Thacker.

And of course, to Honor and Prue.

Pat used the following cameras to photograph this book

Film
Rolleiflex 3.5F
Olympus Pen FT
Nikon 8008s
Polaroid SLR 680
Fuji 645
Pentax 6x7

Digital
Nikon D200
Nikon D700
Leaf Aptus 22 on a Mamiya RZ67 body
Hasselblad H3D

www.patgraham.org